Development Economics in Action

A STUDY OF ECONOMIC
POLICIES IN GHANA

TONY KILLICK

Visiting Professor of Economics
University of Nairobi

LONDON
HEINEMANN
NAIROBI · IBADAN · LUSAKA

Heinemann Educational Books Ltd
48 Charles Street, London W1X 8AH
P.M.B. 5205 Ibadan · P.O. Box 45314 Nairobi
P.O. Box 3966 Lusaka

EDINBURGH MELBOURNE TORONTO AUCKLAND KINGSTON
SINGAPORE HONG KONG KUALA LUMPUR NEW DELHI

ISBN 0 435 97370 3 (Cased)
     0 435 97371 1 (Paper)

Phototypeset by G. A. Pindar & Son Ltd., Scarborough, England
Printed by Cox & Wyman Ltd, Fakenham

*This book
is dedicated to my parents*

Contents

Preface

This book results from an acquaintance with Ghana which began in 1961 and soon developed into an *affaire de coeur*. As is sometimes the case in such matters, however, the affair began after a while to take on a bitter-sweet flavour, for during my tenure at the University of Ghana, from 1961 to 1965, I watched the bright hopes kindled by Kwame Nkrumah dim almost to extinction, with economic growth grinding to a halt and suffering imposed on a people who deserved better.

But the attraction remained strong and 1969 saw me back in Accra, this time as a member of the Harvard Group advising the newly elected government of Dr Busia. One was optimistic again, for in the interim some order had been restored to economic disarray and the new government could claim intellectual distinction. Now, surely, the stagnation of the sixties would be shaken off and the decline in living standard reversed? It was not to be. Within two years the economy was in grave crisis once more and shortly afterwards the military took over again. When I began drafting this manuscript in 1972 the economy seemed as deeply mired in stagnation as it had ever been and while the remarkable cocoa boom of 1973–4 has provided temporary relief, it has done little solve the fundamental problems.

This piece, then, has been written in sadness and occasional anger; trying, with such objectivity as I can muster, to analyse what went wrong. But it also tries to suggest the outlines of an economically and politically feasible solution, for the affair has not ended and there would be few greater pleasures than to be able to contribute, however slightly, to the future prosperity of the Ghanaian people.

I should like to think, though, that what is written here has an interest reaching beyond Ghana; as any villager will tell you, it is not necessary to be involved in an affair to find it interesting and instructive. Many of the things which Nkrumah and his successors tried to do were rather accurate reflections of policies which economists had been urging upon the third world for some time. The Ghanaian experience thus represents a case study in applied development economics and the general conclusion which has been reached will add to the literature on economic development.

The debts I have incurred in preparing this study are many. My former colleagues Sieb Miedema and Joseph J. Stern read the entire manuscript in draft and made a multitude of helpful suggestions. Peter Williams led me firmly through the maze of Ghana's education statistics; and Elon Gilbert tried to restore balance to my chapter on the unbalanced growth of agriculture and industry, besides making a host of other valuable comments. At various stages of the work Y. Adu-Boahene, J. S. Awudu, Jenny Chung and Kevin Makin did excellently all that was asked of them as research assistants. I have imposed myself successfully on the precious time of so many others who have read and commented on various parts of the manuscript that I can only list them below with the assurance that their numbers do not diminish my gratitude to each:

Kwasi Anyemadu	Josephine Milburn
Isaac Bissue	David Morawetz
John Dadson	John Odling-Smee
Batchelor Folson	Nii Noi Omaboe
David Forsyth	Douglas Rimmer
Albert Hirschman	Michael Roemer
Robinson Hollister	Blair Rourke
Simon Kuznets	Yaw Saffu
Harvey Leibenstein	Lance Taylor
Clark Leith	David Williams

Completion of this work would have been impossible without the assistance of many individuals and agencies in Ghana. I received much help from officials of the Ministry of Finance and Planning, the Central Bureau of Statistics, the Bank of Ghana, and the State Gold Mining Corporation. The Auditor General was kind enough to make available to me an advance copy of his report for 1970/71; I should also like to acknowledge the co-operation of the former Ministry of Industries in my study of the Industrial Development Corporation.

Another large debt is owed to the Development Advisory Service of the Center for International Affairs, Harvard University (now the Harvard Institute of International Development) for giving me a year free of teaching and other responsibilities in which to do my writing. Lester Gordon, its Director, gave me every encouragement and generous support; Sophia Stern helped me out in a multitude of ways as only she knows how; and Ann Ringle coped splendidly with typing rather more than a chapter a month while also serving two or three other masters. Mary Wanjiru Kihoro provided equally excellent service in putting the typescript into its final form.

Gratitude also for money: to the US Agency for International Development, which financed part of my time at Harvard; and to the Ford Foundation for enabling me to make a return trip to Accra in 1973. Needless to say, none of the people or agencies mentioned above are responsible for the views and remaining defects in the final product. The buck stops with the author.

To Inge, thanks and apologies. Thanks for putting herself between me and the many household concerns I should have dealt with; for miraculously keeping the children quiet when necessary; for succouring me in so many ways. And apologies to her and the girls for turning what could have been an interesting and relaxed year into a six-days-a-week stay-at-home.

T.K.

University of Nairobi

List of Tables

List of Figures

1 *Introduction*

The Relevance of a Study of Ghana

Among the newly independent states of Africa, Ghana has attracted much international interest. The first colonised black African state to achieve political independence,[1] in March 1975, she was led at that time by a Prime Minister who won attention and influence far beyond his country's boundaries. Kwame Nkrumah represented a new brand of African nationalism; radical, modernizing and socialist in orientation. His successes and failures were carefully watched abroad, as a test of the experiment (as it was then) of political independence in Africa and of his type of ideology. Nkrumah had a vision of the nation-state he wished to create in Ghana and made no bones about wishing to extend it throughout the African continent.

Because he was a nationalist, most African leaders shared many of his views and what was done in Ghana was repeated in other African states as they won their independence. Reduced 'economic dependence,' accelerated industrialization, an expanding role for the state – these were on the agendas of virtually all ex-British colonies and, to a lesser extent (because the French maintained a stronger 'neo-colonial' presence), of the French-speaking states as well. Nationalism, rather than a more outward-looking ideology, was the unifying force, for although it became fashionable in the early sixties for heads of state to talk of 'African socialism', few of them fully shared Nkrumah's ideological commitments. Guinea under Touré, Mali under Keita, Zambia under Kaunda, and Uganda under Obote were the countries where policies most closely resembled those in Nkrumah's Ghana.[2] But Ghana came first and generally led the field, and thus she came to be seen by many as a test case, where Africa's 'readiness for independence' could be assessed but also where an important body of ideas could be put to the test of implementation.

So far as economic policy is concerned, however, the interest of the Ghana case is a wider one. Until the fall of Nkrumah early in 1966,[3] economic strategy in Ghana was inspired by a vision of economic modernization similar to, and influenced by, that of many professional economists who were concerning themselves with the problems of under-developed countries: a 'big push' primarily involving a major investment effort, a strategy centred around an industrialization drive, emphasizing import-substitution, structural change and a less open economy, to be achieved largely through the instrumentalities of the state. A study of the dominant ideas of development economics thus illuminates much of what happened in Ghana in the sixties and, by the same token, what happened there constitutes a case study of development economics in action. After 1966, the country's new rulers began to turn to policies which in some measure reflected the changing concerns of development economists, but which also maintained a strong continuity with those inherited from Nkrumah. The second half of the decade is therefore of considerable interest for the illustrations it provides of the political and economic problems of effecting a transition to a more market-oriented set of policies. Such, at least, is the thesis of this book.

An Outline of the Study

The two chapters which follow are largely an elaboration of the theme of Ghana as a case study in applied development economics. Chapter 2 surveys the leading ideas in the literature on economic development which had come to the fore by the early nineteen-sixties, and the changes which have occurred more recently. Chapter 3 relates these ideas to the economic strategies followed in Ghana during and after the Nkrumah period, and discusses the political and ideological contexts in which they were formulated.

The next step is to record the performance of Ghana's economy during the sixties. Chapters 4 and 5 survey the domestic performance and the balance of payments. The latter chapter also concerns itself with defences of Ghana's performance which attribute failings to factors beyond the control of her governments: adverse terms of trade in the Nkrumah years, and the debt problem inherited by his successors. It is argued that neither was decisive. Chapters 6–10 examine in detail the results of Nkrumah's economic strategy. Development planning, fiscal performance and short-term economic management concern chapter 6, while chapters 7 and 8 study the modernization and industrialization which occurred, and reasons for their failure to generate more rapid economic growth. Chapters 9 and 10 assess the performance of state enterprises established under Nkrumah, and the effects of import and price controls.

The performance and problems of the governments which followed Nkrumah are considered in chapter 11. These governments made little progress in re-establishing an economy depending more upon the operation of market forces, and this chapter explores the difficulties encountered in effecting a transition from a distorted economy. The concluding chapter 12 draws some general lessons from Ghana's experiences and suggests elements of a future development strategy.

Before proceeding to the next chapter, however, it may help the reader to have a brief description of Ghana's economy as it was at the beginning of the sixties and, especially, to survey the resources available for Nkrumah's modernization drive.

Ghana's Economy at the Beginning of the Sixties[4]

In the late fifties Ghana's economy still bore the hallmark of colonization. Physically and as an economy the country was a small one. It had an area of 92,000 square miles, about the same size as the United Kingdom, but in 1960 its population was little more than a tenth and its GDP little more than a fiftieth of the UK's. It was still essentially a rural economy, with more than half its GDP originating in agricultural and related activities. It was a classic case of an open economy, heavily dependent on international commerce. Trade and payments were largely unregulated and tariff levels generally low. Most capital goods and many kinds of consumer goods had to be imported, and exports were dominated by cocoa which was highly volatile but generally provided about three-fifths of total foreign exchange earnings. The ratio of foreign trade to GDP was about 30 per cent.[5]

Most obviously characteristic of its colonial past was the pervasively dualistic structure of the economy. The co-existence of traditional, labour-intensive production techniques with modern, capital-intensive ones occurred not only in the obvious case of manufacturing, but in agriculture, fishing, mining, construction, and trade. At the beginning of the sixties the economy still largely retained a structural framework which emerged at the beginning of the century[6] and, while the cocoa industry was an entirely indigenous one, many of its modern industries remained enclaves, making little use of domestic resources and adding minimally to the national product. In many respects, then, the economy typified most of the African states which were to follow Ghana in achieving political independence.

In other respects, though, it was different, and the differences were generally to Ghana's advantage. For one thing, average incomes, at about $200, were higher than in most other black African countries[7] and, since a basic principle of economics is to every one that hath shall be given, this promised that development might be won more easily than in countries still preoccupied by the provision of a basic subsistence. For all its structural defects, it was also an economy in transition, one in which economic modernization was already under way. A substantial number of industries producing goods which formerly had to be imported were already in operation, the financial system was well established and expanding, and there was virtually no part of the country where money was not in common use. The writ of the government extended throughout the state and tribal divisions were less serious than elsewhere on the continent.

Thus, 'the Ghana experiment' started with advantages. Nkrumah had at his disposal a richer accumulation of economic assets than most of his fellow African statesmen, and this chapter concludes by surveying the stock of human, natural and man-made resources with which he commenced his modernization drive.

Human Resources

It has often been said that Ghana became independent with a more favourable endowment of human resources than practically any other country of tropical Africa, and there is evidence that such was indeed the case. Comparative enrolment ratios in primary and secondary education for thirteen West African states, relating to the late fifties, showed Ghana's primary school rates to be double those of the next highest-ranking country and three times the unweighted mean for the other countries. The secondary school ratio was also the highest, even after correcting an erroneously high figure for Ghana.[8] The educational system, the supply of skilled labour and the efficiency of the public service were all believed to be relatively well developed by the late fifties. Expansion of state intervention and participation in the economy thus stood a better chance of success in Ghana than in most other African states. However, this tells us more about the iniquities of colonialism than it does about the human wealth of Ghana, for it is only by the standards of colonized Africa that she could have been said to be in a favourable position. The supply of skilled workers (defined as craftsmen and workers with more advanced skills) in 1960 was only of the order of three per cent of the total employed labour force – a meagre base upon which to industrialize an economy.[9] There were shortages of various specific skills, such as those of engineers, doctors and secondary school teachers, and even in the fifties these deficiencies had emerged as a serious problem. Extension work, for example, was seriously limited by shortages of junior agriculturalists, with almost half of the Ministry of Agriculture's establishment vacant.[10] Early in the fifties there were grave shortages of professional staff in the Public Works Department, a major cause of high construction costs; the position had further deteriorated by the end of the decade.[11]

Again, while it was true that Ghana's educational system was superior to that of most other tropical African countries, this should not lead anyone to think of it as highly developed.[12] For example, the 1960 census of population revealed that only 16 per cent of the adult population had ever attended school and most of those had only received an elementary education. There were still only about forty secondary schools by 1960 and there were only fourteen secondary school places for every hundred graduates from middle schools. There were only seven university graduates per 10,000 of the population, and scarcely any formal provision for technical training. Thus, even though it had been greatly expanded after the end of the Second World War, the educational system was still inadequate, limiting its ability to increase Ghana's supply of human skills. In short, the small supply of skilled workers, especially those with experience, was a major potential constraint upon the future growth of the economy, a fact which was recognized in the *Seven-year Plan* published in 1964. The supply of skilled manpower would have had to triple during the plan period if its targets were to be fulfilled.[13]

Population growth was another headache for the planners, believed by demographers to be $2\frac{1}{2}$ to $3\frac{1}{2}$ per cent annually at the beginning of the sixties.[14] Although this is not the place to develop the argument, rapid population growth was a major economic problem,[15] even though population density was still low by international standards. The dependency rate was high, with 45 per cent of the population less than fifteen years old, and marginal accretions to the labour force were most likely to be forced into low-productivity traditional farming activities or become unemployed. It was unemployment which most worried the authors of the *Seven-year Plan*. The need to absorb the expansion of the labour force was given as a major explanation of the strategy adopted,[16] and was made all the more urgent by the already considerable volume of under-employment and unemployment at the beginning of the sixties, with the 1960 census showing the number of unemployed to be equivalent to 25 per cent of the total wage labour force.[17]

Ghana thus commenced the sixties with a two-fold manpower problem: a small and inadequate stock of human skills and a fairly fast-growing population. Population policies produce results only over a period of years, and there were limitations to the speed with which the supply of skilled manpower could be increased,[18] so to a large extent these problems were 'given' to the planners and their task was to produce policies which took these constraints adequately into account.

Natural Resources

As with manpower, so with natural resources, Ghana could have been said in 1960 to be neither very poor nor particularly rich. The soils and climate, producing a luxuriant vegetation in the southern forest zone but a much sparser one in the most extensive northern savannah, are suitable for a range of field and tree crops. The basic nutrient value of most of Ghana's soils is poor and rainfall is the most important influence on its farming potential.[19] Fairly heavy rainfall supports a rich vegetational cover in most of the south, which, in turn provides humus to create a high-value topsoil. The savannah vegetation of the north is due to lighter rainfall and, although there is a large potential, is too poor in the dry season to sustain a large and healthy cattle stock. Cattle-breeding in the south is largely prevented by tsetse flies. There are some areas where the traditional system of land rotation is under stress because of increasing population pressure, but this was not a major problem in 1960 and there were large, potentially cultivable areas in the southern savannah scarcely populated at all.[20]

The traditional system of peasant farming represented a rather efficient response to an abundant supply of land, soils which are easily exhausted, and a scarcity of capital funds, for it embodied techniques which maintained the fertility of the soil with large inputs of land (often known as shifting cultivation but better described as land rotation), a more modest application of labour and scarcely any use of purchased capital. Starvation was rare and localized, but malnutrition was endemic.

Most of the economic value of Ghana's land is in the forest zone. The forest itself contains many valuable species, and timber was the country's second most important export. However, most of the extraction in the past had come from virgin forest, with little replanting, and there were fears for the capacity of the forest to sustain the extraction rates which had been achieved by the late fifties. Of even greater importance was the suitability of Ghana's climate for the cultivation of cocoa, and at that time Ghana produced about a third of the total world output. This was an activity which yielded high returns for the economy, for it was still worthwhile for farmers to cultivate and plant cocoa even though the government taxed away about half the total export proceeds. There was access to productive off-shore and deep-sea fishing grounds.

Nor was Ghana without substantial mineral assets. Gold had long been one of her major exports; diamond production was also important, as, to a lesser extent, were bauxite and manganese. Between them, these minerals made up a quarter of the total exports in 1960, at the same time contributing significantly to the national product and industrial employment. But there was a dark side too. Mineral output was static and no new mines had been opened since the 1930s. With indifferent ore qualities and rising costs pressing against a fixed world price, all but the richest gold mines suffered from increasing financial difficulties, and it appeared in 1961 that most of them would close down.[21] There were, it is true, large unexploited deposits of bauxite and iron ore of economic potential, but the quality of the ore was not high and there was no prospect of mining them in the near future. Although close to Nigeria, Ghana was not thought to possess petroleum deposits in economic quantities.[22] In sum, Ghana's known mineral resource base was substantial and diversified, but it was eroding and offered few prospects for rapid expansion.

Capital Resources
Fairly high rates of economic growth were observed in the later nineteen-fifties, accompanied by an even faster expansion of the country's stock of capital assets. Both saving and investment rates were

quite high in this period, estimated gross saving and investment ratios averaging about 18 per cent of GDP in 1958–60, and by 1960 gross investment was up to 20 per cent of GDP. This was substantial by any standard and especially by that of tropical Africa.[23] Szereszewski estimated that the total stock of capital increased by no less than 49 per cent between 1955 and 1960 and, inevitably, this resulted in substantial increases in the ratio of capital to current output.[24]

By 1960, then, Ghana had a substantial and relatively young stock of capital assets and a capital-intensity of output normally associated with an economy at a more advanced stage of development.[25] Many improvements were made to the infrastructure during the fifties, when substantial industrial investments also occurred, although not at rapid enough rates to satisfy Nkrumah and his government.

Mention should also be made of the large accumulation of unutilized savings which still existed in the form of foreign exchange reserves. At the beginning of 1960 these were equivalent to 129 per cent of imports and 174 per cent of gross capital formation in that year, and 21 per cent of the country's entire stock of purchased capital assets. Although deficits had begun to appear on the current account of the balance of payments, there was not yet any serious shortage of foreign exchange.

A large and young capital stock, high saving and investment rates, a major accumulation of reserves and adequate import capacity were Nkrumah's biggest advantages for the industrialization drive he was to launch. But the increasing average capital:output ratio implied incremental ratios that were rising much faster, and declining returns to investment.[26] To some extent, this could be attributed to the heavy infrastructural investments of the period, which would produce their streams of benefits only over a long period and would thus tend to push up the capital:output ratio in the short and medium term. However, there is little evidence of a major change in the composition of the capital stock away from directly productive activities in this period,[27] which suggests the additional explanation that the ratio was rising because of increasingly unfavourable supplies of co-operant factors of production, perhaps in combination with a deteriorating quality of investment. This, at least, is what is suggested by Szereszewski's estimate that the gross capital stock per capita, which we may take as a proxy for the change in capital per worker, rose by 32 per cent between 1955 and 1960.[28] Of course, there was no general shortage of labour, but the supply of specific skills almost certainly failed to keep pace with the rate of expansion of the capital stock, for it is unlikely that the availability of skilled manpower increased by 50 per cent in 1955–60. It was possible to see by 1960 that the capacity of the economy to absorb new investment productively was becoming severely limited.[29] The future ability of investment to generate economic growth would be conditioned by the capacity to increase the supply of such other factors as trained labour, administrative and managerial skills, known natural resources, and foreign exchange. At the time, however, absorptive capacity was not recognized as a general problem – a fact which helps to explain much subsequent history.

Appendix to Chapter 1

A Guide to the History of Ghana's Currency

1. Until 1965 Ghana's currency was the Ghana pound (£G), with shillings and pennies as minor units. The £G exchanged at par with the pound sterling and at £G1 = US$2.80.
2. On 19 July 1965 the currency was decimalized to equal 100 old pennies. The new unit was called the cedi (₵). No alteration of the true external exchange rate was involved and the new unit exchanged at ₵1.00 = $1.17.
3. On 23 February 1967 the currency was again decimalized, this time to be equivalent to ten old shillings, or £G0.5. The unit of currency became the New Cedi (N₵) and was exchanged for the 'old' Cedi at N₵1 = ₵1.20. There was a pro rata change in the external exchange rate so that the effective foreign exchange price of the currency again remained unaltered. The exchange rate against the dollar therefore became N₵1.00 = $1.40. On 19 February 1972 the appellation 'New' was dropped from the official name of the currency unit, which is once more simply called the cedi (₵). *This is the unit which has been used in this book.* The abbreviation ₵ has been used throughout to indicate the 'new' cedi; none of the statistics presented are in 'old' cedis. The cedi is made up of 100 pesewas, the minor unit of value.
4. On 8 July 1967 the external value of the cedi was devalued to ₵1.00 = $0.98.
5. On 27 December 1971 the external value of the cedi was again devalued, to ₵1.00 = $0.55.
6. Following a military *coup d'état*, the external value of the currency was revalued on 7 February 1972 to stand at ₵1.00 = $0.78, or $1.00 = ₵1.28. *Unless otherwise indicated, this is the exchange rate used in this book.*

NOTES

[1] As a British colony the country was known as the Gold Coast. For an excellent political history of Ghana covering 1946–60, see Austin, 1964, and, for a more analytical study of roughly the same period see Apter, 1973.

[2] Tanzania is another African country with a leader seriously committed to a socialist ideology, but Nyerere has chosen a different economic strategy from the other examples just mentioned (see Helleiner, 1972B). Outside Africa, Indonesia in the Sukarno period and Burma are countries that come to mind as having charted a similar course to that chosen by Nkrumah.

[3] At the time of writing there have been three changes of government since independence: (a) A military-police *coup d'état* overthrew Nkrumah in February 1966. Under the title of National Liberation Council (NLC), this government remained in office until September 1969; (b) power was then transferred to a newly elected civilian government under an old-time opponent of Nkrumah, Dr Kofi Busia, leader of the Progress Party; (c) a second military coup was successful in January 1972 and brought to office the National Redemption Council (NRC) under the leadership of Col. I. K. Acheampong.

[4] Birmingham et al. (eds.), 1966, contains a detailed description and analysis of the structure of Ghana's economy at the beginning of the sixties. The bulk of this book was written by the late Robert Szereszewski and myself.

[5] This is the mean of exports plus imports as a proportion of GDP.

[6] For a fuller statement of this thesis see Szereszewski, 1965, *passim*.

[7] See Szereszewski, 1966, Table 2.3.

[8] UN Economic Commission for Africa, 1966, Table 9.

[9] Killick, 1966, pp. 130–1.

[10] According to Bing, 1968, p. 386, 120 posts of the Ministry's total establishment for Agricultural Assistants of 267 were unfilled in 1961.

[11] Killick, 1966, p. 293. See also chapter 12 below on the limitation of the civil service.

[12] See Hurd, 1967, on the growth and nature of Ghana's educational system. Bing, 1968, chapter 10, also contains an interesting discussion of the limitations of the system.

[13] Killick, 1966, pp. 151–3.

[14] The best treatment of this topic is by Caldwell, 1967, especially chapters II and IV, although it now appears that he over-estimated the rate of population growth. The best estimate, based upon the results of the 1970 census, for the 1960–70 growth rate is about 2·6 per cent p.a. See also Gaisie, 1970, and Addo, 1967.

[15] For fuller presentations of this view see Caldwell, 1967, chapter IV, and the NLC's *Population Planning for National Progress and Prosperity*, 1969.

[16] *Seven-year Plan*, chapter 1.

[17] See Killick, 1966, pp. 147–50.

[18] However, chapter 7 below shows that a remarkable expansion did occur in the output of the educational system during the course of the sixties.

[19] Source references for the following paragraphs are Wills, 1962 and Killick, 1966, chapters 9–11 and 15.

[20] See Figure 2.4 of Caldwell, p. 108, which shows large areas with densities below 20 per square mile.

[21] The government averted this by buying up the mines and creating the State Gold Mining Corporation to manage them.

[22] Various oil companies commenced serious off-shore explorations early in the nineteen-seventies, but at the time of writing no oil had been found in economic quantities and the indications were thought to be unpromising. See One-year Plan, 1970/71, pp. 110–11.

[23] The UN Economic Commission for Africa, 1966, Table 13, showed other West African states with gross investment rates of about 10 per cent – the mean was 10·6 per cent – taking 1960 or the year nearest it for which data were presented.

[24] Szereszewski, 1966, Table 8.4, shows the gross capital:output ratio (including cocoa capital) to have risen from 2·2 to 2·5 in this period. However, his figures cannot be taken as much more than rough estimates. This and the following two paragraphs

are largely derived from this source, pp. 192–212.

[25] Ghana's ratio was estimated at 2·5:1 in 1960 whereas Kuznets, 1966, Table 2.7, provides a figure for the US in 1950 of 2·1:1. Ratios he provides for other industrial countries tend to be substantially higher, however, to say nothing of the dangers in making this type of international comparison.

[26] Assuming a one-year time lag, an incremental capital:output ratio (ICOR) of 3·85 for net investments in 1955–60 can be estimated from Szereszewski's figures (Table 8.4, cocoa capital included), as against average ratios rising from 2·2 to 2·5. The ICOR excluding cocoa capital was 3·2.

[27] *ibid.*, Table 8.2, p. 203.

[28] *ibid.*, Table 8.5, p. 208.

[29] *See* Meier and Baldwin, 1957, pp. 351–5, for a discussion of the notion of an economy's absorptive capacity for investment.

2 Development, Disequilibrium and State Interventionism

Attempts during the 1960s to accelerate the development of Ghana's economy did not take place within an intellectual vacuum. Policies there were informed by a set of ideas similar to, and affected by, the leading ideas on development which came to the fore after the Second World War. Until the fall of President Nkrumah early in 1966, a strategy was employed which had many affinities with recommendations then being made by professional economists. Their views thus illuminate much of what happened in Ghana during the sixties, and the core of this book is concerned with a rather close examination of how some of these ideas worked out in practice.

The task of this chapter, then, is to present a statement of what by the beginning of the sixties had come to constitute 'mainstream' development economics, leaving chapter 3 to demonstrate the similarities between these ideas and Nkrumah's strategy of development. Since the chief purpose here is to present a synthesis of the views of important writers on development problems, readers who already have a thorough familiarity with the literature will wish to skim through this chapter quickly. Those less confident of their knowledge in this area will find themselves confronted with a text which, though non-technical in its presentation, seeks to condense a large body of writing. The reader who finds himself on unfamiliar ground is therefore urged to follow up the source references provided in the footnotes, for in the originals he will find the full development of the ideas, and the qualifications with which they were surrounded, to which a brief survey of this kind cannot do justice.

Mainstream development economics is referred to in the past tense. This is not to imply that it is a thing of the past, but that the consensus which characterized the beginning of the sixties no longer exists. In place of a mainstream we now have a network of rivulets, and some strong cross currents. Intriguingly, just as the economics profession began to grow sceptical of the prescriptions of earlier years, so too were Ghana's new policy-makers forming doubts about certain of Nkrumah's policies. The second half of the decade saw a limited attempt to move back to policy instruments operating through the market mechanism, just as many economists were beginning to return to the prescriptions of traditional Western economic theory. This chapter therefore concludes with a very brief discussion of the more recent renascence of neo-classicism in the development literature, and chapter 11 examines the difficulties (and ultimate failure) encountered in Ghana in attempts to revert to a somewhat more freely operating market economy after 1966.

The Nature of the Problem

The poverty of nations is the special concern of development economics. The question it seeks to answer is, 'why some countries should have developed while others remain more or less stagnant, or why some countries remain economically backward while others experience sustained secular advance.'[1] Why does poverty tend to persist, how did the countries that have become wealthy manage to do it, how can poor countries also become rich?

Throughout the 1950s various attempts to answer these questions created the body of literature which established development economics as a distinct specialization.[2] Explanations of the persistence of poverty were fairly unanimous: poverty sets up, or is associated with, various conditions which retard economic progress. It is thus self-perpetuating. We shall see that Nkrumah took a similar view.

The most influential of early explanations along these lines was Nurkse's. He started from two propositions, one ancient, one modern. The first was Adam Smith's thesis that the division of labour is limited by the extent of the market, which Nurkse reinterpreted as the principle that 'the inducement to invest is limited by the size of the market,'[3] i.e. that investment demand is a rising function of national income. The second was a Keynesian consumption function, in which saving is determined by per capita income. A country starting in a state of poverty is thus one with a small supply of investible resources and a small demand for them too. Productivity will therefore remain low and so will income. The vicious circle is complete; poverty is perpetuated.

A later and equally influential theory of self-perpetuating poverty was provided by Leibenstein's notion of the 'low level equilibrium trap.'[4] This was a good deal more subtle than Nurkse's vicious circle and represented an improvement in at least three important respects. Firstly, it did not depend so crucially on simplistic hypotheses about the demand and supply of investible funds, and placed more emphasis on the importance of the creation of human as well as physical capital.

Secondly, it added a major new dimension to the problem in the form of population growth. Thirdly, it was made more dynamic than Nurkse's model by the introduction of the influence of expectations of future rates of growth on investment decisions.[5]

At the risk of doing less than full justice to the sophistication of Leibenstein's model, it might be said that he added to a vicious circle similar to Nurkse's, a neo-Malthusian hypothesis that, at a low initial level of development, improvements in living standards would tend, after a time, to induce an accelerated rate of population growth which would overtake the expansion of total income and thus force per capita income back down again. Since there is a biological limit to the speed with which human population can grow, in the range of $3\frac{1}{2}$ to 4 per cent, continuous increases in per capita income could be sustained at a level above the biological limit but 'at low per capita income levels the income-depressing forces are more significant than the income-raising ones' and thus these economies tend to 'return eventually to a state characterized by a near subsistence level of income.[6]

Three other attempts to explain the persistence of poverty deserve mention. Myrdal developed his notion of circular causation to propound the view that 'market forces will tend cumulatively to accentuate international inequalities.'[7] Rostow stressed the 'income-depressing forces' at work at an early stage of development. The 'central fact' about traditional society, he wrote, 'was that a ceiling existed on the level of attainable output per head. This ceiling resulted from the fact that the potentialities which flow from modern science and technology were either not available or not regularly or systematically applied.'[8] Kuznets also drew attention to the special problems of present-day underdeveloped countries, endeavouring to develop with per capita incomes perhaps only a half or a third of those in the rich countries when they began their industrial revolutions.[9]

The view of the level of investment as being strongly influenced by individual investors' expectations of the future rate of growth of the economy, utilized by Leibenstein, has a long history and an unsavoury one for those of a laissez-faire persuasion. When decisions are made atomistically individuals will take a more pessimistic view of the future expansion of the market than they would if only they were aware of the investments being contemplated by others. By the same logic, a single act of investment will tend to produce a stream of benefits in excess of the private returns to the investor, by expanding the size of the market and thus tending to induce further capital formation by others. Hence, the social value of an act of investment tends to exceed its private value.

This view of the complementary nature of investment decisions was a most powerful contribution to the corpus of economic theory and, as will be seen, was rich in policy implications. Almost all major writers on development in this period embraced it in one form or another,[10] but it was most rigorously formulated by Scitovsky.[11] He argued that the existence of externalities in low-income countries involved a much broader and more important concept than the Marshallian-type external economies usually treated in conventional marginal analysis. There were, in his view, three major reasons why this broader concept of external economies might be important in these countries and why a marginalist, general equilibrium, approach to their problems was inappropriate. Firstly, economies of scale or indivisibilities in investment may induce a producer to choose more or less than profit-maximizing output, and his decision in the face of this dilemma will not necessarily be the best from the point of view of the community.

Secondly, the marginalist approach generally overlooks the dynamic character of an investment decision in raising the rate of return to capital for other, future investors – a factor which later work by Chenery suggested was likely to be of substantial economic importance.[12] Here we are back to Nurkse's axiom that the inducement to invest is limited by the size of the market. Scitovsky's third criticism of conventional marginalist theory was of particular interest to nationalist leaders in former colonies. There was, he said, a big difference between national and international welfare considerations. When national interests predominate, 'investment in exporting industries is always less, and that in import-competing industries is always more desirable from the national, than from the international point of view,'[13] because part of the welfare gains of foreign trade are enjoyed by foreigners who also have to bear some of the costs of import substitution.

We revert to the attack on the relevance of neo-classical marginalism shortly, but at this point the reader is likely to be asking himself whether this gloomy theorizing does not prove too much. Is development impossible, then, and, if so, how is it that the countries of Europe and North America have managed to raise their living standards to levels previously undreamt of? Many of the first countries to industrialize did so upon the basis of a greatly expanded volume of external trade and large importations of foreign capital. The vicious-circle ideas of Nurkse and others seem almost to assume a closed economy, but does not access to the world economy offer an escape route to the low-income countries?

The literature provided an almost unanimously negative answer. Nurkse's attitude is particularly interesting, for he was a committed internationalist of a liberal mould of thought, whose pessimism about the practical possibilities of export-led development in low-income countries was formed despite his intellectual predilections. By 1953 he had become convinced that the growth of world markets for the exports of the low-income countries would be too slow for export-led growth to be feasible for all but a few (the oil-producing countries being the chief exceptions), but it was in his 1959 Wicksell lectures that he developed his argument with a force all the more formidable for the moderation with which it was presented.[14] The structure of production within the industrial countries, he believed, is shifting away from industries with large raw material inputs; the income elasticity of demand for many agricultural products is low; technological progress has achieved substantial economies in the use of material inputs and has made available many synthetics strongly competitive with primary products; the protectionism of industrial states aggravates these problems and also reduces the scope for the low-income countries to switch to the exportation of manufactures.

Nurske confined himself to arguing that the expansion of world demand for primary products was generally slow but others went further. In 1949 a UN study appeared to demonstrate that there was a secular downward trend in the export prices of primary products relative to manufactures[15] and this theme was strongly taken up by Singer:[16]

It is a matter of historical fact that ever since the [eighteen] seventies the trend of prices has been heavily against sellers of food and raw materials and in favour of the sellers of manufactured articles. The statistics are open to doubt and to objection in detail, but the general story which they tell is unmistakeable.

The marginalist response would have been that persistently deteriorating terms of trade would result in adjustments of the pattern of production to take advantage of changing comparative advantages but, as Singer and others[17] pointed out, a characteristic of an underdeveloped economy is an inflexible productive system, a low capacity to transform. Here again, the traditional prescription seemed inapplicable.

Quite apart from any alleged long-term worsening in their terms of trade, the low-income countries were seen to be at a disadvantage because the world markets for primary products are more volatile than for manufactures and because the typical low-income country is heavily dependent on just one or a few such commodities. This combination of circumstances, it was argued, left their economies vulnerable to externally generated instability, which, by increasing uncertainty and risk, discouraged investment.[18]

Nor did foreign private investment offer a promising avenue of escape. Singer and others argued that foreign investment in the low-income countries, being generally concentrated in the production of primary products for export, had led to enclave types of activity having little effect on the general development of the host economy and that the main benefits were enjoyed in the country in which the investment originated.[19] Myint added an additional string to this bow, developing a plausible model in which labour remained low-paid and unskilled in spite of foreign investment.[20] The similarity of these arguments to classical and contemporary attacks on colonialism were very noticeable and this, in the eyes of many of us, made them all the more acceptable. We shall see in the next chapter that Nkrumah found them congenial to his own views.

The Rejection of Marginalism
The broadened concept of external economies deployed by Scitovsky and others to explain the persistence of international poverty dented the defences of traditional neo-classical theory. So too did the seeming inappropriateness of the free trade prescriptions of comparative advantage theory. But the attack of mainstream development economics was launched over a considerably broader front than this. Various additional reasons were advanced for doubting the relevance of a traditional approach to the problems of the low-income countries.

Scitovsky and others noted that the market size of many of these countries was very small by the standards of the industrial states, increasing the problems created by large (relative to the size of the market), indivisible investments and increasing returns to scale.[21] Small markets further tend to increase the incidence of monopolistic or semi-monopolistic industries, thereby further reducing the efficacy of market-oriented policies. Factor markets were also likely to be highly imperfect in the conditions of the underdeveloped countries, creating dualistic economies, and factor prices substantially at variance with their social marginal products.[22] Information flows were also likely to be poor, and these factors would tend to make for low elasticities of supply (which is why deteriorating terms of trade held such serious implications). Thus, the price signals of the market would, at best, meet with weak responses and, at worst, with responses that were socially damaging.

There was pessimism, too, about the supply of entrepreneurial talent. Leibenstein's low-level trap envisaged small incentives for and, therefore, a limited supply of entrepreneurship; Lewis and Nurkse also considered there to be a general shortage of entrepreneurs; and Hirschman based much of his case for unbalanced growth on the view that the capacity to make investment decisions is among the scarcest 'factors' in these countries.[23] If a general shortage existed, it added a further reason for elasticity pessimism and doubts about the efficacy of a market-economy approach to development.

Considerations such as these led the authors of a seminal UN report to conclude in 1951 that the marginal principle, 'though still valid, is often of secondary usefulness'.[24] Unconstrained by the caution which infects the authors of official reports, Myrdal was willing to go much further, arguing that 'criteria for the national planning are . . . entirely outside the price system. There do not exist any "objective" criteria for economic planning.'[25] Myrdal further attacked the hidden value premises of neo-classical theory, which he regarded as 'a rationalisation of the dominant interests in the industrial countries where it was first put forward and later developed'.[26] He was especially hard on trade theory which predicted a gradual international equalization of factor prices and incomes in a world of growing inequalities. Seers was another who attacked conventional theory (and textbooks) as being based upon the 'special case' of an industrial economy.[27]

Finally, and perhaps above all, marginalism was attacked as being too static to be very relevant to the essentially dynamic question of development. Thus, Hirschman:[28]

> Instead of concentrating exclusively on the husbanding of scarce resources such as capital and entrepreneurship, our approach leads us to look for 'pressures' and 'inducement mechanisms' that will elicit and mobilise the largest possible amounts of these resources.

Indeed, the very title of his book, *The Strategy of Economic Development*, implied a break with marginalism, for an economy guided by an Invisible Hand has no need of a development strategy, nor any means of employing one. But no one was able to put it better than Schumpeter. The application of static analysis to the process of growth was fruitless, in his view, for development 'is a distinct phenomenon, entirely foreign to what may be observed in the circular flow or in the tendency towards equilibrium. It is spontaneous and discontinuous change . . . which forever alters and displaces the equilibrium state previously existing.'[29] Capitalist development, as he saw it, was a process of 'Creative Destruction.'[30] General equilibrium theory has little to offer in a process of Creative Destruction.

The Disequilibrium Strategy of Development

It is easier to obtain a consensus among doctors about what ails a patient than about how to cure him. So it is with economists, and it would be idle to pretend that those members of the profession most concerned with development were unanimous in the advice they offered to low-income countries. There was, for example, an extensive debate on the relative merits of balanced and unbalanced growth, especially between Nurkse, urging simultaneous advance on all fronts, and Hirschman, espousing a challenge-and-response argument for the deliberate creation of disequilibria.[31] Despite the disagreements, it is nevertheless suggested that, at the beginning of the sixties, a substantial (but not necessarily identical) majority could have been mustered in support of each of the following propositions – propositions which, as will be shown, Nkrumah also accepted:

1. Economic development is a discontinuous process of structural transformation.
2. Above a certain critical level of per capita income, growth tends to become self-sustaining.

3. To break out of the poverty trap and achieve self-sustaining growth, a 'critical minimum effort' or 'big push' is required.
4. While this push requires many inputs, its single most important component is a massive increase in the ratio of investment to national income.
5. Development entails industrialization, which, by choice or from necessity, will concentrate on satisfying the home market for manufactures.

The remainder of this section is offered by way of elaboration and substantiation.

The first proposition was (and probably remains) the least controversial. In this but not in other respects the profession embraced Schumpeter's vision as its own. Nurkse, Lewis, Leibenstein, Hirschman and Rostow – all can be shown to have expressed sentiments along these lines,[32] and an attempt was made to distinguish between growth and development, with the latter but not the former necessarily involving structural transformation.[33]

The second proposition has already been touched upon, at least by implication, in the description of the views of those who saw the problem of poverty in terms of vicious circles or analogous concepts. If one accepts Nurkse's view that both the inducement to invest and the ability to save are a rising function of per capita income (or the size of the market) and add to it Leibenstein's notion of a rate of population growth which goes up with income until it reaches a biological limit, plus a fairly constant incremental capital:output ratio, then indeed there is a critical point above which society can sustain levels of saving and investment sufficient to induce a growth of income in excess of the expansion of population. All this was demonstrated most elegantly by Leibenstein. Even those who would find it difficult to accept the assumptions necessary for a formal demonstration of the point are nevertheless likely to find it an intuitively appealing one, as expressed in Rostow's notion of the take-off:[34]

> The take-off is the interval when the old blocks and resistances are finally overcome. The forces making for economic progress, which yielded limited bursts and enclaves of modern activity, expand and come to dominate the society. Growth becomes its normal condition. Compound interest becomes built, as it were, into its habits and institutional structure.

The third proposition, the need for a 'big push', is essentially a logical corollary of the second. The theory underpinning it is that an economy which has not achieved the 'take-off' will not merely stagnate, it will retrogress. Until the critical level of income is achieved, income-depressing forces tend to dominate and the economy is constantly oscillating around a subsistence level of income.[35] Thus, there is likely to be a large gap between prevailing income levels and the take-off point, which no effort of everyday dimensions can close.

But of what might the 'big push' consist? This brings us to the fourth proposition. The influence of Keynes was very apparent here. Building on a Keynesian foundation and concerning themselves with the circumstances of industrial capitalist economies, Harrod and Domar had developed a theory of growth featuring a stable incremental capital:output ratio (ICOR),[36] and this proved a powerful simplifying assumption for others who wished to derive a model for the development of low-income countries. Given a constant ICOR, a rate of growth can be determined from a specified rate of investment, or vice versa. This being the case, a doubling, say, in the share of investment in GDP would also double the rate of growth of the economy and propel it towards the take-off point.

In none of the writings was the reasoning as crude or unqualified as this but certainly great stress was placed on capital formation as the prime mover. The 1951 UN report on measures for development stressed the need for net investment rates of at least 10 per cent of national income as compared with 5 per cent or less found in most underdeveloped countries.[37] The emphasis Nurkse placed on this factor is clear from what has already been said. Agreeing with the UN, Rostow saw the take-off as accompanied by a rise in net investment 'from, say, 5 per cent of the national income to 10 per cent or more.'[38] But the most famous formulation was that of Lewis:[39]

> The central problem in the theory of economic development is to understand the process by which a community which was previously saving and investing 4 or 5 per cent of its national income or less, converts itself into an economy where voluntary saving is running at about 12 to 15 per cent of national income or more. This is the central problem because the central fact of economic development is rapid capital accumulation (including knowledge and skills with capital). We cannot explain any 'industrial' revolution (as the economic historians pretend to do) until we can explain why saving increased relatively to national income.

Returning to the literature of the fifties on this topic, one is impressed by the fact that virtually all writers qualified their remarks on physical capital formation by drawing attention to the human and institutional factors that were a necessary complement to it if it were to achieve the desired rates of growth.[40] But it is the inevitable fate of authors to be remembered by their central ideas and not by the qualifying clauses they so carefully insert, so the main message that came across was that a massive investment effort was needed to break out of the poverty trap.

This brings us to the fifth proposition of mainstream development economics, that development entails industrialization. There are two logically distinct ways of understanding this. One can understand it as a *historical* statement, a generalization about the form which development took in the now high-income countries. However, it is easy to slip from the objective patterns of the past to make *prescriptive* statements about the form that development will or should take in the future, and several writers found the journey from positive to normative statements an easy one.

The historical connection between industrialization and development is obvious. After all, the process by which the countries of Europe modernized their economies is called the industrial revolution, and empirical research by Kuznets, Chenery and others has provided ample demonstration of the past importance of the expansion of manufacturing.[41] Undeterred by the dangers of extrapolating history into the future, some found the historical connection so strong that they apparently took it for granted that history would repeat itself. Thus for Rostow the development of one or more substantial manufacturing industries with a high rate of growth was one of the three defining characteristics of the take-off, and Scitovsky simply referred to development theory as 'the theory of industrialisation.'[42]

This is not surprising since, quite apart from historical experiences, there was a powerful battery of a priori arguments to be marshalled in favour of industrialization.[43] It is more likely than agriculture to be associated with a modernization of attitudes and the generation of technical progress.[44] Productivity tends to be higher in industry. The growth of industry generates a demand for agricultural goods, thus stimulating the development of agriculture, and provides material incentives for agricultural expansion in the form of low-cost manufactured consumer goods. Industrialization is a precondition of agricultural progress in countries with high population densities, by providing non-agricultural avenues of employment to relieve pressure on the land. More generally, industrialization is a means of reducing unemployment.

But perhaps the most important argument was that developed by Hirschman.[45] His approach was to examine the power of various types of economic activity to form linkages with other sectors of the economy of the type that would show up in an input:output table, either by creating a demand for their products as inputs or a supply that may lower the costs of other industries – an approach to the subject which was a far cry from that of comparative advantage. He produced evidence by Chenery and Watanabe in which manufacturing scored heavily by these criteria. Primary production naturally comes out poorly, for backward linkages are practically ruled out by definition, and so do various service activities.[46] Hirschman argued in favour of a sequence of development in which investment in directly productive activities was generally in advance of the creation of complementary social overhead capital and, as between industry and agriculture, concluded that the latter

> stands convicted on the count of its lack of direct stimulus to the setting up of new activities through linkage effects: the superiority of manufacturing in this respect is crushing. This may yet be the most important reason militating against any complete specialisation of under-developed countries in primary production.

Hirschman further advocated *import-substituting* industrialization, although several writers anticipated him in this. Prebisch was an early advocate, in one of the first of his UN publications,[47] and we have already noted how writers like Nurkse and Scitovsky stressed the expansion and satisfaction of the domestic market in their own writings. In their view, import-substitution was both necessary in view of the protectionist policies of industrial countries and, given the impracticability of achieving a successful export trade without first establishing a home base, also desirable as a means of internalizing for the economy as a whole the external benefits which they associated with manufacturing.

Again, it is not suggested that the profession was unanimous in advocating the superiority of an industrialization based on manufacturing import-substitutes. Some 'mainstream' writers, notably Lewis,[48] had major reservations about it. But it is contended that there was sufficient agreement to justify saying that this was the predominant view at the beginning of the sixties. I agree with Johnson when he describes an emphasis on the need for industrialization and on the potency of protectionist policies as constituting 'the prevalent strand in the contemporary "conventional wisdom" of the theory of economic development policy.'[49]

It remains in this account of mainstream development economics to examine the view which was taken of the role of the state in the development process.

Planning as a Substitute for the Market

The critique of marginalism set out earlier and the positive advocacy of a big push, disequilibrium strategy of industrialization predetermined a very active role for the state. Arguments concerning externalities described above constituted a powerful theoretical basis for state planning which most of the writers were quick to deploy. The point was put succinctly by Scitovsky:[50]

> In an economy in which economic decisions are decentralized, a system of communications is needed to enable each person who makes economic decisions to learn about the economic decisions of others and co-ordinate his decisions with theirs. In the market economy, prices are the signalling device that informs each person of other people's economic decisions; and the merit of perfect

competition is that it would cause prices to transmit information reliably and people to respond to this information properly. Market prices, however, reflect the economic situation as it is and not as it will be. For this reason, they are much more useful for co-ordinating current production decisions, which are immediately effective and guided by short-run considerations, than they are for co-ordinating investment decisions, which have a delayed effect and – looking ahead to a long future period – should be governed not by what the present economic situation is but by what the future economic situation is expected to be. The proper co-ordination of investment decisions, therefore, would require a signalling device to transmit information about present plans and future considerations as they are determined by present plans; and the pricing system fails to provide this. Hence the belief that there is need either for centralized investment planning or for some additional communication system to supplement the pricing system as a signalling device.

It must be added that the argument of this section applies with especial force to underdeveloped countries.

He regarded the argument particularly relevant to low-income countries because factor and product markets were likely to be even more imperfect than in industrial economies, and entrepreneurial talent was liable to be scarcer.

Even if the profession had taken a more positive view of the efficiency and dynamism of the market system, they were still practically bound to have advocated a greatly enlarged role for the state by their strategy of development. For what institution could give these economies a big push except the state? How could investment rates be doubled, or more, except at the instigation of some central planning authority? And how could industrialization which had been lacking be brought to vigorous life unless, at the very least, the government offered strong inducements for it? Moreover, increased emphasis on the use of mathematical and econometric techniques in economics, including the development of input-output and linear programming methods, meant that economists had more to offer in this area and a professional interest in the application of these techniques.

Thus, there sprang up a consensus in favour of development planning and in 1957 Myrdal could write that it was 'universally urged' that low-income countries 'should have an overall, integrated national plan.' Moreover, he said, 'Because of the various deficiencies in a backward country it is also accepted by everyone that the government will have to take over many functions which in most advanced countries in the Western world were left to private business.'[51] We will see that Nkrumah fully shared these views.

The emphasis in the literature on the development strategies described in the previous section was placed heavily upon macro-economic magnitudes and this had its effect on those who wrote in this

period on the techniques of planning. Stress was placed upon aggrega-
tive concepts like saving and investment ratios, average and incremental capital:output ratios, and import propensities. The planning
literature was also biased towards the development and application of
econometric techniques, with less concern for the policy content of
plans or their micro-economic implementation.[52]

The task of planning included compensation for the distortions of
actual prices, which characteristically over-valued labour (along the
lines of the article by Lewis already cited), and under-valued capital
and foreign exchange. A similar task was to foster import-substituting
industries by reducing the openness of the economy. The planners
were also to impart a longer time-horizon to investment and consumption decisions than the typically myopic view consumers and entrepreneurs of low-income countries would tend to take. And, since
entrepreneurship was generally expected to be scarce, the state would
have to fill the gap with a large investment programme of its own.

Whether its investment programme should take the state into
directly productive activities was a matter on which there was unease.
Several writers identified here as of the mainstream took the view that
it would probably be preferable for state investment to be concentrated on the conventional provision of social overhead capital, but
that it could well happen that the state would often have to play a more
active role in the industrialization drive.[53] A somewhat similar attitude
was displayed towards administrative controls. A few writers advocated import restrictions as a means of buttressing the balance of payments and of stimulating domestic industrialization;[54] others remained
silent or agnostic on the issue.

While most mainstream writers argued in support of more aid from
the industrial nations, they also stressed the importance of a much
improved domestic savings effort to the achievement of self-sustaining
growth. Here, too, the state was seen as having a major responsibility,
in promoting banks and other financial institutions to mobilize voluntary saving, and through tax policies. An increased tax effort was quite
commonly taken as equivalent to an increase in domestic saving, on the
(usually unstated) assumptions that a trivial amount of the additional
revenue would otherwise be saved (or would not be invested productively) and that the government would devote the extra revenue to
capital formation rather than increased public consumption.[55] Others
pointed to the potential of deficit financing as a means of mobilizing
resources for development. Lewis, for example, argued that in a closed
economy the use of inflation to finance productive capital formation
tends to be self-correcting: the supply of goods catches up with
demand and prices cease to rise or may even fall.[56] Similarly, the Latin
American structuralist school saw inflation as an inevitable, if undesir-
able, symptom of an adequately large development effort.[57]

In brief, the mainstream development economics of the fifties was highly interventionist. It established powerful theoretical and practical arguments against reliance upon the market mechanism and advocated a strategy of development which placed the state in the centre of the stage. A central planning agency was to provide inducements or commands superior to the price signals of the market. There was much less agreement on whether the instrumentalities of the state should be largely indirect, i.e. modifying but working through the market mechanism by such means as tariff policy and the provision of tax incentives for investment, or direct, i.e. replacing the market by administrative controls and the establishment of state-owned industries. It is not possible, in my view, to identify a consensus of this issue. But there was virtual unanimity on the large role of the state – a unanimity which extended to Ghana.

Dissident Voices
This survey of the development literature of the fifties would be at fault if it conveyed the impression that the profession was completely agreed about all the ideas presented above. I have tried to indicate in the text and its footnotes the degree of agreement that was achieved on the chief propositions of the literature and some of the reservations that were expressed. The task here has been to identify the main thrust of the writings on development during the period under study. Various writers made important contributions to aspects of this thrust without necessarily agreeing with the rest of it. Probably only a minority of the writers in question could be identified as agreeing with the whole of the mainstream view as here presented. It is nevertheless submitted that there was a sufficient consensus on each of the important elements of the argument for the message to be clear to those studying development or practising it in planning agencies and the like.

The existence of a dissident school should, however, be acknowledged. Its earliest and most vigorous spokesman was Bauer, who has spent most of the last twenty years swimming against the mainstream and now finds himself coming into fashion. His attacks on such hallowed notions as the vicious circle of poverty, central planning and international aid, and his defences of the decentralized decision-making process of the market are well known but perhaps too strongly expressed to command more than minority support.[58] Bruton, Myint and Viner were among more moderate early sceptics, and the outlines were beginning to be discernible of a distinctive Chicago school.[59] But if theirs were not exactly voices in the wilderness, they were too much in the minority to be heard easily, and too much out of fashion to be heeded.

The Congruence with Marxism
The views of Marxist economists have been deliberately neglected in the foregoing paragraphs, for there is clearly a sense in which they

could not plausibly be said to belong to the mainstream of Western economic thought on the problems of development. Yet mainstream development economics was at many points highly congenial to Marxists. This is of considerable importance when we turn to examine economic policies in Ghana during the Nkrumah period, for Nkrumah called himself a Marxist and was clearly influenced by Marxian ideas.

Perhaps the congruence of mainstream and Marxian views was not too surprising, for inequality has long been one of the principal concerns of Marxian thought, and the hidden value premise of development economics is an egalitarian one – that world inequalities in living standards ought to be reduced and that policy alternatives should be assessed chiefly according to whether or not they have the tendency to achieve this result. Whatever the reason, it is probably true to say that contemporary Marxian thought was in general agreement with the main tenets of mainstream development economics.[60] It too regarded poverty as a self-perpetuating vicious circle which could only be broken by structural transformation. Naturally, they embraced the arguments which led to a rejection of marginalism and the open economy. The idea (although not the phraseology) of the big push was also in their writings, together with emphasis on the need for major increases in saving and investment, and a process of development which emphasized industrialization. They were also, of course, among the advocates of centralized planning and of very wide-ranging state involvement in the economy.[61]

However, to the non-Marxian body of thought they brought some distinctive insights of their own. The existence of past colonial exploitation, the economic distortions (dependence on primary production) to which it gave rise, and the highly skewed distribution of income within many low-income countries were dimensions which the Marxists added to the notion of the vicious circle.[62] Similarly, they stressed the large potential that existed for raising national savings by tapping the excess incomes of the wealthy and by expropriating foreign investors.[63] And they went considerably further than most in their arguments for central planning and governmental control of the economy. All in all, though, the congruence of Marxian and non-Marxian thought on the development issue was a rather remarkable and mutually reinforcing one.

The Congruence with Nationalism

We should also note how easily the literature of the fifties could be fitted into the anti-colonial struggle of the same period, from which Ghana had just emerged. The congruence of the ideas of mainstream development economics (reinforced by the Marxian analysis) with those of the new nationalist leaders of Africa and Asia is one which writers as far apart as Myrdal and Johnson have noticed.[64] Some of the economists in question were quite explicit about their anti-colonialism. Lewis, for example, in his celebrated essay on the labour-surplus economy argued that 'the record of every imperial power in Africa in modern times is one of impoverishing the subsistence economy, either by taking away the people's land, or by demanding forced labour in the capitalist sector, or by imposing taxes to drive people to work for capitalist employers.'[65] Myrdal similarly related economic backwardness to colonialism.[66] The arguments deployed to the effect that there was a secular tendency for the terms of trade of low-income countries to deteriorate, and that foreign investment tended merely to create enclaves, the main direct and indirect benefits of which were enjoyed in the investing country, also provided good intellectual ammunition to those embattled against the colonial powers.

The type of development strategy summarized earlier also proved highly attractive to nationalist leaders. The anti-colonial struggle, and the subsequent achievement of independence by many Asian and African countries, generated expectations of rapid improvements in living standards, and the 'big push' type of strategy gave the impression that quick results were there to be had. If the new nations could capitalize upon the patriotic fervour created by the struggle for independence then, after a heroic initial effort, the take-off could be achieved and the benefits enjoyed. The stress on import-substituting industrialization was especially congenial, for a belief in this was (and probably remains) common ground among nationalist leaders seeking also 'economic independence' whose active support and political power is often derived from the growing number of city-dwellers.[67]

The fact that development economics lent support to the nationalist cause in low-income countries ensured that these ideas would have a wide currency and would exert much influence there. This helps to explain why the new nations, Ghana among them, implemented many of the policy recommendations of the literature. Western economists can normally expect to be opposed or (more usually) ignored by their own governments because they are often urging policies involving some real or imagined political unpopularity. In the newly emerging nations of the third world, politics and economics marched together. The profession enjoyed unaccustomed popularity and the leading figures in development economics were in great demand as advisers to the governments of underdeveloped countries.[68]

Destruction of the Consensus

Any major thrust of new ideas generates a counter-revolution, which has duly occurred in development economics. Beginning around the middle of the sixties, it has gathered sufficient force and support so that it is no longer possible to talk of a mainstream of development economics.[69] Instead we have an interplay of many ideas; the consensus has been destroyed.

It would be beyond the scope of this chapter to go at all deeply into the controversies which have arisen since the mid-sixties but, since it will be a contention of a later chapter that economic policies in Ghana in 1966–71 did in some measure reflect the changing fashions in development economics, some account of the new literature should be given. What follows, however, is only a brief, schematic presentation.

To some degree the counter-revolution was based upon a rejection of the theoretical basis of the old orthodoxy. Nurkse's theory of balanced growth was an early casualty, ceasing to have much practical importance with the admission that his theory was 'an exercise in economic development with unlimited supplies of capital'.[70] Unlimited supply of capital is scarcely one of the attributes of low-income countries, with the exception of some of the petroleum producers. Nurkse might also have added that his theory assumed unlimited absorptive capacity for investment, and that assumption, too, scarcely commends itself. Rostow's historical theory of the stages of economic growth was also rejected fairly quickly, especially after a devastating critique by Kuznets[71] which was all the more ironic because Rostow had named Kuznets as father of the child. The hypothesis of a secular deterioration in the terms of trade of low-income countries also came under severe attack and would not today command wide acceptance.[72]

Another factor was the influence of historical findings which appeared to show that factor inputs, as such, were unimportant sources of economic growth by comparison with the accumulation of knowledge and the application of technical progress.[73] The very heavy stress on inputs of new factors, especially capital formation, and the neglect of technological progress was called into question.

Nevertheless, much of the theoretical basis of the early orthodoxy remains intact (a fact which should cause some unease among its critics) and a far more important cause of the counter-revolution was an alleged failure of several of the earlier ideas as *practical* policy solutions. The chief areas of disillusionment concerned the effectiveness of import-substituting industrialization (ISI) and planning. Evidence from Latin America and elsewhere has shown that ISI can impose heavy welfare costs upon the domestic economy without providing the dynamic effects expected of it.[74] Even the political left, influenced by the Chinese model in which 'agriculture is the foundation and industry the leading sector', has begun to adopt a more cautious approach to industrialization.[75]

There is a similarly widespread acceptance that the early advocates of development planning under-emphasized its practical limitations. Waterston provided a coolly detached study drawing attention to the large gap between the promise and performance of planning;[76] we hear now of a 'crisis in planning',[77] and Healey probably speaks for a majority when he describes the results of twenty years of planned development as, 'sadly disillusioning for those who believed that plan-

ning was the only way'.[78] Inadequate flows of information and inefficient administration are now seen as severely limiting the capacity of
planning to reap the benefits which it should theoretically have
achieved, and a fairly common combination of import and exchange
controls plus an over-valued currency is increasingly seen as introducing unwanted distortions into a number of low-income
economies.[79] Similarly, the naive presumption that an increase in tax
revenues is equivalent to an almost equal increase in domestic saving
has given way to a realization that governments also have high marginal propensities to consume.[80]

With this disillusionment has come, from some quarters; a reassertion of the relevance of conventional Western economic theory.
The inefficiencies generated by undiscriminating ISI and by unsuccessful attempts at planning and controlling have led to a revival of interest
in the fundamental concern of neo-classical theory – the efficient
allocation of resources.[81] Bruton's 1965 textbook is largely cast in a
marginalist mould and devotes just one sceptical chapter to strategies
of development, under the heading of 'Some Special Topics'.[82] The
more recent textbook of economic theory written for students in low-
income countries by Bell and Todaro is even more explicit in its
reassertion of marginalism,[83] and the principles of comparative advantage seem to be coming back into favour. However, the debate over the
relevance of conventional economic theory is by no means settled and
the disequilibrium school retains a good deal of support.[84]

This disillusionment and the occurrence of a few 'development
disasters,' such as the break-up of Pakistan, has led many to re-
examine the traditional scope of development economics. A whole
issue of the *Journal of Development Studies* was devoted to the definition and measurement of development,[85] and many researchers have
turned away from the former preoccupation with growth to investigate
the problems of unequal income distribution and unemployment in
low-income countries.[86]

In general, it seems reasonable to characterize the shift in opinions
since the mid-sixties as a movement towards a greater stress on
shorter-term allocative efficiency and equity, which are no longer seen
as antithetical to dynamic growth. Rather little thought, however,
appears to have been devoted to the practical problems of moving
from an economy in which there are large price distortions to one in
which the market more truly reflects relative scarcity values, although
a rapidly burgeoning literature on social cost-benefit analysis seeks to
provide ways for compensating for differences between private and
social valuations.[87] In Ghana, too, there was from the mid-sixties a
greater concern with shorter-run efficiency but there were many
difficulties about attempting a transition from a command to a more
market-oriented economy. Chapters 11 and 12, which deal with this
topic, thus provide a commentary on the practicability of some of the

ideas which have come to the fore in the literature during the last few years. The next task, however, is to examine Nkrumah's development strategy and its affinities with the earlier ideas of mainstream development economics.

NOTES

[1] Leibenstein, 1957, p. 4.

[2] Rosenstein-Rodan's 1943 article perhaps marked the starting point and, of course, earlier writers, especially in the classical period, were also much concerned with development. Keynes and (as will be shown) Schumpeter were also particularly influential on later writers. (*See* Arndt, 1972, on development economics before 1945.) But development economics 'took off' in the fifties, beginning perhaps with the UN's *Measures for the Development of Underdeveloped Countries* (1951) and including major works by Nurkse (1953), Lewis (1954 and 1955), Scitovsky (1954), Myrdal (1956 and 1957), Leibenstein (1957) and Hirschman (1958). This period of 'grand theorising,' strongly marked by the boldness of its ideas, might conveniently be said to have concluded with Rostow's *Stages of Economic Growth* (1960), with Prebisch's 1964 UNCTAD document seen as a late entry into the field.

[3] Nurkse, 1953, p. 6. *See* especially chapter 1 for a statement of the position summarized in this paragraph.

[4] *See* Leibenstein, 1957, especially chapters 3 and 8.

[5] This was well within the Keynesian tradition, as it had been developed by Harrod (1948) and Domar (1957).

[6] Leibenstein, pp. 186–7. He also postulated that beyond some relatively high income level population growth would begin to decline (*see* especially his 1954 *Theory of Economic-Demographic Development*) but that is less relevant to the purposes of the present study.

[7] Myrdal, 1957, p. 55 and *passim. See also* Myrdal, 1956, especially pp. 15–16.

[8] Rostow, 1960, p. 4.

[9] Kuznets, 1964.

[10] The idea can be traced directly back to Allyn Young (1928) – who in turn traces it back to Adam Smith – and is central to the views propounded by Rosenstein-Rodan (1943), Nurkse (1953, *see* especially pp. 13–15), Leibenstein (1957, *see* especially p. 106) and, in a somewhat transmuted form, Hirschman (1958, *see* especially p. 71).

[11] Scitovsky, 1954, *passim. See* Mishan, 1971, pp. 6–7, for a brief, dismissive discussion of this extension of the concept of externalities.

[12] Chenery, 1959.

[13] Scitovsky, p. 307.

[14] Nurkse, 1959, especially lecture 2.

[15] UN, 1949.

[16] Singer, 1950. The quotation is from p.165. While written in quite a different context, Bhagwati's 1958 article on 'immiserizing growth' added another layer of doubt.

[17] Myrdal (1956, chapter XIII), Kindleberger (1962, chapter 7, especially p. 178), and Prebisch (1964, *passim*).

[18] *See* UN, 1953, pp. 6–11 and 14–21, and Myrdal, 1956, pp. 238–46. for examples of this type of argument. The literature is well summarized in Macbean, 1966, chapter 1.

[19] Singer (1950) and Myrdal (1956, chapter XIII and 1957, especially p. 60).

[20] Myint, (1954). *See also* Myint, 1967, chapter 4.

[21] *See* Rosenstein-Rodan, 1943, *passim.*

[22] For a good account of theories of dualism *see* Higgins, 1959, especially pp. 325–33.

[23] Leibenstein (1957, chapter 9), Lewis (1955, pp. 99 and 350), Nurkse (1953, p. 10, n.1), and Hirschman (1958, pp. 24–8).

[24] UN, 1951, p. 49.

[25] Myrdal, 1957, p. 89.

[26] Myrdal, 1957, p. 99. *See also* Joan Robinson, 1969, who deals brilliantly with the value biases of economic theory.

[27] Seers, 1963, *passim.*

[28] Hirschman, 1958, p. 6.

[29] Schumpeter, 1934, p. 66.

[30] Schumpeter, 1950, p. 83.

[31] In practice, Ghana employed a disequilibrium strategy and her experience is discussed in relation to Hirschman's writings in chapters 8 and 12.

[32] Nurkse's notion of balanced growth was an example of a belief in structural transformation, as was Leibenstein's critical minimum effort. Rostow's notion of the 'take-off' involved major changes in the socio-economic structure (*see* Rostow, 1960, p. 39). Lewis (1955, pp. 142–7) also expected growth to occur in discontinuous surges involving major changes in economic institutions and other variables. Hirschman's conception of unbalanced growth can also be interpreted as a theory of induced structural transformation. On the relevance of a Schumpetarian model to the circumstances of low-income countries *see* Wallich, 1958, and Rimmer, 1961.

[33] For an example of the application of this distinction, *see* Clower *et al.,* 1966.

[34] Rostow, 1960, p. 7.

[35] *See* footnote 6, above.

[36] *See* Harrod, 1948, and Domar, 1957; also Kurihara, 1959, especially chapters 3–6.

[37] UN, 1951, p. 35.

[38] Rostow, 1960, p. 8.

[39] Lewis, 1954, p. 416. In this article Lewis developed the theory in which there is a large reserve army of unemployed labour with a zero social margin product, where the rate of growth is determined by the rate of capital formation, and the latter is determined largely by the share of profits in the national income. The belief that many developing countries have a large reservoir of unemployed labour encouraged the view that capital was the key ingredient which was missing in order that they might grow. Lewis was careful to define capital as including knowledge and skills but, again, the main emphasis was on physical capital.

[40] In his 1955 book Lewis discusses many determinants of growth besides capital formation. *See also* Nurkse, 1953, pp. 5 and 156–7. Rostow (1960) has a lot to say about the human and institutional pre-conditions for the take-off, and Leibenstein explicitly declined to give his concept of the critical minimum effort any single specification (1957, p. 105).

[41] *See* Kuznets, 1964, chapter II, and 1965, especially pp. 95–7 and 194–5. In the index of the earlier of these two we find the entry 'Industrialisation. *See* Economic Growth.' Also, Chenery, 1960, *passim.*

[42] Rostow, 1960, p. 39; Scitovsky, 1954, p. 299. Rosenstein-Rodan, 1943 and 1944, was among the earliest of the writers of this persuasion. *See also* Mandlebaum, 1947, *passim.*

[43] For an excellent survey of these arguments and their origin, *see* Sutcliffe, 1971, chapter 3.

[44] Myrdal (1956, p. 227) quotes Galbraith with approval: 'a purely agricultural country is likely to be unprogressive even in its agriculture.'

[45] Hirschman, 1958, *passim.* The following quotation is from pp. 109–10.

[46] Yotopoulos and Nugent, 1973, using improved measurement techniques, confirm the inferior linkage effects of primary and service activities, and the superiority of manufacturing by this criterion (although there are significant differences between individual manufacturing industries).

[47] UN, 1950, p. 6.

[48] Lewis, 1955, especially pp. 276–83.

[49] Johnson, 1967, p. 132.

[50] Scitovsky, 1954, pp. 305–6. Rosenstein-Rodan (1943, p. 248) similarly argued that 'the whole of industry to be created is to be treated and planned like one huge firm or trust', but Nurkse had his reservations and was uncomfortable with the idea that his arguments led to an interventionist conclusion. Whether 'balanced growth' was to be achieved by central planning he preferred to view as a matter of administrative form and, with an obviously greater belief in the efficacy of a market economy, he constantly reverted to the historical example of Japan, where the state played a major initiating role and then gradually phased out of directly productive activities. See, for example, Nurkse, 1953, pp. 15–16.

[51] Myrdal, 1957, p. 79.

[52] Tinbergen and his colleagues were influential in this direction (see for example, Tinbergen, 1958).

[53] See footnote 50. See also Rostow, 1960, p. 25, and Hirschman, 1958, p. 203.

[54] See Myrdal, 1956, p. 283, and Nurkse (with qualifications), 1953, chapter V.

[55] The equation of taxation with saving is particularly strong in Nurkse, 1953, pp. 142–52, and is also evident in the UN, 1951.

[56] Lewis, 1954, pp. 427–31.

[57] See Furtado, 1954, especially pp. 335–6, for an example, and also Hirschman, 1958, pp. 158–9.

[58] See, for example, Bauer and Yamey, 1957, and, more recently Bauer, 1972.

[59] See, for example, Bruton, 1955, Myint, 1967, Viner, 1952, and Wall, 1972.

[60] I have taken the distinguished British economist Maurice Dobb, and Paul Baran as the chief spokesmen of the Marxian school (see especially Dobb, 1963, and Baran, 1952 and 1957). Note that these writers are of the traditional, Soviet-oriented, school; Maoist and other more recent variations take a rather different view on such matters as industrialization and central planning.

[61] On the vicious circle, see, for example, Dobb, 1963, pp. 17–18. On the need for structural transformation and a big push, Baran. 1957, pp. 3–4 and 13–14. For a most subtle and persuasive statement of the Scitovsky-type externalities argument for planning see Dobb, 1960, chapter 1; see also Baran, 1952, pp. 85–6. On the importance of increased investment and saving, see Baran, 1957, pp. 20–21, and Dobb, 1963, p. 41. On industrialization, see Baran, 1957, pp. 273–82, and Dobb, 1963, p. 47 (although both these writers saw the pace of industrialization as being conditioned by the ability of agriculture to generate the surplus needed to provide the resources for industrialization).

[62] Dobb, 1963, pp. 17–18 and 41, and Baran, 1952, pp. 88–91.

[63] Baran, 1957, pp. 261–7.

[64] See Johnson, 1967, pp. 135–6 and Myrdal, 1968, pp. 1150–5.

[65] Lewis, 1954, p. 410.

[66] Myrdal, 1957, p. 60. Myint was another to deploy a modified critique of colonialism to explain the lack of development in certain types of economy, although he falls only rather awkwardly into the mainstream school (see Myint, 1967, especially chapters 3–5).

[67] Sutcliffe, 1971, p. 64, notes in respect of the agriculture versus industry debate, that 'the most widely held and influential opinions on this controversial subject are political or sociological rather than economic,' and goes on to provide examples.

[68] As will be shown in the next chapter, Seers, Lewis, Kaldor and Hirschman were among the leading economists consulted by the Nkrumah government in Ghana, plus the chief Hungarian expert on development, Joszef Bognar. We should notice here a potential conflict between development economics and nationalism in that the former was concerned to argue for more international aid whereas nationalists often professed to be suspicious of the economic dependence it might entail ('we want trade not aid'). In practice, however, development plans looked for inflows of aid, sometimes so large as to be quite unfeasible.

[69] In addition to the works referred to in footnotes 58 and 59, the publication of Bruton's Principles of Development Economics in 1965 and Myrdal's Asian Drama in 1968

may be regarded as of importance in the break-up of the old consensus. A recent article by Healey (1972) surveys the battlefield well, although I would not agree with him that there is yet a new consensus.

[70] Nurkse, 1961, p. 250.

[71] *See* chapter 2 of Rostow (ed.), 1963.

[72] For a highly critical review of Prebisch (1964) *see* Johnson, 1967, pp. 249–50, and the study by Lipsey to which he refers. In similar vein, Macbean (1966, *passim*) was surprised to discover that export instability apparently had few of the adverse effects on development that earlier writers had predicted.

[73] *See* Kuznets, 1964, chapter II, and Dennison, 1967.

[74] Bruton and his colleagues at Williams College have done much work on this (*see* Bruton, 1970). *See also* Hirschman, 1968, and Little *et al.*, 1970.

[75] Sutcliffe, 1971, p. 66.

[76] Waterston, 1966A, particularly chapter IX.

[77] *See* a book of that title edited by Faber and Seers, 1972.

[78] Healey, 1972, p. 761.

[79] *See* Myint, 1967, p. 120, and Johnson, 1967, pp. 69–70.

[80] *See* Please, 1967, and subsequent IBRD papers on this topic.

[81] *See* Little *et al.*, 1970, especially p. 227, and also the associated country studies.

[82] Bruton, 1965.

[83] Bell and Todaro, 1969. *See* especially pp. xii, 3 and 469–70.

[84] For a recent and fairly unabashed statement of a structuralist case *see* Green, 1970, and, with various qualifications, Sutcliffe, 1971. Even in his *Asian Drama* (1968) Myrdal echoes much of the earlier thinking, as well as some of the subsequent disillusionment. *See also* the highly critical review of Bell and Todaro by Stewart, 1971.

[85] When I was an undergraduate a dozen years ago attempts such as that by Frankel (1953) to question the usefulness of national accounting aggregates as measurements of development or its absence were regarded as being deeply reactionary; now this seems in order. The summary of a recent article by Seers probably expresses an important body of opinion:

> Development means creating the conditions for the realisation of human personality. Its evaluation must therefore take into account three linked economic criteria: (i) poverty; (ii) unemployment; (iii) inequality. GNP can grow rapidly without any improvement on these criteria; so development must be measured more directly. (Seers, 1972)

[86] About half of the 'development economists' who attended a meeting at Williams College in October 1972 to describe their research work turned out to be working in the unemployment/income distribution area. Mahbub-el Haq (1971) and Healey (1972) provide good statements of the recent growth of concern with these topics.

[87] *See* Henderson, 1968, for a good general survey of this literature. Little *et al.*, 1970, chapter 10, provide the only explicit discussion of the problems of transition that I have seen.

3   The Economic Strategies of Nkrumah and his Successors

The previous chapter asserted that economic policies in Ghana during the sixties coincided with many of the leading ideas on development policy then in vogue. The task of this chapter, then, is to set out the economic strategies of successive governments in Ghana and to demonstrate their affinities with the ideas surveyed in chapter 2. The emphasis here, as in the whole book, is on the Nkrumah period, because the drive for development was then at its strongest and policies were at their most ambitious.

There is, however, a problem of authentication. The views of Nkrumah, his colleagues and his professional planners did not always coincide, were not always internally consistent or even coherent, and changed with time. The same can be said, although with less force, of those who ruled from 1966. How, then, is it possible to offer a description of these views that has a plausible claim to be accurate? Examination of the declared aims of the development plans will not do, for often they did not accurately state the actual intentions of the governments which published them.[1] For the Nkrumah period I have taken the most consistently expressed views of Nkrumah himself as the basis from which to work. Party publications, the views of other members of his government and party during the last years of his rule makes supplementary sources but only when they were consistent with the known views of The Leader. The complete domination of the man over his government and party during the last last years of his rule makes this a more fruitful way of going about the problem. However, even Nkrumah's public views cannot be taken uncritically, for statesmen's actions frequently depart from their declared intentions.[2] Following the advice of a member of President Nixon's first administration, 'Don't listen to what we say, watch what we do,' I have taken the actions of the governments of Ghana as a better guide to their intentions than their public pronouncements, whenever there was a major difference between the two.

I Nkrumah's Development Strategy

Changes in Ideology and Policy, 1959–62

Ghana became self-governing in 1951 and achieved full independence in 1957. Nkrumah and his Convention People's Party (CPP) were in power continuously from 1951 until the 1966 coup. But the period in which Nkrumah's policies were distinctively different from those of the colonialists he had fought so vehemently was much shorter, and 1961 can conveniently, if a little arbitrarily, be nominated as the year in which Nkrumah broke definitively with the policies inherited from the British.

By 1961 Nkrumah needed a change of direction. Ghanaians had been encouraged to believe that removal of the despised colonialists and their replacement by Ghanaians would bring manna to all. 'If we get self-government,' Nkrumah said in 1949, 'we'll transform the Gold Coast into a paradise in ten years,'[3] and an observer had noted that every trade union meeting he attended was devoted to politics: 'Their standard of living could not be thought of as being separate from their colonial status . . .'[4] With full political independence now achieved and with his party in undisputed control, Nkrumah's dilemma was the classical one of a nationalist leader: how to maintain the momentum and how to satisfy appetites whetted by a successful anti-colonial crusade?

In fact, the growth of the economy in the fifties was far from negligible, as is shown in chapter 4, but still there were unsatisfied expectations, and there is evidence that at the beginning of the sixties Nkrumah was worried about possible loss of support.[5] In particular it was necessary to repay the party activists who had worked in the belief that they would benefit materially. Owusu's description agrees with the finding of most students of the CPP when he says that the hard core of the party's support came from people 'who felt that they were suffering from relative economic deprivation and had strong desires for improving their economic (or class) status.'[6] While the party had some aspects of a genuine mass movement, drawing wide support from most walks of life (except the intelligentsia and the chiefs), it drew in particular from a young generation of Ghanaians with insufficient education to give them literacy or vocational skills, but enough to aspire to a white collar post or at least a city job.[7] 'Standard VII boys' they were called, emphasizing both the significance of their education and its limitations. A more pejorative term was 'verandah boys', for they were said to sleep on the verandahs of their masters or relatives, unable to afford anything better.

The struggle for independence[8] increased political consciousness and speeded up the process of modernization already under way. This brought to the fore relatively well-organized, articulate and politically influential interest groups who put pressures on the government and expected more sympathetic responses than the ones which they received from the colonialists.[9] Since it appeared that paradise would, after all, take a little longer than ten years, Nkrumah was brought face to face with the impossibility of meeting all their claims. One response to this dilemma was to internalize the more powerful pressure groups by making them wings of the party,[10] and (as the distinction between party and state became increasingly blurred) of the government itself. Thus Nkrumah succeeded in capturing the lobbies; in making them dependent on him instead of himself on them. But only up to a point, since they still exerted pressures and wrung concessions.[11]

No one was more acutely aware than Nkrumah of the fragile economic basis of his support:[12]

One may sometimes wonder if the Western Powers fully understand the dilemma facing political leaders in the emergent lands. They have gained independence for their peoples. The hazards and excitements of the struggle lie behind. Ahead lies the workaday world in which people must live and eat and hope and prosper. Independence of itself does not change this world. It simply creates the right political atmosphere for a real effort of national regeneration. But it does not supply all the economic and social tools. The leaders are now expected, simply as a result of having acquired independence, to work miracles.

(He forgot to add that miracles were what he had promised.) Again:[13]

We cannot tell our peoples that material benefits and growth and modern progress are not for them. If we do, they will throw us out and seek other leaders who promise more. And they will abandon us, too, if we do not in reasonable measure respond to their hopes.

Modernization, we have hinted, can be a disintegrative force. Economic specialization throws up powerful interest groups. Urbanization and education, which are almost defining characteristics of modernization, break up traditional authority and create socially chaotic conditions in the cities. Societies which start with a strong sense of identity and cohesion can usually absorb these shocks; nations arbitrarily carved out by colonizing powers, whose citizens' primary loyalites are likely to be to the family, clan or tribe can crumble under the stresses of modernization. As Apter notes, authority is the critical problem confronting the leaders of modernizing societies.[14]

Nkrumah had the task of building a nation despite strong disruptive forces. Organized opposition to Nkrumah during the fifties had been strongest in the Ashanti region, where there had been some resurgence of Ashanti 'nationalism'. In 1953 even CPP Ashanti Members of Parliament voted against their government for a larger Ashanti representation in the legislature[15] and just a few months before independence the opposition National Liberation Movement had threatened to declare a separate independence for Ashanti and called for a partition commission to apportion the assets and liabilities of the country. There were similar divisive tendencies among Ewe-speaking residents in the Volta region, with a substantial movement in favour of seceding from Ghana and joining Togo, also largely Ewe-speaking and administered as a French colony. There were even some rumblings in the North, and the opposition in these three areas joined forces against the CPP in the 1954 election.[16] Even suppression of organized opposition, well under way by the end of the fifties, did not put an end to this type of problem, for Apter notes that after 1961 'the Ashanti regional organisation of the CPP began to take over the grievances which hitherto had been a hallmark of the opposition.'[17]

So the pressure was on Nkrumah. He wanted to build a modern nation-state but to do this he needed power, an undoubted authority. To ensure his authority he had to provide at least a glimpse of that paradise he had promised – he had to make jobs and demonstrate some economic progress – and to do so quickly. This he had to achieve with a world cocoa market turning sour and while maintaining social cohesion. On the other hand, because he was now in charge of a sovereign state, his dominance of the party and government fully assured by the end of 1961, and with many of the opposition having either changed sides, in prison, or destined to go there, he had greater freedom of action than before. A change of direction was thus both politically necessary and possible.

Coincidental with this phase was a shifting balance of power within the ruling party and a movement towards more radical policies. The position of the more conservative old guard of the CPP was weakening. In 1959 Nkrumah delivered a speech to the CPP which placed more stress and urgency on socialism as the ideology of the CPP,[18] in the following year Nkrumah's long-standing but conservative Minister of Finance, Komla Gbedemah, was demoted (and in 1961 fled the country), and various other long-standing members of the party went out of favour. The men who replaced them were often more radical. Some of the old guard were later rehabilitated, but this did not restore the status quo ante, and economic policies after 1961 were little affected by internal power struggles within the ruling party.[20]

The change in the government's attitudes and actions was exemplified by greater efforts to expand trade with Russia and other communist countries.[21] and by the view it took of the roles of private enterprise and the state. During the fifties an Industrial Development Corporation was established which set up a number of publicly owned commercial enterprises. The government had always taken the view that these should be sold to private operators when they had become viable.[22] In 1960, however, Nkrumah announced that his government would henceforth 'place far greater emphasis on the development of Ghanaian cooperatives rather than encourage Ghanaians to start private business enterprises,' the state enterprises would not be handed over to private interests, and that private businesses 'must now stand on their own feet'.[23] Various other measures had been taken to promote and assist Ghanaian entrepreneurs, and as late as 1958 the government set up a committee to investigate the 'best means of assisting Ghanaian businessmen to overcome their difficulties'.[24] But Nkrumah became disillusioned with these efforts and came to believe – correctly in my view – that there was little realistic prospect of fostering an indigenous entrepreneurial class capable of industrializing the country at the speed he wanted.[25]

Even had there been the possibility, it is doubtful whether Nkrumah would have wanted to create such a class, for reasons of ideology and political power. He was very explicit about this, saying, 'we would be hampering our advance to socialism if we were to encourage the growth of Ghanaian private capitalism in our midst.'[26] There is evidence that he also feared the threat that a wealthy class of Ghanaian businessmen might pose to his own political power.[27] On the other hand, he could scarcely prohibit private Ghanaian business altogether, for many small traders had supported the CPP in the fifties and were thus owed economic rewards. Nkrumah conceived an ingenious solution. Ghanaian private enterprise was to be limited to small-scale concerns, 'provided that they are not nominees or sleeping partners for foreign interests.'[28] Its existence was to be contingent upon its willingness to operate within the socialist framework which he wished to create,[29] but the opportunities for Ghanaians to operate small-scale businesses were to be increased by restricting foreigners in this type of activity.[30] It was a brilliant tactic, for most Ghanaian businessmen and women do not aspire to an enterprise larger than one which they can directly control themselves,[31] and the exclusion of 'Lebanese' and 'Nigerians' from small trade would have been a popular move. However, it was left to later governments to implement this policy and win the applause.[32] Given Nkrumah's desire to keep Ghanaian private businesses small, his argument that 'Capital investment must be sought from abroad since there is no bourgeois class amongst us to carry on the necessary investments'[33] was disingenuous. But whilst his attitude to local private enterprise was made clear in the early sixties, his views on foreign private investment remained extremely ambivalent. He urged the need for foreign direct investment, pointing out that it brought in much-needed managerial and technical skills which could be passed on to Ghanaians.[34] A Capital Investments Act was passed in 1963, offering a wide range of fiscal and other concessions to would-be investors. But it was not the old, 'colonial' type of investment that was sought; there were strings to be attached as indicated by Nkrumah:[35]

The Government accepts the operation in the country of large-scale enterprises by foreign interests, provided that they accept the following conditions: first, that foreign private enterprises give the government the first option to buy their shares, whenever it is intended to sell all or part of the equity capital; and secondly that foreign private enterprises and enterprises jointly owned by the state and foreign private interests be required to reinvest 60 per cent of their net profits in Ghana.

No investor, of course, would be allowed to interfere with the domestic or external affairs of the country and, more generally, care should be taken to keep 'sufficient control to prevent undue exploitation' and to preserve 'integrity and sovereignty without crippling economic or political ties to *any* country, bloc, or system.'[36]

While Nkrumah insisted that 'our ideas of socialism can coexist with private enterprise',[37] he also inveighed against neo-colonial foreign domination,[38] his government starved the private sector of imported raw materials, spares and equipment,[39] and used exchange controls to prevent the repatriation of after-tax profits. It was, moreover, difficult to reconcile a coexistence of socialism and foreign investment with his statement that, 'The domestic policy of my government is the complete ownership of the economy by the state . . .'[40] It is hardly surprising, then, that he had little success in persuading investors that Ghana was the country for them, and in order to obtain the participation of foreign aluminium companies in the Volta River Project he was forced to make concessions to them which seemed humiliatingly like the type of neo-colonialist arrangement which he so strongly attacked.[41]

Nkrumah took a similarly schizophrenic view of aid. He asked for foreign aid[42] and it was envisaged that about a quarter of his government's *Seven-year Plan* should be financed by this means. But how to reconcile these facts with the views he published in *Neo-colonialism*? Aid is described there as 'the latest method of holding back the real development of the new countries . . . the paraphernalia of neo-colonialism . . .' Multilateral aid is 'Still another neo-colonialist trap . . .' and the US is 'the very citadel of neo-colonialism', whose objective is to 'achieve colonialism in fact while preaching independence'.[43] And this at a time when the World Bank, the US and the UK were between them financing the external costs of the Volta project! Tormented by the desire for economic independence and the fact of dependence Nkrumah was at his least coherent.

Nkrumah's suspicion of private enterprise and foreign capital sprang from his increasing preoccupation with a need for economic independence and a desire to create a socialist society. The emphasis on socialism was much stronger in the 1962 programme of the CPP than it had been in the past. It described socialism as the 'principle around which the Party is pivoted'[44] and devoted many paragraphs to elaborating the meaning of socialism in the Ghanaian context. And in

introducing the development plan which was prepared shortly afterwards Nkrumah stated that one of its tasks was 'To generate a socialist
transformation of the economy through rapid development of the state
and cooperative sectors'.[45]

Some writers explain Nkrumah's policies almost entirely in terms of
nationalism and regard his socialism as so much rhetoric, without substance. Genoud, for example, argues that to discuss Nkrumah in terms
of socialism is misleading and that there was no significant shift about
1961 to a more socialist orientation. 'Day after day and year after
year,' he complains, 'what is anti-colonial nationalism is being
renamed socialism.'[46] There is something in this. The rhetoric of
socialism, the policies of industrialization and the mechanization of
agriculture can be traced back to what Nkrumah and his party had said
in the fifties and even earlier. After all, Nkrumah in 1947 had concluded the first of his books with a Marxian flourish, 'Peoples of the
Colonies Unite: The working men of all countries are behind you,'[47]
and the 1951 election manifesto of the CPP claimed that 'The
industrialization of the country is one of the principal objectives of the
Party . . .,' envisaging factories 'springing up in all parts of the
country'.[48] Moreover, 'African socialism' claimed some strange adhe-
rents in the early sixties, and one only has to look at the African continent to find countries that did many of the things that Nkrumah did
without any but the most nominal pretence of a socialist ideology.

Nationalism was undoubtedly a major driving force behind the
policies of Nkrumah and his party. Indeed, Owusu argues that,[49]

> Gold Coast nationalism was primarily economic. Politics, or the
> power to decide how economic resources are to be distributed, who
> is to get what job and the like, was seen initially by many as perhaps
> the only effective means, given colonialism, to the real national
> 'good', economic power.

The desire for jobs – urban jobs – was a strong reinforcement to the
nationalist urge to industrialize.[50] Note also that in the fifties the
opposition too was advocating industrialization, the mechanization of
agriculture and more schools, while rejecting the notion of socialism.[51]

Nkrumah's stress on the need for economic independence also had
an obviously nationalistic content. 'The aim of our economic development,' said the CPP 1962 programme 'is to make Ghana free of alien
control of its economy and thus support our political independence
with economic independence.'[52] Nkrumah himself was no less
emphatic. 'We have had enough of European monopoly domination of
our economy,' he wrote, 'We have emancipated ourselves politically,
and now we have to shake off the economic monopoly that was the
objective of foreign political control. This is the crux of our economic
policy, and the essential heart of our endeavours.'[53]

Moreover, Nkrumah and his party often used arguments in favour of socialism (equated in his mind with expanding state economic activity) as if it was simply a superior way of decolonizing and modernizing the country: 'Socialism, because of the heritage of imperialism and colonialism, is the system by which Ghana can progress.'[54] In fact, the most frequently recurring justification for state participation in the economy to be found in Nkrumah's writings of the fifties and early sixties was that there was no alternative if industrialization was to proceed, for indigenous private enterprise would not or could not do it alone and leaving it to foreign investors would leave the country at the mercy of neo-colonialists.[55]

But to deny any serious content to Nkrumah's socialism and to attribute all he did to nationalism is to overstate the case. Economic development, modernization and socialism were so closely connected in his mind that there is little to be gained from trying to differentiate between them. Which is which, for example, in the opening sentence of the *Seven-year Plan*: 'With this first Seven-year Plan Ghana enters upon a period of economic reconstruction and development aimed at creating a socialist society in which the individual Ghanaian will be able to enjoy a modern standard of living in his home supplemented by an advanced level of public services outside'?[56]

One fact which conflicts strongly with a purely nationalist interpretation was Nkrumah's antipathy to the possible emergence of an important indigenous business class. He had no love of foreign capitalists but he preferred to encourage them rather than local entrepreneurs, whom he wished to restrict. It should, moreover, be remembered that Nkrumah was a moderate in his nationalism. When it was expedient, he co-operated with the British colonial government,[57] he did not expropriate foreign investors (as a later government did), the protection granted to import-substituting industries was, in general, not taken to extremes,[58] he did not expel aliens (as the Busia government was to do), and his tirades against neo-colonialists never degenerated into racialism. And if he was a nationalist it was of a pan-African rather than an insular variety, and he is still regarded by many as the most persuasive advocate of African unity.[59] Indeed, it is very possible that his pan-African ambitions provided greater impetus to his drive to develop Ghana's economy, in the belief that the model he built at home would give him a stronger claim to pan-African leadership.

There is a good deal of internal evidence that Nkrumah took his socialism seriously, which perhaps obliges us to do the same. He claims in his autobiography to have been influenced by Hegel, Marx, Engels, Lenin and Mazzini,[60] and the influence of Lenin was particularly apparent – to judge from his newspapers, he liked to be referred to as 'the Lenin of Africa'.[61] It was in his attitudes towards agriculture and industry that Nkrumah's socialism had the clearest impact on policies.

Other nationalist leaders have given low priority to agriculture and have thought of rural improvement largely in terms of mechanization, but few have so deliberately withdrawn assistance from the peasant farmers and pinned their hopes so exclusively on state farms. Similarly, almost all nationalist leaders seek to industrialize their countries but few devote such a large proportion of their governments' resources to creating state enterprises, and few leaders of small countries at an early stage of development begin pushing so early for the development of heavy industry.[62] It was not entirely without meaning that while both the CPP and the opposition were urging industrialization and the mechanization of agriculture, the latter intended to achieve it within a framework of private enterprise whereas the CPP were already talking of creating socialism.[63]

State ownership of farms and factories is admittedly not an exclusively socialist device – take the Japanese example. The other instruments of a command economy – centralized planning and administrative controls – are also to be found in countries which are in no serious sense socialist. Nevertheless, these instrumentalities have come to be regarded as necessary components of Soviet-style socialism, or what has been dismissively described as 'state capitalism'. What convinces me that Nkrumah's socialism had an important effect on his actions was his single-minded pursuit of expanded state activity. Towards the end of his rule there was little of the pragmatist left in him. When his experiments with state farms, state industries and controls were clearly going awry his response was not that of a nationalist searching for the best solution to his country's problems but of an ideologue who believed it was a matter of trying harder to make them work, and of pushing them further. In the sixties Nkrumah's policies were *a prioristic* rather than empirical.[64]

To understand his leadership we must see Nkrumah as both nationalist and socialist. No doubt his philosophizing was crude, inconsistent, and contained the most grievous Marxian heresies,[65] nonetheless it made an impact and became more important in his thinking as time went by. There may have been a theoretical tension between his nationalism and his socialism but there was a good deal of unity in practice, and it was this unity which gave his strategy dynamism. Arguing from a far more ideological point of view than mine, Fitch and Oppenheimer put the point well:[66]

> Socialism, for the CPP, is seen as a superior institutional means for coping with colonialism . . . it is a set of techniques and institutions which enable rapid economic progress and economic independence in the face of a colonial heritage, rather than the mode of operation characteristic of a workers' and peasants' state.

Socialism as a necessary instrument of nationalism is the best way of understanding the ideology of the first half of the sixties.

These, then, were the major factors motivating Nkrumah's policies in the sixties but a third should be added – an urge to modernize Ghana and her economy. If this was a less explicit objective of policy it was no less pervasive than the other two. By the chief socio-demographic indices of modernization – exposure to modern life through demonstrations of machinery, buildings, consumer goods, response to mass media, migration and urbanization, change from agricultural occupations, literacy, and rising per capita incomes[67] – Ghana was already a modernizing society and Nkrumah wishing to accelerate the changes. Take the following extract from his autobiography:[68]

> The ideology of my Party may be formulated as follows: no race, no people, no nation can exist freely and be respected at home and abroad without political freedom. Once this freedom is gained, a greater task comes into view. All dependent territories are backward in education, in science, in agriculture,and in industry. The economic independence that should follow and maintain political independence demands every effort from the people, a total mobilisation of brain and manpower resources. What other countries have taken three hundred years or more to achieve, a once dependant territory must try to accomplish in a generation if it is to survive. Unless it is, as it were, 'jet-propelled' it will lag behind and thus risk everything for which it has fought. Capitalism is too complicated a system for a newly independent state. Hence the need for a socialistic society.

This passage is of more than ordinary interest, for note the political necessity he felt to produce rapid results. And note the sudden transition from the need for speed to the need for socialism. Even by 1957 he seems to have become impatient with the results of essentially liberal-capitalist policies. Private enterprise, after all, had been the rule since the Gold Coast was first created and yet it remained a backward economy. Against this history the successes of the Soviet Union in modernizing its own economy almost literally in a single generation must have seemed an attractive alternative.[69] Certainly, Nkrumah's later policies suggested that it was a Soviet style of socialism that he had in mind.

It is interesting to note from this passage how socialism, economic independence and modernization become meshed as a mutually reinforcing set of objectives. Modernization implies industrialization,[70] which entails at least a partial closing of the economy, as protection from foreign competition. This, in turn, promotes greater economic independence by reducing reliance upon imports. But since there was practically nothing of a ready-made indigenous modern entrepreneurial class, the only way to create an industrial sector which was not wholly in foreign hands, and thus in conflict with the desire for economic independence, was for the state itself to fill the entrepreneurial gap. Thus, socialism came, in its economic dimension, to mean a large and growing share of the state in economic activities.

To sum up, it is contended that around the turn of the decade there was political pressure on Nkrumah to produce better economic results and that at the same time fundamental changes occurred in the power structure and ideology of Nkrumah's party and government, dating, perhaps, from his 1959 speech and culminating with the publication in 1962 of the party's *Programme for Work and Happiness*. For these reasons we draw a distinction between the new policies and those of the fifties, concentrating in this book on the last five years or so of Nkrumah's rule.[71] The nationalist and socialist objectives, combined with the desire to change Ghana into a modern nation-state, were seen as entailing a break with the 'colonial' policies of the past and resulted in the formulation of a new strategy of economic development. What was this strategy and how were the problems perceived that it was intended to solve?

The New Economic Strategy

Nkrumah's diagnosis of his nation's economic problems defies rigorous presentation but can be described as a mixture of anti-imperialism and the type of stagnationism attributed in the previous chapter to mainstream development economics.

The anti-imperialism was a vulgarized and modified form of the classical Hobsonian/Leninist critique. The most succinct statement of Nkrumah's view of the economics of colonialism is in this passage from his *Towards Colonial Freedom*:[72]

> The purpose of founding colonies was mainly to secure raw materials. To safeguard the measures for securing such raw materials the following policies were indirectly put into action: (i) to make the colonies non-manufacturing dependencies; (ii) to prevent the colonial subjects from acquiring the knowledge of modern means and techniques for developing their own industries; (iii) to make colonial 'subjects' simple producers of raw materials through cheap labour; (iv) to prohibit the colonies from trading with other nations except through the 'mother country'.

He also referred in the same work to a 'two-way fixed price system, basic in colonial economies', whose object is to 'buy cheap raw materials and labour from the colonies and to sell high-priced manufactured goods back to the colonies'[73] (the possible tensions between these motives were not noticed). These themes recur in Nkrumah's writings on colonialism and were faithfully reflected in the CPP's 1962 programme.[74] The colonialists had left behind a distorted economy: oriented to the export of raw materials, based on cheap labour, starved of modern know-how and industries, a dumping-ground for the surplus manufactured goods of the industrial nations, exploited both in the prices received for exports and in those paid for imports, and excessively dependent on trade with the metropolitan power.

However, anti-colonialism spilled over into other explanations of underdevelopment strongly reminiscent of the views of development economists. Nkrumah drew attention to the vulnerability of an economy heavily dependent on the single export crop, cocoa, and to the lack of balance with which it was associated.[75] He was pessimistic about prospects for his country's terms of trade[76] and about the effects of synthetic substitutes for primary products.[77] He was also, as we have shown, pessimistic about the availability of local entrepreneurship and finance to push the economy forward rapidly. Perhaps most significantly of all, he shared with the economics profession a view of poverty as self-perpetuating: 'The vicious circle of poverty, which keeps us in our rut of impoverishment, can only be broken by a massively planned industrial undertaking.'[78]

He similarly shared the scepticism of many economists about the efficacy of the market mechanism in inducing the economic development he was determined to achieve, writing of the 'uncounted advantages' of planning and that 'Government interference in all matters affecting economic growth in less developed countries is today a universally accepted principle . . .'[79] This is the interventionism of mainstream development economics and it is no coincidence that Nkrumah cited Myrdal in support of the contentions just quoted.[80]

The task, then, was to throw off the distorting effects of the colonial system, escape from dependence on primary product exports and break out of the vicious circle of poverty. A private enterprise solution was neither possible nor, in general, desirable. Planning and 'government interference' were to spearhead the attack – but what strategy was to be followed?

It was a revolutionary rather than evolutionary strategy. This much was implied in Nkrumah's view that a 'massively planned industrial undertaking' was necessary to break out of the poverty trap. It was a fundamental social and economic transformation which was sought, for, in the words of the CPP programme, 'Socialism can be achieved only by a rapid change in the socio-economic structure of the country.'[81] Socialism, economic independence and modernization called for large changes in various aspects of the socio-economic structure, in the composition of production and employment, the composition and geographical direction of external trade; for the large-scale infusion of modern knowledge and technology; and for a rapid expansion in the role of the state in the economy.

There was to be a shift in the end-use of capital formation, away from the former emphasis on the creation of social overhead capital (SOC), in favour of directly productive activities (DPA). This, a modernization of agriculture, and an accelerated process of industrialization were to be the chief changes.[82] We will therefore concentrate on some elaboration of these elements, dealing more briefly with other aspects later.

A seriously deficient infrastructure had been identified as the chief development constraint in the fifties and the development plans of that decade might, in the terminology of Hirschman, have been described as building up the SOC in the hope of inducing a comparable expansion in directly productive activities.[83] New roads were built, and hospitals, schools, power stations and a modern artificial harbour at Tema near the capital, Accra. The number of telephones tripled, the number of persons served by piped water more than doubled.[84] The development plans adopted by the Nkrumah government in the fifties allocated eighty per cent or more of planned government investments to SOC projects.[85] However, the response of the productive sectors to these infrastructural improvements did not satisfy the politicians or the planners. E. N. Omaboe, who acted as chairman for most meetings of the Planning Commission (Nkrumah was formally the chairman but did not attend most working sessions), wrote that 'Ghana is in possession of an infrastructure that is capable of supporting a higher level of productive services . . .'[86] and J. H. Mensah, Executive Secretary of the Commission and chief draughtsman of the Seven-year Plan, held a similar view.[87] Hence, the plan sought to increase government spending on DPA, and the share of SOC projects in planned expenditures fell to 63 per cent.

There was, however, one massive exception to this general strategy: the Volta River Project, which involved the creation of a large hydro-electric power plant and the simultaneous construction by private investors of an aluminium smelter utilizing a large proportion of the power.[88] Nkrumah had made the Volta project his own (although, contrary to popular belief, he did not originate it) and he was very clear about why he wanted it: 'Electricity is the basis for industrialization. That, basically, is the justification for the Volta River Project.'[89] Generating capacity was being built ahead of demand in the hope of stimulating industrial growth and thus the new strategy was not purely one of emphasis on DPA. Nevertheless, the shift was clear and characteristic of the new approach. Nkrumah himself was explicit about this and saw it as essential to the realization of his political objectives, arguing that 'we still have to lay the actual foundations upon which socialism can be built, namely, the complete industrialization of our country . . .' and that 'We must try and establish factories in large numbers at great speed . . .'[90] In this he was probably influenced by the Russian example, for on returning from a visit there in 1961 he said, 'I am convinced we have much to learn from them on how to speed up our industrialization.'[91]

But what *economic* arguments were deployed in favour of industrialization? We have already seen that Nkrumah believed massive industrialization to be the only hope of breaking out of the poverty trap. Another major theme was the transformation of the colonial structure of production and increasing economic independence (a) by processing materials before export and (b) by producing local substitutes for imported manufactures. Of these, priority was to be given to import-substitution.[92] As Nkrumah put it, 'Every time we import goods that we could manufacture if all the conditions were available, we are continuing our economic dependence and delaying our industrial growth.'[93]

The need to industrialize in order to reduce the unemployment problem was the dominant rationale offered by the *Seven-year Plan*[94] (although it was given relatively little emphasis by politicians in this period), an argument which can be directly traced to the influence of Mensah, the man who wrote much of it.[95] Unemployment had not at the beginning of the sixties become the highly sensitive issue it was to be later, although there was some discussion of the need to encourage small industries in rural areas to reduce the pace of urbanization.[96]

Ghana was a basically agricultural economy so the question arises, where did agriculture fit into Nkrumah's scheme of thought? Because he identified development with industrialization, Nkrumah tended to view agriculture as an inferior form of activity,[97] and those who criticized a strategy of industrialization did so for sinister motives:[98]

> industry rather than agriculture is the means by which rapid improvement in Africa's living standards is possible. There are, however, imperial specialists and apologists who urge the less developed countries to concentrate on agriculture and leave industrialisation for some later time when their populations shall be well fed. The world's economic development, however, shows that it is only with advanced industrialisation that it has been possible to raise the nutritional level of the people by raising their levels of income.

He did not, of course, deny the desirability of raising agricultural productivity, simply the notion that industrialization should wait upon this development. In fact, he believed that the best thing to do with agriculture was to industrialize that too. He called for 'a total break with primitive methods'[99] and for 'gigantic agricultural schemes',[100] and we shall show later that his agricultural policy was essentially one of mechanization. He had little faith in the modernizing capabilities of Ghana's millions of small-scale peasant farmers. 'Small-scale private farming,' he was to write later, 'is an obstacle to the spread of socialist ideas. It makes for conservatism and acquisitiveness and the development of a bourgeois mentality.'[101] This, no doubt, helps to explain why he dismantled agricultural extension services designed to help the peasant farmers.

In brief, then, Nkrumah's strategy was one of accelerated industrialization, and later chapters show that a rapid expansion of manufacturing was actually achieved during the first half of the sixties. But that is not the whole story and we should refer briefly to two other important aspects.

One was a rapid expansion of education and the supply of skilled manpower – necessary, of course, for successful industrialization but desired also for its own sake. Elementary school education was free and was made compulsory in 1961; fees for secondary education were abolished in 1965. The *Seven-year Plan* proposed to double the number of pupils entering secondary schools during the plan period and to increase sixfold the output of the universities.[102] Moreover, the targets of the plan implied a 100 to 300 per cent increase in the number of skilled workers over its seven years, depending on whose figures were to be believed.[103]

Second, there was to be an increasing share of economic activity by the state, which was how socialism was understood. Thus the *Seven-year Plan* (p. 3):

> The building of socialism imposes especially heavy responsibilities on the state in the field of economic policy and development ... As the state finances each year out of budget surpluses a large proportion of the productive investment made in the country the economy will become progressively socialised until by the end of the transition period the state will be controlling on behalf of the community the dominant share of the economy.

Forty-four per cent of all planned investment was to be undertaken by the government, public consumption was to grow twice as fast as private consumption, and public-sector output of various agricultural crops was to increase more rapidly than the output of the private sector by multiples of $1\frac{1}{2}$ to 28.[104] The share of the state in industrial output was also to grow, although no precise target was set. Moreover, this was not just wishful thinking by the politicians; later chapters show that much socialization of economic activity actually occurred. The foreign exchange budgets for 1965 and 1966 illustrate yet other aspects of this socialization, for chapter 10 shows that these envisaged transferring large amounts of foreign exchange from the private to the public sector, and the import licensing system was expected to give priority to state enterprises in the allocation of licences for raw materials, spares and capital equipment.

The Instrumentalities
We have seen already how Nkrumah regarded planning as a means of achieving industrialization superior to the laissez-faire methods of the nineteenth century, and central to the implementation of the strategy described above. According to the CPP, 'Socialism implies central planning in order to ensure that the entire resources of the State, both

human and material, are employed in the best interests of all the people.'[105]

Interestingly, direct participation of the state in the productive system was to be achieved by creating new enterprises rather than by nationalizing private concerns. A few failing gold mines and a large trading company were bought out by the government on agreed terms but the general approach adopted was well put in a 'Guide to the Implementation of the Seven-year Plan', that socialism should not be achieved 'by hindering the growth of the private sector, but by maximizing the growth of the public sector. Private enterprise will not be killed; it will be surpassed.'[106] Socialist writers were subsequently to criticize Nkrumah for what they regarded as this suicidal attempt to sup with the devil.[107]

Legislative controls – on imports, capital transfers, on the licensing of industry, on minimum wages, on the rights and powers of trade unions, on prices, on rents and on interest rates – were also used. Of course, not all this was new. Despite Nkrumah's beliefs, colonial policy had not been one of laissez-faire. Attempts to control prices, rents and interest were all initiated in the colonial period and there were other major pieces of interventionism, notably the war-time creation of a statutory marketing board with a legal monopoly over the exportation of cocoa.[108] Szereszewski has shown the key role of the colonial government in an earlier period of the Gold Coast's development[109] and another writer observed that 'Nkrumah did not need a socialist ideology in order to follow and improve on a well-beaten track.'[110] But socialist ideology he had, nonetheless, and the extent and pace of interventionism greatly expanded in the early sixties. There was, in other words, a real sense in which Nkrumah was turning Ghana into a 'command economy' in which the state was gradually taking over all major economic initiatives.[111]

A second question under the heading of instrumentalities concerns Nkrumah's views on the mobilization of resources for development. Here Nkrumah was caught in a dilemma, although a common one for leaders of low-income countries. Under political pressure to satisfy the material aspirations aroused among Ghanaians by the struggle for independence and, especially, to reward his party activists, he was constrained in the extent to which he could squeeze the Ghanaian consumer. But he believed that 'The vicious circle of poverty . . . can only be broken by a massively planned industrial undertaking,' and his objective of greater economic independence naturally disposed him to favour the maximum possible domestic financing of this 'massive undertaking'.[112]

His attempted resolution of this dilemma was characteristically bold. Some outside assistance was essential but the bulk of Ghana's big push was to be achieved from domestic resources. Despite the resulting necessity to raise domestic saving, the material aspirations of the people were also to be satisfied, (a) by achieving a high overall growth rate which would enable appreciable improvements in consumption standards (and the creation of more jobs) even while the domestic saving ratio was being raised, and (b) by emphasizing the expansion of collective consumption, through the creation and improvement of social services (thus also satisfying the socialization objective).

Chapter 6 gives reasons for not taking the specific numbers very seriously but, nevertheless, the overall macro-strategy of the *Seven-year Plan* provides a useful illustration of the approach just summarized. The *Plan* shows that, even though gross investment was quite high by the standards of low-income countries immediately prior to the plan period (over 19 per cent), the intention was a heroic investment effort to raise the ratio to over 23 per cent. Moreover, the proportion of capital investment financed from abroad was intended to go down a little and the gross domestic saving ratio was to rise from under 14 per cent to nearly 19 per cent.

Despite this, private per capita consumption was planned to rise in real terms, with the total growing at 4·5 per cent while annual population growth was taken as 2·4 per cent. There was also to be a socialization of consumption, with the share of GDP claimed by private consumption falling and the share of public consumption rising. Finally, the marginal saving rate implicit in the plan was almost 0·3; a full 77 per cent of total planned investment was intended to come out of domestic saving.[113] This was the arithmetic of economic independence. Nor were these the mere pipe dreams of planners, as will be shown later.

Given the economic pressures upon him, Nkrumah's willingness to squeeze the domestic consumer was courageous, some would say foolhardy. He had some appreciation of what was involved if he was to reconcile his objectives of industrialization and economic independence:[114]

> The Welfare State is the climax of a highly developed industrialism. To assure its benefits in a less developed country is to promise merely a division of poverty. Undoubtedly there must be an investment of a proportion of the capital reserves in the establishment of minimum wage levels to assure proper diet, as well as minimum health and housing facilities. But poverty is progressively reduced only as productivity progresses and part of its surplus can be made available in increased wages, better housing and generally improved social conditions.

One source of surpluses he had been squeezing for some time was the cocoa farmers. Large proportions of the export proceeds of cocoa had been withheld from the farmers and used by the state, and the squeeze was tightened drastically during the first half of the sixties.

Since much of the active opposition to the CPP had come from cocoa-growing areas, aspecially in Ashanti, to tax the farmers was politically easier than it would have been otherwise,[115] but he was also willing to spread his net to the urban proletariat. For example, he saw the trade unions in independent Ghana as playing quite a different role from that during the colonial period. Thus, the CPP:[116] 'In the present stage of our development, Trade Union officials must discard their colonial mentality and methods and remember that they are not struggling against capitalists . . . The Trade Union Movement must spearhead their efforts to raise production and productivity and cease to be advocates for outmoded conditions'. Here again Nkrumah matched his words with deeds. On the advice of Nicholas Kaldor, the 1961 budget raised taxes and introduced a compulsory saving scheme, intended, as Nkrumah was later to explain, 'to make the people aware of the false standards and illusory ideas of wealth in an economy which has not yet got off to a real start on the road of reconstruction and development.'[117] When workers struck in protest, their nominal leader, the General Secretary of the Trades Union Council, berated them as, 'Frightened by measures taken by the Government to streamline the nation's pattern of expenditure, demonstrate the soundness of our finances and gear both on to a programme of industrialization . . .'[118], and the strike leaders were imprisoned.

Even in 1965, when there was much inflation and shortage of consumer goods, the budget substantially raised taxes, and Nkrumah called for reductions in consumption expenditures to make resources available for investment.[119] The foreign exchange budget for that year cryptically illustrated the government's priorities: 'The allocation of consumer goods imports by the private sector is the residual after the minimum requirements for health, primary industries, manufacturing industries and government consumption have been fully met.'[120] Besides overt taxation, the government also resorted to the 'inflation tax' as an additional means of mobilizing resources, and there was large deficit financing in 1965.[121]

Nkrumah's Policies as a Case Study of Applied Development Economics

In an interesting article published in 1966 Rimmer made the point that development was not necessarily understood in Ghana in the way in which economists view it, but was thought of rather in terms of the creation of jobs and of certain physical manifestations of economic change, such as the building or roads, schools, water supplies, and so on.[122] This point of view does not necessarily conflict with the view that Ghana's leaders were also pursuing economic growth and development as it is more usually thought of by economists. In a later article, however, Rimmer threw down a much more fundamental challenge to the idea that economic development was an important objective of economic policies in countries such as Ghana.[123] He would challenge the conceptual framework of this chapter, which views economic policies in Ghana as development-oriented, and it is a challenge which cannot be ignored. Briefly, his argument is that the chief concerns of policy-makers in West Africa are, 'first, the enrichment of the government itself (i.e. of the ruler, of Ministers, of party leaders, of top civil servants, and possibly of numerous subordinate ranks of public officers and party workers), and secondly the buying of political support which will enable the government to maintain itself in power.' Those in power live 'not by creating a surplus but by taking economic advantage . . . of political power' and indigenous businessmen usually have parasitical relationships to governments. This view, he states, is particularly applicable to Nkrumah's Ghana.[124] By implication, the use of terms such as socialism is a mere diversionary tactic. The real ideology is acquisitiveness – the amassing of wealth by the leaders and their closer followers through graft, and the creation of jobs and social services for party supporters. These are the politics of cynicism, but do they fit the case we have been describing?

That there is truth in it must be conceded. It is shown in a later chapter that, for all his talk of planning, Nkrumah showed little understanding of it and took little notice of his planners. Subsequent commissions of enquiry were to establish that there was a good deal of corruption in Nkrumah's government, from which the leader himself was not immune.[125] It is also the case that the government devoted considerable resources to the 'uneconomic' creation of employment,[126] and that it expanded the social services. But this is not the complete story and, in my view, Rimmer's analysis does not provide a balanced interpretation of Ghana's economic policies under Nkrumah or, indeed, under any other government.

It is interesting to recall, first, that it was neither Nkrumah nor his ministerial colleagues who stressed employment creation in the early sixties, but the Executive Secretary of the Planning Commission – a civil servant, not a politician.[127] Relatively little emphasis was placed on unemployment in Nkrumah's writings and after his overthrow he actually made the extraordinary claim that 'In Ghana, before 24th February 1966, unemployment was virtually unknown.[128] The 1962 CPP programme proclaimed that unemployment would be abolished by the end of the sixties but seemed as concerned with ensuring the release of surplus labour from the rural areas to man the factories that were to be set up.[129] Second, corruption does not emerge as a factor of primary importance in this book and was not a special characteristic of the Nkrumah period.

However, these are quibbles. More fundamentally, major aspects of the policies of the period we are concerned with simply do not fit Rimmer's framework. The big push, the intensity of the drive to industrialise, the shift away from infrastructural investments, the emphasis on the need to transform the colonial structure of the economy, the pan-African crusade are not factors which can easily be explained in terms of a desire to redistribute wealth in favour of those in power. Neither can Nkrumah's policies regarding the ownership and control of assets. We have shown that he sought to limit the size of Ghanaian businesses and, if he had to choose, preferred foreign entrepreneurs to Ghanaians. He did not expropriate foreign businesses to transfer wealth and jobs to his friends, and the management of many public enterprises was in the hands of expatriates rather than Ghanaians. Finally, Nkrumah adopted tough measures to restrain private consumption, even in times of hardship, rather than give up his vision of an industrialized Ghana. Nkrumah's response to group demands was to ingest them more often than to buy them off.

In short, Rimmer provides us with a picture of politics as preoccupied with aggrandizement, reward and economic appeasement. These were certainly parts of the scene; it would be naive in any setting to think of policy as being directed solely towards the pursuit of development. But his thesis fails to explain the undoubted dynamism of the late Nkrumah period, fits only some of the facts and conflicts rather strongly with Nkrumah's willingness to impose hardships in pursuit of a long-term vision of a modernized Ghana. It is impossible to obtain a rounded view of his policies unless we accept long-term economic development as being one of his chief objectives. We conclude, then, by summarizing the case in favour of viewing Nkrumah's policies in the sixties in terms of applied development economics.

In stressing the nationalist and socialist influences on Nkrumah's thinking and policies we have perhaps neglected the impact of the leading ideas of economists on the problems of low-income countries. Nkrumah showed some awareness of their writings and used their arguments,[130] although their direct influence on him was probably no more than marginal. Of potentially much more importance was their influence through the advice he received from his civil servants and advisers. Two Ghanaian civil servants who were particularly involved in the preparation of the *Seven-year Plan*, Omaboe and Mensah, were relatively recent graduates from university, well aware of the literature on development economics at that time. We have already mentioned the influence of Mensah's writings on the Plan; Omaboe, who stated that successful implementation of the plan would 'catapult the nation to the threshold of the take-off stage', was also an important figure.[131] In addition, over the years the Planning Commission and the Bank of Ghana (another important source of economic advice) built up a staff of recently graduated economists versed in the ideas of mainstream development economics and they too had some influence on what went on in Ghana during this period.[132]

Mention might also be made of the considerable quantity of outside advice which was received in these years. Among the most prominent of the foreign economists who at one time or another advised Nkrumah were Dudley Seers, W. Arthur Lewis and Nicholas Kaldor. A conference of experts was held in April 1963 to discuss a draft of the *Seven-year Plan* attended by these scholars and by such other well-known names as Albert Hirschman, K. N. Raj, H. C. Bos and the Hungarian economist Joszef Bognar. The strategy outlined in that draft was virtually identical with the one published in the final document and it is interesting to see what attitude the participants of the conference took towards it.[133] Their chief criticisms of the draft were:

(a) The plan was over-ambitious, especially with regard to agriculture and the supply of skilled manpower;
(b) It did not contain enough specific projects (it was in this respect the opposite of 'colonial planning', which essentially consisted of a shopping-list of projects);
(c) Insufficient work had been done on the internal consistency of the plan (a working group proposed a simple form of input:output table that might be used for this purpose);
(d) The plan covered too long a period.

In short, constructive professional advice was offered but very little by way of fundamental criticism of the strategy. Nkrumah's planners could reasonably go away from that meeting in the belief that the principal ideas of the plan had found general acceptance.[134]

This suggests what indeed is a chief contention of this study, that what Nkrumah was trying to do in the sixties was in consonance with the ideas of most development economists. The views of the economists themselves had some influence on Nkrumah's decisions but what was decisive was the congruence that existed at the beginning of the sixties between the ideas of mainstream development economists, Marxists and nationalists. The mutual reinforcement of economics, socialism and nationalism gave this set of ideas an intense attraction to statesmen such as Nkrumah. The claim, then, is not that Nkrumah adopted his strategy primarily because it was being adovcated in the development literature, but rather than the prescriptions of the literature coincided in most essentials with the natural predilections of a leader of Nkrumah's background and persuasions.

We have already shown strong similarities between Nkrumah's analysis of the obstacles to Ghana's development and the pessimistic diagnoses of the literature of the fifties. Recalling now the description in chapter 2 of the chief prescriptions of mainstream development economics at the beginning of the sixties,[135] consider the similarities between these and Nkrumah's views.

First, they agreed that development was a discontinuous process of structural transformation; we have seen how insistent the Ghanaians were in their desire to remove the distortions created by the colonial structure of the economy, based upon primary production. Second, they were agreed that a big push was necessary in order to achieve the desired transformation – recall Nkrumah's call for a 'massively planned industrial undertaking' if Ghana was to break out of 'the vicious circle of poverty.'[136] Third, they were apparently agreed that a very high level of investment was a crucial component of the big push, with Ghana's gross investment ratio planned to rise to 23 per cent. Fourth, there was agreement on the necessity for industrialization, concentrating on the manufacture of import substitutes: Nkrumah, in common with many economists, was convinced by the industrial revolutions of the nineteenth century that industrialization was the path to prosperity and that, by comparison with agriculture and other forms of primary production, industry was a much more potent modernizing force.

Finally, note the agreement of the economics profession and of Ghana's leader on the need for planning and the inadequacies of the market system. The centralized planning envisaged by the CPP was, in general, intended to replace markets rather than improve upon them – import controls, foreign exchange regulations, industrial licensing, price controls – although there were exceptions like the Capital Investment Act, which offered pecuniary incentives to foreign investors. Given a shortage (and suspicion) of local entrepreneurs, the state was to fill the vacuum by setting up its own farming, trading and industrial enterprises; it was also to play a major role in mobilizing the savings necessary for the big push – through taxation and, in the last resort, through deficit financing.

This, then, is the case for treating Nkrumah's policies as a study in applied development economics. Much of the remainder of this book is taken up with an examination of how the application worked out in practice, but the present chapter concludes with a brief examination of the strategies adopted after Nkrumah was deposed early in 1966.

II Economic Strategies after Nkrumah

The preoccupation of the military and police officers who overthrew Nkrumah and formed the National Liberation Council (NLC) was to restore some order to what they saw as a chaotic economic situation. The civilian administration under Dr Busia's Progress Party which followed the NLC in 1969 concerned itself more with development but had only a little more than two years in office before another coup swept the National Redemption Council into power early in 1972.

The NLC took a more pragmatic approach to the country's economic problems than had formerly been the case. It was not interested in socialism or, indeed, in any other ideology. It set out to restore 'efficiency' to the economy and was not much concerned with the elaboration of a coherent body of economic ideas. Throughout it saw itself as a transitional government and adhered with remarkable consistency to its stated intention to hand power back to an elected civilian government. As soldiers and policemen they were, in general, happy to leave the mysteries of economic management to past and present civil servants, and for most of their period Omaboe (Nkrumah's former Government Statistician) dominated the formulation of economic policies. In his view, the chief problems facing the country at the time of the coup were:[137]

'1. the correction of the present imbalance in the country's foreign payments position;
2. the arrest of the inflationary pressures to which the economy has been subjected during the past few years;
3. the provision of more job openings for the rising population of the country; and
4. the restoration of balance to the Government's Budget.'

Their overall strategy for dealing with these, put together with the advice of the IMF,[138] was to pursue orthodox disinflationary fiscal and monetary policies while avoiding an adverse effect on production, by improving capacity utilization, and preparing the economy for another development effort to be launched as soon as stabilization had been achieved. The following summarizes the chief policies adopted in pursuit of this strategy.[139]

First, to reduce the pressure of demand on available resources, thus improving the balance of payments and easing inflationary pressures, major cuts were made in public-sector investments. The general principle was adopted that economically sound projects already under way should be completed but that few, if any, new ones should be commenced. This, of course, also reduced the budget deficit and removed the need for inflationary deficit financing. Second, the NLC pursued a policy of cautious liberalization. Their stated intention was the eventual abolition of import, price and exchange controls but, in practice, the most that was achieved was a modest reduction in the coverage of import licensing. In fact, it is doubtful whether they accepted a consistent liberalizing philosophy, as is shown in chapter 11. Third, rather more emphasis was placed on the role of private enterprise, especially Ghanaian. Special measures were introduced to assist Ghanaian businessmen, including legislation to restrict certain activities exclusively to Ghanaians. But again the approach was pragmatic. State participation would be undertaken when private capital was not available for certain 'basic projects'. A few state enterprises were sold off to private investors, some state farms closed down, and an Industrial Holding Corporation was set up to improve the economic performance of remaining state enterprises. Redundant workers in organizations such as the Workers' Brigade and a state construction corporation were laid off. Industrial capacity utilization, public and private, was improved by providing more import licences for raw materials and spare parts, and import restrictions on these items were lifted.

A fourth strand in the policies of the NLC was a major effort to secure external aid and debt relief, especially from Western countries. The response of these countries, as is shown later, was the partly self-defeating one of being generous with aid and parsimonious with debt relief. Nevertheless, appreciable net assistance was received in both forms from 1966 to 1972. Finally, the soldiers sought to prepare the economy for a fresh development drive (a) by stabilizing the economy and improving the balance of payments, (b) by creating an atmosphere of confidence conducive to higher levels of private investment, (c) by beginning to repair the neglect suffered by the country's peasant farmers under Nkrumah, and (d) by strengthening the economic planning capabilities of the public service.[140] Indeed, the NLC itself began to feel the need for more growth-oriented policies towards the end of its period and prepared a two-year plan with the sub-title, *From Stabilization to Development*.[141] A family planning programme was also adopted, making Ghana one of the first African states to have a population policy – although one that has yet to have much concrete content.[142] On handing over to the newly elected Busia administration in October 1969 the NLC claimed that 'Ghana has achieved a sufficient measure of economic stability and restored conditions for new growth,' while conceding the major problems still awaited solution.[143]

In spite of their long wait for power, Busia and his colleagues came to office with little by way of an economic policy. It was, as those advising them quickly discovered, impossible to derive from the election manifesto of the Progress Party a meaningful economic programme, although it seemed generally in favour of private enterprise and placed considerable stress on giving Ghanaians a 'greater stake in the economy of their own country.'[144] In spite of an apparently positive attitude to the freer operation of market forces, a large role was also envisaged for the state – an ambiguity neatly illustrated by the co-existence on the same page of pledges to move away from trade controls and to improve the enforcement of price controls.

J. H. Mensah, who immediately emerged as Busia's chief economic policy-maker, took over the portfolios of finance and planning, giving his virtual monopoly in the area of macro-economic policy making, and quickly assumed a domination of the cabinet on economic matters which only weakened in the last months of the Busia administration. What were Mensah's objectives and how did he intend to achieve them?

He was preoccupied with three problems: growth, employment and equality. He saw that Ghana, after nearly a decade of stagnation, needed more rapid growth; and that the future of the government to which he belonged depended upon improved economic performance.[145] If forced to choose, he would sacrifice economic stability for faster growth and did so, as we will see. His concern with unemployment was, of course, completely consistent with the approach he had taken in the early sixties while preparing the *Seven-year Plan*, and it is no coincidence that of the three governments discussed so far, Busia's displayed the greatest sensitivity on the employment issue. Mensah's concern with equity (shared by the government as a whole) is a relatively new theme for this chapter, although it had received some attention in earlier years.[146] The concern focused on the large disparities believed to exist between rural and urban living standards. For Mensah,[147]

> the principal task that has to be accomplished in the search for social justice in Ghana is to raise the levels of rural income as a whole vis-à-vis the levels in urban income as a whole, rather [than] to make adjustment within the structure of urban incomes.

For the lower-paid urban workers who were asking for a higher minimum wage he had but cold comfort:[148]

> At the present time incomes policy is based on the assumption that the lower paid urban workers are . . . an under-privileged group on whose behalf state intervention should be used in the pursuit of a more equitable income distribution. If instead of that hypothesis we substitute the more realistic assumption that the lower-paid urban workers are simply the less well-off members of a relatively wealthy urban minority in the country as a whole then our conclusion about a viable and realistic minimum wage . . . would be quite different.

Discussing the strategy adopted for dealing with these problems is more than usually difficult for it was never clearly articulated, so we are forced to deduce the government's strategy, insofar as it had one, from what it did.[149] Four main imperatives can be identified:
   (a) substantially to raise domestic investment and saving rates;
   (b) to expand export earnings and attract more external assistance;
   (c) to accelerate the Ghanaianization of economic activities;
   (d) to place special emphasis on rural development.
These objectives were taken to entail greater public investment, especially in agriculture and other rural programmes, but while the state was to play a more prominent role in the development effort, some moves were made partially to dismantle the instrumentalities of the command economy. Imports were rapidly liberalized and interest rates were increased. Wages were restrained and the 1971 budget substantially reduced the real incomes of public servants.[150] Various small-scale service activities were reserved for Ghanaians and aliens were summarily expelled from the country.

Finally, when high public expenditure and a large import boom brought the economy once again to crisis point, the government devalued the cedi by a massive 90 per cent in local currency terms. Even though accompanied by other measures intended to assuage public opinion – such as large increases in the wages of lower-paid government workers, a 25 per cent increase in the cocoa producer price and various tax reductions – this drastic medicine could only be unpopular and a group of army officers seized this as the opportunity they had been waiting for and staged a second *coup d'état* in January 1972.

Styling themselves the National Redemption Council (NRC), they partially revalued the currency, restored comprehensive import controls, widened the scope of price controls, subsidized certain imported consumer goods, and generally moved rapidly back towards a command economy. Economic policies had come full circle and some of Nkrumah's old colleagues began to emerge in positions of influence, if not power.

From this sketch of economic strategies in the post-Nkrumah years, two features emerge of particular interest to the theme of this book. First, just as the consensus of mainstream development economics began to break up and more attention was being paid to ways of making market forces operate more efficiently, and as concern with unemployment and income distribution began to increase, Ghana's policy-makers were moving tentatively in the same direction. So, just as Nkrumah's policies had coincided with strategies then propounded by many economists, the policies of the two subsequent administrations at least partly mirrored the shifts of emphasis discernable in writings on development. Secondly, however, limited progress had been made by the time of the second coup in changing the policies inherited from Nkrumah. There remained much continuity after 1966; attempts to move towards greater use of the market mechanism were half-hearted and partial; and the soldiers who otherthrew Busia in 1972 rapidly demonstrated a faith in a command economy similar to Nkrumah's, even though they displayed little interest in his socialism.

Several questions arise. Why was there so much continuity of policy after 1966? To the extent that policies did alter, did the changes promise better results than Nkrumah achieved? Was the heightened concern with equity and unemployment justified? We will revert to these questions later, especially in chapters 11 and 12, but the next step is to examine the performance of the economy, which is undertaken in the two following chapters.

NOTES

[1] It is often said, no doubt rightly, that development plans are written mainly to impress foreign aid donors, but it sometimes seems to me that they are written for academics. Many scholars solemnly quote national development plans to describe public priorities and policies when a nodding acquaintance with the country in question would show that the plan was not regarded as performing any operational function. *See* the first part of chapter 6 for a discussion of the political realism of the *Seven-year Plan*.

[2] His common resort to ghost writers adds to the difficulties of distilling what Nkrumah's views were. It is scarcely a secret in Ghana that a variety of writers contributed substantially to several of the works written under his name while he was in power (*see* Rimmer's review of one of them in the *Economic Bulletin of Ghana*, 1966, No. 3). On the other hand, there is a good deal of uniformity of expressions and opinion in them, and also in the books he published after he was deposed (which we can more safely assume to have come largely from his own pen). They should be used carefully but are certainly more reliable guides to his thinking than development plans and similar official documents.

[3] *Ashanti Pioneer* (Kumasi), 5 March 1949, cited by Fitch and Oppenheimer, p. 25.

[4] Richard Wright cited by Fitch and Oppenheimer, p. 99. Even as late as 1964, when it should have known better, the CPP was pushing the slogan, 'Vote for the Party and all other things shall be added unto you' (*Ghanaian Times*, 24 January 1964).

[5] *See* Kraus, 1971, p. 44.

[6] Owusu, 1970, p. 299.

[7] *See* Austin, 1964, especially pp. 12–28, and also Apter, 1973.

[8] It was not much of a struggle, for the British bulldog was growing weaker and perhaps wiser.

[9] *See* Kraus, *passim*.

[10] Organizations representing the trade unions, the farmers and their cooperative movement, the market women, and the youth were all formed into 'integral wings' of the CPP.

[11] *See* Kraus, 1973, pp. 73–86.

[12] Nkrumah, 1958, p. 51.

[13] Nkrumah, 1961, p. 145. Abandon him they did and when Uphoff (1970, pp. 715–16) conducted an opinion poll on 'reasons why Ghanaians were happy about Nkrumah's overthrow' economic reasons came top of the list, with corruption second.

[14] Apter, 1965, p. 42.

[15] Austin, pp. 176–80.

[16] A good account of these regional movements is to be found in Austin, *passim*.

[17] Apter, 1973, chapter 15. I am much obliged to Professor Apter for making the proofs of this revised edition available to me prior to publication. *See also* Frimpong, 1970, *passim*.

[18] *See* Folson, 1971, part 2, p. 1.

[19] *See* Legum, 1964, *passim*, and also Lewis, 1965, p. 60.

[20] Some have placed significance on a visit which Nkrumah paid to the Soviet Union in 1961, and it probably is true that it was this event that induced him to give the country's new development plan a seven-year span (*see* Omaboe, 1966, pp. 450–1). But his decision to scrap the extant five-year plan after less than two years of its currency was made before he went to Russia, having described it as 'piecemeal and unpurposeful' (Uphoff, 1970, p. 101), and the visit was probably as much a symptom of the shifting ideological emphasis as a cause of it. Another manifestation was the rift that appeared between Nkrumah and Professor W. Arthur Lewis, who had acted as Nkrumah's economic adviser on several occasions in the fifties. For advice on tax questions Nkrumah turned instead to Nicholas Kaldor (an unhappy experiment which created a first-order political crisis) and on planning to the Hungarian economist, Jozsef Bognar. Fitch and Oppenheimer (1966, especially chapter 6) make much of this change, and divide Nkrumah's economic policies into a 'Lewis era' and a post-Lewis, pro-socialist era.

[21] Nkrumah made his first diplomatic and trade contacts with the Eastern countries in 1959, and several trade and payments agreements were signed during 1960 and 1961 (*see* Uphoff, 1970, p. 278).

[22] *See* Killick, 1972–3, Pt. I, p. 19.

[23] *Legislative Assembly Debates*, 2 September 1960, cols. 1071–73, and *Ghanaian Times* (Accra), 10 October, 1960.

60 DEVELOPMENT ECONOMICS IN ACTION

[24] Esseks, 1971, p. 13.

[25] *See* chapter 12 for a discussion of Ghanaian entrepreneurship.

[26] *National Assembly Debates*, 11 March 1964.

[27] After the 1966 coup one of Nkrumah's senior economic advisers stated that Nkrumah 'informed me that if he permitted African business to grow, it will grow to the extent of becoming a rival power to his and the party's prestige, and he would do everything to stop it, which he actually did' (E. Ayeh-Kumi quoted in *West Africa*, 19 March 1966, p. 330).

[28] *See* CPP, 1962, para. 109.

[29] 'The initiative of Ghanaian businessmen would not be cramped, but we intended to take steps to see that it was channelled towards desirable social ends and was not expanded on the exploitation of the community. We would discourage anything which threatened our socialist objectives.' Nkrumah, 1968, pp. 86–7.

[30] In March 1962 Nkrumah announced that, 'In future the private small-scale personal enterprise sector will be exclusively reserved for Ghanaians. Foreign concerns already established in this sector will be allowed to continue operation, on condition that they do not expand their present establishment and scale of operations.' Reproduced in Friedland and Rosberg (eds.), 1964, p. 272.

[31] This, at least, is regarded by Garlick (1971, p. 139 and *passim*) as one of the major findings of his research into Ghanaian entrepreneurship, and is consistent with casual observations. He also notes (pp. 128–9) that, despite all the difficulties, most Ghanaian traders were able to hang onto their businesses during the first half of the sixties.

[32] *See* chapter 11 for a brief discussion of the 'Ghanaianization' of small businesses after 1966.

[33] Nkrumah, 1963, p. 98.

[34] *National Assembly Debates*, 11 March 1964, vol. 25.

[35] Nkrumah in Friedland and Rosberg (eds.), p. 271.

[36] Nkrumah, 'Speech to Businessmen', 22 February 1963, Flagstaff House, Accra (emphasis in original).

[37] ibid.

[38] He wrote a whole book about it: *Neo-Colonialism: The Last Stage of Imperialism* (1965).

[39] *See* chapter 10 below, which shows that the 1965 and 1966 foreign exchange budgets envisaged massive transfers of foreign exchange from the private sector to the state, and that private industry was particularly hard hit by the import shortages which occurred.

[40] *National Assembly Debates*, 2 October 1962, Col. 2.

[41] *See* Killick, 1966, pp. 402–4.

[42] 'The leaders of the New Africa have no alternative but to look for outside assistance.' (Nkrumah in *Foreign Affairs*, October 1958, p. 52). Also: 'Aid is a necessary form of insurance to make it certain that the development plan can continue despite fluctuations in the prices of raw materials' (Nkrumah, 1961, p. 87).

[43] The quotations are from Nkrumah, 1965, pp. 50, 242 and 241.

[44] *See* CPP, 1962 paragraph 7.

[45] *National Assembly Debates*, 11 March 1964, col. 21.

[46] *See* Genoud, *passim*, especially chapter 6. The quotation is from p. 219.

[47] Nkrumah, 1962, p. 43. This was originally written in 1947 but did not find a publisher until 1962.

[48] Quoted by Krobo Edusei, then Minister of Industries, to Parliament (*see National Assembly Debates*, 6 February 1962, col. 197).

[49] Owusu, p. 171. See also Austin, pp. 42–3 and *passim*.

[50] Myrdal, 1968, p. 1150, notes a nationalist identification of industrialization with development in South Asia. *See also* an interesting essay on this topic by Kahan in Johnson (ed.), 1967.

[51] *See* Genoud, pp. 94–6.

[52] *See* CPP, 1962, paragraph 72.

[53] Nkrumah, 1963, p. 102.

[54] *See* CPP, 1962, paragraph 7(2).

[55] *See* Nkrumah, 1963, p. 119, for an example.

[56] *Seven-year Plan*, p. 1.

[57] Fitch and Oppenheimer (pp. 26–35) are caustic about this collaborationism.

[58] *See* chapter 8, pp. 186–7.

[59] It was the pan-Africanist who came to the fore in the official definition of 'Nkrumaism': 'Nkrumaism is the ideology for the New Africa, independent and absolutely free from imperialism, organised on a continental scale, founded upon the conception of One and United Africa, drawing its strength from modern science and technology and from the traditional African belief that the free development of each is conditioned by the free development of all' (Quoted by Legum in Friedland and Rosberg, p. 141).

[60] Nkrumah, 1957, p. 45.

[61] It is, however, characteristic of the impossibility of placing him neatly into any Western ideological category that he should also have said in his autobiography that the writings of Marcus Garvey – a West Indian who proclaimed the cause of black Americans after the end of the first world war – did more than any others to fire his enthusiasm (p. 45). But the influence of Lenin and of the USSR was certainly important – note his stress on the importance of electrification, the derivative title of his book, *Neo-colonialism, The Last Stage of Imperialism*, and his endeavours to combine the roles of philosopher and man of action.

[62] In this he was outdoing the Marxian writers. Even the normally strident Baran is cautious about the creation of heavy industries in small underdeveloped countries such as Ghana. *See* Baran, 1957, p. 284, n. 77.

[63] Genoud, p. 95.

[64] The distinction is from Tinbergen, 1955, p. 3. In Tinbergen's terminology, *a prioristic* policies are based on theories, whereas empirical policies are derived from experience with alternatives.

[65] *Consciencism* (1964) was Nkrumah's most ambitious attempt to provide a formal statement of his political philosophy. *See* Folson, 1971, for a detailed and somewhat caustic account of the development of the ideology of Nkrumah and the CPP in the fifties. Fitch and Oppenheimer are scathing about the limitations of Nkrumah's concept of socialism (*see* especially chapter 8) and Grundy, 1963, also has an interesting discussion on the conflicts between Nkrumah's views and Marxist-Leninist orthodoxy. One of Nkrumah's practical heresies, of course, was that he did not expropriate foreign companies, nor did he attempt any serious attack on the property of wealthy Ghanaians.

[66] Fitch and Oppenheimer, p. 109.

[67] These are the chief indicators of modernization listed by Deutsch, 1961, pp. 463–551.

[68] Nkrumah, 1957, pp. xv–xvi. His statement that, 'we lay stress on education because it is the antidote to feudalist despotism and ignorance and superstition' (Nkrumah, 1961, p. 45) and many of his other writings and speeches have the same powerfully modernizing emphasis, and it was consistent with this that the CPP theologians should have defined the ideology of 'Nkrumaism' as, 'drawing its strength from modern science and technology' (quoted by Legum, p. 141).

[69] Dobb (1963, p. 64) was not the first nor the most reluctant to point out this attractive aspect of the Soviet model for leaders of the low-income countries.

[70] Both Eisenstadt (1963, p. 3) and Apter (1971, p. 18) stress the close interconnections between modernization, urbanization and industrialization.

[71] Omaboe (1966, p. 452) also stresses the change that occurred in the sixties:
> Firstly, it could be claimed that the Seven-year Plan is the first real plan which sets out the policies and objectives of the CPP Government. The first plan had already been prepared when the CPP came into power in 1951. Although the

second plan was introduced in 1959, two years after the attainment of independence, it could be said with some degree of justification that in 1959 the
Government had not been able to break with the past. This came after the
institution of a republican form of government in July 1960 when the Government took some radical decisions which Ghanaianised the top posts of the civil
service. By the time the Seven-year Plan was launched in 1964 political
independence had been forcibly asserted in many ways, both domestically and
internationally. The plan is therefore the first true reflection of the economic
and social objectives of the CPP.

[72] Nkrumah, 1962, p. 10. This was first written when he was a young student in 1947 but
was not published until 1962. However, in a foreword to the 1962 publication
Nkrumah states, 'the views I expressed then are precisely the views I hold today
concerning the unspeakably inhuman nature of imperialism and colonialism' (p.
x). It is also of some interest that in Consciencism he reaffirmed his continued
adherence to the 'economic analysis' just quoted (Nkrumah, 1964, p. 98). What
was generally absent from his writing on this topic was a view that the colonies had
also served as an outlet for the surplus capital of the imperial powers, and he
apparently did not believe that imperialism would inevitably lead to war. In these
respects his analysis was a departure from those of Hobson and Lenin.
[73] One catches echoes here of the cheap labour arguments of Lewis and Myint, and of
Myrdal's use of colonialism as an explanation of underdevelopment described in
the previous chapter (p. 26).
[74] See CPP, 1962, paragraphs 28–31.
[75] Nkrumah, 1963, p. 108.
[76] 'Each year the western world pays less for its imports and each year charges more for
its exports,' Nkrumah, 1968, p. 73.
[77] Nkrumah, 1963, p. 63.
[78] Nkrumah, 1963, p. 167.
[79] Nkrumah, 1963, pp. 109–10 and 165.
[80] See ibid., pp. 109–10 where Myrdal is quoted in support of the manipulation of
market forces.
[81] See CPP, 1962, paragraph 7. In similar vein, the Seven-year Plan (p. 5) argued that
the 'colonial structure of production based on exports of primary commodities
which largely accounts for the present low level of income must be completely
altered.'
[82] Seven-year Plan, pp. 7–12.
[83] Scott, 1967, is the most comprehensive source for this period. See also Seers and
Ross, 1952, who wrote at length about the adverse consequences for the development of the economy of the inadequacies of the ports and other transport facilities,
and of the construction industry.
[84] For a useful statistical summary of these developments see Seven-year Plan, p. 26.
[85] It was estimated by Omaboe, 1966, Table 18–3, that 89 per cent and 80 per cent
respectively of planned expenditures were allocated to social services and
infrastructure in the first and second plans. The proportions for agriculture and
industry were 11 and 20 per cent, compared with 37 per cent in the Seven-year
Plan.
[86] Omaboe, 1966, p. 454.
[87] J. H. Mensah, 'Comprehensive Economic Planning in Ghana: paper prepared for
ECA conference on planning.' mimeo, n.d., (ca. September 1962) p. 20:
a general presumption of planning for the next seven years has been that the
existing level of social services is under-utilized in terms of the volume of
economic activity which it could support, and that a good deal of expansion
could take place without any need for corresponding increases in social and
administrative services.
[88] See Killick, 1966, ch. 16 on the Volta River Project; also chapter 9 below.
[89] Nkrumah was speaking to Parliament; National Assembly Debates, 21 February
1961. Note again the influence of Lenin.
[90] Nkrumah addressing a CPP meeting in April 1961, 'On Building a Socialist State'
[Ministry of Information and Broadcasting, Accra, 1961]. Later, in exile, he was
to develop another political argument for industrialization: 'Urbanization is at the

core of social change. Therefore, industrialization, which is the main cause of urban growth, determines the social pattern. With growing industrialization the African proletariat will increase in numbers and become more class conscious' (Nkrumah, 1970, p. 70). It is doubtful, though, whether this consideration had much influence on his thinking in the earlier sixties. Egala, one of Nkrumah's senior ministers, put the case in more nationalistic terms. According to him, the programme of industrialization would free Ghana from 'the unfeeling heel of imperialism and colonialism' (*Ghanaian Times*, 25 May 1962).

[91] *Ghanaian Times*, 3 October 1961.

[92] *See Seven-year Plan*, p. 93, which nominated the production of manufactured consumer goods as the type of industrialization on which 'it is intended to lay the main emphasis . . . under this plan.'

[93] Nkrumah, 1963, p. 112.

[94] *Seven-year Plan*, pp. 4–12.

[95] The section of the plan just cited reproduces practically word-for-word an article which Mensah wrote explaining the rapid growth of the labour force and the need to generate more jobs as an argument for industrialization. *See* Mensah, 1962. In another publication, Mensah introduced the historical argument for industrialization that attracted attention in chapter 2: 'That the division of the world into industrialised and non-industrialised countries corresponds exactly to that into rich and poor countries is one of the few well-established generalisations in economics . . .'

[96] Nkrumah in an address sent to Parliament, reported in the *Ghanaian Times*, 26 September 1963.

[97] This emerges very strongly from a reading of *Towards Colonial Freedom* (1962). Several Ghanaians have mentioned to me that Nkrumah referred to cocoa farming as 'a poor nigger's business' (compare with Marx's reference to 'the idiocy of rural life'), although I have not been able to trace a source for this statement.

[98] Nkrumah, 1965, p. 7.

[99] In a lecture ironically entitled 'Africa Needs her Farmers', Government Printer, Accra, 1962 (cited Apter, 1973).

[100] Nkrumah, 1961, p. 28.

[101] Nkrumah, 1970. p. 79. A lack of faith in the peasant is, of course, firmly in the Soviet tradition. *See* Baran, 1957, p. 273: 'The subsistence peasant in backward areas . . . has neither the means for acquiring the necessary implements, nor – and this is even more important – would he be able to employ them on his dwarf plots.'

[102] *See Seven-year Plan*, chapter 7, and also Bissue, 1967, pp. 38–40.

[103] *See Seven-year Plan*, Table 7.1, and Killick, 1966, pp. 150–3.

[104] Computed from *Seven-year Plan*, Chapters 4 and 13. *See also* Killick and Szereszewski, 1969, pp. 111–12.

[105] *See* CPP, 1962, paragraph 54.

[106] Quoted by Mensah, 1965, p. 14.

[107] *See* Fitch and Oppenheimer, chapter 8.

[108] Bauer, 1963, especially in chapter 11, deals with the history of cocoa marketing and with various other aspects of the interventionism of colonial governments.

[109] Szereszewski, 1965, *passim*.

[110] J. C. de Graft-Johnson in *Economic Bulletin of Ghana*, 1972, No. 1, p. 58.

[111] For a development of the notion of a command economy *see* Wiles, 1962, p. 18 and *passim*.

[112] 'It has been well pointed out that political independence is but an empty facade if economic freedom is not possible also. I must emphasize again, however, that economic freedom can only be purchased by capital development, it cannot be given from the outside.' Nkrumah in 1955, quoted by Grundy, 1963, p. 445.

[113] These figures were computed from the *Seven-year Plan*, chapter 13, and Table 4.A.

[114] Nkrumah, 1963, pp. 105–06. Note that he characteristically treats industrialization as synonymous with development.

[115] Mohan, 1967, p. 206. *See also* Table 5.6 below.
[116] *See* CPP, 1962, paragraph 121.
[117] Nkrumah, 1963, p. 100.
[118] John K. Tettegah reported in *Ghanaian Times*, 20 September 1961.
[119] Nkrumah reported in *Ghanaian Times*, 13 January 1965. *See also* chapter 6 below.
[120] *The Budget, 1965*, Part III, p. 8.
[121] *See* chapter 6 below.
[122] Rimmer, 1966, *passim.*
[123] Rimmer, 1969, *passim.*
[124] Ibid., pp. 201–2.
[125] *See* chapters 9 and 10 below, and the *Apaloo Report.*
[126] *See* chapter 9 below.
[127] *See* p. 45.
[128] Nkrumah, 1968, p. 92.
[129] *See* CPP, 1962, paragraphs 125–7.
[130] For example, he quoted and paraphrased Myrdal on the inappropriateness of free trade policies, on the need for planning and for intervening in normal market processes (*see* Nkrumah, 1963, pp. 109–10 and 161.
[131] *See* his interesting account of planning in Ghana in Omaboe, 1966, chapter 18; the quotation is from p. 459. *See also* Mensah's 1962 article.
[132] The author was at that time on the teaching staff of the Department of Economics at the University of Ghana and was involved in attempts to 'de-colonize' the curriculum and to give it more of a development orientation.
[133] I am here relying on my notes taken while a participant at this conference.
[134] To avoid any contrary impression, I should state that I was among those in agreement with the plan's broad strategy.
[135] *See* pp. 26–9.
[136] Nkrumah, 1963, p. 167.
[137] The key documents upon which the following account of NLC policies are based are NLC, *Rebuilding the National Economy* (March 1966); NLC, *New Deal for Ghana's Economy* (July 1967); NLC, *Outline of Government Economic Policy* (August 1967). The quotation is from a statement by Omaboe in the March 1966 document, p. 9. Two other useful background documents are entitled *Ghana's Economy and Aid Reguirements* and cover 1968 and 1969–70 respectively.
[138] A resident representative of the Fund had an office in the Bank of Ghana from 1966 until early 1970, and in this period the Fund provided substantial financial assistance to Ghana.
[139] *See* chapter 11 for a more extensive discussion.
[140] The government requested the assistance of the Harvard Development Advisory Service in strengthening its economic planning potential and an advisory team worked in Accra from mid-1967 until September 1972. This writer was a member of the Harvard Group and worked in the planning agency from October 1969 to July 1972.
[141] NLC, *Two-year Development Plan: From Stabilization to Development*, July 1968.
[142] NLC, *Population Planning for National Progress and Prosperity*, March 1969.
[143] Commissioner for Economic Affairs, *Developments in the Ghanaian Economy, 1960–68*, p. 7 and *passim.*
[144] *Progress Party Manifesto*, August 1969, p. 5.
[145] This point was particularly stressed by him in a document submitted to the creditor countries in 1970.
[146] By Lewis among others. *See* Rimmer, 1970, pp. 33–5.
[147] *See* Mensah, 1971.
[148] Ibid.
[149] The following paragraphs are largely gleaned from Mensah's budget statements and other speeches, and, to a lesser extent, from the *One-year Plan, 1970/71* (which, however, was largely written by officials and is a poor guide to the real thinking of

Mensah and his ministerial colleagues).

[150] Higher rents for government housing and reduced allowances were estimated to have cut the effective incomes of higher-paid civil servants by about a quarter.

4 *Domestic Economic Performance in the 1960s*

That Nkrumah was under pressure for improved economic performance at the beginning of the sixties is an eloquent comment on the high expectations of the Ghanaian public, for it appears that the economy grew quite rapidly in the second half of the fifties.[1] The GDP apparently expanded at well over 5 per cent a year (in constant prices) between 1955 and 1960,[2] the infrastructure was considerably strengthened, and industrialization began to gather pace.[3] The gross investment rate, at around 20 per cent of GDP in 1960, was high by the standards of low-income countries, but domestic saving was sufficient to finance most of it. A serious foreign exchange constraint had not yet emerged and the cost of living was drifting only very slowly upwards.

These achievements perhaps only served to whet the appetites of people who had been led to hold unrealistic views of the extent to which colonialism had held them back and independence could propel them forward. More was demanded of Nkrumah – but in most respect he delivered less during his remaining years in office. The purpose of this chapter, therefore, is to discuss the domestic performance of the economy during the sixties, during and after Nkrumah, leaving for the next chapter the examination of the critical foreign exchange shortage that emerged early in the decade.

No single indicator can adequately summarize the performance of an economy, nor it is satisfactory to limit the assessment to aggregates provided in the national accounts. The following discussion does make extensive use of national accounting data but, in order to record the multi-faceted changes that can occur in an economy, supplementary evidence is presented on the financial system, wages and prices, the expansion of collective consumption, trends in unemployment, and changes in the distribution of income. We commence conventionally, however, with an examination of overall growth trends in the economy.

Growth, Saving and Investment

The most outstanding feature of the Ghanaian economy in the sixties was its failure to grow. In fact, it probably retrogressed, for the national accounts indicate a decline in per capita GNP, as can be seen in Table 4.1, line 9.[4] In constant prices, GNP per head fell from about ₵140 in 1960 to a little under ₵125 in 1969.[5] In the first half of the decade, i.e. during the Nkrumah period, expansion of the GNP is estimated as approximately keeping pace with population growth, believed to have been about 2.6 per cent annually; in the post-Nkrumah years the position deteriorated when, conceding the unreliability of the national accounts, it appears that there was very little growth in total GNP, and a decline in GNP per head.[6] However, the less unfavourable result for the Nkrumah years may be misleading, for recorded growth in GNP can be entirely attributed to an expansion of public consumption in these years, which may be a rather spurious indicator of economic progress[7].

Stagnation is scarcely an experience unique to Ghana but what is remarkable is that it occurred in spite of a massive development effort during the first half of the decade. From figures on gross capital formation (line 2 of Table 4.1), it can be seen that by 1964–5 the investment ratio had been raised from the already considerable 16 per cent in 1958–9 to an extraordinary 23 per cent and (from line 5) net investment from 12 to 16 per cent of NNP.[8] This was Ghana's 'big push', seen then by many economists as a massive investment effort. Nkrumah outdid even the 50 per cent increase in the country's capital stock that occurred in the second half of the fifties, with net capital accumulation in 1960–5 estimated as equivalent to no less than 80 per cent of the 1960 capital stock.[9]

It is against this effort that Nkrumah's failure to produce economic growth must be assessed. That the growth record was no better after he had left the scene may be less surprising, because very sharp reductions in investment meant that by the end of the decade the country was only just maintaining the existing stock of capital assets, with negligible net investment.[10] On the other hand, earlier experiences showed that there was no strict connection between investment and growth, and it is a convincing testimony to the low productivity of earlier investments that the economy failed to expand later, for it was only then that many of the investments of the Nkrumah years could begin to produce their benefits and real efforts were made to improve capacity utilization.

The sheer arithmetic of the investment failure of the earlier sixties is remarkable. Attempts to measure incremental capital: output ratios for this period result in figures which are either absurdly large or even negative, and Table 4.2 shows that even the *average* ratio doubled

TABLE 4.1
Key National Accounting Performance Indicators, Selected Periods
(Derived from constant price estimates)[a]

	1958–9 av.	1964–5 av.	1968–9 av.	1958–9 to 1964–5	1964–5 to 1968–9	1958–9 to 1968–9
	(% of GNP or NNP)[a]			(growth rates – % p.a.)		
1. Total Consumption of which:	82	85	83	3.5	0.2	2.3
(a) private	72	70	68	2.4	0.0	1.5
(b) public	10	15	15	10.0	0.9	6.9
2. Gross Domestic Fixed Capital Formation	16	23	13	—	—	—
3. Gross Domestic Saving	18	15	17	2.5	0.3	2.1
4. Gross Domestic Product[b]	—	—	—	—	—	—
5. Net Fixed Capital Formation	12	16	0	—	—	—
6. Net National Saving	14	5	4	1.8	0.3	0.9
7. Net National Product	—	—	—	2.6	2.6	2.6
8. Population[c]	—	—	—	0.2	–2.3	–0.8
9. Per Capita GNP[b]	—	—	—			

Sources: Appendix Tables 4.A and 4.B.

NOTES:

[a] The consumption, gross capital formation and gross savings items are expressed as percentages of GNP, and the net capital formation and net savings items as percentages of NNP. Both GNP and NNP are from constant-price estimates but adjusted for terms of trade effects – see Appendix, Table 4.B.

[b] Adjusted for terms of trade effects.

[c] Assumed to grow throughout at 2·6 per cent p.a. – see note e of Appendix, Table 4.B.

between 1960 and the peak year of 1967.[11] It may be wondered whether any other country has achieved the dubious distinction of quite so steep a trend in a coefficient which can normally be expected to change only rather gradually. The reasons for this failure are the subject-matter of several of the chapters which follow.

TABLE 4.2
Capital and Output, 1960–9
(Columns 1 and 2 in millions of cedis, in constant (1960) prices)

Year	Gross Capital Stock[a] (1)	GNP[b] (2)	(1) as a multiple of (2) (3)
1960	1684	946	1·78
1961	1959	939	2·09
1962	2183	955	2·29
1963	2460	1004	2·45
1964	2727	1048	2·60
1965	3034	974	3·11
1966	3232	923	3·50
1967	3312	928	3·57
1968	3363	990	3·40
1969	3420	1055	3·24

[a] Taken from T. M. Brown, 1972, Table D–1 and multiplied by 2 to convert from net to gross capital stock. Brown's estimates utilize official capital formation data.
[b] From Appendix, Table 4.B.

Discussions of the behaviour of saving must be qualified by the fact that the saving data are derived as residuals and are thus among the least reliable of the statistics presented here; the figures on *net* saving (Table 4.1, line 6) are liable to particularly large errors because of the difficulties of obtaining accurate estimates of capital consumption. What they show is that both the gross and net saving ratios declined in the first half of the decade (lines 3 and 6), when investment ratios were going up. The gap between the two gross ratios changed from a saving surplus of 2 per cent of GNP in 1958–9 to a deficit of 8 per cent in 1964–5. In the first sub-period Ghana was adding to her external reserves but by the mid-sixties about a third of gross investment had to be financed by inflows of capital from abroad. Large balance of payments deficits were a consequence of these trends, culminating in a major foreign exchange crisis in 1965–6, which is examined in chapter 5.

In the later sixties, it will be seen, gross saving rose somewhat as a proportion of GNP, but the net ratio declined further to only 4 per cent. With an even greater proportionate cut in investment, the savings-investment gap was eliminated, and the balance of payments improved. But it was an improvement won almost exclusively by reduced capital formation. Attempts by the Busia government to achieve higher rates of investment and growth in 1970 and 1971 were not supported by adequate measures to increase domestic saving. This and the resulting deficit financing rapidly restored an excess of investment over saving, generating a new balance of payments crisis and inflation at home.

The Financial System

The savings situation deteriorated in spite of an effort in the Nkrumah period to develop the financial system. Some indicators of financial development are presented in Appendix Table 4.C (p.92). This shows (col. 3) an increase in money supply as a proportion of GDP in the first half of the decade, followed by a later decline. A number of factors influence the demand for money and velocity of circulation but the substantial rise in the money/GDP ratio is consistent with an increasing monetization of economic activity and, by the same token, the subsequent decline, while influenced by more restrictive monetary policies, might also indicate retrogression to a relatively larger volume of subsistence production and barter transactions, as per capita incomes declined.[12] Secondly, in a developing financial system we expect the share of currency in total money supply to decline gradually, until a fairly advanced stage of development is achieved. Column 5 of Table 4.C shows this to have occurred between the years shown, so by this indicator there was fairly consistent 'progress' throughout.

Column 9 deals more directly with the development of the financial system. There was in the first half of the decade a very substantial increase in the real value of total financial assets but much slower expansion thereafter. Regression analysis suggests that easily the most important reason for this was the more rapid increase in the number of bank branches during the earlier years, attributable largely to the expansion of the government-owned Ghana Commercial Bank (although it would be unwise to conclude from this that the response to future bank expansion would remain as strong as in the sixties). Changes in real interest rates were also significant and these two variables provide a good statistical explanation of the growth of financial assets, with a corrected R^2 of 0.94. It was thought that changes in real per capita income might also have been an explanatory variable but, upon testing, this was found not to be significant.[13]

The ability of the financial system to attract a larger volume of real resources does not, of course, necessarily entail a *net* increase in aggregate saving. It may be that savers switched to financial from non-financial assets, such as gold trinkets or cattle. The fact remains, however, that on most indicators the organized financial system was a developing one in the sixties, especially in the earlier years.

Living Standards

The decline in the saving ratio was due partly to trends in living standards during the sixties. Returning to Table 4.1 (item 1), two facts stand out: (a) that total consumption, private plus public, declined slightly on a per capita basis taking the decade as a whole, although the deterioration occurred in the later years, but (b) there was throughout a socialization of consumption, with public consumption growing more rapidly than that of the private sector, especially in the earlier part of the decade. Concentrating for the time being on personal consumption, there was a serious decline during the sixties: measured in 1960 prices, per capita private consumption went down from ₵96 in 1958–9 to ₵86 in 1968–9.[14] The average Ghanaian, on this evidence, was struggling in vain to maintain living standards he had achieved in the late fifties. The deterioration appears from Appendix Table 4.B to have commenced about 1962, to have continued until about 1966 and then, taking one year with the next, to have roughly stabilized until the end of the decade.[15]

As explained in the Appendix, the national accounts are not very reliable, especially on the subject of local foods, which account for roughly half of total consumption, so the figures should be treated with reserve. There is, however, independent evidence for believing that a serious worsening did occur in living standards during this period. The behaviour of price data, for example, suggests that in several years the production of local foods did not keep pace with the expansion of population, as it was assumed to do by the national accountants, so that the accounts probably understated the decline. Figure 4.1 shows trends in consumer-goods prices since 1960 and it can be seen that in all but one year the prices of local foods rose relative to other consumer prices and, with per capita incomes stagnant or declining, this suggests that population growth was outstripping food output. Since in most of these years there were also restraints on food imports, it is a reasonable conclusion that there was a deterioration in average food intake. This is reinforced by a private estimate that total local food consumption expanded at about 1·6 per cent p.a. in 1960–5, implying a decline per capita of 1·0 per cent a year.[16] After 1965, and with the exception of the 1967 bumper crop, food prices continued to rise faster than the general rate of inflation, suggesting that the decline in per capita consumption may have continued in the second half of the decade – an inference not contradicted by the limited success of government efforts to improve the techniques and productivitiy of peasant farmers.[17]

Data on real wages and other forms of income provide further evidence of worsening living standards in the sixties. It seems that Mensah's view, reported in the previous chapter, that 'the lower paid urban workers are simply the less well-off members of a relatively wealthy urban minority . . .' is not well supported by the facts. Lines 8–11 of Appendix Table 4.D (p.94) present a variety of indices of real incomes. All show declines from 1960 to 1966 (the trough year), which were serious for all urban workers, drastic for unskilled workers earning the minimum wage, and for the cocoa farmers. Although there was some improvement by 1970, all the indices remained below the 1960 level.[18] The enigma in this picture is the self-employed food farmer.[19] On the assumption that increased retail prices were passed back to the farmer, it seems that he did well out of the inflation of the sixties, as indicated on the lowest curve of Figure 4.1 and lines 12 and 13 of Table 4.D[20]. His terms of trade improved in these years and, on reasonable assumptions about supply and demand elasticities, this probably meant that his real income also improved. Certainly, the production of food increased enormously in attractiveness by comparison with cocoa farming in those areas where the two were alternatives, although it is not known how much switching actually occurred between them.

FIGURE 4.1. *Consumer Price Indices*

If we accept that for the nation as a whole a clear deterioration occurred in private living standards during the sixties, the next question is whether increased consumption of public goods was sufficient to compensate for this. Major improvements undoubtedly occurred in public services, as indicated by socio-economic indicators of the most important items of collective consumption in Table 4.3. Each of these shows improvement – in most cases very substantial – during the decade. The most dramatic of the achievements was in education, although this was essentially a continuation of a trend from the previous decade. The 1970 population census revealed a major improvement in school enrolment rates, as compared with ten years previously. Enrolments in secondary schools practically tripled over the period and expansion of the universities was scarcely less rapid.

Progress in the provision of health services was slower but still clearly discernible, as was the extension of piped water supplies. Housing standards also appear to have improved considerably over the decade, in both rural and urban communities. Since most housing remained in private hands, this trend is rather surprising and appears to conflict with evidence of declining private living standards, although increasing inequalities of income in the urban economy and the sub-economic rents charged by public housing authorities provide some explanation.[21]

The lower section of Table 4.3 presents some of the more significant of these trends in the form of indices and these are averaged in lines 22 to 24. A crude and subjective attempt to provide a weighted average is given in line 24, which shows (a) that the greater part of the progress had been recorded by 1965, i.e. in the Nkrumah period. Those who distrust this lapse from scientific objectivity will see that both lines 22 and 23 also record substantial overall improvements and, again, that the Nkrumah years were the years of most rapid improvement.

This progress notwithstanding, expansion of the social services was probably not sufficient to compensate for the decline in per capita private consumption. The national accounts indicate that the expansion of public consumption was only sufficient to compensate for worsening private consumption for a few years and that total per capita consumption then began to fall.[22] Moreover, the estimates of public consumption are based on the standard, but questionable, assumption that the utility of government services is accurately expressed by the cost of providing them. Moreover, the assumption in the accounts of constant real per capita consumption of local foods was probably optimistic for this period. Taking all the evidence presented in this chapter, there seems every reason to believe that over the decade there was a discernible decline in average consumption standards.

Unemployment
During the course of the sixties the unemployment problem prompted increasing governmental concern, to a point where the Busia administration became almost obsessional about it. The general view,• shared by the author, was that unemployment was going up[23] for a number of reasons. The labour force was believed to be expanding quite rapidly while the economy was stagnant. Attempts by the NLC to bring the budget under control resulted in substantial lay-offs in 1966

TABLE 4.3
Selected Socio-economic Indicators

	Unit	1960	1965	Latest	(Year)
Education					
1. Percentage of 6–14 age group currently attending school[a]	percentages	40·1%	—	58·1%	(1970)
2. Numbers enrolled in schools:[b]					
a. Primary and middle schools	thousands	586	1,405	1,400	(1969/70)
b. Secondary schools	,,	17	43	49	,,
c. Universities	,,	2·0	4·3	4·8	,,
d. Total of above	,,	605	1,452	1,454	,,
Health					
3. Persons per doctor	thousands	18·7	13·5	14·7	(1969)
4. Persons per nurse[c]	,,	2·4	1·8	1·1	,,
5. Persons per hospital bed[d]	hundreds	10·9	10·6	9·5	(1970)
6. Infant mortality rate[e]	see note	95·1	94·9	87·5	(1967)
7. Crude death rate[e]	,,	13·1	12·8	12·6	(1967)
Water Supplies					
8. Percentage of total population served by public pipe-borne supplies[f]	percentages	19%	20%	20%	(1969)
9. No. of rural water supplies[g]	number	4,056	4,241	4,299	(1969)
Housing					
10. Number of persons per house[h]					
a. Urban	persons	14·91	—	14·29	(1970)
b. Rural	,,	9·60	—	7·27	(1970)
c. Total	,,	10·62	—	8·61	(1970)

Table 4.3 continued

	Unit	1960	1965	Latest	(Year)
Transportation					
11. Road mileages[i]					
a. Hard-top	miles	2,050	2,347	2,470	(ca. 1968)
b. Laterite and gravel	"		6,283	6,800	" (1969)
12. Total number of vehicles with valid licences[j]	thousands	45·9	52·6	61·2	(1969)
Power					
13. Sales to domestic consumers[k]	Kilowatt hours (000's)	53·0	102·7	153·2	(1969)
Communications					
14. Letters carried by postal services[l]	millions	63·4	118·6	184·6	(1969)
Indices[m]	*Weight*[p]				
15. Education (line 1)	30	100	(145)[n]	145	
16. Health (line 3)	15	100	128	121	
17. Water (line 8)	15	100	105	105	
18. Housing (line 10c)	20	100	(110)[o]	119	
19. Transport (line 12)	5	100	115	133	
20. Power (line 13)	10	100	194	289	
21. Communications (line 14)	5	100	187	291	
	100				
22. Unweighted mean		100	141	172	
23. Median		100	128	133	
24. Weighted mean		100	135	151	

For notes see page 76

NOTES: To Table 4.3

a Source: Central Bureau of Statistics, *1970 Population Census of Ghana,* Vol. II, Table 2.

b Figures refer to fiscal years 1960/61, 1965/66 and 1969/70 and relate only to students in public institutions. Source: Central Bureau of Statistics, *Statistical Yearbooks and Handbooks* (various issues).

c Figures for nurses include midwives. Source: CBS, *Statistical Yearbooks and Handbooks* (various issues).

d Figures refer to 1961, 1964 and 1970 respectively. Sources: 1961 – *Seven-year Plan,* Table 2.1; 1964 and 1970 – Ministry of Health. Figures exclude cots.

e Data based upon very incomplete coverage of compulsory registration areas. These largely cover the towns and cities and the mortality rates are therefore likely to be biased downward. Figures refer to 1961, 1964 and 1967. Source: Kpedekpo, 1970, Vol. 1, Table 5.19.

f Figures relate to population served by Ghana Water and Sewerage Corporation. First figure is for 1962. Source: CBS: *Economic Survey,* 1968 and 1969.

g Number of wells, boreholes and ponds. Source: CBS, *Economic Survey,* 1963 and 1969.

h Based upon CBS census returns for all regions except Northern and Upper. Source: *Report of Housing and Town Planning Committee,* 1971, Table 3.

i Sources: Ghana National Construction Corporation (1965); Nathan Sector Study Report (1968).

j Source: CBS, *Motor Vehicle Statistics,* 1969.

k First two columns refer to 1959/60 and 1964/65. Sources: CBS, *Statistical Yearbooks,* and Electricity Corporation of Ghana. Figures exclude sales to industrial users.

l Source: CBS, *Economic Surveys.*

m All indices have been calculated so that a larger index-number records an improvement.

n Since it appears from lines 2a–d that there was little change in school enrolment between 1965 and 1970, the 1970 figure has been imputed to 1965.

o This figure was obtained by linear interpolation and rounded up.

p Subjectively determined by author taking into account (a) the reliability of the indicator and (b) the importance of its subject to personal welfare.

A dash indicates data not available.

and 1967.[24] The educational system was thought to be producing a growing number of people unable to find the jobs to which they aspired and unwilling to accept anything of lesser status. Statistics showed only slow growth of urban employment.[25] Moreover, even in 1960 the problem had been a very substantial one, with the number recorded as unemployed in that year's census equivalent to about 6 per cent of the total labour force and, more to the point, about 25 per cent of the wage labour force.[26] In 1969 an alarming figure of 600,000 unemployed was mentioned by the Prime Minister, which would have represented a four-fold increase over 1960.[27]

However, the 1970 census did not confirm the general view, as shown in Table 4.4. Employment grew at 2·2 per cent, about the same annual rate as the labour force, and the overall unemployment ratio actually declined fractionally – from 6·4 per cent in 1960 to 6·3 in 1970. Further examination of the data provides an interesting picture.

TABLE 4.4

Employment Trends, 1960–70
(in thousands, except where indicated otherwise)

	Sex	1960	1970[a]	Annual Growth(%)
1. Total labour force[b]	Total	2723	3396	2·2
2. Total employment	Total	2559	3196	2·2
3. Agricultural employment[c] (a)	M	1002	1041	0·4
(b)	F	579	777	2·9
(c)	Total	1581	1818	1·4
4. Non-agricultural employment (a)	M	566	725	2·5
(b)	F	412	652	4·6
(c)	Total	978	1377	3·4
5. Unemployed (a)	M	109	146	2·9
(b)	F	55	56	0·2
(c)	Total	164	202	2·1
Ratios (percentages)				
6. Participation rates (a)	M	89·0	83·7	—
(b)	F	56·7	63·2	—
(c)	Total	73·0	73·3	—
7. Unemployment as per cent of employment (all sectors) (a)	M	7·0	8·3	—
(b)	F	5·5	3·9	—
(c)	Total	6·4	6·3	—
8. Unemployment as per cent of non-agricultural employment (a)	M	19·3	20·1	—
(b)	F	13·4	8·6	—
(c)	Total	16·8	14·7	—

NOTES:

[a] In the view of the Census office there was an under-enumeration in the 1970 census and the figures in this column have been adjusted for this. We take the Census Office estimate that the true growth of total population was at 2·6 per cent p.a. during the sixties and assume the 1960 population to have been accurately counted. This results in a hypothetical under-enumeration of 136,000 in 1970, caused chiefly by a strong and sometimes violent anti-alien campaign that was in full swing at the time of the census. We therefore assume the 136,000 to be non-Ghanaians.

We have further assumed the non-Ghanaian population to have retained the characteristics recorded in the 1960 census. The chief of these were (1) a ratio of males to females of 59·5 per cent to 40·5 per cent; (2) proportions of age fifteen and over of 70 per cent and 58 per cent for males and females respectively; (3) participation rates of 66 and 25 per cent, respectively; (4) the same proportions engaged in agriculture as in 1960, viz 48 per cent for men and 29 per cent for women. It would be easy to vary these assumptions but it should be stressed that the effects of the adjustments were minor for all variables and were in no sense crucial to the substance of the trends discussed in the main text. Some of the figures in this column have had to be calculated from data shown by the CBS as ratios. They are therefore subject to larger than normal rounding errors.

[b] Total employed plus unemployed.

[c] Employment in agriculture, forestry, hunting and fishing.

Sources:

For 1960: *1960 Census Reports*, Vols. III and IV. *Post-emuneration Survey Report.*
For 1970: *1970 Census Report*, Vol. II.

While the overall participation rate remained constant between 1960 and 1970, at 73 per cent of the adult population, there was a substantial decline in male participation compensated, however, by an increase in the female rate (item 6 of Table 4.4). The drop in the male rate can be attributed to larger numbers in full-time education but the rise in the female rate occurred in spite of an increase in the number of women in education.[28] This substitution of women for men was particularly apparent in agriculture, where there was hardly any increase in the number of men but a 34 per cent increase in female workers. Ghana's food supplies depended increasingly upon her womenfolk. In view of this, it is surprising that there was an increase in the proportion of unemployed men (offset by a decline in female unemployment), for with relatively more men being absorbed by the educational system, one might have expected the opposite.

Relative to the volume of employment, then, unemployment did not increase between the censal years, although there was an absolute increase of about 40,000. Since the definition of unemployment used for the census was essentially only relevant for wage employment, it may be less misleading to relate the unemployment statistics to jobs in the modern sector.[29] In the absence of full census results, the best we can do is to use non-agricultural employment as a proxy and if unemployment is related to this magnitude it appears as a *declining* problem, with the overall rate going down from 16·8 to 14·7 per cent (item 8 of Table 4.4).

What reasons might be given for the apparent failure of unemployment to worsen as people thought it did? Firstly, the labour force did not grow as rapidly as expected, perhaps because of the effects of educational expansion in absorbing young people.[30] Secondly, it does not appear that the products of the educational system were as prone to hold unrealistic job expectations or as reluctant to accept manual work as was generally thought to be the case; the evidence is that potential job-seekers were relatively, well-informed about their prospects and realistic in their aspirations.[31] Thirdly, it is probable that urbanization and the concentration of unemployment in the cities was mitigated by some return to farming, induced by the improvement in the barter terms of trade of food farmers shown earlier. Incentives to leave the farms and go to town in search of work were diminishing and, while urbanization still proceeded, the agricultural labour force did not suffer to the extent that had been predicted.[32] Fourthly, average output per man was apparently static, with employment growing at much the same pace as GNP, which gave a high absorption of labour from a given rate of economic growth – although static productivity is hardly good news. Finally, the state was expanding rapidly as an employer in the first half of the sixties – recorded public sector employment went up by 93,000 or 63 per cent between 1960 and 1965 and by the end of the decade stood at about the 1965 level.[33] This increase alone was equivalent to well over half the unemployment recorded in 1960.

While they are the best sources available, not too much weight should be placed on inter-censal comparisons. That the 1960 and 1970 censuses were held at the same time of year and the relevant questions were the same reduces the difficulties, as does the absence of obvious abnormalities in economic conditions at the time of both censuses. However, there are difficult conceptual and practical problems in measuring unemployment in countries like Ghana, arising from imperfect specialization and the existence of various informal types of work.[34] One may be particularly uneasy about the major changes recorded in female participation and unemployment between the two censal years, which strongly influenced the results reported here.

One obvious limitation of census data is that they can tell nothing about trends within the decade. Given that the expansion of public sector employment was concentrated in the first half of the decade, it is probable that unemployment went down in that period and then rose in the later sixties. This is consistent with evidence that secondary-school leavers began to experience growing difficulties in finding work towards the end of the decade.[35] It may well be, then, that governments had a more accurate impression of what was going on than the census figures suggest, although alarmist views of the size of the problem are contradicted by evidence that there were labour *shortages* in the rural economy[36] and that, contrary to official statements, there was no unemployment among university graduates at the beginning of the seventies.[37]

To suggest that unemployment may not be the problem it is often thought to be is not, of course, to deny that it is a problem at all. On the contrary, to have nearly 15 per cent of the non-agricultural labour force unemployed is both a waste of productive resources and a symptom of real social distress.[38] What is more, unemployment, as conventionally defined, records only part of the story – it leaves out the disguised unemployment and underemployment that are also prevalent. Even though there is little hard data, it is probable that much seasonal unemployment occurs in agriculture during the dry months of the year,[39] and much of the petty trading in the towns can best be regarded as disguised unemployment. This latter problem may well have worsened, for some of the increase in non-agricultural female employment probably took place as a result of the squeeze on real wages discussed earlier, with wives taking up petty trade to eke out the increasingly inadequate wages of their menfolk. In this situation, even tiny profits would be better than none – but would tend to diminish the profits of others.

In conclusion, we can ponder that the phase of most rapid educational expansion is now over, that in the years to come the labour force will expand more rapidly, that net saving and investment rates (and hence the likely future growth of the economy) have fallen to miserable levels, and that the public sector – with an already swollen payroll and acute budgetary problems – is unlikely in the future to absorb more than a small proportion of those entering the labour market.[40] The realities may shortly catch up with the pessimists.

Income Distribution

Traditional African society is often thought of as naturally egalitarian – a consideration which stimulated writers to stress 'African socialism' as being inherent in society and distinct from other forms of socialism.[41] Certainly, there are plausible *a priori* reasons for expecting incomes in Ghana to have a relatively low inequality. There are no large landowners who could be compared with those of the Indian sub-continent, the latifundia of Latin America, or the former white settlers of East Africa. Also lacking is an entrepreneurial élite with command over accumulations of wealth and income comparable, let us say, to the small number of families who have controlled so much of Pakistan's industry.[42] There is no powerful aristocracy, as in Ethiopia, nor has the exploitation of the peoples of the hinterland by a coastal elite been characteristic of Ghana, as it has of Liberia.[43] There is, of course, an élite but in former times this was based more on education and status than on wealth as such, and the emergence of a modern élite has been a recent outcome of industrialization and political independence. Extended family obligations, while they may be weakening, remain a potent redistributive device.[44]

The importance of income transfers, large numbers of self-employed, incomplete occupational specialization, and poor statistics conspire to prevent even the roughest estimates of the overall distribution of the national income, but something can be said about particular groups within society. One study examined the distribution of income among wage and salary earners employed in relatively large-scale establishments, almost entirely in urban centres. Figures are also available on the situation among cocoa farmers in 1967–70. The Ghana estimates are compared with data on average income distribution in other low-income countries in Table 4.5.

It will be seen that all the data on Ghana show a less unequal distribution than in the other low-income countries, providing support for the view of Ghana as a relatively egalitarian society. Moreover, being studies of income rather than of expenditures, the results probably overstate the degree of inequality, for income transfers arising from extended family obligations are likely to have effected some redistribution in favour of poorer Ghanaians and to have fallen relatively heavily upon the upper income earners within each group.[45]

No comparable data can be presented for food farmers but a study of agricultural incomes in Ghana concluded that:[46]

levels of income in various groups in the agricultural sector are not as

TABLE 4.5
Distribution of Income in Ghana and other Low-income Countries

Income Receivers	Lowest 50%	Highest 20%	Highest 10%
	percentage of total income		
GHANA			
Wage and salary earners:[a] 1956	33	37	22
1962	29	43	30
1968	26	50	27
Cocoa farmers, 1967–70[b]	22	49	33
OTHER LOW-INCOME COUNTRIES[c]	19	55	41

NOTES:
[a] Source: Ewusi, 1971, graph 6 and Appendixes I to VI.
[b] Source: Buxton, 1973, Table 4, who provides estimates of the distribution of all types of cash income, supplemented by provision for the value of subsistence production estimated from Dutta-Roy, 1969, Table A.12.
[c] Source: Healey, 1972, Table 5. The figures are the mean values of all available observations for the 18 developing countries in his table. When more than one observation was available the latest was selected. There were 15, 12 and 13 observations respectively for the three proportions shown above and almost all of these related to the early or mid-sixties. Alternative means were calculated for the eight sets of observations which were complete for the 50%, 20% and 10% categories but these were little different from those shown above, viz 20, 55 and 39.

different as might have been expected. Probably more than two-thirds of the farmers receive less than ₡500 per annum in cash income. While most sharecroppers receive less cash income than farmers in the localities where they work, they frequently receive more than farmers in other parts of the country. Annual labourers receive a low level of cash income but receive a wide range of fringe benefits.

This study went on to argue that income inequalities in non-cocoa agriculture were too small for redistribution to be an effective way of improving the position of the poorest members of rural communities. Another study of two farming areas in the Ashanti Region found that the most important 15–20 per cent of the farmers accounted for not less than half of *marketed* output,[47] which implies a fairly skewed distribution but which would be significantly modified if subsistence production were also included.

What is perhaps more relevant to this chapter is the *trend* in income distribution during the sixties. Economists are expressing concern about the tendency for inequalities to increase in developing countries[48] and we saw in the last chapter that this was a concern shared by the Busia administration in 1969–71. In particular, it was believed that rural-urban disparities were getting greater.[49] It was perfectly reasonable to expect growing inequalities. Large profits – legitimate and otherwise – were being made out of industrial protection, import licensing, and the corrupt practices of some politicians and public servants. The coverage of the income tax was highly imperfect.[50] Government expenditure policies had a strong urban bias, especially during the Nkrumah years.[51] Extended family ties were probably weakening in the cities.

As regards urban wage and salary earners, the results in Table 4.5 are unambiguous: inequalities grew considerably. One of the standard measures of inequality is the Gini coefficient and Ewusi calculated this to have risen from 14.59 in 1956 to 17.66 in 1968, or about 20 per cent.[52] Despite all the qualifications which could surround these results, they are large and consistent enough to leave little doubt that the distribution did worsen within this group. Some reasons are already apparent. We saw earlier that the real value of the statutory minimum wage – which determined the wages of many unskilled labourers – fell much more drastically in the sixties than other indices of urban earnings.[53] It was the hapless labourer who was being squeezed. Other differentials tended to widen in the same period. For example, the money incomes of senior Ghanaian civil servants rose nearly twice as fast as those of the junior grades,[54] and greater pressure for jobs probably depressed wages in junior private sector posts, relative to jobs demanding higher education.[55]

The other aspect on which it is possible to be fairly confident was the trend in urban-rural differentials, which the Busia administration believed to have become intolerably large. Table 4.D presents some highly relevant evidence. The real earnings of urban wage-workers declined during the first half of the sixties, as also did those of cocoa farmers. In the same period the barter terms of trade, and probably the real incomes, of food farmers improved substantially. With food production a far larger component of GDP than the receipts of cocoa farmers,[56] this suggests that, overall, discrepancies between urban and rural incomes tended to diminish. It also suggests that inequalities may have been reduced within the rural economy, for income is probably more highly skewed in cocoa than in food farming.[57] Examining similar data but with greater refinement Knight concluded that between 1960 and 1967 urban real incomes declined slightly while rural incomes grew by 20 per cent.[58] Data in a study of agricultural workers suggested that, once allowance was made for the free provision of food and other 'perks', their earnings were comparable to those of urban labourers[59] and although this finding was qualified by the possibility that agricultural labourers are more prone to temporary unemployment, later findings suggested that they can usually find work all through the year.[60] Finally, a survey of the Eastern Region showed average incomes to be only a little lower in rural households than in the towns.[61] We should, of course, remember the urban bias to social services, tending to raise the real value of wages in the towns, but it

nevertheless seems probable that the allegedly large inequalities between the towns and the villages were largely mythical, and the view
that these were becoming larger was almost certainly wrong.

Overall, the very incomplete evidence defies any neat generalization
about trends in the distribution of Ghana's national income. There is
evidence in both directions and there are enormous measurement
problems. All that can be said is that the pattern was complex and
diffuse, and the changes seemed to be generally well tolerated by society, failing to give rise to the fierce political tensions generated by this
issue in other countries.

Conclusion

The performance of an economy has many dimensions, and alternative
indicators for Ghana pointed in different directions during the sixties.
Is it, then, possible to characterize this period in a general way? Surely
the overwhelming impression is of failure – to generate growth, to
invest resources wisely, to raise productivity. By the standards of other
low-income countries, the performance of Ghana's economy was
appalling. In a (largely unsuccessful) attempt to convey a sense of the
urgency of the problem, a former colleague in the Ministry of Finance
and Planning presented comparisons of sixteen different indicators of
Ghana's economic performance in 1966–9 with those of other low-
income countries and showed Ghana to come near the bottom of the
list in all but a few cases. Her mean ranking was seventeenth out of 22
countries.[62]

The worst aspect of Ghana's poor showing was the failure of the big
push of the Nkrumah years. High levels of capital formation failed to
generate growth either in the short run or later in the decade. The
simultaneous tendency for saving ratios to decline resulted in a
growing gap between investment and domestic saving, intense
pressures on the balance of payments (as will be shown in the next
chapter), and inflation. Those who took over from Nkrumah inherited
a sorry mess and their successes in restoring some balance to the
economy were considerable. Nevertheless, their response was the
essentially negative one of cutting investment (and imports); the
improved utilization of productive capacity was not sufficient to impart
greater dynamism to the economy and, by running net investment
down to negligible amounts, they left the economy ill-prepared for
another development effort. When the Busia administration nevertheless attempted one, the old problems of a saving-investment gap, inflation and foreign exchange shortages reappeared and by 1972 the
economy seemed as mired in stagnation as it had been during the
preceding decade.

Two governments were penalized for these failures by being
deposed. But it was the Ghanaian public who really paid, especially the
urban poor. Improved social services were inadequate compensation

for the shrinking value of take-home pay, and poverty increased. To some extent, though, the present generation was protected at the expense of its children, for the post-1966 response to the saving-investment gap was to shield the consumer by cutting investment rather than raising saving.

Appendix to Chapter 4

The National Accounts and other Statistical Sources

(a) *The National Accounts*
Official estimates of Ghana's national accounts begin with 1955, although unofficial estimates have been made back to 1950.[63] Rather unusually, they were derived from expenditure estimates; the first official estimates of the industrial origin of the GNP begin only in 1965[64] and no estimates have yet been attempted of the national accounts by factor incomes. At the time of writing, published estimates do not extend beyond 1969, which is a serious handicap in discussing the post-Nkrumah record.

Various components of the estimates of expenditure on GNP are subject to substantial margins of error. A basic weakness of them all is that there is no meaningful series on the production or consumtpion of local foodstuffs – an item which alone is believed to comprise 30–40 per cent of total GNP. In an attempt to overcome this deficiency, a nation-wide sample household expenditure survey was conducted in 1962 and from this it was possible to obtain an estimate of national food consumption.[65] The expenditure estimate for this item in the national accounts, as published in the annual *Economic Surveys*, is said to be based on the assumption of a constant real per capita consumption of local foods (although the published figures do not always seem to tally with this procedure) and, for the current-price series, is inflated by a national index of local food prices.[66] Since there are several indications that food production and consumption failed to keep pace with the growth of population in the first half of the sixties, and perhaps in some later years too, this procedure, besides being arbitrary and useless for showing year-by-year variations, probably gave an upward bias to estimates of private consumption and GDP in this period.

Other items in the series are also subject to large error margins, although they are less important in relation to total GDP. Estimates of the construction component of fixed capital formation are largely based on imports of construction materials and, in the case of rural communities, assume the housing stock to expand at the same pace as population.[67] The item for changes in stocks has a very limited coverage, being restricted to cocoa and the inventory position of a few major trading companies. There is also known to have been considerable over-estimation of public consumption, due to double-counting of the consumption expenditure of various para-statal organizations, beginning around 1966, biasing the accounts upwards to a significant degree.[68] Finally, the price indices used for constructing a constant-price series were of dubious quality, especially for public consumption, capital formation and external trade.

Appreciating the weaknesses of their estimates, the Central Bureau of Statistics (CBS) undertook a major revision of the national accounts, concentrating on the development of a series of accounts by industrial origin but also providing expenditure estimates consistent with those by industrial origin. To date, this new series only covers 1965 to 1968.[69] Prepared in meticulous detail, this revised set of estimates must be regarded as a major improvement on most figures in the old series, although its authors were still gravely handicapped by an absence of tolerably accurate data on foodstuffs production.[70] The new estimates showed total GNP to be about 15 per cent smaller than had previously been thought, taking the four years as a whole. As well as having a smaller absolute size, these estimates (which I call the Singal/Nartey estimates, after their authors) showed that the constant-price GNP fell a little over the four-year period, as compared with a 6 per cent rise indicated by the earlier series.

The substantial differences between the two sets of estimates and the brief span of the Singal/Nartey accounts created considerable problems for this writer because he needed a series that would cover at least the whole of the sixties. It was therefore necessary to reconcile the Singal/Nartey figures with the earlier ones, and the results are set out in Tables 4.A and 4.B, with the methodology explained in the table notes.

A feature which greatly assisted reconciliation of the two series was that for 1965, which was used as the base, the proportional composition of expenditures on the GDP was very similar in the two cases. Total consumption was 90·8 per cent and 91·7 per cent, fixed capital formation 16·9 and 18·1 per cent and domestic savings 9·2 and 8·3 per cent. Moreover, they both showed the share of private consumption and of fixed capital formation to decline over the period, with the share of public consumption growing (but more slowly in the Singal/Nartey figures), and domestic savings displaying similar trends.

Given these points of agreement and the fact that the general trends indicated by the series are consistent with independent indicators of the same features, the figures presented here are probably reliable enough to portray broad medium-term trends in the economy, which is the chief use made of them in this study. However, it is important to have an appreciation of the serious deficiencies of the data, so as to avoid placing weight on any set of numbers which will not bear it. For this reason, for example, particularly cautious use is made of the data on capital consumption and on NNP, for the depreciation estimates must be judged among the least reliable,[71] even though the resulting estimates of net saving and investment are generally consistent with what one would have expected.

Despite all the weaknesses mentioned and the difficulties of reconciling the two sets of estimates, there is, in my judgment, little doubt that the broad trends discussed in the main body of this chapter did really occur, even though no great precision can be claimed for their measurement.

(b) *Financial Developments*

Table 4.C presents various indicators of financial development, covering roughly the same period as the national accounts. The notes to the table provide sources and other details.

(c) *Incomes and Prices*

Table 4.D provides a full presentation of the data utilized for Figure 4.1 and discussed in the main text. Sources and other explanations are provided in the notes to the table.

TABLE 4.A
Expenditures on National Product in Current Prices[a] (millions of cedis)

	1958	1959	1960	1961	1962	1963	1964	1965	1966	1967	1968	1969[b]
1. Total Consumption	642	728	790	914	942	1054	1147	1460	1558	1529	1658	1849
of which:												
a) private	572	650	694	804	830	916	987	1255	1367	1311	1382	1536
b) public	70	78	96	110	112	138	160	205	191	218	276	313
2. Gross Fixed Capital Formation	110	154	194	210	184	218	232	271	200	178	191	206
3. Change in Stocks	-2	+20	+22	-20	-12	-8	+14	-3	-1	-19	+2	+17
4. Exports minus Imports	+30	-12	-50	-82	-30	-56	-36	-141	-76	-41	+27	+45
of which:												
a) Exports of goods and non-factor services	220	240	246	244	240	234	247	251	222	274	396	456
b) Imports of goods and non-factor services	-190	-252	-296	-326	-270	-290	-283	-392	-298	-315	-369	-411
5. Gross Domestic Product	780	890	956	1022	1084	1208	1357	1587	1681	1647	1878	2117
6. Consumption of Fixed Capital[c]	-38	-43	-53	-66	-71	-78	-92	-105	-128	-158	-184	-195
7. Net Domestic Product	742	847	903	956	1013	1130	1265	1482	1553	1489	1694	1922
8. Net Factor Payments Abroad	-4	-6	-10	-14	-10	-18	-12	-19	-14	-25	-50	-55
9. Net National Product	738	841	893	942	1003	1112	1253	1463	1539	1464	1644	1867
10. Net Fixed Capital Formation (2+6)	72	111	141	144	113	140	140	166	72	20	7	11

TABLE 4.A continued

	1958	1959	1960	1961	1962	1963	1964	1965	1966	1967	1968	1969[b]
11. Gross Domestic Savings (5 minus 1)	138	162	166	108	142	154	210	127	123	118	220	268
12. Net National Savings (11+ (6+8))	96	113	103	28	61	58	106	3	−19	−65	−14	18
Analyses – percentages of total												
13. Total Consumption/GDP	82·3	81·8	82·6	89·4	86·9	87·3	84·5	92·0	92·7	92·8	88·3	87·3
14. Private Consumption/GDP	73·3	73·0	72·6	78·7	76·6	75·8	72·7	79·1	81·3	79·6	73·6	72·6
15. Gross Fixed Capital Formation/GDP	14·1	17·3	20·3	20·5	17·0	18·0	17·1	17·1	11·9	10·8	10·2	9·7
16. Gross Domestic Savings/GDP	17·7	18·2	17·4	10·6	13·1	12·7	15·5	8·0	7·3	7·2	11·7	12·7
17. Net Fixed Capital Formation/NNP	9·8	13·2	15·8	15·3	11·3	12·6	11·2	11·3	4·7	1·4	0·4	0·6
18. Net National Savings/NNP	13.0	13·4	11·5	3·0	6·1	5·2	8·5	0·2	−1·2	−4·4	−0·9	1·0

NOTES:

[a] The basic sources for this table are the CBS *Economic Surveys* (various issues) and Singal and Nartey, 1971, tables 16·5 and 16·6. However, the Singal/Nartey estimates, which cover 1965-8, are smaller than earlier estimates and are even less satisfactory in their treatment of consumption of local foods than the earlier series. To produce continuous and comparable series the following procedures were adopted:

  i. In the cases of public consumption and gross fixed capital formation the Singal/-Nartey estimates were chained to the old series by taking the earlier figures for 1965 and assuming that thereafter these changed in each year by the proportions shown in the Singal/Nartey figures. For example, they estimate that public consumption fell by 6·6 per cent between 1965 and 1966. The earlier CBS estimate for public consumption in 1965 was ₵205 million and this was reduced by 6·6 per cent to give a figure of ₵191 million for 1966.

  ii. The Singal/Nartey figures for changes in stocks, imports and net factor payments to the rest of the world were accepted as they stood and incorporated in Table 4·A.

  iii The figures on private consumption were given special treatment. The Singal/Nartey figures on consumption of items other than local foods were used, adjusted in the same manner as those on public consumption and capital formation. However, the earlier estimates of local food consumption have been preferred to those by Singal/Nartey (taken from *Economic Survey*, 1969, Table 6) and have been added to the adjusted Singal/Nartey figures on consumption of items other than local foods. This unsatisfactory procedure was necessitated because the Ministry of Agriculture data on food production used by Singal and Nartey (assumed equivalent to consumption) were markedly less plausible than the results of earlier CBS estimating procedures, and less consistent with independent evidence. For example, their data indicate an 18 per cent increase in food production in 1965-6, which remarkable expansion was, according to the Ministry's data, accompanied by a 46 per cent rate of price inflation! In the following year the growth of output apparently slumped to 8 per cent – but was accompanied by a 27 per cent fall in prices. Arbitrary though it is, the earlier series, based on an assumption of constant real per capita consumption, at least is more consistent with common sense.

[b] Since the Singal/Nartey estimates do not cover 1969, the figures shown in this year are derived by raising the 1968 figures by the proportions implicit in the 1968–9 estimates in the *Economic Survey, 1969*, Table 3. The exception to this is changes in stocks, in which case the figure shown for 1969 in the *Survey* has been accepted.

[c] Taken from T. M. Brown, 1972, Tables C·3 and D·1.

TABLE 4.B
Expenditures on National Product in Constant (1960) Prices[a] (millions of cedis)

	1958	1959	1960	1961	1962	1963	1964	1965	1966	1967	1968	1969	Growth Rate 1958–9 to 1968–9 (% p.a.)
1. Total Consumption	670	734	790	855	823	870	849	886	836	870	866	902	2·3
of which:													
a) private	590	650	694	751	709	745	715	721	693	726	708	734	1·5
b) public	80	84	96	104	114	125	134	165	143	144	158	168	6·9
2. Gross Fixed Capital Formation	116	166	194	200	182	216	221	251	179	139	133	138	−0·4
3. Change in Stocks	−2	+20	+22	−20	−10	−8	+26	−3	−2	−19	+1	+11	—
4. Exports minus Imports	−6	−34	−50	−46	+43	−4	−1	−31	+30	+28	+52	+18	—
of which:													
a) Exports of goods and non-factor services	188	218	246	277	324	308	271	335	299	272	297	283	—
b) Imports of goods and non-factor services	−194	−252	−296	−323	−281	−312	−272	−366	−269	−244	−245	−265	—
5. Gross Domestic Product	778	886	956	989	1038	1074	1095	1103	1043	1018	1052	1069	2·4
6. Terms of trade effect[b]	+36	+20	0	0	−73	−52	−35	−110	−106	−69	−24	+27	
7. Adjusted GDP*	814	906	956	953	965	1022	1060	993	937	949	1028	1097	2·1
8. Net Factor Payments Abroad	−4	−6	−10	−14	−10	−18	−12	−19	−14	−21	−38	−42	
9. Gross National Product*	810	900	946	939	955	1004	1048	974	923	928	990	1055	1·8
10. Consumption of Fixed Capital	−40	−46	−53	−63	−70	−77	−88	−97	−114	−124	−129	−134	
11. Net National Product*	770	854	893	876	885	927	960	877	809	804	861	921	0·9
12. Net Fixed Capital Formation*	76	120	141	137	112	139	133	154	65	15	4	4	—
13. Gross Domestic Savings*[c]	144	172	166	98	142	152	211	107	101	79	162	195	—
14. Net National Savings*[d]	100	120	103	21	62	57	111	−9	−13	−45	33	61	—

TABLE 4.B continued

	1958	1959	1960	1961	1962	1963	1964	1965	1966	1967	1968	1969	Growth Rate 1958–9 to 1968–9 (% p.a.)
15. Population[e] (000 s)	6391	6557	6727	6902	7081	7265	7454	7648	7847	8051	8260	8475	2·6
16. Total Consumption Per Capita ($\mathcal{C}$)	104·8	111·9	117·4	123·9	116·2	119·8	113·9	115·8	106·5	108·1	104·8	106·4	−0·3
17. Private Consumption Per Capita ($\mathcal{C}$)	92·3	99·1	103·2	108·8	100·1	102·5	95·9	94·3	88·3	90·2	85·7	86·6	−1·0
18. GNP[a] Per Capita ($\mathcal{C}$)	126·7	137·3	140·6	136·0	134·9	138·2	140·6	127·4	117·6	115·3	119·9	124·5	−0·8
Analysis – percentages of total													
19. Total Consumption/GDP*	82·3	81·0	82·6	89·7	85·3	85·1	80·1	89·2	89·2	91·7	84·2	82·2	—
20. Private Consumption/GDP*	72·5	71·7	72·6	78·8	73·5	72·9	67·5	72·6	74·0	76·5	68·9	66·9	—
21. Gross Fixed Capital Formation/GDP*	14·3	18·3	20·3	21·0	18·9	21·1	20·8	25·3	19·1	14·6	12·9	12·6	—
22. Gross Domestic Savings/GDP*	17·7	19·0	17·4	10·3	14·7	14·9	19·9	10·8	10·8	8·3	15·8	17·8	—
23. Net Fixed Capital Formation/NNP*	9·9	14·1	15·8	15·6	12·7	15·0	13·9	17·6	8·0	1·9	0·5	0·4	—
24. Net National Savings/NNP*	13·0	14·1	11·5	2·4	7·0	6·1	11·6	−1·0	−1·6	−5·6	3·8	6·6	—

NOTES:
[a] Derived from *Economic Surveys* for 1958–65 and 1969 and from pre-publication estimates based on the Singal/Nartey figures for 1965–8 kindly supplied by the CBS. For 1966 to 1969 private consumption estimates were deflated by the national consumer price index, recalculated to a 1960 base. Import and export figures for 1969 were deflated by price indices in Stern, 1972.

[b] Difference between exports minus imports in constant prices and in current prices.

[c] Item 7 *minus* item 1.

[d] Item 13 *plus* items 8 + 10.

[e] Assumes linear growth rate of 2·6 per cent p.a. from the 1960 census. The 1970 census counted a population of 8,559,000 but was known to have under-enumerated. Continuation of our series to 1970 provides a population of 8,695,000 which implies under-enumeration of 136,000 in the 1970 census. The 2·6 per cent growth rate was taken after consultations with K.T. de Graft-Johnson, former head of the CBS Census Office.

The symbol * is used to denote an aggregate that has been adjusted for the terms of trade effect.

TABLE 4.C
Financial Indicators, 1958–71
(millions of cedis except where otherwise indicated)

	GDP[a] (current prices)	Money Supply[b]	(2) as % of(1)	Currency in Circulation[b]	(4) as % of (2)	Other Financial Assets[c]	Total Financial Assets (2) + (6)	Price Index[e]	(7) Divided by (8)	(9) As an Index	Interest on Savings deposits[f]	Real Rate of Interest[g]	No. of Commercial Bank Branches[h]
	(1)	(2)	(3)	(4)	(5)	(6)	(7)	(8)	(9)	(10)	(11)	(12)	(13)
1958	780	91	11·7%	52	57%	32[i]	123	96	128	87	3·0%	—	—
1959	890	95	10·7%	55	58%	38[i]	133	99	134	91	2·5%	-0·1%	93
1960	956	107	11·2%	62	58%	40[d]	147	100	147	100	3·0%	+2·0%	104
1961	1022	125	12·2%	71	57%	48	173	106	163	111	3·5%	-2·5%	113
1962	1084	134	12·4%	78	58%	67	201	116	173	118	3·5%	-5·9%	134
1963	1208	151	12·5%	79	52%	78	229	121	189	129	3·5%	-0·8%	149
1964	1357	185	13·6%	97	52%	91	276	134	206	140	3·5%	-7·2%	170
1965	1587	228	14·4%	114	50%	122	350	169	207	141	3·5%	-22·6%	181
1966	1644	224	13·6%	103	46%	142	366	192	191	130	3·5%	-10·1%	188
1967	1622	220	13·6%	92	42%	144	364	176	207	141	3·5%	+11·8%	190
1968	1824	232	12·7%	101	44%	168	400	189	212	144	3·5%	-3·9%	188
1969	2056	245	11·9%	111	45%	182	427	203	210	143	3·5%	-3·9%	189
1970		283		126	44%	208	491	208	236	161	3·5%	+1·0%	191
1971		281		128	46%	234	515	227	227	154	7·5%[j]	-1·6%	188

NOTES:
(a) Derived from Appendix Table 4.A.
(b) Mean values of end-of-month figures. Source: Ahmad, 1970, p. 137, for 1959–65; Killick, 1966, Table 13.7 for 1958; Bank of Ghana, *Quarterly Economic Bulletin*, various issues, for 1966–71.
(c) Time and savings deposits and 'other liabilities' of commercial banks plus deposits with Ghana Savings Bank and First Ghana Building Society. Figures are means of month-end values.
(d) Mean of March, June, September and December.
(e) Consumer price index. Sources: Table 4.D, line 7; *Statistical Yearbook, 1962*, Table 108.
(f) Source: Bank of Ghana, *Quarterly Economic Bulletin*, various issues. When a range of rates was available the highest figure has been shown in the table.
(g) Column (11) *minus* current year's increase in price index given in column (8).
(h) Number as at end-June. Source: Bank of Ghana, *Annual Reports*, various years.
(i) End-of-year figures.
(j) Higher rate introduced September 1971.

TABLE 4.D
Indices of Incomes and Prices, 1960–71

	1960	1961	1962	1963	1964	1965	1966	1967	1968	1969	1970	1971
INCOMES												
1. Minimum Wage[a]	100	100	100	100	100	100	108	108	115	115	115	115
2. Monthly Earnings in Private Sector[b]	100	114	117	119	126	136	156	161	178	189	201	—
3. Industrial Earnings[c]	100	(114)	(117)	122	125	135	144	156	167	181	196	—
4. Cocoa Farmer Incomes[d]	100	85	88	84	106	63	65	104	90	126	125	137
RETAIL PRICES[e]												
5. Local Foods	100	106	117	122	137	188	216	184	201	218	228	256
6. Other Items	100	106	115	120	131	148	164	163	173	186	184	194
7. All items	100	106	116	121	134	169	192	176	189	203	208	227
REAL INCOMES[f]												
8. Minimum Wage	100	94	86	83	75	59	56	61	61	57	55	51
9. Monthly Earnings in Private Sector	100	108	101	98	94	80	81	91	94	93	97	—
10. Industrial Earnings	100	(108)	(101)	101	93	80	75	89	88	89	94	—
11. Cocoa Incomes	100	80	76	69	79	37	34	59	48	62	60	61
OTHER												
12. Terms of Trade of Food Farmers[g]	100	100	102	102	105	127	132	113	116	117	124	132
13. Index of Relative Attractiveness of Food Farming Over Cocoa Farming (12 divided by 11)[h]	100	125	134	148	133	343	388	192	242	189	207	216
14. Index of Industrial Earnings Relative to the Minimum Wage (10 divided by 8)	100	115	117	122	124	136	134	146	144	156	171	—

NOTES:

a Index of the statutory minimum wage for non-agricultural unskilled workers, as at year-end.

b Index of monthly earnings of male Africans in establishments with ten or more workers – average of March, June, September and December (Source: *Labour Statistics, 1968; Statistical Handbook, 1969;* 1970 figure is provisional, from CBS.)

c Index of average wage and salary payments per person employed in mining, manufacturing and power (Source: *Industrial Statistics, 1966–68* and *1969*). This series commenced in 1962 and the entries for 1960–2 assume that in these years industrial earnings moved the same way as in line 2.

d Index of total payments by Cocoa Marketing Board to cocoa farmers. Note this is *not* an index of payments per farmer, except on the assumption that there was no change in the number of farmers over the period (Source: Gill and Duffus, *Cocoa Market Reports,* various issues).

e Accra retail price index used for 1960–3. The national retail price index, which commenced in 1963, was used from 1964 and the two joined by the 'chaining' method. (Source: *Economic Surveys,* various issues).

f Items 1 to 4 deflated by item 7.

g Item 5 divided by item 6. This would provide an index of the real value of farmers' cash incomes if we assume a constant volume of commodities marketed per farmer, with a rise in the index showing an improvement in the purchasing power of his marketed output.

h This index is obtained by dividing the terms of trade of the food farmers (line 12) by the index of real cocoa incomes (line 11). Making the simplifying (but inaccurate) assumption that farmers specialize exclusively in growing either food-stuffs or cocoa, this series provides an index of changes in the relative attractiveness of these alternatives. A rise in the index shows an improvement in the attractiveness of food farming over cocoa growing. Of course, the possibility for switching between the alternatives only exists in areas capable of producing both types of crop, i.e. large parts of the forest zone.

All indices converted to a 1960 base.

NOTES

[1] This paragraph is largely based on Killick and Szereszewski, 1969, especially pp. 86–93.

[2] Somewhat faster if we add terms of trade effects, which were generally positive in this period. *See* Ord, 1964, Table S.1.

[3] Fifty-six per cent of the 234 manufacturing establishments recorded in the 1958 *Industrial Statistics* had commenced operations during the fifties.

[4] Table 4.1 is derived from data presented in the Appendix to this chapter, which also contains a discussion of the reliability of the national accounts and the methods used in preparing the data.

[5] *See* Appendix Table 4.B. At the official exchange rate then in force, the 1969 value in current prices was equivalent to $243 per capita in 1969 but a more realistic exchange rate would result in a figure well below $200. All values in this book are expressed in Ghana's present unit of currenty, the cedi ($\mathbb{C}$). The appendix ot chapter 1 provides a guide to the bewilderingly eventful history of Ghana's currency.

[6] At the time of writing, the national accounts do not extend beyond 1969 but examination of price, fiscal, and balance of payments data for 1970 and 1971 indicates the stagnation to have continued despite a revival of investment. After adjusting for changes in the terms of trade, it appears fairly safe to say that constant-price GNP per capita was no higher in 1971 than it was two years earlier.

[7] *See* Kuznets, 1966, pp. 224–5.

[8] The gross ratios may be compared with data for 35 other low-income countries for 1953–63, provided by the UN, 1966, Table I.1. Only three of these had gross investment ratios larger than 23 per cent, and the average value for all of them was 16 per cent.

[9] This figure is calculated from estimates of the capital stock by T. M. Brown, 1972, Table D.1.

[10] Import and fiscal statistics strongly suggest, however, that there was a considerable revival of investment in 1970 and 1971.

[11] The *Seven-year Plan* assumed an *incremental* ratio of 3·5!

[12] Blomqvist, 1971, has provisionally estimated a lagged income elasticity of demand for money of around 1·3. Although this is subject to large margins of error, his figures show that the elasticity is very probably in excess of 1·0. However, he failed to find a significant time trend for the demand for money to increase independently of real income.

[13] Where S = total financial assets in constant (1960) prices
   Y = per capita GNP in constant prices
   B = number of commercial bank branches
   R = real rate of interest on savings deposits
a lagged regression of the form $S = a + bY + cB + dR_{(t-1)}$ was run on data for 1958–1970. The resulting coefficients, with t-values in brackets, were:

$$S = -16\cdot37 + 0\cdot518Y + 0\cdot898B + 0\cdot750R_{(t-1)}$$
$$(1\cdot52)\quad(11\cdot66)\quad(2\cdot40)$$

The t-value of B was significant at well above the 0·1 per cent level and of R was significant at the 5 per cent level. This result was somewhat at variance with Blomqvist's finding that the demand for money was not significantly influenced by the rate of inflation.

[14] Averages calculated from Appendix Table 4.B.

[15] Available data for 1970 and 1971 suggest there was little change in average private consumption per head between 1969 and 1971.

[16] *See* Stoces, 1966, especially Table 11. This article provides an excellent review of agricultural trends to the mid-sixties, although it now appears that the author underestimated the expansion of the agricultural labour force.

[17] A rapid expansion of rice farming in the north did, however, provide a welcome

exception to the general stagnation, becoming significant about 1970. The record of the agricultural sector is dealt with in more detail in chapter 8.

[18] Addo, 1972 Table 11, provides data showing indices of the real wages of agricultural labourers of about 75 (1960 = 100), considerably better than their counterparts in the towns but still well down over the decade.

[19] In cocoa-growing areas virtually all cocoa farmers also produce food, at least for their own subsistence. To talk of 'the food farmer' is, therefore, an oversimplification, but a convenient one.

[20] Some argue however that the farmer profited little and that it was the middleman who did well out of the inflation. This issue is taken up in chapter 8.

[21] Public provision of domestic housing was largely confined to a State Housing Corporation and the Tema Development Corporation, and their activities were concentrated exclusively in the cities and towns. Perhaps two-fifths of total new urban housing in 1960–70 may be attributed to these agencies, which charged sub-economic rents. See Report of Housing and Town Planning Committee, 1971, passim.

[22] Total per capita consumption in 1960 prices was estimated at ₵117.4 in 1960 and ₵106.4 in 1969 – see Appendix Table 4.B, line 1b.

[23] Williams and Ntim, 1973, for example, refer to a period up to 1968 of 'manifestly increasing unemployment'. Peil, 1972, p. 70, found no clear evidence of a deterioration in the employment situation but nevertheless continued to assume that there had been one in later passages in her book.

[24] It was estimated that almost 59,000 workers were laid off between July 1966 and August 1967, although more than half of these were probably dismissed by private employers (in spite of pleas by the NLC that this should not be done). See Employment Market Situation Report, August 1967.

[25] Total recorded employment grew at under 2 per cent p.a. and industrial statistics showed a 3·5 per cent growth to 1970.

[26] Killick, 1966, pp. 147–50.

[27] However, see attempts in the 1970/71 One-year Plan, p. 146, to strike a more moderate note.

[28] Among adults (15+), the proportion currently attending school rose from 6·3 to 11·9 per cent for men and from 1·8 to 5·5 for women.

[29] For a discussion of this point, see Killick, 1966, pp. 147–9. The definition of unemployment used in 1970 was the same as that of 1960.

[30] See Caldwell, 1967, Table 4.16, who projected the labour force to expand at 3 to 4 per cent annually, against the actual of 2·2 per cent.

[31] See Foster, 1965, pp. 282–3 and passim, and also Peil, 1972, p. 45.

[32] Stoces, 1966, Table 6, estimated the agricultural labour force to have expanded at less than one per cent a year in 1960–5. It is interesting that only about a fifth of those laid off in 1966–7 (see footnote 24) registered as unemployed at employment centres and a sample survey indicated that many had apparently returned to their villages. Peil also found that industrial workers returned to farming between factory jobs and as an alternative to unemployment.

[33] Calculated from various issues of the Labour Statistics. I have preferred to use census data over the official labour statistics because the latter are not very meaningful. Their limitations are clear from the fact that the official 1970 figures of recorded employment represented only 12 per cent of total employment as recorded in the 1970 census (after adjustment), and only 28 per cent of non-agricultural employment. Moreover, the trends shown are also likely to be unreliable because of incomplete and variable reporting coverage. These statistics show total recorded employment to have increased 17 per cent in 1960–70, whereas the census returns indicate a 41 per cent increase in non-agricultural employment in the same period. See Williams and Ntim, 1973, and Killick, 1966, chapter 6, and 1972, for discussion of the reliability and interpretation of the labour statistics.

[34] See Hart, 1973, for a very interesting treatment of this problem in the Ghana case.

[35] Bezanson, 1971, pp. 43–7, shows that the proportion still without work 12 months after leaving school rose from 6 per cent in 1965 to over 50 per cent in 1968 and 1969.

[36] Addo, 1972, Table 5, shows for a sample of cocoa farmers that they were only able to hire about two-thirds the amount of labour they desired. Rourke and Obeng, 1973, found agricultural labourers to be able to find work easily, and the author was told by a member of a commission enquiring into wages that the commission had heard many complaints of labour shortages in rural areas.

[37] Bezanson, 1973B, p. 64.

[38] Bezanson, 1973A, records, for example, that about 30 per cent of 1970 middle-school leavers were still unemployed 22 months after completing their schooling.

[39] Rourke and Obeng's results suggest, however, that the seasonality of agricultural employment may not be as marked as is generally thought, although their research related only to hired labour.

[40] Bezanson, 1973B, expresses strong fears for the future ability of the public sector to absorb university graduates on the scale of past years. *See also* Addo, 1967, p. 26.

[41] Nkrumah (1964 p. 78), for example, refers to the 'socialist egalitarianism of the traditional African society'. Myrdal, 1956, p. 399, states flatly that in Ghana (the Gold Coast) income was less unevenly distributed than in the United States.

[42] Papanek, 1967, pp. 67–72.

[43] Clower *et al.*, 1966, chapter 1 and *passim*.

[44] Peil, 1972, p. 217, concludes from her study of Ghanaian factory workers that, 'The regular remittances of large numbers of urban workers are an important factor in equalising rural and urban incomes . . .' and (p. 212) cites an estimate by Caldwell that roughly ₵10 million is remitted from Accra each year, mostly, it may be presumed, to rural communities.

[45] The article by Hart, op. cit., suggests other ways in which income is redistributed from the middle class to the poor in the cities.

[46] Rourke, 1971, pp. 101–2.

[47] Nyanteng and van Apeldoorn, 1971, pp. 63–4.

[48] Healey, 1972, Table 5, shows several developing countries in which inequalities have apparently worsened over time and none in which the distribution had clearly become more equal.

[49] *See* Mensah, 1971.

[50] Examination of tax returns in 1970 revealed widespread evasion of the income tax by the self-employed and smaller companies. Only one of the country's legions of private lawyers had filed a tax return!

[51] Per capita government expenditures on health provided an extreme example, with the level in Accra being estimated for 1968/69 at four times the national average (Sharpston, 1969). Public works expenditures were also biased in favour of the capital, although to a lesser extent.

[52] Ewusi, p. 95. He presents five alternative statistical measurements of changes in inequality and all show the same general trend toward a less equal distribution.

[53] *See* Appendix, Table 4.D, line 14.

[54] In an unpublished draft, Knight shows that the average money salaries of junior civil servants rose 10 per cent in 1958–68 while those of senior Ghanaian civil servants went up by 17 per cent. Lorenz curves drawn from 1969–70 data on the size distributions of civil service and other public-sector employees indicate a more skewed distribution than that shown in Table 4.5 for all wage and salary earners. Twenty-six and 23 per cent of total payments went to the lowest 50 per cent earners and 34 and 36 per cent to the top 10 per cent.

[55] *See* Bezanson, 1971, 1973A and 1973B.

[56] In 1960, food production (taken as equivalent to food consumption) comprised 30 per cent of GDP, while payments to cocoa farmers were equal to only 11 per cent of GDP.

[57] Beckman, 1972, pp. 28-9.

[58] Knight, 1972, p. 213.

[59] Rourke and Sakyi-Gyinae, 1972, *passim. See also* Addo, 1972.

[60] Rourke and Obeng, 1973.

[61] Dutta-Roy, 1969, pp. 28–37, shows average monthly household incomes to have been ₵33.1 in rural communities and ₵37.5 in urban areas. Converted to a per capita basis, the difference was even smaller: ₵7.69 as agaainst ₵7.82.

[62] I am indebted to Michael Roemer for the data. A comparison was also made limited to African countries – ten in all. In all but one of the seven indicators for which the data permitted a comparison, Ghana's showing was much worse than the median of the other nine.

[63] *See* Ord, 1964.

[64] However, some semi-official estimates were prepared by Walters, 1962, and are discussed by Szereszewski, 1966, chapter 2.

[65] The results of this survey have never been fully published but the main results are given by Golding, 1962. *See also* Szereszewski, 1966, chapter 5.

[66] No official account of the methods of estimation was published. The best discussion of this topic is by Szereszewski, 1966, chapter 2.

[67] This last assumption may have biased the statistics downwards, for rural housing standards apparently improved during the sixties – *see* Table 4.B, and accompanying text.

[68] About a fifth of the total increase in current-price GNP shown in the old series between 1965 and 1968 can be attributed to over-estimation of public-sector consumption.

[69] *See* Singal and Nartey, 1971, supplemented by constant-price series kindly provided by the CBS.

[70] Estimates were prepared by the Ministry of Agriculture, but the sampling techniques were poor and reliability of results, even on casual examination, was questionable. A much-improved sample survey was conducted in 1970 and this should provide the basis for a better series of estimates for later years.

[71] These figures were derived independently by T. M. Brown, 1972, using official capital formation data and Szereszewski's estimate of the capital stock in 1960. Singal and Nartey also produced capital consumption estimates but only for 1965–8. Their figure for 1965 is ₵89 million against Brown's ₵105 million, although the difference becomes progressively larger over the years. In my view, Brown's figures make more realistic provision for the inflation of capital good prices (especially that caused by a devaluation in 1967) than those by Singal and Nartey. On the other hand, the indicated rise in the ratio of capital consumption to NNP, from about 4 per cent in 1958 to 11 per cent in 1969 is surprisingly rapid, even remembering the high rates of capital formation of the earlier sixties.

5 External Performance: The Foreign Exchange Constraint and its Causes

Its acute balance of payments problem is perhaps the most widely known feature of Ghana's economy and it is to this subject that we now turn, beginning with a brief description of trends in the sixties and then going on to a more analytical treatment. Was Nkrumah the helpless victim of adverse forces in the world economy over which he had no control, as some have claimed? Were the governments that followed him as seriously hamstrung by the external debt problem he left behind as has generally been thought? To what extent can poor balance of payments results be blamed upon domestic policy weaknesses? These questions will be the concern of later sections in this chapter, together with concluding discussions of the effects of foreign exchange shortages on the growth of the economy and of the extent to which the objective of economic independence was successfully advanced during the sixties.

Balance of Payments Trends

In every year bar one since 1960, there has been an overall deficit in Ghana's external payments, and in every year bar none a deficit on current account. Beginning the decade with valuable external assets she ended it with negative reserves, i.e. with short-term obligations to the IMF and commercial banks in excess of the value of the central bank's foreign exchange assets. These and other facts are presented in Table 5.1, which summarizes the main trends in the balance of payments. There were two major payments crises. Both, in appearance if not in substance, were resolved by a military coup – in 1966 and in 1972 – and it is convenient to divide the discussion into the years leading up to these crises: the Nkrumah years and the post-Nkrumah period, 1966–71.

The Nkrumah Years

Perhaps the best way of conveying the drastic deterioration that occurred in the external payments situation in the first half of the decade is to examine column 6 of Table 5.1, which shows that between end-1960 and end-1965 Ghana's estimated international liquidity balance was drawn down from ₵544 million to ₵59 million, the latter figure being only about a tenth of the value of that year's imports.[1] Starting with reserves equal to more than a year's supply of imports, she had within a short span been reduced to practically no reserves at all. Furthermore, very large foreign debts had been incurred in the same period. At the time of the February 1966 coup these debts amounted to about ₵640 million, a figure which excludes a substantial backlog of unpaid bills and similar short-term obligations. Of this amount, four-fifths were medium-term suppliers' credits, almost all of them accumulated during the preceding five years (see Table 5.4 below).[2] If we take the debt and liquidity positions together, therefore, the overall deterioration in Ghana's net asset situation was of the order of ₵1100 millions. Since in the same period total imports (f.o.b.) amounted to about ₵2500 millions, Ghana financed about two-fifths of her imports by running down her reserves and obtaining foreign credits of a largely medium-term nature.

Paradoxically, these were not, with the major exception of 1965, years of large and expanding import bills, as can be seen from Part A of Figure 5.1. Imports in 1962 to 1964 were substantially below 1960–1 levels. They were, moreover, increasingly used in ways which should in principle have eased the payments pressures. Table 5.2 shows that remarkable changes in the end-use composition of imports occurred in the first half of the decade, with drastic reductions in the share of consumer goods and corresponding increases in imports of capital goods and raw materials, many of them intended for import-substituting industries. These changes were a reflection of Nkrumah's determination to invest heavily in an industrialization programme and his willingness, if necessary, to squeeze the Ghanaian consumer in order to do so. So while reserves were spent and debts accumulated ordinary Ghanaians found it increasingly difficult and expensive to buy imported consumables; in real terms, per capita imports of finished consumer goods approximately halved between 1959–61 and 1964–6, despite the 1965 import boom.[3] Overall, then, the country's payments difficulties could not be blamed upon high imports, certainly not upon the Ghanaian consumer.

We are thus led to examine the other side of the trading account and in doing so we come nearer to an explanation of the problem, for export earnings were stagnant in these years (Figure 5.1). One explanation for this was the poor performance of the cocoa industry,

TABLE 5.1

Summary Statistics of Ghana's Balance of Payments, 1960–71
(millions of cedis calculated at ₵1.28 = $1.00)[a]

	Trade Balance[b] (1)	Net Invisibles[c] (2)	Current account(1+2) (3)	Non-monetary capital(net)[d] (4)	Overall Balance (3+4)[e] (5)	Implicit International Liquidity[g] (6)
1960	−10	−118	−129	+59	−70	544
1961	−72	−131	−203	−16	−219	325
1962	+13	−122	−109	+97	−12	313
1963	−41	−136	−177	+75	−102	211
1964	0	−130	−130	+89	−41	170
1965	−163	−147	−310	+199	−111	59
1966	−55	−117	−173	+136	−37	22
1967	+26	−143	−117	+73	−44	−22
1968	+59	−128	−69	+63	−6	−28
1969	+81	−151	−70	+57	−13	−41
1970[f]	+143	−164	−21	+95	+74	33
1971	−36	−155	−191	+97[h]	−94[h]	−61

NOTES:

[a] i.e. calculated throughout at the exchange rate established on 7 February 1972.

[b] Includes exports of non-monetary gold. All items f.o.b. Excludes imports and exports of Valco aluminium smelter, the net balance of which is treated as a service item.

[c] Includes net transfer payments.

[d] Direct investment, other private long-term capital, trade credits, commercial credits and long-term loans to government, and errors and omissions. The allocation to this entry of all errors and omissions is somewhat arbitrary but the largest mistakes are likely to have occurred with respect to capital flows.

[e] Equivalent (with opposite sign) to the balance on monetary account, defined as the net balance on assets of government, sterling balances, bilateral balances, assets/liabilities of commercial banks, central bank and changes in IMF position.

[f] 'Imports' of oil exploration equipment have been netted out on current and capital accounts.

[g] It is impossible to construct a meaningful series on Ghana's international liquidity or external reserve situation from published sources, which contain many inconsistencies over time and with the balance of payments accounts. The procedure adopted has been to take as correct the Bank of Ghana's figure for foreign exchange reserves as at end-1960 and to add to it the 1960 value of Ghana's gold tranche position with the International Monetary Fund (=25% of quota). The figures for subsequent years have been derived by adding the overall balance (subtracting in the case of deficit years) from the liquidity poition at the end of the previous year. E.g. to obtain end-1961 liquidity subtract the 1961 deficit of ₵219 million from end-1960 liquidity of ₵544 million = ₵325 million. The resulting figures are similar to unpublished estimates prepared by the IMF, but the latter show a more rapid deterioration in the early years and a correspondingly less favourable liquidity position thereafter. The 1969 estimate in Table 5.1 of −₵41 million may be compared with the IMF estimate of −₵93 million.

[h] Involuntary short-term credit in the form of unpaid import bills, amounting to ₵79 million, has been treated as a monetary item in this year because of the grossly misleading impression conveyed by treating it as a net capital inflow.

Source: Bank of Ghana.

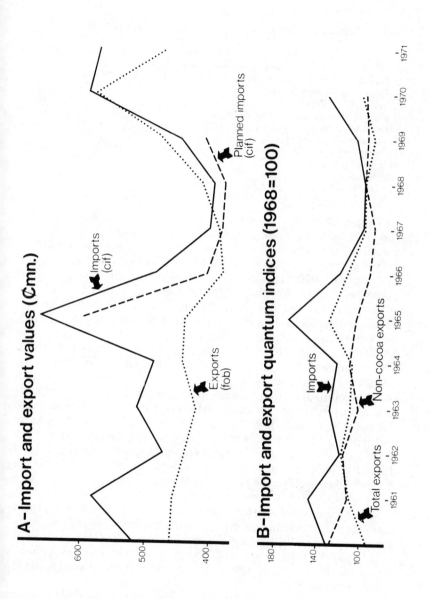

FIGURE 5.1(A) *Import and Export Values*
FIGURE 5.1(B) *Import and Export Quantum Indices*

TABLE 5.2
The End-use Composition of Imports, 1952–1969
(percentages of total imports)

	1952–4	1959–61	1964–6	1967–9
1. Non-durable consumers' goods	49	42	28	25
2. Durable consumers' goods	7	8	5	5
3. Fuels and lubricants	7	5	5	6
4. Non-durable producers' materials	12	14	18	29
5. Durable producers' materials[a]	12	20	16	10
6. Producers' equipment	13	12	28	24

NOTE:
[a]Chiefly construction materials.
Source: CBS annual *Economic Surveys*.

the output of which fluctuated around a trend that was at best static and in the later sixties seemed to be gently declining.[4] With other producer countries still expanding their output, the consequence was that Ghana's former standing as the world's leading producer began to slip, so that by the 1970/71 season she contributed only 26 per cent of world output, as compared with 37 per cent ten years earlier.[5]

This situation did not, however, mean that Ghana became less dependent on cocoa exports, for the other export industries scarcely did better; an index of the volume of non-cocoa exports, with 1960=100, stood at 83 in 1965 and 79 in 1970, and cocoa exports in 1969 comprised a larger proportion of the total than in 1960.[6] The quantity of timber and gold exports went down and, with the exception of the aluminium smelter towards the end of the decade, no significant new export industries, either in agriculture or in industry, emerged to compensate for these declines. These failures and the general tendency for export trade to diminish relative to total economic activity are shown in Table 5.3, calculated from input:output tables for 1960 and 1968. Exporting shrank in relation to total sales, overall and in most of the individual sectors; the poor performance of non-cocoa agriculture and manufacturing is particularly noteworthy.

Starting the decade with an already substantial trade deficit, export earnings remained consistently well below import levels and this, combined with normally substantial deficit on invisibles (largely attributable to payments for freight and insurance, and net transfers abroad), produced generally large deficits on current account. But what of the capital account?

The ambivalence of Nkrumah's attitudes towards foreign direct investment and official aid – asking for it while simultaneously condemning it as neo-colonialist – was mentioned in an earlier chapter. The results, so far as the official statistics reveal them, were fairly

TABLE 5.3

Exports as Percentage of Total Sales, by Sector

	1960	1968
Cocoa[a]	78·0	88·2
Other agriculture	2·0	0·8
Forestry	39·8	17·6
Mining	99·0	100·0
Construction	0·0	0·0
Manufacturing	26·9	21·2
Electricity and fuels	0·0	2·1
Transport and services	6·1	2·6
ALL SECTORS	19·9	14·7

Sources: 1960: Szereszewski, 1966 Table 3.1;
   1968: Central Bureau of Statistics (unpublished).
NOTE:

[a] In fact, virtually all Ghana's cocoa is exported; the figures in the table are less than 100 per cent because of sales to the manufacturing sector for processing into cocoa butter and paste before export.

predictable: little private investment or official long-term aid. Net receipts from private direct investments totalled ₵124 millions for the six years, and there was about ₵130 million in long-term aid.[7] The combined total of these two items was equivalent only to about 10 per cent of total fixed investment over the period[8] and if we net against them payments by Ghana of profit remittances and interest, the grand total for the entire period is negligible, a mere ₵30 millions. Almost all the long-term aid and much of the private investment was attributable to the Volta river project. The direct foreign exchange costs of this were financed by aid loans from the World Bank, and the US and UK governments; associated with the project was the construction of a large aluminium smelter by a consortium styled as Valco, 90 per cent owned by Kaisers of America.

We saw in the preceding chapter that the gap between domestic saving and gross investment grew in the first half of the sixties; we have now seen that Nkrumah was only able to finance a small part of his investment programme with long-term capital. His and his colleagues' response was characteristic:[9] to press ahead with the investment programme notwithstanding, to try to contain the payments problem through the use of import controls, to finance the remainder by using up reserves and obtaining medium-term suppliers' credits, and to gamble that import substitution and the processing of exports would improve the balance of payments in time to avert a crisis. The odds were heavily against such a gamble, for Latin American and Asian countries were already discovering that import-substituting industrialization places heavy initial burdens on the balance of payments while bringing only moderate relief (if any) in the longer run.[10]

But if there was a chance that the gamble could have paid off it was destroyed during 1965.

As is shown in later chapters, highly expansionary fiscal and monetary policies were pursued during 1965, adding substantially to aggregate demand. With virtually all imports subject to licensing, this should not theoretically have affected the volume of imports, but in practice even licensed imports were affected by the state of demand. Moreover, inventories had been run down to abnormally low levels during 1964, which added further pressures for larger licence allocations. Nkrumah's pan-African ambitions also played a role, for an important meeting of the Organisation for African Unity was due to be held in Accra in the autumn and Nkrumah, who had been running into much opposition to his ideas within the Organisation, resolved to spare no expense to impress his distinguished guests. A huge new conference centre was constructed at remarkable speed and expense, a large fleet of new government cars was imported and, just before the visitors arrived, shops were filled with imported consumer goods of a quantity and variety that had not been seen for a long time.[11]

The consequence was a record high import bill in 1965, which the country simply could not afford. Reserves were further reduced (Table 5.1) and large new debts incurred. It was obvious by the end of the year that Ghana would be unable to meet her obligations in the months ahead and that drastic action would be necessary. The IMF was called for in the hope of a rescheduling of medium-term debts and substantial financial assistance,[12] but Nkrumah and his colleagues baulked at the stabilization measures that were a precondition of Fund support. Finally, in February 1966, with Nkrumah out of the country, a military coup brought the National Liberation Council (NLC) to power.

1966 to 1971
Reference back to Table 5.1 shows that the NLC had considerable success in improving the foreign payments situation. The trading account moved out of the red and the current account deficits were greatly reduced, as was the deterioration of the country's international liquidity. That these improvements were achieved while export earnings declined (Figure 5.1(A)) underlines the achievements but also draws attention to their limitations. By a combination of disinflationary policies at home, which drastically reduced domestic investment (chapter 4), a devaluation in 1967, and tighter control over licences, very large reductions were achieved in imports as is shown in Figure 5.1(A).[13] In the short run the NLC had little alternative, but holding down imports was only a palliative; improved export performance was essential to any long-run solution of the payments problem.

Despite their domestic measures the NLC still needed large-scale external assistance, and they sought more aid, stand-by credits from the IMF, and the re-scheduling of medium-term debt obligations. In all respects they achieved considerable success, as is recorded later, and when the Busia government was elected to office in October 1969 the balance of payments position, if still delicately poised, had at least been stabilized. The new government inherited the further advantage that exports had at last begun to rise in value, if not in quantity, in response to more favourable world cocoa prices (Figure 5.1).

Within two years the government was nevertheless confronting a payments crisis scarcely less severe than that of 1965. Cocoa prices, and hence export earnings, were returning to historically more normal levels,[14] increased imports had been allowed to absorb most of the windfall foreign exchange earned in 1969 and 1970 but did not go down much when exports declined in 1971. After four years of surpluses the country experienced its third-largest deficit ever on current account (Table 5.1). Reserves slumped, unpaid import bills piled up and the IMF was sent for again. A desperately large devaluation in December 1971 was followed almost at once by another coup and Ghana's second 'democratic experiment' was at an end.

It was also Ghana's second experiment with growth policies, for while the NLC had concentrated on stabilizing the economy, the Busia government raised investment levels to obtain more rapid economic growth. It was then that the basically unchanged weaknesses of the external sector swam rapidly to the surface again; as domestic expansion generated increased demand for imports the export sector remained stagnant as ever. The resulting payments crisis, accelerated though it was by poor economic management, was thus entirely predictable.

Influence of the Terms of Trade
Returning now to the earlier sixties, Nkrumah and others have argued that many of the economic difficulties which Ghana found herself in during his period were due to worsening terms of trade, a circumstance entirely outside Ghana's control.[15] This point of view is most fully stated in an article by Eshag and Richards.[16] They compare the performance of Ghana's economy with that of neighbouring Ivory Coast during the period 1960–5 to gauge the extent to which differences in performance may be attributed to contrasting economic policies or to factors over which the governments had little or no control. They conclude that the 'most significant development in the demand for Ghana's exports . . . was a fall in the export price of cocoa' and they nominate this fall as the 'dominant factor responsible for slowing down the rate of growth of the Ghanaian economy.' Their 'chief conclusion' is that the poor showing of Ghana's economy by comparison with the Ivory Coast's was due to changing conditions of external demand outside Ghana's control,[17] although policies in Ghana, especially on taxation, tended to make things worse. Others, however, have disputed that the terms of trade were so important.[18]

To help clarify this issue, indices of export and import prices, and of the terms of trade are displayed in Figure 5.2. It is easy to see from this that if the decade is viewed as a whole it is impossible to argue that there was any consistent long-term tendency, favourable or unfavourable. The commodity terms of trade in 1970 were almost exactly the same, at 124, as in 1960, when the index stood at 126. However, there was a major deterioration from 1960 to 1966, caused very largely by declining world prices for cocoa.

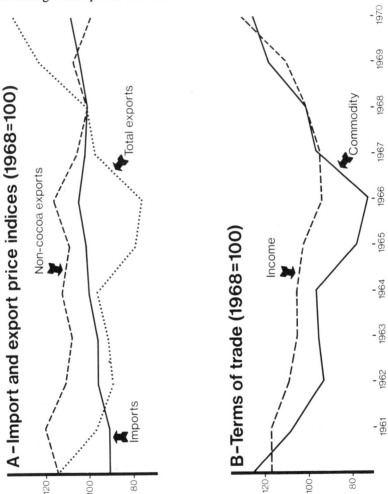

FIGURE 5.2(A) *Import and Export Price Indices*
FIGURE 5.2(B) *Terms of Trade*

In assessing the economic impact of this, it is important to note that Eshag and Richards were wrong to attribute the declines in the world price of cocoa to developments in world demand for this product. World demand for cocoa grew more rapidly in the first half of the sixties than in the preceding decade and in the following five years.[19] However, as world supply increased rather more, inventories accumulated and prices plummeted.

Now this is more than a quibble. If the cause of falling prices was on the supply side of the market two implications follow: (a) that it was not entirely true that this was beyond the control of the producing countries,[20] and (b) that when gauging the effect of changing conditions in the world cocoa market it is necessary to look at the volume exported as well as the price received. This is important, for the year in which the world price declined the most sharply was also the year in which Ghana had a record crop (557,000 tons in 1964/65 compared with an average of about 425,000 tons in the preceding four seasons), with the one tending to offset the other. In fact, the elasticity of demand for Ghana's cocoa throughout the first half of the decade appears to have been about unitary, with changes in price offsetting changes in output and resulting in a remarkably stable value of export earnings.[21] It of course remains true that had prices not fallen in this manner, ie, had demand been more elastic, Ghana would have benefited more from her cocoa exports, but it is quite unrealistic not to expect major increases in sales, such as those of 1964/65, to have depressing effects on prices.

Leaving cocoa aside for a moment, what was happening to the prices of other exports and of imports? Looking back at Figure 5.2(A), it is evident that trends in these other prices were adverse to Ghana, although only rather gently so. There was a clear downward drift throughout the decade in a composite price index of Ghana's traditional exports other than cocoa, accompanied by an upward drift in import prices. The case of non-cocoa exports was, however, worsened by a downward trend in volumes during the first half of the decade, as is evident from Figure 5.1(B). For all exports other than cocoa, Ghana is a small supplier relative to total world consumption and she is therefore faced with large price elasticities of demand. Total earnings could therefore be raised by increasing the quantity of sales, so the decline in the volume of these exports worsened the effects of declining world prices.[22]

The importance of supply conditions draws attention to the fact that in controversies of this kind much depends upon which concept of the terms of trade one uses. The argument is conventionally made with respect to the *commodity* terms of trade, i.e. the ratio of export prices to import prices. The unbroken curve in Figure 5.2(B) shows that there were indeed serious declines in this index in 1960–6 and it is by reference to this that writers have defended Nkrumah. However, changes in world cocoa prices were easily the strongest influence on this deterioration and, in my view, it is unhelpful to view this without also attending to the quantities of cocoa Ghana was placing on the market.

To take account of this type of consideration it is preferable to employ *income* terms of trade. This is an index of the purchasing power of total export proceeds and is obtained by deflating an index of export earnings by an index of import prices.[23] Such an index is displayed in the broken curve of Figure 5.2(B), and it is evident that any argument concerning the economic effects of deteriorating terms of trade in the Nkrumah years has to be substantially modified if we use the income series. There was still a downward trend but it was much milder – a decline of 13 per cent in 1960–5, compared with a 39 per cent drop in the commodity terms of trade. It is a matter of judgment as to which is the more appropriate index but my conclusion is that; while adverse terms of trade did undoubtedly worsen things in the first half of the decade, they did not have so serious an impact as some have argued. Defective policies had more serious effects, as will be argued shortly. In particular, the terms of trade argument overlooks the crucial fact that the official objective of diversifying Ghana's exports by developing non-traditional exports failed completely, so that the volume of exports other than cocoa actually declined. Ghana's balance of payments problems throughout the sixties are more easily explained by this failure and the policies which caused it than by reference to adverse trends in world prices.

The Debt Problem and External Assistance
If trends in the terms of trade could be used in defence of Nkrumah, the same could certainly not be done for the governments which followed him, for Figure 5.2 shows that on either measure the terms of trade improved substantially during the NLC period and the first of Busia's two years of office. After 1966, however, attention focused on another aspect of the payments problem that was not the making of those who had taken over the responsibilities of government: the burden of external debts.

Some stress was placed earlier on the magnitude of the foreign debts accumulated under Nkrumah, and in the acutely difficult period after he was deposed it was clear that Ghana would be simply unable to meet her contractual obligations as they then stood.[24] As scheduled, the servicing of these debts would have absorbed about 19 per cent of Ghana's export earnings in 1967 and 1968 and, in spite of their demonstrated willingness to cut back severely on imports (Figure 5.1), the NLC simply could not afford that. They therefore went to the creditor countries in search of a negotiated rearrangement of the debt obligations within Ghana's ability to pay. Rescheduling conferences were held in 1966, 1968 and 1970, and at each of them a new tranche of relief was agreed.

The case which successive governments made for debt relief can be summarized as follows.[25] Firstly, there was the question of ability to pay: that on any reasonable projections of Ghana's balance of payments and import needs, she would be unable to meet her obligations as they then stood. Secondly, there was the nature of the debts in question: many of them had been incurred for projects of a long-term nature, inappropriate for medium-term financing; many of the loans had been pressed on the Nkrumah government by fast-talking 'project-mongers' after quite inadequate pre-investment feasibility studies (see chapter 9); and a number of the contracts were signed as a result of bribery and other malpractices. The first aspect of this argument was illustrated by an analysis of contractor-financed projects according to the time-span over which they could be expected to yield measurable economic benefits, the premise being that the repayment period of a credit should bear a reasonable relationship to the economic life-span of the project it is financing. The average length of the contractor credits in question was about $8\frac{1}{2}$ years, with a maximum of 12 years, but it was found that less than half the projects analysed could be expected to generate their incomes within a 12-year span.[26] Even if the projects had all been financially viable, which was far from being the case, a problem would still have arisen regarding the unsuitability of their financing.

The Busia administration pleaded two further considerations.[27] The first was a straightforward application of an argument associated with Prebisch's report to the first UNCTAD meeting:[28] that during the sixties the net effect of the commodity terms of trade on the balance of payments was negative and that this constituted a transfer of resources from Ghana to her trading partners, the creditor countries. The other argument was developmental: the economic growth and structural changes needed for fundamental improvements in the payments position depended critically upon the availability of foreign exchange; a long-term debt agreement was needed for the development of the economy and its debt-servicing capacity. It was also politically essential if Ghana's newly restored democracy was to survive.

Ever since the 1966 coup there had been a strong popular sentiment in Ghana that the NLC ought to have repudiated all or some of the debts.[29] The Busia administration did not do that but it did believe strongly that the 1966 and 1968 agreements had been unfavourable, even though after the latter the Ghana delegation had claimed to have brought back a 'final' solution. Two aspects of these agreements evoked especial ire. Firstly, they provided only short-term relief, for $2\frac{1}{2}$ and $3\frac{1}{2}$ years respectively, thus merely postponing the problem rather than providing a solution geared to reasonable projections of Ghana's future debt-servicing capacity.[30] Secondly, the creditors insisted in both years that a clear distinction be drawn between the provision of development aid, which was appropriate on soft terms, and debt relief, which they saw as essentially a commercial matter. In consequence, the 1966 and 1968 agreements required the payment of moratorium interest, ie interest on all deferred payments (principal *and* the original contractual interest), at rates of 5 to 6 per cent. Thus, an additional debt-servicing burden was created and Minister of Finance Mensah showed that moratorium interest had added to the original contractual obligations by 35 per cent.[31] This, in his view, was not good enough and he made a strong attempt in 1970 to negotiate a longer-term and softer agreement. Two significant advances were made. The creditors gave up their insistence that soft terms were inappropriate for debt relief and, in a complex formula, agreed to terms incorporating a larger grant element – 61 per cent – than any country had hitherto received from a debt settlement.[32] Second, although they did not offer a long-term settlement, providing relief for only two years, they did agree to meet Ghana again before mid-1972 'to review Ghana's debt situation in the longer-term'. However grudgingly, they seemed to have conceded the eventual necessity for a long-term settlement, even though they could not bring themselves to do it then. In the event, after the January 1972 coup the National Redemption Council repudiated some medium-term debts and unilaterally rescheduled the remainder on terms similar to those asked for in 1970. The planned meeting with the creditors did not take place.

If Ghana found the Western governments to be demanding creditors, they were relatively generous aid donors. During the years after 1966 the US, the UK, Germany, the World Bank group and others provided considerable long-term development aid, all the more valuable for being on soft terms and largely in the form of programme support, i.e. not tied to particular projects.[33] Total aid commitments in 1968–69 were equivalent to 19 per cent of imports in those years, 20 per cent of government revenues and 27 per cent of gross investment. On a per capita basis, this worked out to an annual figure of $7·1, compared with an average for all low-income countries of $3·9.[34]

Thus, the balance of payments impact of the debt problem can only be adequately assessed in the context of the overall flow of financial assistance to Ghana, and an attempt is made in Table 5.4 to consolidate all resource transfers during the post-Nkrumah years.[35] As the table notes explain, some of the figures are subject to substantial margins of error, but the accuracy is sufficient to portray the general picture. The first three lines show the net effect of the debt agreements negotiated in 1966, 1968 and 1970; despite the limitations of these, substantial net relief was provided in the later sixties, although the figures in line 3 would have been substantially negative throughout most of the seventies.[36] Large credits were also received from the IMF in 1966–8, although there was a return-flow in the later years, as shown in line 4.

Lines 5 and 6, which deal with long-term aid, need some explanation. Line 5 records new aid commitments, whereas line 6 shows the amounts of aid that Ghana actually spent in each year. Comparison of these shows that the rate of spending did not catch up with new commitments until 1969-70 – a fact which slowed down the pace at which the economy could benefit from the aid and embarrassed the Ghana government when asking for more, although much of the delay was caused by the highly complex disbursement procedures of the various lending agencies.

Lines 7, 9 and 10 of Table 5.4 provide measures of total resource transfers to Ghana in 1966–71. Line 7 is the total value of debt relief, net credit from the IMF and gross aid expenditures; from these sums are deducted actual debt service payments (on medium- and long-term debts) to provide an estimate of the net capital receipts of the government in line 9; line 10 provides an indication of net long-term aid by deducting debt service payments from gross aid receipts.

TABLE 5.4
Financial Assistance to Ghana, 1966–71 (millions of cedis[a])

	1966	1967	1968	1969	1970	1971[j]
1. Contractual medium-term debt obligations (P+I)[b]	46	72	80	64	52	39
2. Negotiated medium-term debt obligations (P+I)[c]	5[h]	12	41	22	27	20
3. Debt relief (1–2)	41	60	39	42	25	19
4. Net credit from IMF[d]	58	26	15	−7	−32	−40
5. Gross long-term aid commitments[e]	28	69	89	79	73	n.a.
6. Gross long-term aid receipts[e]	14	14	61	71	75	54
7. Gross total assistance (3+4+6)	113	100	115	106	68	33
8. Actual debt service payments (P+I)[f]	24	19	36	30	30	35
9. Net total assistance (7–8)	89	81	79	76	38	−2
10. Net long-term aid (6–8)	−10	−5	25	41	45	19
11. External indebtedness[g]						
(i) medium-term	509				394[i]	
(ii) long-term	130				338	
(iii) total	639				732	

NOTES:
[a] Calculated throughout at ₵1.28=$1.00.
[b] P+I signifies principal plus interest payments.
[c] As negotiated at 1966, 1968 and 1970 debt conferences. Not all these payments were actually made, however, due to delays in completing bilateral agreements and various disputed items. Due to imperfect data these are order-of-magnitude estimates only.
[d] Excludes use of Special Drawing Rights.

e 'Receipts' differ from 'commitments' because of delays in utilizing the aid in question.
f These figures relate to servicing of medium- and long-term debts. They are derived from balance of payments data but, because of various inconsistencies in the data, are subject to substantial margins of error.
g This excludes indebtedness to the IMF and various short-term debts. At the end of 1970 there were arrears on current payments of about ₵72 million and various other obligations (chiefly arrears on profit and dividend payments) amounting to about ₵70 million. The 1966 figures refer to the position as at 24 February 1966. The 1970 statistics relate to the end of the year.
h Estimated *actual* payments in 1966.
i Certain disputed debts have been excluded and arrears in certain other payments have been added.
j Most of the estimates for this year are provisional.
Sources: Bank of Ghana balance of payments estimates and various unpublished sources.

By the first two measures, Ghana received very substantial financial assistance during the later sixties, tailing off rather rapidly in 1970 and 1971 as debt relief diminished and as the IMF was repaid. The amounts in question may be compared with the annual average value of imports (f.o.b.) in these years of ₵432 millions, and with the very small amounts received during the Nkrumah era. While Ghana could reasonably complain about the attitudes of her creditors, she could not claim to have done badly in other respects. In fact, Ghana was generously treated in the provision of long-term development aid, permitting a radical restructuring of her external debt in the five years following the first coup, (see item 11 of Table 5.4). The country's total medium- and long-term indebtedness went up about ₵100 million in this period but the composition changed radically, in favour of a longer-term portfolio; the share of long-term debts in the total rose from 20 per cent in February 1966 to 46 per cent. at the end of 1970. Thus, if the total magnitude of the debt problem had increased it at least had a more reasonable time profile.[37]

There are many, inside and outside Ghana, who blame the continued economic difficulties after 1966 and the fall of the Busia government upon the debt problem and the attitudes of the creditor countries. This will not stand up to detailed examination. Certainly, the creditors' insistence on drawing a distinction between the terms for aid and for debt relief was logically absurd; by their unsympathetic treatment of the debt issue they were undermining their own endeavours as aid donors, both economically and politically. Preoccupied with an imagined danger of providing hostages to fortune and legalistic notions like *caveat emptor*,[38] the creditors at no stage seriously came to grips with the realities of Ghana's limited long-term debt servicing capacity, nor did they ever attempt to offer an economic justification for what they were offering. Greater generosity would have been more harmonious with their own aid policies and would have offered significant additional support to Ghana.

It has, on the other hand, proved easy to exaggerate the seriousness of the debt problem. The magnitudes in question were large but by no means of Indonesian proportions[39] and the debt problem was not fundamental to Ghana's payments problems. As Mensah himself admitted, 'Even if we obtained 100 per cent medium-term debt relief, our external accounts would remain unbalanced.'[40] Indeed they would. Various independently prepared balance of payments and national accounts projections all showed that even if there were no medium-term debts the country would remain in need of larger long-term aid receipts than those of the late sixties in order to achieve even a modest rate of economic growth – so large as to call into question both the feasibility of obtaining them and Ghana's capacity to absorb them.[41] To put the matter another way, it was estimated that 100 per cent debt relief could be expected to raise the rate of growth of the economy by less than half of one per cent annually.

The main theme of this chapter has been that the chief proximate cause of Ghana's payments problems was the poor performance of her exports, and that is very relevant here. The debt problem looked so grave because export prospects seemed so poor; had exports been dynamic the shorter-term aspect of the problem could have been solved. By the same logic, a debt settlement, while it could provide relief, could not in any way solve the payments problem; only improved export performance could do that. The debt problem was a symptom more than a cause of the foreign exchange constraint.

The Influence of Economic Policies

Having discounted arguments to the effect that Ghana's foreign exchange problems were essentially due to circumstances beyond her control, the implication is that domestic conditions had more effect on these problems. The following paragraphs therefore attempt to assess the impact of domestic policies. Refreshingly, we can start on a positive note.

Nkrumah has been criticized for his attempts to redirect Ghana's trade towards Russia and other Eastern European countries,[42] but for the record there is little evidence that this policy was against Ghana's interests. From available, admittedly partial, data it appears that the prices Ghana received and paid in her trade with the East were comparable with the terms of trade with Western Countries.[43] It may well be that bilateral trade agreements with Ghana stimulated the very rapid expansion of cocoa consumption in East Europe in the sixties, from which addition to world demand Ghana was a major beneficiary.[44] Ghana's experience of Eastern aid does not seem to have been unfavourable. There were, it is true, complaints about quality and after-sales service, and also that these countries were mostly concerned to use their aid as an export promotion device (but that criticism would apply equally to Western donors). There were also cases in which the Eastern countries were more particular about the viability of proposed aid projects than the Ghana government.[45] The terms of Eastern aid were less favourable than aid from the West in the later sixties, because they were repayable over only ten years, but they were considerably better than Western suppliers' credits during Nkrumah's period of office.[46] There is no reason to disagree with the conclusion of a detailed study by Uphoff that, 'Generally speaking, aid from the East was straight-forward and sober . . .'[47]

It has been shown that there was a persistent tendency for an import surplus in the sixties, and we should turn now to try to explain the import and export trends reviewed earlier. Although the export failure lay at the root of the problem, import policies also had an aggravating effect, especially those affecting the relative prices of imports and domestically produced goods. The maintenance until 1967 of an unchanged parity for the cedi in the face of domestic inflation had the effect, of course, of making imported goods attractive relative to local goods, thus adding to demand. There was admittedly a real attempt during the Nkrumah period to increase import duty collections, which rose as a proportion of the landed costs of imports from 17·4 per cent in 1960 to 33·8 per cent in 1965, but the NLC cut back on these very substantially so that by 1969 duty collections were only 18·9 per cent of imports.[48] The NLC did, in the other hand, devalue the cedi by 43 per cent (in local currency terms) in 1967.

We can take this matter further by referring to calculations by Professor Leith of the 'effective' exchange rates (i.e. the official exchange rate adjusted for the effects of taxation) for imports and exports, displayed in Figure 5.3. This shows that the effective exchange rate for imports in the sixties was always well above the official rate. That is to say, importers had to pay duties and other taxes in addition to the official rate of exchange; the effective rate for exporters, on the other hand, was almost invariably below the official rate because part of the proceeds were taxed.[49] This structure of course had a strong tendency to encourage import substitution as against exporting. In fact, at the end of the period the effective rate for imports ($\mathbb{C}1.35 = \$1.00$) was practically double the average for exports ($\mathbb{C}0.70 = \$1.00$).

However, the incentive to import remained very strong throughout the period because of increases in the general price level relative to the after-tax cost of imports, and this inflation further discouraged exports. One way of illustrating this is to convert the effective rates in Figure 5.3 into index series and to deflate these by the consumer price index.[50] The results are set out in Table 5.5. A decline in the import index shows that the after-tax cost of imports fell relative to the general level of domestic consumer-good prices, ie that the incentive to import increased. A fall in the export index shows that the after-tax value of exports declined relative to the cost of living, ie that the incentive to export was going down.[51]

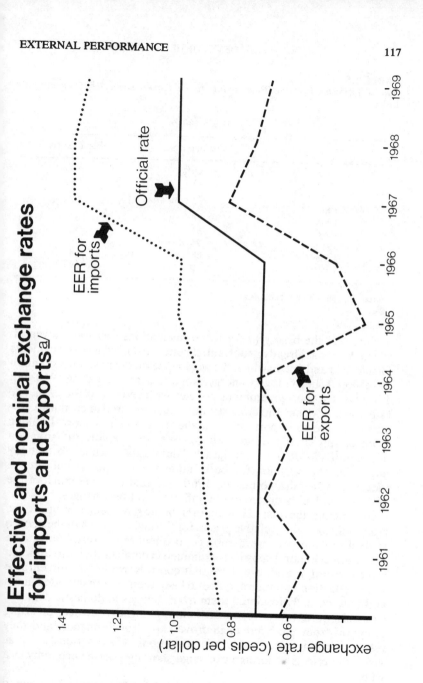

FIGURE 5.3 *Effective and Nominal Exchange Rates for Imports and Exports*

TABLE 5.5
Indices of Effective Exchange Rates for Imports and Exports, Deflated by Consumer Price Index

(1960=100)

	For Imports	For Exports
1961	98	80
1962	93	96
1963	91	79
1964	83	87
1965	75	33
1966	63	38
1967	94	76
1968	88	64
1969	80	56

Source: Figure 5.3 and Table 4.D

Note that the base year for these calculations was 1960, a year in which there was already a substantial deficit in the balance of payments (Table 5.1) and one in which the weaknesses in the payments situation were already beginning to emerge. Nevertheless, comparing 1960 with 1969 we see that government policies with respect to the exchange rate, the tax system and domestic inflation conspired to produce a greater incentive to import and a smaller incentive to export. Looking more closely at the trends, we can see how rapidly the situation deteriorated in 1964–6, that the 1967 devaluation, while substantially improving the situation for both imports and exports, still left the indices less favourable than in 1960, and that by 1969 much of the devaluation had been eroded by inflation and tax changes.

In principle, the quantity of imports should have been immune to the effects of changes in relative prices, for throughout much of the decade virtually all imports were subject to quantitative restrictions. The operation of import licensing is examined in detail in chapter 10 and, to refer forward, it is shown there that controls, while they did enforce some reduction in imports, failed to keep them within intended limits and only partially insulated them from changes in domestic demand. Controls were, moreover, an essentially negative device, diverting attention from the need to improve export performance, and they resulted in micro-economic mis-allocations which seriously aggravated the effects of foreign exchange shortages on the economy as a whole.

Export policies were no more successful, a failure which stemmed from the low priority attaching to exports in Nkrumah's development strategy. Take the example of the country's major export, cocoa. There was a very strong case against a rapid expansion of cocoa production, most of the benefits of which would be lost to the consuming countries by depressing world prices, as happened in 1964/5. On the other hand, there was very little to be said in favour of actually cutting back on production, a policy from which other producers would stand to gain at Ghana's expense. A policy of gradually expanding output in line with world demand seemed the sensible one. Nkrumah, however, seemed to regard the industry essentially as a milch cow, convenient to exploit because much of the opposition to his party had been centred in cocoa-growing areas. Table 5.6 brings out some of the results of this attitude. The real value of the price paid to the cocoa farmers and their total incomes from cocoa were cut by nearly two-thirds between 1960 and 1965 (lines 1 and 2). Real government spending on the industry also plummeted in the same period (line 4) and supplies of insecticides, essential to maintain the farms in good health, were cut back to almost nothing (line 5). Ghana's main earner of foreign exchange could not even get the very small allocations of imported supplies that it needed. The rather limited progress in restoring the situation after 1965 is also noteworthy: a large proportion of cocoa receipts was still taxed and government spending on the industry expanded only rather moderately. One consequence was that for most of the decade the real value of the producer price was too low to induce the farmers to undertake sufficient new planting to maintain moderate growth in the industry.[52]

TABLE 5.6
Government and the Cocoa Industry: Selected Indicators[a]

	1960	1961	1962	1963	1964	1965	1966	1967	1968	1969	1970
1. Index of real producer prices (1960=100)[b]	100	87	77	61	46	37	45	60	59	65	64
2. Index of real value of total payments to cocoa farmers (1960=100)[c]	100	80	76	69	79	37	34	59	48	62	60
3. Payments to cocoa farmers as % of total export proceeds from cocoa[d]	72	58	60	57	71	41	55	65	41	50	37
4. Index of real value of budgeted government expenditures on cocoa industry (1960=100)[e]	100	70	16	20	18	30	39	26	31	44	41
5. Index of quantity of insecticide sales to cocoa farmers (1960=100)[f]	100	63	67	86	63	2	9	33	57	68	118

NOTES AND SOURCES
[a]Date on producer prices and payments to cocoa farmers in lines 1–3 relate to crop years commencing in the year indicated at the head of the column. Data in line 4 relate to fiscal years commencing in year shown at head of column.

^b Index of nominal producer price (adjusted for 'voluntary contributions') deflated by consumer price index.
^c Taken from Table 4.D, line 11.
^d Adjusted to exclude 'voluntary contributions' to government. Export proceeds include cocoa products.
^e Recurrent and capital expenditure estimates deflated by price index for government consumption expenditures. Sources: Pantanali, 1970, Table 8.2; *Economic Survey, 1969*; annual budget estimates. A 7 per cent increase in the price index was assumed for 1970.
^f These figures relate to sales of the anti-capsid spray, Gammalin 20. Source: Cocoa Division of Ministry of Agriculture.

Attempts to raise the unit value of Ghana's traditional exports by processing them at home were largely unsuccessful. An increasing proportion of cocoa and timber exports were processed before shipping and at the time of the 1966 coup a gold refinery was under construction.[53] The evidence suggests that the processing of cocoa in Ghana led to a net loss of export earnings because of inefficiency and unfavourable prices for cocoa butter.[54] It also appears that the country earned more foreign exchange for a log exported unsawn than it did from a sawn log, because of high wastage rates.[55]

Faith in the benefits of statutory marketing boards for export commodities was similarly misplaced.[56] The most important was the Cocoa Marketing Board, which pursued a rather rigid policy of selling in advance a substantial proportion of each crop, apparently regardless of world market conditions – a successful policy when the market was falling but resulting in large losses of foreign exchange when the market was rising, for example, from 1966 to 1969.[57] The Timber Marketing Board was unpopular within the industry, which claimed that the Board fulfilled no useful function in return for a 3 per cent levy on exports of prime species;[58] attempts to give it an export monopoly in the middle of the decade led to disruption of the trade and losses of foreign exchange, and had to be abandoned. The Diamond Marketing Board similarly entered into dispute with producers and probably contributed to the drastic tailing-off of declared production by African diggers and a general stagnation of production from the country's major diamond mine.[59]

Perhaps most serious of all was the absence of effective measures to stimulate the emergence of new export industries, prior to the introduction of a generous export bonus scheme in 1971. We have already seen in Table 5.5 that potential new exporters were faced with unfavourable relative prices, by contrast with production for the home market. Indeed, the chief emphasis of Nkrumah's development strategy was on import-substitution rather than exports and, to a lesser extent, this was true of the NLC.[60] Although industrialization did result in a substitution of local manufactures for imported consumer goods, this brought little net relief to the external payments because local industry tended to be capital-intensive and based upon the processing of imported materials and components – a point taken up in chapter 8. Little official attention was paid to the development of non-traditional exports, with the result that the product-composition of exports was frozen (*see* Table 5.8 below).

Falling import and export policies were compounded by the reluctance of both the Nkrumah and Busia administrations to accept that the foreign exchange position constituted a major constraint upon their freedom to pursue expansionary policies at home. Both sought to raise the level of investment above domestic saving, with major payments deficits an inevitable consequence. Nkrumah's response was the rapid accumulation of an insupportable and inappropriately structured external debt; Busia's the short-term consumption of windfall foreign exchange earnings accruing from the 1968–70 cocoa boom. The most spectacular (and irresponsible) example of the politicians' refusal to live within the limits imposed by the foreign exchange shortage was the import boom of 1965, although Mensah's 1971 budget had the dubious distinction of being more explicit in its rejection of the import constraint (*see* chapter 11). Poor coordination of domestic and external policies also had adverse effects, a case in point being the neglect to reinforce the 1967 devaluation with domestic fiscal and monetary policies to prevent inflation from eroding the change in exchange rate.[61]

All in all, then, it is not surprising that Ghana so consistently faced balance of payment difficulties, for government policies had negative effects throughout most of the sixties. Policies generally increased incentives to import and reduced incentives to export, and the substitution of controls and marketing boards tended to be counter-productive. The stress on the control and replacement of imports, with a relative neglect of exports, was especially serious. Imposed on this very weak structure, the adverse movements of the terms of trade in the first half of the decade turned a serious situation into a desperate one; in the later years it was the debt problem which became the external bogey but that this was regarded as being so serious was due as much to export stagnation as to the magnitude of the debts.

Effect on Domestic Economic Performance
Allusion has been made several times to the harmful effects of the foreign exchange position on the performance of the domestic economy. That this was a critical constraint can be argued on both historical and *a priori* grounds.

Consider first the nature of Ghana's economy: small, still at an early stage of development, dominated by primary production and associated service activities, still with an inflexible and dualistic structure of production, and heavily dependent on commerce with the outside world. Obviously the level of economic activity and its rate of expansion were liable to be crucially dependent on being able to sustain an adequate level of imports. The most important connection between import capacity and growth in such an economy results from the high import content of capital formation. At the beginning of the sixties (and indeed at the present time) Ghana was almost wholly reliant on imports for all types of capital goods except certain construction materials. In the absence of a substantial domestic capital-goods sector, she was dependent on transforming resources into investment goods through the intermediation of foreign trade. But current domestic production was also reliant upon imports of raw materials and other inputs. The most heavily dependent sector was manufacturing which, apart from a substantial wood-processing industry, typically produced the simpler types of consumer goods from imported materials and components.[62] Mining, power generation and transportation relied similarly on imported materials and spares. Farming, it is true, used hardly any foreign inputs but was also affected by import shortages because of the reduced ability of the transport system to carry produce to the markets with reasonable speed and efficiency. It could even be argued that imports of finished consumer goods had a positive effect on economic growth, by acting as incentive goods. This was probably crucial in an earlier stage of the economy's development[63] and it is plausible, if speculative, that the willingness of cocoa and food farmers to invest labour in expanding their productive capacities is positively correlated with the availability and relative cheapness of imported goods which bring some luxury into their lives.

We might further hypothesize that balance of payments problems are likely to emerge sooner or later when an economy such as this embarks upon a major development effort. Import needs are likely to grow at least as fast as the domestic product but there may be severe structural difficulties in inducing a parallel growth in exports. With an export sector already over-dependent on a single commodity and with a diminishing base of known natural resources (chapter 1), the creation of non-traditional export industries is necessary but even with strong incentives this is likely to take considerable time. The manufacture of import substitutes appears to offer a quicker solution but, as already noted, it is only after a rather long time-lag that such a strategy can actually be expected to result in substantial net savings of foreign exchange. Thus, an increasingly wide gap is likely to open up between export earnings and import demand; unless this is filled by an inflow of foreign capital (and the use of foreign exchange reserves) economic growth is likely to be retarded.

Ghana's post-war history accords well with *a priori* expectations. Compare first economic performance in the fifties with that of the sixties. In the fifties there was no foreign exchange constraint: in seven of the ten years there was surpluses on current accounts and the decade ended with a large excess of foreign exchange reserves.[64] In the same period, it appears that the GDP grew annually at about 5·0 per cent in real terms, or around 2·5 per cent per capita.[65] By contrast, there were almost unceasing shortages of foreign exchange in the sixties and the expansion of GDP failed even to keep pace with population growth. If the simple juxtaposition of these facts is less than conclusive, it is at least highly suggestive, especially looking at the statistical relationships between economic growth and imports in the fifties. Since in these years there were no important administrative controls we may take actual imports as reflecting changes in demand and may derive from them estimates of the income elasticity of import demand. Two independently derived set of estimates resulted in elasticity estimates in the range of 1·2–1·7, implying that import capacity would have to grow considerably faster than domestic incomes if local demand was to be satisfied.[66] It is also possible to estimate the import requirements of investment in 1955–60. It appears that in these years the marginal import component of capital formation was 44 per cent, and the elasticity of demand for imported capital goods with respect to total capital formation was 1·02.[67] Extrapolating these relationships into the sixties, an increase in capital formation by, say ₵100 would generate an additional demand for imported capital goods of ₵44, and a given proportional increase in capital formation would result in roughly the same proportional increase in capital-good imports. However, because the composition changed in favour of industrial investments, the import content of capital formation actually rose in the first half of the sixties, so that figures from 1955–60 rather understate the requirements.

Other aspects of the record of the sixties support the view that shortages of foreign exchange had a critical effect on the performance of the economy. The main way in which these had their effect in the Nkrumah years was by creating shortages of raw materials and spare parts, which, in turn, contributed to a large-scale under-utilization of productive capacity.[68] The disruption of output and large reductions in imports of finished consumer goods meant a smaller supply of 'incentive goods' which was liable to have harmful effects on agricultural output. From 1966 the NLC made major efforts to ensure more adequate supplies of raw materials and spares but the foreign exchange situation was such that they could only do this by cutting back on imports of capital goods. The result meant large reductions in the level of investment, so that by the end of the decade there was virtually no net investment (*see* Table 4.1).

At the risk of appearing to labour the obvious, it is possible to demonstrate the seriousness of the foreign exchange constraint more formally by the application of two-gap analysis.[69] The starting point is the standard Keynesian position that while the saving-investment gap and the export-import gap are identical *ex post* they may differ *ex ante*. When a shortage of domestic saving is the more important problem the saving-investment gap will, *ex ante*, be the larger; when a foreign exchange shortage is the more important, the *ex ante* export-import gap will be greater. The difficulty,of course, is to measure *ex ante* magnitudes, i.e. the *desired* levels; only actual magnitudes are revealed in hard data.

The problem becomes tractable if we make the simplifying assumptions (a) that in the short and medium term export earnings are exogenously determined so that the adjustment of *ex ante* differences in the two gaps is not brought about by changes in this magnitude, and (b) that actual investment is the same as the *ex ante* magnitude. The first of these is probably innocuous in the Ghana case, the second more questionable. On these assumptions, there are only two variables which can bring the gaps into *ex post* identity: domestic savings and imports. When the shortage of saving is the larger of the two gaps, actual imports are more than the intended level and the saving-investment gap is filled by additional receipts of foreign capital (or by running down reserves). In this case, actual imports are positively correlated with the inflow of foreign capital and this inflow supplements domestic saving, with saving independent of foreign capital receipts. When foreign exchange is the binding constraint, the process of adjustment occurs through reductions in saving below the potential level. In this case, foreign capital substitutes for domestic saving, i.e. the two are negatively correlated. There are now two alternative functional relationships which can be tested empirically. Either imports are positively correlated with, and saving is independent of, foreign capital receipts (the saving constraint case); or saving is negatively correlated with, and imports independent of, foreign capital (the import constraint case). Regression analysis of actual saving and imports can indicate which of the two constitutes the binding constraint.

Application of this methodology to current-price data for Ghana in 1960-9, the period in which severe payments problems were experienced, clearly indicates that foreign exchange was the binding constraint. There was a significantly negative correlation between saving and foreign capital receipts, and the coefficient of imports with respect to these receipts did not differ significantly from zero.[70]

We may conclude, then, that the payments difficulties, and the policy failings which contributed to them, had a crucial bearing upon the poor performance of the economy in the sixties. Some qualifications should, however, be remembered. The limited capacity of the system to put capital to productive use was also of key importance, especially in the Nkrumah years, and would quickly re-emerge as a constraint were investment to be raised back to the high levels of the earlier sixties. Two-gap analysis does not catch this dimension. Secondly, the assumption of two-gap analysis that *ex ante* and *ex post* investment were always identical is probably not valid, for government investment was used as an adjustment mechanism by the NLC. Third, domestic saving fell in the course of the sixties so that by the end of the decade it was not much more than sufficient to cover depreciation expenditures. If export performances suddenly improved, a parallel improvement in saving would be necessary if the economy were not rapidly to run into a saving constraint. The capacities to invest wisely, to save, and to import were *all* weak by the end of the sixties.

Progress Towards Economic Independence

It emerged in chapter 3 that greater economic independence was among Nkrumah's chief policy objectives, and that an accelerated Ghanaianization of economic activity featured prominently in the policies of the NLC and the Busia governments. Economic independence is not a clearly defined concept, easily rendered into statistics. Nevertheless, various objective indicators can be provided and it may be appropriate to conclude this chapter by examining these, although they take us beyond external trade and payments data.

Economic independence has to do with the degree of Ghanaian control over the domestic economy. Viewed this way, economic independence necessitates but goes beyond the achievement of political sovereignty; clearly the domestic economy could not be said to be under Ghana's control so long as she was governed by, or under the supervision of, the British colonial service. There is also a (less strong) sense in which domination of the civil service by expatriate officers conflicts with the desire for economic independence, since they would exert influence upon economic policies. Thus, the achievement of political independence and the Ghanaianization of the civil service which occurred in the fifties and early sixties[71] were major steps towards economic independence.

Nevertheless, at the beginning of the sixties Ghana still had several attributes of economic dependence. Must of the country's industry and commerce was foreign-owned, and a very wide range of manufactured goods still had to be imported. Exports were heavily dominated by cocoa[72] and the geographical distribution of trade still showed a markedly 'colonial' orientation, with the United Kingdom accounting for about a third of the total.[73] Nkrumah was also worried about the 'neo-colonial' dangers of allowing much of the country's investment to be financed from abroad, and chapter 3 showed the stress placed on the domestic financing of investment in the *Seven-year Plan*.[74]

On this latter aspect, enough has already been said to show that Nkrumah was completely unsuccessful in preventing the accumulation of large-scale foreign debts which were liable to make the country's policy-makers beholden to the creditors. These and the need for external assistance permitted the governments of the major creditors and aid donors, and the IMF to exert leverage on economic policies in Ghana, although it is easy to exaggerate the extent to which that leverage had effect except during the NLC period. Overall, though, the

large-scale financing of domestic investment with foreign loans defi-
nitely tended to reduce Ghana's economic independence.

Trends in the ownership of the productive system, however, were in
the desired direction. For example, the industrialization of the sixties
was accompanied by an apparent reduction in the degree of foreign
ownership, as shown in Table 5.7, with the share of gross manufacturing output originating in wholly foreign-owned factories declining
from 63 per cent in 1962 to 40 per cent in 1970, and a corresponding
increase in the share of joint Ghanaian/foreign enterprises. The same
tendency was observable in other sectors. In banking, for instance, the
share of the government-owned Ghana Commercial Bank in the total
commercial bank deposit liabilities went up from 28 per cent in mid-
1960 to 68 per cent twelve years later.[75] The relative importance of
domestically owned trading enterprises also increased, as a result of
the acquisition by the government of a large Greek-owned company to
form the Ghana National Trading Corporation,[76] the rapid expansion
of that corporation and, later in the decade, the acquisition by private
Ghanaians of many small-scale trading enterprises following legistla-
tion excluding foreigners from these activities.[77] The acquisition of
various gold mines to form the State Gold Mining Corporation in 1961
should also be mentioned, although these were known to be of dubious
economic value.[78]

TABLE 5.7
Manufacturing Output by Type of Ownership, 1962–70

Type of Ownership	Percentage of Gross Output		
	1962	1966	1970
Ghanaian			
Private	13·0	9·7	6·0
State	11·8	19·5	15·6
TOTAL GHANAIAN	24·8	29·2	21·6
Mixed			
Private/Foreign	4·8	8·7	20·9
State/Foreign[a]	7·1	12·7	17·3
TOTAL MIXED	11·9	21·4	38·2
Foreign	63·2	48·3	40·2

Source: Central Bureau of Statistics, *Industrial Statistics.*
NOTE:
[a] Based on assumption that private partners with government are all foreign.

One aspect of the quest for economic independence emphasized in
chapter 3 was what might be called the internalization of economic
activity, i.e. increased trade barriers and domestic production of
import substitutes. Reliance of the economy on international trade
could be reduced in this way and hence its dependence on conditions
beyond the control of the government. There is no simple way of

measuring the degree of internalization but relevant indicators are present in the first four lines of Table 5.8 below.

TABLE 5.8
Indicators of Internalization and Trade Diversification, 1960–69[a]

	1960	1966	1969
Ratios			
1. Ratio of trade to GNP[b]	29·3	14·2	17·9
2. Ratio of imported consumer goods to private consumption[c]	32·2	15·5	21·3
3. Ratio of manufacturing value-added to imports[d]	14·5[h]	32·2	23·4
4. Ratio of competitive to complementary imports[e]	2·55	—	1·19[i]
Concentration coefficents			
5. Commodity composition of exports[j]	62·3	64·7	65·7
6. Geographical origin of imports[g]	51·1	45·0	45·6
7. Geographical destination of exports[g]	54·0	45·7	46·8

Sources: *Economic Surveys* (various issues). Szereszewski, 1966 Table 3.1 and CBS input:output table for 1968.
NOTES:
[a] 1966 has been preferred as the intermediate year over 1965 because of the abnormally large cocoa crop and import volume in 1965 (*see* Figure 5.1).
[b] The mean value of exports and imports expressed as a percentage of GNP.
[c] Excluding consumption of local foods.
[d] Calculated in constant prices. The use of this indicator was suggested to me by reading Steel, 1970.
[e] Calculated from input:output tables for 1960 and 1968. Complementary imports are those used as inputs for domestic production, the remaining imports being classified as competitive with domestic production.
[f] Calculated throughout according to the classification of exports provided in Table 18 of the *Economic Survey, 1969*. Cocoa and cocoa products, and sawn and unsawn timber were both treated as single commodities.
[g] Calculated throughout according to the classification provided in Table 21 of the *Economic Survey, 1969*.
[h] 1962 data.
[i] 1968 figure.

We can note first the marked decline in the trade ratio during the first half of the sixties, only slightly offset by a rise later. These, it is true, are somewhat artificial trends, since in most years after 1961 the economy was unable to import enough to satisfy domestic demand, but there is little doubt that some genuine import substitution did occur. Lines 2–4 attempt to measure this more directly. Line 2 shows the very sharp fall in consumer-goods imports relative to total private consumption (excluding consumption of local foods) in 1960–6, again only partly offset by an increase in 1966–9; the country's consumption needs were increasingly being met by domestic producers. The figures in lines 3 and 4 provide perhaps the best measurements of import substitution. They show a rise in value-added by domestic manufacturing industries relative to import volumes, rising by 60 per cent in the first half of the decade and then levelling off; and a halving of the ratio of competitive to complementary imports, which means that an increasing proportion of total imports were being used as inputs for domestic production rather than going straight to the final user.

To these indicators of increased internalization of economic activity must be added a major qualification: most of Ghana's import-substituting industries are based upon the processing of imported raw materials and components, and often on capital-intensive techiques (chapter 8). They and their customers thus had to rely upon the availability of foreign exchange for raw materials and spares. Shortages of these had disruptive effects on domestic output and consumption, and there was a genuine sense in which this development made the economy more rather than less dependent.

The country's overwhelming reliance upon cocoa exports was another important dimension of dependence and it had been official policy since the 1920s to diversify exports, a policy endorsed by the governments of the sixties. [79] Line 5 of Table 5.8 measures the trend in the diversification of exports. Presented there (and in lines 6 and 7) are Gini coefficients of concentration, a reduction in which would indicate reduced reliance on one or a small number of exports (or trade partners in the case of lines 6 and 7). [80] As can be seen from the increases in these coefficients, the commodity concentration of exports, far from diversifying, actually increased a little over the decade, despite the emergence at the end of the period of aluminium as a significant new export, [81] and even though neighbouring Ivory Coast was having substantial success in this direction. [82] The extreme dependence on cocoa continued.

A final aspect of the 'colonial' structure of trade which Nkrumah wished to eliminate was reliance upon a small number of trade partners, almost exclusively Western countries and very heavily weighted towards Britain. Considerably greater success was achieved in this regard. Britain's share in Ghana's import and export trade declined from 34 per cent in 1960 to 27 per cent in 1969 and new trading partners were found. During the Nkrumah years the shift was in favour of the Eastern European countries, whose share rose from a meagre 6 per cent in 1960 to 24 per cent five years later; trade with these countries declined after the 1966 coup but did not return completely to its former level, and other countries, notably the United States and Japan, assumed relatively greater importance. These trends are reflected in lines 6 and 7 of Table 5.8, where it is shown that the geographical concentration of import and export trade declined in the first half of the decade and then roughly stabilized.

It is impossible to form from the foregoing any simple generalization about trends in economic dependence; while most indicators show increased independence, the accumulation for foreign-owned debt, the limited use by industry of domestic raw materials, and the failure of export policies moved the economy in the opposite direction. On balance, the evidence does suggest that Ghanaian control over the economy increased during the sixties, bringing economic independence nearer. Whether that was necessarily in Ghana's interest is, however, another matter, for if it brought benefits it also imposed rather heavy costs. This will become clear in the chapters that follow, analysing various aspects of economic policy, especially in the Nkrumah period.

NOTES

[1] Since there have been two devaluations and one revaluation of Ghana's currency, it is necessary to convert balance of payments data to a uniform exchange rate in order to make comparisons over time. All figures in this chapter, unless indicated otherwise, have been calculated at the 1972 exchange rate of ₡1.28 = $1.00 and they therefore differ numerically from most published statistics. For details of exchange rate changes *see* the Appendix to chapter 1.

[2] The total recorded externally held public debt at the end of 1960 was about ₡24 million – calculated from 1969 *Economic Survey*, table 12.

[3] Using 1968 prices and the 1972 exchange rate, per capita imports of consumer goods can be estimated at ₡40.4 in 1959–61 and ₡22.5 in 1964–5.

[4] There was, however, a record crop in 1964/65 and there were good crops in 1971/72 and 1972/73..

[5] Calculated from Gill and Duffus, *Cocoa Market Report*, January 1972, p. 14.

[6] *See* Stern, 1972, Table 2–b. The predominance of cocoa in total exports was even larger in 1970, due to exceptionally high world prices.

[7] In addition, Ghana received 'soft' loans from Russia and other communist countries amounting to ₡94 million but these were medium-term credits, typically repayable over ten years, rather than long-term development aid. So far as American aid is concerned, Schlesinger, 1965, pp. 573–4, reported that in 1963 President Kennedy, concerned at Nkrumah's violent anti-Western attitude and increasingly totalitarian stance at home, instructed AID to extend no further long-term credits to Ghana. Nkrumah, 1968, p. 96 states that after the publication of *Neocolonialism* in 1965 'The American Government sent me a note of protest, and promptly refused Ghana $35 million of aid.'

[8] As given in the national accounts in current prices and after converting capital inflows back into the exchange rate prevailing at that time.

[9] To be fair, it is not clear that Nkrumah's increasingly sycophantic advisers had kept him informed of the gravity of Ghana's payments situation. When in March 1965 some courageous officials who did not belong to his usual coterie of personal advisers finally got to Nkrumah and advised him of the true situation it is said that he was 'stunned' by the gravity of the news. He nevertheless failed to follow up with adequate corrective measures and his subsequent actions suggest that he had not absorbed this lesson in economic realities (*see* Uphoff, 1970, p. 695 and n. 8).

[10] *See* Sutcliffe, 1971, p. 265, and Little, *et al.*, 1970, pp. 62–3.

[11] *See Economic Survey, 1965*, paragraphs 126–7.

[12] *See* Minister of Finance Amoako-Attah, as reported in the *Ghanaian Times*, 6 May 1965.

[13] *See* NLC, *Developments in the Ghanaian Economy*, 1969, especially p. 5.

[14] Between 1967 and 1969 the average world price for cocoa rose by 58 per cent to its highest level for fifteen years. .The average London spot price for Ghana cocoa in 1971 of £236 per ton may be compared with a post-war average of £245 per ton. *See* Gill and Duffus, *Cocoa Market Report*, January 1972, p. 24.

[15] Nkrumah, 1968, p. 89. *See also* Bing, 1968, chapter 11 and *passim*.

[16] Eshag and Richards, 1967.

[17] *ibid.*, pp. 358 and 370.

[18] Berg, 1971, p. 198, for example, asserts that 'external factors made growth more difficult in the period 1960–65 . . . But the impact was not very great . . .' In the same volume, Green, a writer generally sympathetic to Nkrumah's political standpoint, accepts that the effect of the terms of trade was merely to speed the inevitable arrival of a major economic crisis (p. 258).

[19] Growth rates computed from a three-year moving average of total world grindings of cocoa beans (the conventional measure of cocoa consumption) were 0·4 per cent in 1950–5, 4·3 per cent in 1955–60 and 6·7 per cent in 1960–5 (computed from various issues of the Gill and Duffus *Cocoa Market Report*).

[20] In fact, an alliance of the major cocoa producing countries sought to hold up world prices in 1964/65 by refusing to sell below an agreed minimum price. Unfortunately, this price was settled before the abnormally large size of the 1964/65 crop was fully realized and this placed unbearable strains on the collective unity of the countries in question. The policy collapsed in ruins and producers were forced to sell at prices lower than would have occurred had a more orderly selling policy been pursued.

[21] This is only a rough indication of the price elasticity of demand because the outcome was also affected by changing income effects in the consuming countries. *See* Leith, 1971A, for a discussion of export instability.

[22] Leith, 1971B, shows that the competitive performance of Ghana's exports other than cocoa was generally poor and concludes that 'this limited competitive success clearly dampened the net effect of the import substitution policies on the overall growth of the economy'.

[23] *See* Viner, 1937, pp. 558–64, for a discussion of alternative concepts of the terms of trade.

[24] *See* Grayson, 1973(B), for a discussion of the supplier credit issue.

[25] The author was an active participant, as a government adviser, in the preparations for the 1968 and 1970 debt conferences.

[26] The full statistics of this analysis are in Mensah, 1970, pp. 6–7.

[27] For an authoritative statement of their point of view, *see* ibid.

[28] *See* UN, 1964, Part Two, chapters I and III.

[29] A journal published by faculty members of the University of Ghana, *The Legon Observer*, was the most persistent and articulate advocate of this view.

[30] Details of these and the 1970 agreement are given by Klein, 1973, Table 2.

[31] Mensah, 1970, p. 10, shows the original contractual obligations (principal plus interest) covered by the 1966 and 1968 re-scheduling agreements to have been ₵250 million and that moratorium interest on deferred payments totalled ₵90 million, or 35·6 per cent of the original – calculations which, however, fail to take account of the effects of discounting future streams. Excluding 'non-IMF member countries' (a euphemism for communist countries), the position was even less favourable, with moratorium interest equal to almost 40 per cent of the original contractual obligations. (Note that the sums quoted above were as given by Mensah; converted at the 1972 exchange rate used throughout this chapter they would have read ₵337 millions and ₵121 millions respectively.)

[32] *See* Klein, 1973, Table 2, which covers all agreements up to end–1972. Grant elements were calculated at a 10 per cent discount rate. The 1970 agreement with Ghana provided for three alternative ways of providing this assistance, each to have not less than a 61 per cent grant element.

[33] Weighted average terms for aid in 1967–70 were a 32-year maturity, an 8-year grace period and a 2·7 per cent rate of interest. Discounted at 10 per cent, these terms contain a 59 per cent grant element. These terms may be compared with the 1968 average of all aid provided by OECD-member countries, of 25 years maturity, 3·3 per cent interest and 48 per cent grant element (*see Pearson Report*, 1969, p. 163).

World Bank aid was on IDA terms.

[34] Calculated from data in the 1968 *Annual Report* of the World Bank.

[35] Objection may be made to treating interest and amortization payments as a deduction from new capital receipts, on the grounds that interest is an income flow, and past investments should have earned or released sufficient foreign exchange to cover the return flows. However, given the circumstances in which many of these debts were incurred and the fact that the focus here is on the net foreign exchange impact of the debt/aid issue, it seems less misleading to follow this procedure than the alternative.

[36] Negative debt relief, i.e. the net addition to debt servicing obligations resulting from the three rescheduling agreements, would have averaged ₵25 million annually in the seventies.

[37] The average maturity of the external debt went up from 12 years in February 1966 to about 20 years at the end of 1970.

[38] 'Let the buyer beware, you buy at your own risk.'

[39] At their peak Indonesia's original debt servicing obligations would have been about 29 per cent of expected export earnings, as compared with 19 per cent in Ghana's case.

[40] Mensah, 1970, p. 5.

[41] Projections prepared within the Ministry of Finance and Planning, and independently by the World Bank all pointed to this conclusion.

[42] The IMF tended to take a strong line on this and the NLC was put under some pressure to place more of Ghana'a trade on a multilateral basis. It may have been under pressure from the IMF that even Nkrumah announced in August 1965 that cocoa would not in future be sold under bilateral agreements (*see Daily Graphic,* 25 August 1965).

[43] Goodman, 1966, Table 4, has shown that in 1955–64 Russia and East Germany were among the countries paying above-average prices for imports from Ghana, although Bulgaria, China and Czechoslovakia were paying below the average. Stevens, 1974, Table 5, has shown that when the world price is declining, the price paid by Russia for Ghana cocoa tends to be above the world price, and that the opposite is the case when the world price is rising. He has also calculated (Table 7) that crude petroleum imports from Russia in 1967–70 were marginally cheaper than the same product from other sources – 6.375 pesewas per gallon as against 6.252.

[44] Gill and Duffus, January 1972, p. 15, show that cocoa consumption in Eastern Europe and the USSR rose at 9 per cent annually in 1961–71 whereas in the rest of the world consumption went up at just over 3 per cent a year. In absolute terms, the expanded consumption of the communist countries represented 28 per cent of the total growth of world consumption in the same period.

[45] Stevens, 1974.

[46] Credits from communist countries had an average maturity of 10 years, a 3·0 per cent rate of interest and a grant element of 34 per cent (discounted at 10 per cent).

[47] Uphoff, 1970, p. 278.

[48] *See* Table 8.6 below.

[49] The chief export taxes were on cocoa; exporters of other commodities received effective rates only a little below the official rate.

[50] Taken from Table 4–D, line 7. I have preferred this to Leith's use of the GDP deflator on the grounds that the consumer price index, while more partial, is considerably more reliable than other price indices used in the national accounts.

[51] Ideally one should deflate the effective rate for exports by an index of costs but no such index is available nor can it readily be compiled.

[52] This, at least, was the conclusion of Merrill Bateman, an economist who has specialized in a study of the world cocoa market, in an unpublished report prepared for the World Bank. *See also* Eshag and Richards, 1967.

[53] This project, which threatened to be a poor investment, partly because it would be too small to benefit from the substantial economies of scale to be obtained in gold

refining, was abandoned by the NLC but the NRC announced in 1972 that the possibility of bringing it into production was being re-examined.

[54] This was the outcome of an investigation by the World Bank in 1968 and published data is consistent with this. Between 1963 and 1970 the price received for Ghana's cocoa butter averaged only 73 per cent of the average price for 'Prime English' butter, as reported by Gill and Duffus. A Ministry of Finance estimate for 1967 showed the major cocoa factory to have local resource costs of ₵7.50 for every cedi's worth of net foreign exchange earned.

[55] See Richardson, 1969. Pearson and Page, 1972, p. 23 and Tables II–24 and II–31, show domestic resource costs per unit of foreign exchange earned to be generally three to four times greater in saw-milling than in logging.

[56] Nkrumah stated that state monopolies for cocoa and other exports could prevent the terms of trade from turning against Ghana – see Ghanaian Times, 26 August 1963.

[57] By comparing the prices received by Ghana with the average third position London price (converted to an f.o.b. basis), it can be estimated that Ghana would have earned about 12 per cent more from her exports of cocoa beans in 1966–9 if the Marketing Board had been able to achieve this average price. In 1965, 1970 and 1971, on the other hand, Ghana did better than the world average.

[58] See Richardson, 1969.

[59] See One-Year Plan, 1970/71, pp. 107–9.

[60] See chapter 11.

[61] See Leith, 1973, chapter 5, for an excellent discussion of this theme, which is also elaborated in chapters 6 and 11 of this study.

[62] See Szereszewski, 1966, pp. 72–4. See chapter 8 for further evidence on the import-dependence of manufacturing.

[63] Szereszewski, 1965, chapter 5 and passim.

[64] Trends in Ghana's balance of payments during the fifties are discussed in Killick, 1966, chapter 14.

[65] See Killick and Szereszewski, 1969, pp. 86–8.

[66] Nypan, 1960, estimated elasticities of $1\cdot2$ and $1\cdot7$ from 1950–8 data, the higher figure being derived from a regression which included import prices as a second explanatory variable. Scott, 1967, p. 152, reports an income elasticity of $1\cdot4$ in 1955–8.

[67] These estimates were calculated from data in the 1961 Statistical Year Book, Szereszewski, 1966, chapter 2, and Ord, 1964.

[68] See chapters 7, 8 and 10 below.

[69] The following analysis follows a methodology developed by Landau (1971) and the reader is referred to that source for a fuller explanation.

[70] The equations fitted were:

$$S = a_1 + b_1 Y + dF \qquad (1) \text{ and}$$
$$M = a_2 + b_2 C + c_2 I + d_2 F \qquad (2)$$

where S=gross domestic saving, Y=GNP, F=net inflow of foreign capital (including use of reserves), M=imports, C=total consumption, and I=gross domestic capital formation (including changes in inventories). The resulting values were:

$$S = 154\cdot3 + 0\cdot222\,Y - 0\cdot661\,F \qquad \text{with } R^2 = 0\cdot524 \qquad (1)$$
$$(0\cdot680)\ (-2\cdot47)$$
$$M = 87\cdot82 + 0\cdot131\,C + 0\cdot492\,I - 0\cdot136\,F \qquad \text{with } R^2 = 0\cdot630 \qquad (2)$$
$$(2\cdot83) \qquad (0\cdot94)\ (-0\cdot34)$$

(t values in brackets). The coefficient for F in equation (1) with 7 degrees of freedom is significant at the 95 per cent level; the coefficient for F in equation (2) does not differ significantly from zero. In both cases, the values of R were significant at well above the 95 per cent level.

For a contrary finding see Weisskopf, 1972, who places Ghana among the countries constrained primarily by domestic saving. However, his data cover 1955–65, during which period Ghana was transformed from an export-surplus into an import-surplus country and it is difficult to place much relevance on an analysis of such a heterogeneous period.

[71] 'In 1952 there was only one Ghanaian head of (a government) department. By 1957 the figure had risen to twenty-two. Now all the permanent and pensionable posts are held by Ghanaians,' Nkrumah, 1967, p. 95. Bing, 1968, contains a good account of colonial resistance to Ghanaianization but also draws attention (pp. 387–8) to some of the costs of rapid Ghanaianization.

[72] Michaely, 1962, Table 1, found Ghana's coefficient of commodity concentration to be the fifth largest of 44 countries covered.

[73] The UK's share of Ghana's trade in 1960 was 36·7 per cent of imports and 31·3 per cent of exports – see Economic Survey, 1961, table 104.

[74] 'We shall not go bankrupt. We shall not allow our savings to run down in order to get into a position where we have to beg for money, cap in hand, and be "saved" by their generous financial assistance, given on conditions – economic, political or ideological – which deprive us of our independence.' Nkrumah to Parliament, 4 July 1961, quoted by Uphoff, p. 303.

[75] Calculated from data in Ghana Commercial Bank, 1963, p. 116, Legon Observer, 22 September 1972, and Bank of Ghana, Quarterly Economics Bulletin, March 1962 and June 1972.

[76] This take-over is often seen as an attempt to break foreign domination of large-scale trading activities, although the Apaloo Report (p. 222) suggests the initiative probably came from the former owners, who were getting into financial difficulties. Nkrumah, 1963, p. 108, cites a British report to the effect that in 1959 '85 per cent of all Ghana's import trade was in the hands of European firms (mainly British), 10 per cent in the hands of Asians (sic) (Indians, Syrians and Lebanese), and only 5 per cent in Ghanaian hands'.

[77] Under the Ghanaian Business (Promotion) Act, 1970, which superseded a 1968 decree along similar lines, only Ghanaians were permitted to own trading enterprises with an annual turnover of less than ₵500,000, overseas business representation and taxi services from August 1970. This monopoly was extended to commercial land transportation, bakeries, printing, beauty culture, produce brokerage, advertising, and manufacture of cement blocks from June 1971. See chapter 11.

[78] At the end of 1972 the National Redemption Council announced that it was compulsorily acquiring controlling interests in the major foreign-owned mining and timber companies, although this fell outside the period covered here (see West Africa, 18 December 1972).

[79] See Killick, 1966, p. 333 on the history of export diversification as a policy objective, where I quote Governor Guggisberg in 1919: 'We have all our eggs in one basket. The cocoa baskets are full – what about the other baskets if anything goes wrong with the cocoa crop or the cocoa market?' For a more recent version see the One-Year Plan, 1970/71, p. 36.

[80] The Gini coefficient measures concentration by weighting large individual shares in a given total. It is derived by squaring the ratios of individual items to a given total, summing the squares and taking the square-root of the sum. The results are expressed as percentages in Table 5.8.

[81] The Valco aluminium smelter came into production in 1968 and by the end of the decade its exports were worth about ₵55 million annually (at the 1972 exchange rate). Due, however, to a variety of tax and other concessions in the agreement negotiated with the Ghana government, net foreign exchange earnings were much smaller, at about ₵20 million.

[82] See Eshag and Richards, Table 1. It can be calculated from their data that the concentration coefficient of Ivory Coast exports fell from 55·0 per cent in 1960 to 50·9 per cent in 1965.

6 Planning, Saving and Economic Management

Among the characteristics of mainstream development economics surveyed in chapter 2 were a belief in the necessity for large-scale mobilization of resources by the state for a big development push, faith in the advantages of planning, and relative disinterest in short-term economic management. This chapter reviews Ghana's experiences in these areas, comparing actual results with the arguments presented in the literature. It falls into three parts.

The first examines the content and effectiveness of the *Seven-Year Development Plan, 1963/64 to 1969/70*[1] and includes a note on planning after the 1966 coup. The efforts of Nkrumah's government to mobilize budgetary resources for development are taken up in Part II, while Part III turns to analyse more broadly the record of short-term fiscal and monetary management, and its effects on economic performance.

I The Planning Experience

If planning is defined as an attempt to exercise forethought to select optimal means of securing specified ends then the remainder of this book is about Ghana's planning experience. 'Development planning' has, however, become used to refer to the preparation and implementation of a planning document seeking to determine the pace and pattern of an economy's development in the medium-term, and the economic policies to secure these results. It is useful for present purposes to adopt this narrower definition in examining Ghana's experiences with development planning in the sixties, leaving other aspects of economic policy for later treatment.

It was shown in chapter 3 that Nkrumah fully embraced the conclusions of mainstream development economics that planning was an essential feature of a serious development effort[2]: 'The greatest single lesson that can be drawn from the history of industrial development in the world today is the uncounted advantages which planning has in the first place over the laissez-faire go-as-you-please policies of the early pioneers of industrialization.'

It will be useful to recall briefly the arguments deployed in chapter 2 in favour of planning.[3] Negatively, there was a distrust of markets in allocating resources, in guiding the economy on to a dynamic growth path, and in securing these results with a tolerably equitable distribution of the benefits. Positively, planning was seen as providing a superior set of decision-making signals: internalizing the externalities discussed by Scitovsky and others, reconciling differences between private and social valuations, correcting the tendency of the private sector towards myopic consumption and investment decisions and mobilizing resources on the scale necessary for a 'big push' to self-sustaining growth, as only a centralized planning effort could hope to do.

Planning, in this view, represented an alternative to the market for allocating resources between alternative uses. Nkrumah and his party saw the matter in much the same light. According to the party's 1962 *Programme for Work and Happiness*, planners should decide how resources were to be mobilized and how these should be used.[4] They should decide the relative shares of saving and consumption and how to attract labour. They should 'ration some raw materials'. The organization of education, decisions as to what form of agriculture and industry should be encouraged, where they should be located, and how they should be attracted and financed were further responsibilities of the planners. Another authoritative document stated as Nkrumah's 'second principle' of socialist development that, 'national economic planning is the principal lever for all-round progress', that the plan shuld be all-embracing and that it should reflect 'the strictest control to safeguard against unrelated over-spending on any project'.[5]

Ostensibly, then, the urge for comprehensive economic planning came from the highest political sources and it appeared that Ghana was not among those countries that were merely going through the motions of 'having a plan'. The *7YP* was not written, as plans so often are, in a political vacuum, for its authors could derive fairly explicit policy guidance from the *Programme for Work and Happiness*.[6]

Enough was perhaps said in chapter 3 for the reader to be generally familiar with the main thrust of the plan: major increases in the level of investment, accelerated industrialization, the modernization of agriculture, a shift of government investment away from social overhead capital in favour of the directly productive sectors of the economy, and a greatly expanded output of trained manpower. The following pages do not go over this ground but have the more limited intention to offer an assessment of the plan as a technical document and examine the problems encountered in implementing it.

An Assessment of the 7YP

Since assessments inevitably turn out to be critiques, we should begin by pointing out the difficulties with which the authors of the 7YP were confronted and the considerable fruits of their labours. Ghana's is not a very 'plannable' economy, not least because its export sector is peculiarly sensitive to the behaviour of one of the world's most volatile commodity markets.[7] The extreme and unpredictable variability of the world cocoa price de-stabilizes not only the country's import capacity, but also the tax revenues of the government. These effects and the natural dependence of a still essentially agricultural economy on the vagaries of the weather, subject key economic variables to considerable year-by-year instability, which, in turn, induces a preoccupation with the short-term inimical to the development of settled medium- and long-run economic policies.[8] A dearth of relevant and reliable statistics was another of the planners' severest problems.[9] Production data were (and remain) very weak, especially for food-stuffs, and the national accounts were consequently an unreliable basis upon which to prepare a serious macro-economic plan.[10] There were major statistical lacunae on manpower, saving and international capital flows. In other cases, for example fiscal statistics, the data were not presented in a manner suited to the needs of economists. A grave shortage of qualified Ghanaian economists was equally serious; when the 7YP was being formulated the Office of the Planning Commission included only four qualified Ghanaians, reinforced by 16 foreign advisers of varying expertise and command of the English language, but having in common only a limited knowledge of the national economy.[11] Finally, there were all the familiar difficulties of planning an economy in which many important economic decisions remained in private hands.

In the face of these difficulties, the 7YP was something of a triumph. It contained incisive analyses of the economy's weaknesses and mapped out a persuasively argued long-term development perspective which offered a reasonably balanced and orderly process of growth, of which the 7YP was to represent only a first instalment. There were illuminating discussions of the state of major sectors of the economy, and it was at the time the most useful source of information and analysis on the economy. It was sensible and specific about institutional arrangements for plan implementation, explicit about the rather stringent budgetary implications of the government's ambitions, and laid down sensible principles for the acceptance of external finance. These were no mean achievements and, if there were weaknesses, the strengths should be remembered too.

But weaknesses there were and to these we must now turn. One was to attempt a plan covering as long as seven years, which was too long in view of the uncertainties already mentioned. It seems that this was Nkrumah's decision,[12] resulting from a visit to Russia which launched its own first seven-year plan in 1959, but Ghana's plan could have been more flexible than it was, for example by sub-division.[13] As it was, year-by-year projections and targets for such variables as consumption, imports, investment, the structure of output, and government expenditures and revenues seemed somewhat fanciful beyond the first year or two, and there was an obviously high probability that events beyond Ghana's control would undermine the plan rather quickly.[14] Provision was made for a series of annual plans (although only one ever appeared[15]) but it seemed doubtful whether they could introduce enough flexibility.

In common with many plans, the 7YP was overly preoccupied with macro-economic variables and paid insufficient attention to sector programmes and projects. One manifestation of this was the use made of an aggregate gross incremental capital:output ratio to derive overall investment requirements for the plan period. A ratio of 3·5:1 was used, which together with a targeted annual growth rate of 5·5 per cent, implied gross investments of slightly above ₵2 billion. From this figure were derived detailed estimates of financing, imports of capital goods, and so on.[16] No sectoral ratios being available, the figure of 3·5 was said to be estimated from macro-economic data on Ghana's recent past performance. Objections to such use of aggregate ratios have since become sufficiently well known to need no more than a mention here[17]: that there is no necessary causal relationship between investment and output growth;[18] that many factors other than physical capital formation influence the rate of growth; that such ratios are liable to be unstable in the short run and to change over time; that they cannot easily be adjusted to reflect changes in the economic structure that plans invariably seek to bring about. It is, moreover, difficult to find evidence to support the choice of a ratio of 3·5. For example, constant-price national accounts for 1955–62, assuming a two-year gestation lag, indicate a gross incremental ratio of 6·0 and various alternative calculations all show ratios substantially in excess of 3·5.[19] And, as Bissue points out, while the planners were using an aggregate ratio for macro-economic purposes, the sectoral allocations were made on entirely different criteria.[20] The same writer also draws attention to errors in the macro-arithmetic of the plan which caused aggregate investment needs to be over-estimated by about a fifth and indicated a misleadingly rapid growth of GDP.[21]

It was rightly claimed of the 7YP that it broke with the 'shopping list' or 'colonial' plans of the past but in retrospect one wonders whether this was a strength or a weakness. For if the colonial planners erred in neglecting the macro-economic aspects of their task, the 7YP was noticably deficient in specific public sector projects. Even the sectoral chapters were rather general, tending to express aspirations unsubstantiated by specific proposals. One is bound to agree with the government minister who said, 'It were better to spend two years out of the seven years of the Plan to get proper projects based on the natural resources available rather than to rush with hastily thought out plans.'[22] As is shown in the next two chapters, projects based on Ghana's natural resources were rather few; project identification and appraisal were treated more as a matter of implementation than as part of the plan itself.

Doubts were also expressed about the realism of some aspects of the plan. For example, its treatment of private investment was unsatisfactory, being derived simply as the difference between aggregate and government investment. [23] Included in the figures for private investment and saving was ₵200 million as the capitalized value of surplus agricultural labour – an application of the surplus labour theories of Lewis and others, the empirical basis for which was not, however, immediately apparent.[24] Aside from the aluminium smelter, foreign private capital inflows were projected to rise substantially, despite the emergence by 1963 of a distinctly frosty investment climate.

The manpower and educational aspects of the plan were similarly open to complaints of unrealism. High-level manpower projections were based on data on the skill composition of the labour force in the 1960 population census, with all the status optimism these could be expected to contain, when there were better – though smaller – estimates available from a special survey conducted in the same year.[25] The plan was also unrealistic in its projected output of trained teachers, with actual graduations from teachers' training colleges numbering less than half the planned number.[26] Provision for depreciation, at about 14 per cent of gross investment, also looked too small and later estimates suggest that for the beginning of the plan period it covered less than half of actual requirements.[27] It is also noteworthy that almost all these examples of unrealism had an optimistic bias, so that taken together they gave a misleading rosy view of potential growth.

Despite the plan's recognition of the critical importance of agriculture, the chapter dealing with it was among the least satisfactory. Handicapped by an absence of statistics on private food production, it nevertheless presented production targets which, besides starting from unreliable base data,[28] could not be monitored. The targets were ambitious and various observers raised doubts about the practicability of achieving the desired expansion, since it was largely to be secured through mechanization and other technological innovations which would normally have rather lengthy gestation periods, and few specific projects were proposed. The share of total government investment in agriculture, at 16 per cent, seemed small, relative to the improvements that were expected[29] and, while the composition of government spending is not necessarily a good guide to relative priorities, the fact is that the Ministry of Agriculture's draft submission for the plan included spending proposals which were cut by the Planning Commission. A large sum for a cocoa disease unit was eliminated and, in fact, the plan made no specific provision for cocoa at all. This industry, the most important of Ghana's exports, claimed just two paragraphs of the whole chapter. There was also evidence of unease among the planners about the balance between assistance to peasant farmers and investment in mechanized, government-owned farms. It seems from the text that the authors were inclined to place most emphasis on helping the peasants but were aware that the political tide was flowing in the other direction.[30]

In a number of respects, then, the plan was flawed, and seriously so. In practice, however, these defects were of little consequence, for while the plan remained officially in operation it was never actually implemented.

Implementation problems

Consider the government's budgets for 1962/4 and 1965.[31] As Waterston observes, the budget is a key element in giving effect to a development plan,[32] but this received little recognition in Ghana. Although the 7YP provided detailed fiscal projections, it was conspicuously silent on the co-ordination of it, and its annual plans, with the annual budgets, and in practice Ministers of Finance paid little heed to it. The budget speech for 1963/64 made only one passing reference to the 7YP and, in direct opposition to its strategy, proposed an increase in government consumption relative to capital expenditure.[33] The case of the 1965 budget was more curious. For that year an *Annual Plan* was prepared by the Planning Commission which could be expected to be specifically related to that year's budget proposals. In fact, the connection between the two exercises appears to have been tenuous, for the *Annual Plan* was coy about the budget and the budget speech made no reference even to the existence of an annual plan.[34] To be fair, the circumstances of 1965 would have made co-ordination of the budget and plan very difficult, as is explained in Part III, and the main thrust of the budget's expenditure proposals was at least consistent with the intentions of the planners. Nevertheless in practice it was not found possible to shift the composition of government investment towards directly productive activities in the manner envisaged by the planners, and the 1966 budget retreated from economic services towards spending on general administration and social services.[35]

Similarly, the planners seem to have been unable to exert much influence on balance of payments policy. The 7YP stated that the country's external reserves should not be significantly reduced below end-1963 levels[36] but Table 5.1 shows a substantial decline in international liquidity during 1964 and an enormous one in 1965. The preparation of a foreign exchange budget for 1965 was a potentially valuable innovation – but it was prepared under the direction of the Minister of Finance, not the Planning Commission, whose *Annual Plan* had little to say about the specifics of balance of payments policies.[37] Indeed, the *Annual Plan* was more of a review of performance in 1963 and 1964 than a blueprint for 1965.

It is scarcely surprising, then, that the Planning Commission was unable to enforce its eminently desirable proposals for the screening of government investment projects. According to the *7YP*, all projects and contracts had first to be subjected to careful economic and financial screening by the Planning Commission and the Ministry of Finance before they could even be considered by the Cabinet, and the government, it said, intended 'to enforce these rules rigidly'.[38] The reality was different. From the outset the Commission found it impossible to hold other ministries to these procedures[39] and, if he exaggerates a little, Rimmer is basically right about the way government investment decisions were actually made:[40]

> New projects appeared which had never been envisaged in the Plan but were now being pushed by contractors willing to pay commissions to the persons who accepted them. Projects were begun without feasibility studies and without competitive tendering. New enterprises were distributed among party functionaries as private fiefs, enabling them to give patronage to relatives, friends, and supporters. By the middle of 1965 the development programme, so far as the Central government was concerned, was effectively reduced to the completion of a new conference hall in Accra in time for the meeting in November of the heads of state of the Organisation of African Unity.

The refusal of the politicians to submit to the discipline of planning was reflected in *de facto* policies towards the expansion of state industries almost exactly the opposite of those which they had formally adopted in the *7YP*. According to the plan, the priorities for the development of government industries were:[41]

> *First*, the attainment of the maximum utilisation of existing plant capacity; *Secondly*, an expansion wherever possible of the productive capacity of existing enterprises in preference to the setting up of entirely new factories for the production of the same commodity; *Thirdly*, the completion of projects in the process of construction; and *Finally*, the erection of new buildings and installation of new machinery to commence entirely new industries.

In reality, as is shown in later chapters, first priority was given to the construction of new projects, and in the allocation of foreign exchange this was given precedence over the supply of industrial raw materials and spare parts to raise utilization levels.

The *7YP*, then, was a piece of paper, with an operational impact close to zero. Why? It could be argued that this was due to defects in the plan itself, to shortages of staff to monitor and implement it, and to the intervention of factors beyond Ghana's control, especially the falling world cocoa prices of the early and mid-sixties. This last point is certainly not without substance, for while the plan assumed an average cocoa price of ₵400 per ton[42] the actual prices received in 1964 and 1965 were only ₵356 and ₵276 respectively. This had serious consequences for government tax receipts, although the impact on export earnings was less severe because of a bumper crop in 1965, with the value of cocoa exports, at ₵136 million in each of the two years, only about ₵25 million less than planned.[43]

The falling cocoa price would have made the original document unworkable without modification, although adjustments could have been made through annual plans, but it seems evident from the illustrations already provided that the real reasons for the neglect of implementation were political. We mentioned at the outset that there was an ostensible political desire for effective planning and that the 7YP was able to draw upon a rather detailed party programme as a political guide. A conscientious effort was made by the plan's authors to adhere to this but tensions inevitably arose between political aspirations and economic realities, so that the plan only partly reflected the aspirations of the government. This was especially true of some aspects of the basic strategy of the plan.

We saw in chapter 3 that for Nkrumah development was synonymous with industrialization and that he had a low opinion of primary production. The 7YP, on the other hand, took the view that, 'the most readily available way of raising the national income is by concentrating our efforts in the coming seven years first and foremost on the modernisation of agriculture'.[44] Later:

> however much progress is made in the non-agricultural sectors of the economy the general level of prosperity in Ghana cannot increase significantly unless agriculture which employs nearly two-thirds of the labour force also undergoes a revolutionary change. During the next two decades the rate of growth in agriculture will condition the rate of growth of the whole economy.

Agricultural development, the planners believed, was necessary to improve nutritional standards, to raise the level of rural incomes, to increase the supply of raw materials, and to reduce dependence on imported food-stuffs. But in placing such emphasis on agriculture they were out of step with Nkrumah and his colleagues.

A further divergence showed up in the phasing of industrial development. The long-term perspective in the 7YP was to start with the simpler manufactured consumer goods, building materials and the processing of Ghana's traditional exports; then to progress to basic industries such as metals and chemicals; and finally to proceed to the creation of heavy industries and the manufacture of sophisticated products like electronic equipment.[45] Even though Nkrumah was the nominal chairman of the Planning Commission, it is clear that neither in principle nor in practice did he agree with this sequence:[46]

> secondary industries, important as they are to making us economically independent, will still leave us heavily reliant on outside sources and skill unless we build up those heavy industries *which alone provide the fundamental basis of industrialization.*

In the end the planners bowed to the view of their President, so that, whereas the industrialization described in the *7YP* was phased over twenty years, the *Annual Plan* for 1965 shifted dramatically into higher gear and stated that 'the time has now come to devote more attention to the development of basic industries . . .'[47] Published only a year later than the master document, this made nonsense of the perspective of the *7YP*. A serious rift between Mensah, Executive Secretary of the Planning Commission and chief author of the *7YP*, and the more militant wing of the ruling party came into the open, and he later left to take up a post with the United Nations.[48]

The reluctance of individual Ministers to submit to the disciplines of a plan was even more serious for implementation. A struggle for control over the capital budget quickly developed between the Planning Commission and the Ministry of Finance, in which Mensah's technical expertise proved no match for the drive and political weight of Finance Minister Amoako-Atta, who was able to announce in his 1965 budget speech that preparation of the capital budget was to be transferred to his Ministry.[49] Other Ministers also resisted the endeavours of the planners:[50]

> Cabinet Ministers appear so little inclined to accept the Commission's authority that it is intended to appoint as its Vice-Chairman a minister who will be politically responsible for planning.

This was not done, however, and Ministers continued to go their own way:[51]

> For example, the deputy Minister of Works and Communications thought it an excellent idea for his own region (the East) to draw up a regional seven-year development plan and attempt to have its projects inserted in the development plans of the relevant ministries. In mid-1962 the CPP Regional Steering Committee accepted the idea and had all DCs prepare lists of projects for their areas. They were examined and pared in a series of conferences over a fortnight and printed as a 'plan.' The deputy Minister then persuaded each of the relevant ministries to include these projects in their own segment of the Seven-Year Plan. At no time did he contact the State Control Commission. Naturally, not all his projects fitted in with the Seven-

Year Plan then being prepared. Within a short time, the flow from the cabinet of development projects requiring State Planning Committee investigation and approval began to slow down.

The absence of Ministers from membership of the Planning Commission probably contributed to the estrangement between the planners and politicians but Nkrumah, who was its Chairman, was no better at keeping within the limitations of the plan. I was told that he explicitly stated that he did not regard himself as bound by it, and when told that one of his decisions ran counter to the plan is said to have retorted, 'Who decides, Mensah or me?'[52] His belief in planning as an allocative device appears to have lacked much consistency.[53]

> One thing that puzzled me and other persons who knew Nkrumah was his capacity to approve things without really intending to adhere to them. This is borne out vividly by the episodes of the Seven Year Development Plan. I have a feeling that Nkrumah approved the document and the discipline which it was likely to impose on his economic policies and actions knowing very well that he would not accept the constraints imposed by the Plan.

Ironically, private investors may have taken the plan more seriously than the government, for it is suggested in a later chapter that acceptance of the plan's optimism about the future rate of industrialization and growth contributed to over-investment in industrial plant.

In retrospect, we see an almost total gap between the theoretical advantages of planning and the record of the 7YP. Far from providing a superior set of signals, it was seriously flawed as a technical document and, in any case, subsequent actions of government bore little relation to it. Far from counteracting the alleged myopia of private decision-takers, government decisions tended to be dominated by short-term expediency and were rarely based upon careful appraisals of their economic consequences. The plan was subverted, as most plans are, by insufficient political determination to make it work[54] but, in fairness to the politicians, we should add that the notion of medium-term planning is based upon a rather naive view of political decision-making processes.[55] On either explanation, Ghana's experience with the 7YP strongly supports the conclusion of a recent article on planning in Africa, that:[56]

> those engaged in planning activities must be sufficiently close to the seat of political power to be relevant to the actual process of political decision making . . . [and] neither the existence of a Planning Ministry nor the periodic construction of a national plan necessarily has anything to do with meaningful planning . . .

A Note on Planning after Nkrumah

Although the preoccupation of the NLC after the 1966 coup was with economic stabilization, they gradually sought to move to a more developmental stance. A *Two-year Plan 1968/69–1969/70* was prepared and, as its sub-title – 'From Stabilisation to Development' – indicated, was regarded as the 'forerunner of a more comprehensive development plan',[57] the preparation of which would, however, be a task for the civilian government elected into power in September 1969. In the event the Busia administration decided against the immediate preparation of a medium-term plan but did publish a *One-year Plan* for 1970–1.[58] Preparations were subsequently begun of a medium-term plan, which was nearing completion when aborted by the 1972 military take-over.

Given the intrinsic limitations of one- and two-year plans devised without the benefit of a longer-term perspective, it would not be very helpful to examine these documents in detail here.

We might instead ask whether the planning capabilities of the public administration and policital commitment to planning improved much in the post-Nkrumah period. Real progress was made within the civil service. The staff of the planning agency was strengthened with Ghanaian and foreign economists, a regional planning administration was set up, together with planning units in a few of the more important functional ministries, such as education and agriculture. Besides producing the two-year and one-year plans, the agency published a document on progress during the first year of the former, and was heavily involved in the preparation and evaluation of the annual capital budgets.

But all this meant little unless there was a parallel improvement in governmental commitment to make planning work and, so far as the Busia period was concerned, it seemed to this writer that the position had improved little upon the Nkrumah era, even though none other than J. H. Mensah had become Minister of Finance and Planning and exercised something of a monopoly in the formulation of economic policies.[59] The following extract from a'note on economic planning in Ghana' written in the first half of 1971 in response to an elaborate proposal for plan organization records the situation as I saw it then and also, perhaps, conveys some of the frustrations felt by Ghanaians and non-Ghanaians working within the planning agency:

We start by making a distinction: between planning in the broad sense of exercising forethought about an economic operation and the results it may have, on the one hand, and the writing of development plans on the other. In the former sense there is rather little planning in Ghana. In the latter sense there is a long history of planning which has, however, tended to have a rather minimal impact on the actual development of the economy. The principal thesis of this note is that the utility of writing development plans is bound to remain slight so long as the everyday decision-making processes and the short-term management of the economy remain in their present unsatisfactory state.

The unsatisfactory nature of the present situation can be indicated by some examples:

(a) The annual budget of the central Government is coordinated with monetary policy in a highly imperfect manner and is scarcely co-ordinated with balance of payments policy at all [*see* chapter 11].

(b) The annual import licensing programmes are largely paper exercises, only remotely connected with the licences issued, and do not provide an adequate safeguard against an insupportable volume of imports [*see* chapter 10].

(c) Economic statistics of a type useful for the management of the economy are produced by a variety of agencies but they are often badly out of date, are rarely accompanied by any analysis, they remain fragmented rather than being considered in relation to each other, and are little used.

(d) At the official level there are no formal arrangements for the overall co-ordination of economic policies. At the political level there does exist a Cabinet Economic Committee but it is not clear whether this is able to perform an effective co-ordinating function.

(e) That written development plans are not taken seriously is clear from two recent occurrences: that the draft *One-year Plan, 1970–1* had to be re-written to make it consistent with the budget (instead of the other way round); and the decision to produce from scratch and with no overall policy guidance a draft *Five-year Plan* between December, 1970 and June, 1971.[60]

In this situation questions concerning the ideal organisational structure and status of the agency responsible for 'development planning' are of limited importance. If conditions are such that development plans cannot or will not be implemented it would be far better not to bother with plan-writing at all and to use the manpower thereby released for more productive activities. Thus, anyone concerned with the creation of an *effective* planning agency must necessarily concern himself with far broader issues than that of merely devising the best organisational arrangements for the preparation of development plans.

This conclusion is reinforced by consideration of the current personnel situation. The economics personnel employed in the Ministry of Finance and Planning are of generally indifferent calibre, morale is low and motivation is weak. Among the reasons for this are low salaries, an absence of effective supervision and communication, a tendency to give the most interesting work to advisers, a training and promotion policy that emphasises seniority rather than merit, and a scepticism about the utility of the work that is undertaken . . . It might be added that the staffing position of the Bureau of Statistics is no more satisfactory than that of the Ministry itself.

Neglect of the Bureau of Statistics continued to the point where by 1972 it was practically bereft of professional staff and seemed near to complete collapse. No machinery for implementing the specific policies of the *One-year Plan*, of which there was a considerable number, was set up and they were largely ignored.[61] In the end, preparation of the draft five-year plan became more serious than was at first threatened but there remained in the mind of this participant a large doubt about the government's amenability to operating within the constraints of a plan it had had little part in preparing.

II The Mobilization of Resources

One of the arguments in favour of planning mentioned earlier was that only the state could mobilize resources on a scale large enough to undertake a big push, and Part II examines the record of the Nkrumah government by this criterion, focusing on the financing strategy of the *7YP* but utilizing data for the entire first half of the sixties.

The Strategy
The broad strategy was described in chapter 3: promote economic independence by financing a high proportion of the investment effort from domestic resources; restrain the expansion of consumption, especially private consumption; achieve a high marginal saving rate.[62] Chapter 4 presented data showing the actual record: that the private consumer (especially the cocoa farmers and the urban proletariat) was successfully squeezed; that there was a substantial socialization of consumption, with the expansion of social services partly compensating for declining private living standards; that a large proportion of gross investment was financed by domestic saving despite very high investment rates and a tendency for gross saving to decline as a proportion of GNP.[63]

The purpose here, however, is to go beyond these macro-economic indicators and to focus on the record of the government itself in its use of the budget and the banking system for the mobilization of resources, using the fiscal policies enunciated in the *7YP* as a yardstick by which to assess achievements. A central feature of the financing scheme of the plan was that savings on the current budget should be enough to finance a substantial proportion of government investment.[64] This, it was recognized, would involve restraining the growth of current ('consumption') expenditures and a larger tax effort. Only very limited borrowing from the private sector was envisaged, the implication being that most private saving should be utilized to finance private investment, and deficit financing was not to be carried to the point of generating 'an inflationary collapse or a balance of payment crisis'.[65] Foreign loans and grants would be sought to cover the direct foreign exchange costs of the government's investments; loans should be on

soft terms and should preferably be in support of the whole programme rather than tied to specific projects. How did the realities
accord with these aspirations?

The Record

With regard first to the tax effort, Table 6.1 presents three alternative
measures of tax revenues, all expressed as percentages of current-price
GDP. In the first column, concentrating for the time being on the years
up to 1965, it can be seen that there was a relatively low tax effort in
1962 and 1963, and that the opposite was true of 1964 and 1965.
Reference forward to Table 6.2, col. 2 (p. 150) shows that the value of
total receipts was relatively static in the early sixties and then recorded
a large jump. Various attempts have been made to construct indices of
tax effort for developing countries and it is instructive to compare
Ghana's record with those of other countries.[66] The most recent and
sophisticated study of this kind presented data on 49 developing countries, Ghana included, using data for 1966-8, and it emerged that
Ghana's tax effort was somewhat above the average of the countries
studied. Comparison of actual tax yields with that of a representative
tax system gave Ghana a yield slightly above that of the representative
system and a ranking of 17th out of 49.[67] Four alternative criteria gave
Ghana rankings of 26, 25, 21 and 20, all out of 49.[68] What is particularly interesting about this result is that Ghana's tax effort in 1966-8
was substantially below the levels which had prevailed in 1964-5, the
implication being that in the late Nkrumah years Ghana was making a
large tax effort by the standards of developing countries.

TABLE 6.1
Tax Revenues as Percentages of Current-price GDP

	Total tax revenues (1)	Non-cocoa tax revenues (2)	Domestic tax revenues[a] (3)
1961	14·3[b]	9·4	3·6
1962	11·8	9·5	3·8
1963	11·9	9·5	3·8
1964	16·4[b]	11·5	6·4
1965	15·9	14·7	7·9
1966	12·6	11·7	7·0
1967	13·5	11·4	7·2
1968	14·3	10·5	7·4
1969	14·6	9·8	6·9
Unweighted mean	13·9	10·9	6·0

Sources: *Economic Surveys*, 1968 and 1969, Tables III and VI; for GDP *see* Chapter 4,
Table 4.A, line 5.
NOTES:
[a] Total tax revenue less taxes on international trade.
[b] Includes 'voluntary contributions' by cocoa farmers.

What makes the 1964–5 record even more remarkable is that the tax ratio was raised in the teeth of highly adverse trends in world cocoa prices and a tax structure with an exceptionally low elasticity with respect to increases in monetary GDP.[69] In these respects, columns (2) and (3) of Table 6.1 give a better impression of the tax effort. Comparison of columns (1) and (2) indicates that the decline in the overall ratio in the early sixties was wholly attributable to a decline in cocoa revenues and that the ratio of non-cocoa tax revenues was stable in 1961–3. Chapter 5 showed that there was a sharp downward trend in world cocoa prices in the first half of the sixties, to which revenues from the cocoa duty were particularly vulnerable because the rate of duty was highly progressive with respect to the price realized on the world market. Successive cuts in the producer price could not prevent large reductions in revenues from this source.[70]

Even the ratios in column (2) are not immune from the effects of trends in the world cocoa price, for this variable affects Ghana's import capacity and hence the tax base for the collection of import duties (although import capacity was less directly related to export earnings in the early years because of excess reserves and the availability of suppliers' credits). The third column of the table is therefore confined to revenues from taxes other than those on external trade, and it is there that one sees most clearly the effort that was made in 1964 and 1965. Comparing with 1963, the ratio was more than doubled, with the value of receipts rising from ₵27·0 million in 1963 to ₵123.2 million two years later.[71] This increase was achieved by a variety of means in the 1963–4 and 1965 budgets, of which higher rates of personal and company income tax, increases in excise rates, and the introduction of a sales tax were the most important.[72]

All in all, then, it cannot be said of the Nkrumah government that it lacked the will to tax the country to finance its expenditure proposals. Leaving aside the economic desirability of transferring resources to the state budget, the question arises next as to whether the government's will to tax was matched by control over its expenditures to generate the savings needed for its development programmes. Table 6.2 gives statistics on this, presenting a conventional classification of expenditures into current and capital items, with budgetary saving defined as the surplus of current receipts over current expenditures. An alternative will be offered shortly, but the conventional classification has the considerable advantage of being the one used by Ghana's fiscal planners, with recurrent expenditures treated as having a first claim on budgetary resources.

For the time being it is most useful to concentrate on columns (1) to (3) of the table. They show a rapid expansion of both current revenues and expenditures, and a tendency beginning in the late fifties for current savings to diminish almost to zero until arrested by the 1963–4 and 1965 budgets. The restraint of current expenditures called for in the 7YP did not materialize; as conventionally measured, government consumption grew in real terms at 10·0 per cent annually from 1958–9 to 1964–5 – four times as fast as private consumption.[73] The government held down private consumption but, as Bissue ironically observed, 'Government consumption has refused to succumb to the restraining influence of this policy.'[74] The consequence, of course, was that only a modest part of the increased tax effort remained available for the government's investment programme, an illustration of the 'Please effect', according to which 'the attempt to increase domestic savings by increased tax performance had been frustrated by the growth of current governmental expenditure.'[75] Column (6) of the table dramatizes this by expressing budget savings relative to capital expenditures. Starting in 1957–8 with savings in excess of capital spending, the ratio declined steeply under the influence of falling savings and growing capital expenditures to only 5 per cent in 1962–3, but with a major revival beginning in 1963–4. Taking 1960–1 to 1965 as a whole, budget savings were equivalent to 28 per cent of capital spending. The 7YP called for savings of 44 per cent and, despite the adverse trend in current expenditures, that target was approximately achieved during the two years in which the plan was nominally in force.

The conventional classification of government spending into current and capital items is, however, only a poor indicator of the consumption and development contents of the budget. Ghana's Ministry of Finance classified all capital spending as being synonymous with development, but this was misleading. The current budget includes spending on the agricultural extension services, the educational system, community development, and other items which might be more appropriately thought of as developmental, and the capital budget includes the building of government offices, military equipment and a host of other things with few directly developmental returns. There is something very unsatisfactory about a classification which, for example, counts the cost of building a technical college as 'development' and the cost of running it as 'consumption'. Of course, any classification of expenditures as 'developmental' or 'non-developmental' is arbitrary and none can be presented which is not open to that criticism. But some schemata are more arbitrary than others and an attempt is made in Table 6.3 to present an alternative which dispenses with the current/capital dichotomy and instead classifies government expenditures roughly by end-use. The definitions used are explained in the table notes. Even these are far from perfect and a good deal of the spending classified as 'developmental' actually brought few economic returns – the cost of state farms, for example.

This table indicates that development and consumption expenditures claimed roughly equal shares of fiscal resources throughout the first half of the sixties, and comparison of column (3) with Table 6.2, column (7) shows that this re-classification attributes a larger develop-

TABLE 6.2
Budgetary Trends, 1957/58–1971/72

(₵ million and percentages)

	Current Expenditures (1)	Current Receipts (2)	Current Balance (3)	Capital Expenditures (4)	Overall Balance (5)	(3) as % of (4) (6)	(4) as % of (1) (7)
1957/58	78·4	120·0	+41·6	38·7	+2·9	107%	49%
1958/59	91·3	133·7	+42·4	54·7[d]	−12·3	78%	60%
1959/60	100·6	140·1[a]	+39·5	73·6	−34·1	54%	73%
1960/61	134·0	166·2[a]	+32·2	89·0	−56·8	36%[a]	66%
1961/62[b]	180·7	193·8	+13·1	125·4	−112·3	10%	69%
1962/63	159·6	164·6	+5·0	105·8	−100·8	5%	66%
1963/64[b]	236·1	292·6[a]	+56·5	141·3	−84·8	40%	60%
1965	219·8	282·6	+62·8	141·8	−79·0	44%	65%
1966	203·6	230·2	+26·6	64·8	−38·2	41%	32%
1967	245·1	253·5	+8·4	68·6	−60·2	12%	28%
1968	300·2	297·7	−2·5	67·0	−69·5	−4%	22%
1969	315·0	331·7	+16·7	56·2	−39·5	30%	18%
1970[c]	362·5	436·9	+74·4	79·3	−4·9	94%	22%
1970/71[c]	378·1	480·5	+102·4	108·6[e]	−6·2	94%	29%
1971/72	431·0	409·0	−22·0	103·5[e]	−125·5	−21%	24%

Sources: *Economic Surveys*, various issues; *Ghana Gazette*, No. 64, 1972; No. 22, 1973.

NOTES

[a] Includes 'voluntary contributions' by cocoa farmers.

[b] Fifteen-month period.

[c] There is a six-month overlap between the 1970 calendar year and 1970/71 fiscal year data.

[d] Excludes ₵8.0 million loan to Government of Guinea.

[e] Because the *Gazette* treats capital expenditures differently from the *Economic Surveys*, these figures would probably need adjusting downward to make them strictly comparable with the earlier ones.

mental component to total spending than does the conventional current/capital distinction. The re-classification also gives a different impression of trends over time, with development spending growing a little faster than consumption.[76] At least partially, then, claims that the growth of public consumption was incompatible with the government's development plans were based upon a statistical artefact,[77] and the 'Please effect' may have been exaggerated.

TABLE 6.3

Alternative Classification of Government Expenditures, Selected Years[a]

	Consumption[b] ₡ million	Development[c] ₡ million	(2) as % of (1)
	(1)	(2)	(3)
1960/61	106·4	106·1	99·7%
1962/63	132·2	128·0	96·8%
1965	167·7	179·7	107·2%
1967	161·0	127·6	79·3%
1969	224·3	117·7	52·5%

NOTES

[a] These figures exclude total public debt servicing payments (principal and interest), and loans and advances.

[b] Defined as total expenditures (current and capital) on general administration; defence; justice and police; social services other than education; transfers to local government; minor unallocated items; half of expenditures on community services; one-third of expenditures on education.

[c] Total expenditures on economic services; half of expenditures on community development; two-thirds of expenditures on education.

Sources: *Economic Surveys,* various issues.

Another way in which budgetary data did not fully record the magnitude of the development effort in the first half of the sixties was because most expenditure on government projects – largely industrial – financed by suppliers' credits was not recorded in the annual budgets at all. For most of the time only cash payments to service the credits themselves were recorded, not the value of work completed.[78] Some idea of the magnitude of this can be gained from comparison of data on the financing of budget deficits with independent information on the total growth of the public debt, in Table 6.4. Part A of the table presents aggregated data on deficit financing in 1960–5 inclusive derived from budgetary statistics, indicating an overall deficit (comparable with the figures in Table 6.2, column 5) of ₡570 million. Part B records the total growth in the public debt over the same period, indicating total net government borrowings of ₡838 million. The difference between these two totals, ₡268 million, may be used as an indicator of the amount of unrecorded expenditures although, for a number of reasons, this figure should only be taken as an order of magnitude. Notice, however, the enormous discrepancy between the figures for

external borrowing, indicating the large volume of government investment in projects financed from external sources which were not
recorded in the budget, although it should be added that the developmental value of some of these projects was slight.

TABLE 6.4
Aggregate Budget Deficits and their Financing, 1960–5: Alternative Figures[a]

		ℂ million
A **From budget data**		
1. Capital receipts		22
2. Use of government reserves		83
3. Domestic borrowing		425
4. External borrowing		36
5. Balancing item		4
6. Total (=aggregate recorded budget deficit)		570
B **From public debt and monetary data**		
7. Capital receipts[b]		22
8. Use of government reserves[b]		83
9. Domestic borrowing		377
of which, net borrowing from banking system	157	
other domestic borrowing	220	
10. External borrowing[c]		356
of which, short-term	8	
suppliers' credits	284	
long-term	64	
11. Total (=aggregate recorded and unrecorded budget deficit)		838
12. Unrecorded deficit (11–6)		268

Sources: *Economic Surveys*, various issues. Ahmad, 1970, Tables VII and XVI. Unpublished data on external debt.
NOTES:
[a] Figures include provision for estimated deficit of ℂ23 million in January-June 1960.
[b] Reproduced from lines 1 and 2.
[c] External debt as at 24 February 1966 expressed in the then existing exchange rate,
   adjusted for external debt outstanding at end-1959. The figure for suppliers' credits
   includes a minor sum for credits obtained by private borrowers.

It was in the size of budget deficits and the manner in which they
were financed that the government departed most radically from the
strategy announced in the *7YP*. For if the magnitude of the government's development effort was larger than is often thought, it is also
true that *all* categories of spending went up very rapidly so that, despite
the tax effort, large deficits remained to be filled by whatever means
were available. As far as domestic borrowing was concerned, the
government violated the strategy (a) by borrowing from the general
public on a much larger scale than had been envisaged, and (b) by
borrowing large sums from the banking system, with consequences
which are discussed in Part III. As regards borrowing from abroad, the
heavy reliance on suppliers' credits violated the principles of the *7YP*

that financing should not be tied to specific projects and – much more important – that loans should be long-term and at low interest rates. We saw in the previous chapter that the credits generally conformed to neither criteria.

To sum up, the Nkrumah government made a major developmental thrust through its own powers of taxation and spending. An above-average tax level was achieved despite adverse trends in the world cocoa market and an inelastic tax system, and the pattern of government spending retained a large developmental content, especially taking into account investments that were not recorded in the budgets. But other types of spending also went up fast, resulting in total expenditures that could only be financed by violating the sensible domestic and foreign borrowing policies of the *7YP*. This violation resulted in large borrowings from the private sector, expansionary money creation, and an insupportably large and inappropriately structured external debt. These deviations might well have been justified had the government succeeded in generating economic growth but enough has been said earlier to indicate that they were not successful, for reasons explored in the following chapter. The will was there, but not the capacity to spend wisely: that is the tragedy of Nkrumah's economic policies.

III Short-run Economic Management

The instability of the economy mentioned at the beginning of this chapter, plus the absence of the built-in stabilizers found in more advanced economies (especially the absence of an income-elastic tax structure), show up in a number of ways. First, economic activity is subject to strong but variable seasonal fluctuations – in supply and demand, in prices, in money supply, in the balance of trade, and in government revenues and expenditures. Between years there is also much variability – in government revenues, in export receipts,[79] and in the overall growth rate of the economy.

If, for the time being, we assume this instability to be detrimental to the economy, it follows that economic policies should be used as instruments of stabilization. In this part, then, we will examine the extent to which fiscal and monetary policies in the first half of the sixties affected economic instability. It should be borne in mind, however, that there were bound to be severe limitations on the use of these instruments for stabilization. Knowledge of the short-run behavioural characteristics of the economy, and therefore its responsiveness to any given policy action, was poor. The range, quality and punctuality of information on current trends in the economy, and the utilization of it for economic management, left much to be desired.[80] And the unpredictability of tax receipts obviously increased the difficulties of using the budget as a sensitive instrument of economic stabilization.[81]

Frequent changes in the periodicity of the fiscal year added to the problems.[82] Monetary policy was similarly constrained, because it was bound to be strongly influenced by the fiscal situation, because the organized financial system was still at a fairly early stage of development, and for the well-known reasons that make monetary policy a suspect instrument of short-term stabilization everywhere.[83] But to point to the obstacles is not to argue that stabilization should not be attempted. On the contrary, an even stronger effort is necessary than in a more amenable environment. What, then, was the response of those who devised the fiscal policies?

Fiscal Management
There was a clear shift of emphasis in fiscal policies at the beginning of the sixties, resulting from changes in the balance of power in the CPP. Under the strong but conservative hand of Minister of Finance Gbedemah, fiscal policy was used as an orthodox tool of economic stabilization in the late fifties. The first two years of independence were designated as a period of 'consolidation' and the overall budget was kept approximately in balance, partly as a response to the first signs of an emerging balance of payments problem.[84] In 1959, a new development plan was launched that signalled a substantially increased level of government capital formation. Much more important was the departure of Gbedemah during 1961, which removed a major restraint on Nkrumah's large spending ambitions.[85] First taking over responsibility for preparation of the budget himself and later appointing more amenable Finance Ministers, Nkrumah was able to shift the whole emphasis of fiscal policy from a pursuit of domestic and external equilibrium to nothing much more than a search for resources to match the government's expenditure plans. From 1961/62 to 1965 budgets incorporating large deficits were brought before parliament, and increasingly chaotic decision-making processes prevented the budget from being employed to stabilize an economy that was moving ever further from equilibrium. What is more, budget proposals tended systematically to under-estimate the actual deficits experienced up to 1964, because of over-optimistic estimates of tax revenue and reduced fiscal discipline leading to larger expenditures than originally planned.[86]
    The 1965 budget provides the plainest example of Nkrumah's approach to these matters. In the face of an increasingly grave balance of payments crisis and accelerating inflation (*see* chapters 4 and 5), it became obvious during 1964 that a disinflationary budget was required for 1965. Nkrumah took the initiative. Referring to the need for restraint in government spending, he announced, apparently to the great surprise of his Minister of Finance and budget officials, that total government spending in 1965 should not be allowed to exceed ₵400 million. But ₵400 million exceeded estimated expenditures in the pre-

vious budget by almost two-fifths![87] This was too much even for an expansionist Minister of Finance like Amoako-Atta who, at no little risk to himself, doctored the estimates so that, while appearing to sum to ₵400 million, they actually envisaged an increase on the previous budget of only about 8 per cent. Even so, and despite swingeing tax increases in this and earlier budgets, there was a large overall deficit in 1965, as there had been in previous years (*see* Table 6.2), to which should be added substantial unrecorded expenditures financed by suppliers' credits.

The condition of the economy worsened predictably but drastically during 1965, aggravated by a severe slump in world cocoa prices. The rate of inflation went up again and it became obvious that in a little time the country would be forced to default on its external debts. These realities were brought home to the government sufficiently for them to re-examine their policies and to call for missions from the International Monetary Fund and World Bank. The policy advice these organizations would give was obvious: reduce government spending, halt the acceptance of more suppliers' credits, improve the financial performance of state enterprises, slow down on new investments until existing productive capacity was brought to a higher level of utilization.[88] It seemed, moreover, that the government had become reconciled to the need for a change.

Nkrumah spoke of a need 'to improve the efficiency of our economic administration' and for 'co-ordination between our planning, executing, commercial and banking agencies,' and publicly directed that the size of the 1966 budget should be brought down 'to levels which can be contained by our resources.[89] That budget appeared to contain considerably reduced expenditures and was said by the Minister to be within the limits of available cash resources and to have been framed in the light of Fund-Bank recommendations. The use of the fiscal instrument for stabilization was apparently being re-asserted.

This was an illusion, however. The apparent cut in expenditures was partly spurious, arising from Amoako-Atta's strategems of the previous year, and comparison of the 1966 spending proposals with the 1965 budget indicated that there would actually be another increase.[90] Furthermore, spending had not been confined to available resources (other than bank borrowing), for there was an unfilled gap of ₵37 million and all the Minister could say about this was that, 'It is hoped . . . that we may close the gap if we succeed in getting consumer goods on credit.'[91] In addition, the budget envisaged a further ₵23 million of suppliers' credits during the year, so in this respect too the budget was at variance with the urgings of the IMF and World Bank. Finally and above all, Nkrumah had not accepted the necessity for restraint, public utterances notwithstanding:[92]

Ghana was in somewhat desperate financial straits, and a visiting

International Monetary Fund mission strongly suggested a top limit to the budget which would have left a more manageable deficit. Planning committee members, especially the principal politician/Ministers, took this warning seriously and severely cut the budgets of the other Ministers who appeared before them. The committee had full decision-making powers, for the cabinet no longer discussed development projects; it required only Nkrumah's approval. In February 1966 committee members anticipated that, given the cuts they had made, Ministers would go to Nkrumah seeking supplementary budgets. They decided to forestall this possibility by reiterating the importance of the budget limit, which Nkrumah had already publicly asserted. A subcommittee, the Central Treasury Committee, approached Nkrumah, who in the next two days undid their disciplined efforts and wantonly restored all the cuts that had been made (including that in the military's budget). . . .

Little wonder that Amoako-Atta, one of the few of Nkrumah's close colleagues who did not retract their previous actions or beliefs after the 1966 coup, nevertheless complained of his former leader that he ignored financial advice.[93] Symbolically, Nkrumah's decision to defy the economic realities and spend more was one of his final acts as President.

Monetary Policy

The government's fiscal management inevitably caused considerable repercussions in the monetary system. In 1961–3 and, especially in 1965, the government undertook a considerable volume of deficit financing, defined as net government borrowing from the central and commercial banks.[94] Table 6.5 records that deficit financing, so defined, amounted to ₵149 million for the whole period 1960–5; since at the beginning of the period the total money supply amounted to only ₵114 million, this method of balancing the budget had a strong expansionary impact on the monetary situation. This was all the greater because for much of this period the form of government borrowings from the banks – largely the sale of Treasury Bills – kept the commercial banks highly liquid and thus able to expand their lending to other borrowers while at the same time extending more credit to the government.[95] Table 6.5 shows the emergence in the early sixties of the government as a major borrower from the banking system but shows also that from 1962 the shares of government and non-government borrowers remained roughly constant despite the continued growth of the former.

The central bank did not play an effective role in this situation.[96] Being newly established, the Bank of Ghana was initially more concerned to effect a smooth transition from the currency board system than to pursue an active monetary policy, although by 1962 it was describing monetary trends as potentially inflationary.[97] In 1963 and especially 1964 it did attempt more actively to restrain the growth of bank credit to non-government borrowers, by reducing bank liquidity and raising statutory reserve ratios, but that these endeavours were ineffectual is shown by Table 6.5. In fact, lending to non-government borrowers accelerated continuously from 1963 to 1965 and added to monetary expansion in a major way.

TABLE 6.5
Total Bank Lending by Type of Borrower, 1960–72[a]
(℃ million)

| | Borrower | | | |
	Central Government[b] (1)	Non-Government (2)	Total (3)	(1) as % of (3) (4)
1960	1·8	27·2	29·0	6%
1961	18·8	48·2	67·0	28%
1962	46·6	50·0	96·6	48%
1963	75·0	70·6	145·6	52%
1964	85·2	104·6	189·8	45%
1965	151·2	155·0	306·2	49%
1966	217·6	164·0	381·6	57%
1967	232·9	158·0	390·9	60%
1968	247·1	166·2	413·3	60%
1969	257·4	187·3	444·7	58%
1970	274·4	227·3	501·7	55%
1971	223·5	365·7	589·2	38%
1972	330·9	442·1	773·0	43%

Sources: Ahmad, 1970, Tables VII and IX; Bank of Ghana *Quarterly Economic Bulletins* (various issues).
NOTES:
[a] Figures are averages of monthly data and relate to total lending by the central and commercial banks.
[b] Net of government deposits.

Three factors particularly undermined the Bank of Ghana's attempts at credit control. Firstly, there was a change in the method of financing the cocoa crop which, combined with the increasingly serious financial difficulties of the Cocoa Marketing Board, was a major source of new domestic credit.[98] Secondly, the government-owned Ghana Commercial Bank did not observe the reserve ratios laid down by the central bank, which, in turn, was unable or unwilling to insist that they be observed. A third and related point is that most 'non-government' borrowing was being undertaken by other public bodies, and to control their borrowing was politically almost as difficult as limiting credit to the central government itself. The overwhelming importance of the public sector as a user of bank credit is demonstrated by an estimate that by the end of 1965 the public sector had 86 per cent of total bank credit.[99]

The more than ten-fold expansion in total bank credit between 1960 and 1965, recorded in Table 6.5, whilst partly offset by a liquidation of overseas assets, led naturally to a large increase in money supply, which more than doubled between 1960 and 1965.[100] In practice, then, monetary trends were even more expansionary than fiscal policies, insofar as it is realistic to separate the two.

The Inflationary Process

At the beginning of the decade it was still possible for the economy to absorb this monetary stimulus, and the increase in economic activity with which it was associated, without serious inflation. Shortages of foreign exchange had not yet become serious and excess foreign exchange reserves were able to absorb the growing gap between aggregate demand and domestic supplies. The cost, of course, was a deterioration in the balance of payments but it was not until controls were imposed and the volume of imports was cut that excess demand began to spill over into domestic inflation.[101] Ahmad's analysis shows this clearly, with most monetary expansion being absorbed by deficits on the balance of payments until 1963.[102] From then on, the extent of monetary expansion became too great to be absorbed by imports, even though large payments deficits continued, and the rate of inflation accelerated. Indeed, there would have been more inflation but for the public's willingness to hold larger money-balances or, to express the matter in more old-fashioioned terms, a decline in the velocity of circulation, mitigating the impact of monetary expansion.[103] The government's ability to hold down urban wages and cocoa incomes (chapter 4) was also an important disinflationary factor.

However, to attempt to explain the inflation of 1963–5 largely by reference to deficit financing and monetary expansion, as Ahmad and Scott tend to do, misses some important aspects of the situation. The effects of deficit financing seem to have been exaggerated, for only in 1965 do Ahmad's figures indicate a clear connection both between deficit financing and increased money supply, *and* between monetary expansion and inflation.[104] In the earlier years deficit financing either was not the chief source of monetary expansion or the monetary expansion had only a muted effect on the price level. Larger credits to the rest of the public sector added fuel to the inflationary fire but, even so, an exclusively monetary explanation, focused on the expansion of aggregate demand, is incomplete. It is also necessary to examine supply conditions.

The inelastic supply of marketed food-stuffs was particularly important. For reasons given in chapter 8, government agricultural policies were most unsuccessful in this period and there were powerful demographic and techological forces at work causing food production to stagnate. Given generally low price elasticities for local foods, this inevitably meant relative increases in their prices – a tendency strengthened by a decline in the efficiency of the distributive system. If we trace the pattern of price increases in the inflationary years 1963–5, the outstanding fact is the rise of food prices relative to other consumer goods, with the former rising almost twice as fast as the latter (see Figure 4.1).

The import-substituting industrialization of the first half of the sixties was another important element in the situation; Ghana was exhibiting the characteristic symptoms of 'structural' inflation, with the domestic structure of industrial production proving too inflexible to accommodate major new demands being made on it as a result of import restrictions. It was not merely that industry could not catch up quickly enough with demand: as is shown in chapter 8, the industrialization was highly inefficient, fostering the emergence of high-cost producers charging prices well in excess of the imports they were replacing.

As between the monetarist and structuralist explanations of inflation, the following points might be made: (a) there presumably was some smaller quantity of money which would have permitted adjustments to relative prices while leaving the general price level unchanged; but (b) the demand for money was probably too unstable in the short run for policy-makers to have been able to predetermine the quantity of money that would have this effect; (c) given that import-substituting industrialization was also taking place, there was no realistic way of achieving the necessary changes in relative prices without some overall increase in the general price level; (d) a monetary policy so restrictive as to prevent general price increases would probably have imposed a high cost in terms of output and employment forgone relative to the benefits of avoiding inflation; but (e) expansionary fiscal and monetary policies pursued in the last two or three years of the Nkrumah period added to the effects of an inelastic productive system to an extent that seriously worsened the economic situation, especially in 1965.

Consequences

The survey of the mainstream development economics in chapter 2 drew attention to the lack of concern in the literature with the task of short-run economic management, even to some hostility to the notion that this was an important task of policy.[105] There was a general presumption that the state had high marginal propensities to save and invest, Lewis was arguing (admittedly for a closed economy) that the use of inflation to finance productive investment was self-liquidating, and as an undergraduate of that period I well remember the generally low opinion that was held of the policy biases of the IMF, which invariably lent its weight to stabilization. Put more positively, the whole emphasis of the big-push, structural transformation school was on disequilibrium as an essential, if uncomfortable, part of the development process. In its inattention to economic management and stability, then, the Nkrumah government was mirroring the general opinion prevailing in the economics profession at the time. But was this inattention justified by the results? Did the forces which generated instability also accelerate the pace of development?

The analysis of this section suggests the contrary. Superimposed on an inherently unstable economy and a productive structure which was unable, partly because of other policy mistakes, to adjust to the increasing demands being made upon it, large-scale credits to the central government and the rest of the public sector were inimical to the development effort. Combined with a constant exchange rate, the most serious effect of the expansion was to weaken the balance of payments, undermining import and exchange controls (chapter 10) and bringing the country to the point of being unable to honour its external obligations.[106] As surplus import capacity was eliminated, excess demand spilled over into inflation, which became severe by the standards of Ghana's past in 1965 and into 1966. These effects had the further consequences of making the possibility of effective medium-term planning even more remote than it already was and of creating an economic climate that placed efficiency at a discount.

Whether, as Ahmad argues,[107] the deficit financing, credit expansion and inflation merely permitted a transfer of resources from private to government consumption is more doubtful. His analysis relies too heavily upon the conventional distinction between the government's capital and recurrent expenditures, and Table 6.3 showed that on an alternative classification developmental spending actually grew a little faster than government consumption in the first half of the sixties. It is at least possible that the deficit financing permitted more saving and productive capital formation than would otherwise have occurred, especially if we recall that the urban proletariat and the cocoa farmers were the main sufferers from the forced saving imposed by price increases.

But this issue is beside the point. If the argument of the previous chapter is accepted, that import capacity rather than domestic saving was the binding constraint on the growth of the economy, and given the undoubted harm that monetary expansion did to the balance of payments, it follows as a matter of logic that the expansion undermined the growth of the economy, whatever its effects on domestic saving.[108] Besides avoiding other adverse consequences, better short-term economic management would have improved import capacity. Thus, the pusuit of stability, not as an end in itself but as a complement to longer-term policies, emerges as a necessary part of Ghana's development effort. One suspects that this also holds for many other developing countries.

NOTES

[1] For convenience hereafter abbreviated to *7YP*.

[2] Nkrumah, 1963, pp. 109–10.

[3] *See* above, pp. 39–44

[4] The remainder of this paragraph is summarized from the CPP, 1962, paragraphs 56–64.

[5] *The Spark,* 1964, p. 22.

[6] *See* Omaboe, 1966, chapter 18, p. 452. This chapter contains a useful history of planning and illuminating comments on the *7YP. See also* Bissue, 1965 and 1967.

[7] In a study of export structures Michaely, 1962, Tables 8 and 10, found Ghana to have the fourth highest index of export price instability and the second largest fluctuation in national income derived from changes in the terms of trade. Work by Coppock, 1962, and Macbean, 1966, also demonstrated the instability of Ghana's exports.

[8] *See* Killick, 1966, chapter 17, for an elaboration of this argument.

[9] *See* Omaboe, 1963. *passim.*

[10] *See* the Appendix to chapter 4 for a discussion of the reliability of the national accounts.

[11] Waterston, 1966A, pp. 532–3. Joszef Bognar was the most influential of the foreign advisers on the eventual content of the plan.

[12] Omaboe, 1966, pp. 450–1.

[13] Sub-division of the plan was proposed by a working party of an international conference of economists which discussed a draft of the *7YP*. The suggestion was that a plan for the second half of the period, revised to take account of changed circumstance, should be prepared during the first half. *See* Waterston, 1966B, for the case in favour of short planning periods in Ghana.

[14] Arthur Lewis told a cautionary tale about plan targets in Ghana: 'The second development plan, with which I was associated, did not give a lot of targets. We had thought at one stage of putting in a lot of targets, but we had a salutary experience which stopped that. One of the earlier chapters which came to be written was the chapter on manufacturing industry. That chapter had a modest target, that in the course of five years 100 new factories would be started in Ghana. There was a list of the things which would be done. Even when we made the list of 100, we thought the target was too high. We nevertheless made the list because we were trying to pin down the Industrial Development Corporation, whose staff were spending their time running all over Europe on political missions, doing everything except trying to get industry started in Ghana. We thought if we gave them a target of 100 industries they would really have to buckle to this. If at the end of 5 years they were very far from this, they would be in serious trouble. When we took this to the Ministerial group of which I spoke, all that happened was that they cut out 100 and 600 was put in its place. After this we did not put any more targets in' (quoted by Scott, 1967, p. 78).

[15] *Annual Plan, 1965.*

[16] *See 7YP,* chapter 13, especially p.242.

[17] The argument is developed extensively by Bissue, 1965. *See also* Streeten, 1972, chapter 6.

[18] *See* Cairncross, 1962, chapter 6.

[19] Calculated from Szereszewski, 1966, Table 2–7. The data which he used (Walters, 1962) were available when the plan was in preparation. Ratios calculated from current price data are much lower – even lower, at around 2·0, than the 3·5 used in the plan – but this merely reflects the tendency for the prices of capital goods to rise more slowly than the general price level. Calculations of ICORs in the later fifties and early sixties also show them to be highly unstable from one year to the next.

[20] Bissue, 1965, pp. 30–1.

[21] 'First, with a base year figure of ₵1014 million for GDP and an annual average growth

rate of 5·5 per cent, the GDP at the end of seven years is ₵1476 million and not
₵1592 as the planners imagined. Incremental income is then given as ₵1476 –
₵1014 million=₵462 million. Applying this to the capital coefficient of 3·5, gross
investment, assuming no gestation lags, is equal to ₵462×3·5=₵1617 million.
This means that investment requirements were over-estimated by as much as ₵414
million through a mere arithmetical error. Alternatively, with an investment of
₵2030 million, an initial income of ₵1014, and a capital coefficient of 3·5 the
implicit annual average growth rate works out to be 6·9 per cent, implying that the
growth potentialities of the economy were grossly under-estimated.'
'A second error relates to what might be termed "the missing year" . . . the bases of
the projections (of the plan) were the average values for 1960–62. Naturally, the
first year covered by the forward projections should have been 1962/63 and not
1963/64 as was the case. In other words, the seven–year period should properly
have covered the period 1962/63–1968/69 and not 1963/64–1969/70. Alternatively, one could assume that the Plan covered an eight-year period, implying an
annual rate of growth of GDP of 5·8 per cent and not 6·9 per cent obtained for a
seven-year period. Simple arithmetical slips such as these detracted immensely
from the technical correctness of the Plan.'
(Bissue, 1967, pp. 23–4.) I have taken the liberty of correcting a small numerical
error and of converting his figures from pounds into cedi equivalents.

[22] Krobo Edusei, Minister of Industries in *Parliamentary Debates,* 12 March 1964.

[23] I owe this point to Bissue, 1965; *see also* the *7YP*, p. 31.

[24] According to the plan (p. 269) this was based on an assumed capitalization of approximately 5 per cent 'of the total value of rural labour time' but estimates by Szereszewski, 1966, Table 3.7, suggest that this sum was equivalent to about 12 per
cent of value-added by labour in agriculture and related activities in 1960.

[25] *See* Killick, 1966, pp. 130–1 and 150–3 for a fuller discussion of this point.

[26] Calculated by comparing *7YP*, Table 7–6 with data kindly provided by P. Williams.

[27] Compare the *7YP*, Table 13.8, line 4, figure for 1963/64 of ₵34 million with T. M.
Brown's estimate of ₵77 million for 1963 (Brown, 1972, Table D–1).

[28] *See* Bissue, 1967, Table 6, showing very large discrepancies between the plan's base
figures and subsequent estimates of 1963 production. Comparison of the plan's
figures with Rourke, 1973A, Tables 1 and 2, suggests that the planners greatly
underestimated the volume of output of most staple foods in the early sixties.

[29] See Bissue, 1967, 25–7.

[30] The plan made provision for the creation of an extension service within the Ministry of
Agriculture, but the government had already decided in 1962 to transfer responsibility for extension to the more political Farmers' Council (*see* chapter 8).

[31] 1963/64 was intended as the initial year of the plan period. The plan was not actually
published until early 1964 but had reached a sufficiently advanced stage of drafting
to enable it to be used as the basis for the 1963/64 budget had the Minister so
desired. The coverage of the fiscal year was then changed so that the 1963/64
budget was in operation for 15 months and the next one related to the 1965
calendar year.

[32] Waterston, 1966A, chapter VII.

[33] *See 1963/64 Budget Statement,* and Killick, 1964, pp. 48–9 and especially Table IV.

[34] *See Annual Plan, 1965,* and *The Budget, 1965.*

[35] *Annual Plan, 1965,* p. 13 and *Economic Surveys,* 1964, paragraph 98, and 1965,
paragraph 108. The share of total government expenditures on economic services
fell from 39 per cent in the 1965 budget to 27 per cent in 1966, with general and
social services claiming enlarged shares (*see* Uphoff, 1970, p. 709).

[36] *7YP,* p. 220.

[37] Compare *Annual Plan, 1965,* pp. 29–33 with the section of *The Budget, 1965* containing the foreign exchange budget.

[38] *7YP,* pp. 288–90 and 295–9.

[39] J. H. Mensah, its Executive Secretary, was already complaining in 1963 that the Plan-

ning Commission had not thus far been able to influence the choice of government projects (from my notes of the April 1963 conference on the draft plan).

[40] Rimmer, 1969, p. 195. He adds that the cost of the conference hall was three to ten times as large as the provision for it in the plan. Another example was a decision a few weeks after the plan was launched to sign a protocol with a foreign government for the construction of a ₵14 million 'Olympic sports complex', which would have been incompatible with the investment programmes of the plan. *See also* Omaboe, 1966, pp. 460–1.

[41] *7YP*, p. 105 (italics in original).

[42] *7YP*, p. 233. The figure of ₵480 mentioned by Bissue was a desirable level mentioned in the plan but was not used in its foreign exchange and fiscal projections.

[43] It may be judged from the *7YP*, pp. 233–4, that export proceeds from cocoa were expected to average about ₵160 million in the first two years of the plan period.

[44] These references are from the *7YP*, pp. 14, 54, 61 and 55–6.

[45] *7YP*, pp. 11–12.

[46] Nkrumah quoted in Friedland and Rosberg, 1964, p. 260 (my emphasis). When cutting the sod at the site of a steel mill he similarly asserted that 'Ghana must go into basic industries so as to produce machines and tools for further industrialization . . .' (*Ghanaian Times*, 4 June 1962).

[47] *Annual Plan, 1965*, p. 23.

[48] In a courageous open lecture Mensah argued that Marxian concepts and class analysis had a limited applicability to the Ghanaian situation (*see* Mensah, 1965), which brought strong attacks upon him by some of the party ideologues (*see* for example, an extended critique of Mensah's lecture in the *Ghanaian Times*, 4–7 August 1964).

[49] *The Budget, 1965*, p. 13.

[50] Waterston, 1966A, p. 501, quoting a UN report on the administration of planning in Ghana.

[51] Kraus in Foster and Zolberg, 1971, p. 63.

[52] Mensah in an interview with Uphoff, 1970, p. 151.

[53] E. N. Omaboe, who acted as chairman of day-to-day meetings of the Planning Commission, in correspondence with the author.

[54] Waterston, 1966A, p. 367, observes that 'lack of adequate government support for the plans is the prime reason why most are never carried out.' Higgins, 1965, pp. 371–2, contains an illuminating discussion of the role of the planner according to the type of government with which he is working:

'1. A government with strong popular support, placing economic development high on its priority list, establishes a "decision-function" with priorities reasonably well quantified and expressed in terms of measurable economic objectives – income, employment, balance of payments, distribution of income among groups and regions, etc. This situation is "bliss" for the development planner and he can work along familiar lines.

'2. The same government adds to its list of development objectives certain goals that until recently, at any rate, were considered "non-economic"; levels of literacy and general education, standards of pulic health, national security, prestige items, etc. Here the task of the development planner is a little more complicated, mainly because it is difficult to determine the appropriate accounting prices for education, health, national security, and the like. Conceptually, however, the planner's situation is no different in this case from the first one. It is a matter of measuring costs and benefits, determining opportunity costs, complementarities and linkages, etc. and the same tools of analysis can be used.

'3. Through sheer incompetence the politicians, while sincerely aiming at national welfare, fail to see planning as a problem of resource allocation and continue to insist on mutually incompatible goals, making systemative preparation and implementation of plans impossible. The planner then has two essential choices. He may stay on the job and do his best to educate the politicians, or he may resign

and try to educate the general public to the need of replacing the government.
'4. The politicians are pursuing goals which in the opinion of the planners, are contrary to the national welfare, not through ignorance but through genuine lack of
concern for it. They may be concerned simply with staying in power, or getting rich,
or preserving the privileges of a privileged class, or acquiring new territory not
worth the cost of getting it or using it, etc. In this case the planner as a technician can
have no function. As a citizen, he has a responsibility to help "get the rascals out";
and as a citizen, not as a planner, he must decide whether he can be more effective
boring from within or attacking from without. Nothing in economic science, and
little in the other social sciences, is of much help to him here.'
Nkrumah's government may best be placed in the third category, although some
would put it in the fourth.
55 See Leys, 1969, pp. 247–75, and Leys in Faber and Seers, 1972, chapter 3, for
illuminating essays on this theme.
56 Helleiner, 1972A, p. 354.
57 Two-year Plan, foreword.
58 One-year Development Plan, 1970/71.
59 Formal responsibility for planning was transferred to the Prime Minister early in 1971
but Mensah remained dominant in the formulation of government economic
policies until shortly before the 1972 coup.
60 This deadline was later extended to June 1972 but at no stage was any meaningful
political guidance offered by the government on what the thrust and policies of the
plan should be.
61 A document was prepared detailing 52 policy decisions announced in the 1970–1
budget but a high proportion of these was also not implemented.
62 See pp. 79–89. Some 77 per cent of the investment programme of the 7YP was to be
financed from domestic resources and the implicit marginal saving rate was 0·3.
63 See chapter 4, passim. It can be calculated from Table 4.A that 69 per cent of gross
domestic fixed capital formation in 1960–5 was financed by domestic saving.
64 The following summarizes the main features of chapter 13 of the 7YP. The plan
envisaged budgetary savings equivalent to 41 per cent of government capital
expenditures.
65 ibid., p. 276. Deficit financing was to amount to ₵112 million over the seven-year
period, commencing at an annual rate of ₵20 million and tapering off to ₵14
million p.a. in the last three plan years. Domestic non-bank borrowing, net of
domestic public debt servicing, was to total only ₵24 million over the plan period.
66 In particular, see Lotz and Morss, 1967; Chelliah, 1971; and Bahl, 1972.
67 Bahl, Table 3.
68 ibid., Table 5.
69 Chelliah, 1971, studied the income elasticities of tax revenues for 27 developing
countries from 1953–5 to 1966–6 (see his Table 1). Of these Ghana's elasticity was
far lower than any of the others, with a value of 0·69 against a median value for the
group of 1·3.
70 Revenue from the cocoa export duty went down from ₵30.6 million in 1960–1 to
₵19.7 million in 1965. See Ahmad, 1965, pp. 13–15, on the structure of the cocoa
duty, and Killick, 1966, p. 382, on the instability of this revenue source.
71 See Economic Survey, 1969, Table III.
72 The tax proposals of the 1963–4 and 1965 budgets were estimated at the time to raise
new revenues equivalent to 27 per cent and 29 per cent of the expected receipts
from the previous year's tax structure. The 1961–2 budget, under the influence of
advice by Nicholas Kaldor, also envisaged a major increase in the general level of
taxation, estimated at the time as equivalent to 35 per cent of receipts from the
previous year's tax structure (including revenue from a compulsory saving
scheme).
73 See Table 4.1.
74 Bissue, 1965 p. 150.

[75] Please, 1967.

[76] The increases in development and consumption expenditures between 1960–1 and 1965 recorded in Table 6.3 were 69 per cent and 58 per cent respectively; in Table 6.2 over the same period capital and current expenditures grew by 59 per cent and 64 per cent.

[77] Ahmad, 1970, Chapters III and IV, for example, places heavy emphasis on the adverse effects of the rapid growth of government consumption.

[78] *See* Scott, 1967, p. 119.

[79] Although there was a remarkable stability in export earnings from 1959 to 1965 this was much less true in the following and preceding years.

[80] The deficiencies in the data were particularly serious on investment and production. The situation was worsened during the first half of the sixties by an increasing tendency for Nkrumah to be shielded from the real truth on the state of the economy by sycophantic or apprehensive colleagues and advisers (*see* Kraus, 1971, p. 61, and Green, 1971, p. 257.) It required a major and courageous effort by officials who did not number among Nkrumah's confidants to inform him of the gravity of the situation in 1965.

[81] Ahmad, 1966, Table I, gives figures indicating that in 1957–8 to 1965 actual revenues deviated from planned revenues by an annual average of ± 21·5 per cent.

[82] The timing of the fiscal year was changed four times between 1961–2 and 1966–7.

[83] Even the Chicago school holds this point of view, arguing that the short-run connection between money supply and the level of economic activity is not well enough understood (or stable enough) for monetary policy to be a reliable weapon of stabilization except in the longer term. This was validated for Ghana by the researches of Blomqvist, 1971, who found a lagged demand function for real money balances which was fairly stable in the longer run but was unpredictable on a year-by-year basis. For more discussion of the possibilities of effective monetary policies in Ghana in the circumstances of the early sixties *see* Killick, 1966, pp. 430–4.

[84] Gbedemah explicitly linked the planned budgetary suplus of 1957/8 with the deficits on the current account of the balance of payments, which first appeared in 1956 – see *Parliamentary Debates*, 29 May 1957, cols. 306–323. *See* also Nkrumah's foreword to the *Second Development Plan*, 1959–64.

[85] As a rift emerged between Nkrumah and Gbedemah, the latter was first demoted to Minister of Health and then, after making a speech in opposition to the government's policy of 'preventive detention', went into exile in the autumn of 1961. For accounts of fiscal policy in the late fifties and early sixties *see* Scott, 1967, Chapter III, and Ahmad, 1966, *passim*.

[86] Scott. p. 93, shows that large supplementary estimates were passed during the course of each fiscal year to make provision for items not included in the original budgets. Ahmad, 1966, Table 1, shows that in 1960–1 to 1963–6 actual expenditures exceeded the budgeted figures by an average of nearly 9 per cent, and revenues fell short of expectations by about 7 per cent.

[87] The expenditure provisions of the 1963–4 budget totalled ₵288 million. *See* Ahmad, 1966, pp. 5–6, and Killick, 1965, pp. 42–6, for discussions of the 1965 budget; *see also* Nkrumah's sessional address to Parliament, 12 January 1965.

[88] *See* Amoako-Atta's summary of their recommendations in the *1965 Supplementary Budget*, pp. 3–4.

[89] Nkrumah in his sessional address to Parliament, 1 February 1966.

[90] Ahmad, 1966, pp. 6–8.

[91] *1966 Budget Statement*, paragraph 115.

[92] Kraus, 1971, pp. 64–5.

[93] As quoted by Uphoff, 1970, pp. 743–4.

[94] For a lucid and valuable study of the deficit financing of this period *see* Ahmad, 1970, whose data and analysis are used extensively in the following paragraphs.

[95] *See* Killick, 1965, pp. 36–40, for an elaboration of this point. Ahmad, 1970, Table 2, shows that in 1964 and 1965 the banks' liquidity ratios were above 60 per cent.

[96] For a discussion of the early policies of the Bank of Ghana and the operation of the currency board system, *see* Killick, 1966, chapter 13.

[97] *See* Bank of Ghana *Annual Report, 1961–2*, p. 23.

[98] For an explanation of this *see* Ahmad, 1970, pp. 61–4.

[99] From Scott, 1967, Tables D.3 and D.4, and the Bank of Ghana *Annual Report, 1966–7*, Table 9, it can be estimated that the public sector (including para-statal bodies) was indebted to the banks by ₵310 million, out of total bank credit of ₵359 million. Scott (p. 109) suggests that credit policies discriminated against the private sector. It is more likely, however, that the private sector was simply not very interested in borrowing. Foreign firms tended to be excessively liquid because they were unable to repatriate their profits. There was a much reduced volume of importation by the private sector, there was much under-utilization of capacity, and inventory levels were generally low. The expatriate commercial banks, which handled the accounts of most private companies, were generally under-lent and could probably have extended more credit to private borrowers had there been a demand for it.

[100] *See* Table 4.C, column (2).

[101] Kindleberger, 1963, p. 250, makes the interesting point that, by reducing the marginal propensity to import to zero, the imposition of import controls increases the size of the multiplier and hence the impact on money incomes of any domestic expansionary impulse. With inelastic aggregate supply, this effect would intensify inflationary pressures.

[102] Ahmad, 1970, Table 5.

[103] Blomqvist, p. 21 and Appendix I, shows that actual price increases in 1962 to 1965 were somewhat less than could be predicted from the monetary expansion of those years. If in the quantity theory equation $MV = PT$ we make current-price GDP proxy for PT then it can be calculated that V fell in every year from 1960 to 1965, from 8.9 at the beginning to 7.0 at the end.

[104] Compare his Tables 3 and 5.

[105] *See* pp.23–4

[106] *See* Table 5.5 and the accompanying text, and especially Leith, 1973, chapter 2.

[107] Ahmad, 1970, especially pp. 110–11.

[108] The various ways in which the shortage of foreign exchange held back the growth of the economy are traced in succeeding chapters, especially chapters 8 and 10. *See also* Leith, 1973, chapter 4.

7 Modernization without Growth

Earlier chapters have shown that Nkrumah shared with mainstream development economists a belief in the necessity for fundamental structural changes if the economy was to be modernized, and in the efficacy of a big investment push to achieve this result. It has also been shown that a very large investment effort was indeed undertaken, with estimated net investment rising as high as 16 per cent of NNP in 1964–5,[1] but that the economy failed to grow in response.

Other observers have commented on this phenomenon of 'investment without growth' in Ghana, and the task of this chapter is to examine the structural changes that occurred in the economy and to begin to account for the growth failure. This task is taken further in chapter 8 and the two chapters are best read together.

Structural Changes in The Sixties
In his researches into past patterns of growth Professor Kuznets has identified the chief types of structural change that were associated with modern economic growth – changes much more marked than in premodern eras.[2] The most important included a shift in production and employment in favour of industry, an infusion of industries embodying modern techniques of production, a change in factor proportions in favour of human and physical capital, a growing importance of public utilities and social services, an increasingly complex network of intersectoral flows, and development of the institutional framework of economic activity. Changes along each of these lines occurred in Ghana during the period under review.

First, there was industrialization. This is dealt with more fully in the next chapter, but some indicators can be mentioned here. The first is that while the GNP was growing at around 2·5 per cent annually, constant-price manufacturing value-added grew at 8·8 per cent in 1962–70.[3] As stated, these figures tend to exaggerate the relative rise of manufacturing, for domestically priced value-added (even in constant prices) tends to be over-stated because of protection. Valued in world prices, output and growth would be smaller.[4] On the other hand, figures of value-added fail to indicate the full extent of the industrial expansion that occurred in the first half of the sixties, because, for reasons discussed later, output tended to lag far behind the productive capacity that was built.

In fact, the industrial base was expanded so rapidly that by the end of the decade the manufacturing sector was dominated by plants that did not exist ten years earlier. Thus, of Steel's sample of manufacturing firms, almost four-fifths had been established during the sixties and other data are roughly consistent with his sample.[5] As another illustration we may take a calculation that of the 43 import items having a value of ₡1 million or more in 1960, only 11 were then also being produced in Ghana in significant quantities; by 1970 I estimate that 33 of these same items were locally produced, most of the remainder being machinery and transport equipment.[6]

The structure of employment was also being industrialized. Recorded employment in manufacturing rose at about 8·0 per cent a year in 1962–70, as compared with 2·2 per cent growth of total employment in 1960–70.[7] We have already seen in chapter 4 that non-agricultural employment grew nearly two-and-a-half times as fast as agricultural employment between the two census years. The infusion of modern technologies that Kuznets refers to of course went with the industrialization and will be commented on rather extensively in chapter 8. However, it was not confined to the industrial sector. Large sums were spent on the transfer of modern technology to agriculture, and on attempts to replace traditional distributive and other service activities with more modern, capital-intensive substitutes – all points that will be taken up later.

As regards changing factor proportions, data presented in chapter 4 have already indicated the enormous growth in the stock of fixed capital, especially in the first half of the decade, with an estimated 80 per cent increase between 1960 and 1965. Physical capital increased relative both to the labour force and national product. However, human capital formation, in the form of educational expansion, was also proceeding at a rapid pace, producing by the end of the decade a greatly expanded flow of 'high-level' manpower. This is illustrated in Table 7.1 below, with fuller details in Appendix Table 7.A. Most of the educational expansion took place in the first half of the decade[8] and by 1970 had resulted in an expansion of the stock of educated high-level manpower of between 70 and 169 per cent, depending upon which figure one starts with. Here again, then, Ghana was exhibiting one of the traits of modernization.

The growth of public utilities and social services identified as characterizing modern economic growth also occurred in Ghana, as already recorded in the discussion of Table 4.3. To judge from the weighted index presented there, the output of public goods went up at about 4·5 per cent per annum in real terms in 1960–9 – about three times as fast as total GNP. Again, Ghana conformed to past processes of modernization by developing a more complex network of inter-sectoral transactions. Comparison of input:output tables for 1960 and 1968 shows inter-sectoral flows rising as a proportion of value-added from 9·5 per cent to 13·2 per cent.[9] It will be shown later that achievements in this direction were much less than they might and ought to have been but Ghana was nevertheless losing some of the simplicity of structure characteristic of underdeveloped economies.

TABLE 7.1
Stocks of Capital and Educated High-level Manpower: Illustrative Estimates, Selected Years[a]

	1960	1965	1970
1. Fixed capital stock (₵ mn.)	1,684	3,034	3,500
2. Educated high-level manpower stock			
(a) High estimate	48,829	56,269	83,043
(b) Low estimate	24,107	35,033	64,814
3. Index of (2) (1960 = 100)			
(a) High estimate	100	115	170
(b) Low estimate	100	145	269
4. Fixed capital per high-level worker (₵000)			
(a) With high manpower estimate	34·5	53·9	42·1
(b) With low manpower estimate	69·9	86·6	54·0

NOTE:
[a] For sources and further details see appendix Table 7.A.

Finally, there was a development of the institutional framework of the economy, associated with modernization. There was, for example, a significant growth of the financial system, with the creation and development of a larger number of financial intermediaries – the Bank of Ghana, Ghana Commercial Bank, the National Investment Bank, the Agricultural Development Bank, a building society, and so on – and with an improved network of commercial bank branches attracting a substantial rise in the real value of savings.[10] We should refer also to other para-statal bodies created in this period, like the Volta River Authority, the Electricity Corporation and the various marketing boards, which affected the institutional structure of the economy in major ways.[11]

The developments just mentioned were all manifestations of the large increase in state involvement in the economy during the later Nkrumah years – an increase which itself represented a major institutional change. Besides creating many public institutions, the central government itself became much more involved in economic life, through the introduction of administrative controls, a widened tax base,[12] and a greatly increased share of total investment activity. The data are not good enough to permit more than the roughest estimate of its overall share of investment but it appears to have been at least 60 per cent in 1960–5, and 80 per cent or more if we exclude house-building.[13] When state investment was cut back after 1966 the small amount of private investment was laid bare, for net investment plunged almost to zero in the latter part of the decade.[14]

In appearance, then, Ghana's economy was being modernized in conformity with the classical patterns of development. 'Investment without growth' does not adequately describe the paradox of the Ghanaian economy, for it was also a case of 'modernization without growth'. Why should these changes have failed to generate the growth that was associated with prior experiences of modernization?

Time Lags and Utilization Problems

Various writers have argued that Nkrumah's investments could only be expected to generate significant growth in the longer term and that he should not, therefore, be assessed on the performance of the six-ties.[15] The first strand of the argument is that the composition of government investment tended to be rather heavily weighted towards infrastructure and, since the state took over most investment in the first half of the sixties, this was liable to bias total capital formation away from directly productive activities in favour of projects yielding their returns only over a long period. The *Seven-year Plan*, it is true, intended to change the pattern of government capital expenditures in favour of productive activities but this shift proved difficult to achieve.[16] The massive Volta river hydro-electricity project, which was largely constructed in 1963–5 and cost well over ₵100 million, was the most obvious case in point. Here was a major addition to the country's capital assets whose benefits would only be enjoyed over many years.

It could secondly be argued that physical capital formation was outstripping the availability of co-operant factors of production, so that diminished returns could be anticipated in the short run. The large investments in education would restore a better balance between cap-ital and skill availabilities, but only after a substantial time-lag, as young people progressed through the educational system and began to acquire experience at work. Over time, shortages of skill would be alleviated, past investments would become more productive, and the growth rate would increase.

It could, thirdly, be argued that gestation periods of investment in the first half of the sixties were unusually long, again having the effect of deferring the benefits of investments to a later date. Here again, the Volta project could be invoked, involving large expenditures over several years before the power turbines could be switched on and the associated aluminum smelter could go into production.[17] But there were additional reasons for thinking that gestation periods were lengthening, at least for government projects. These had to do with the difficulties that were experienced in planning the construction of capital projects in a sensibly phased manner. As the 1963 *Economic Survey* put it:[18]

> although the government has signed many agreements for factories with overseas companies or governments, and although in some cases the plant and machinery have arrived in the country, the civil engineering works have not been carried out and as a result the factories have not gone into production.

Finally, such arguments pointed to the diminishing rate of utilization of the capital stock during the late Nkrumah years. Two distinct reasons could be given. One was that many projects had been built ahead of demand and could only hope to gradually achieve their theoretical capacity output. The Volta project and other examples could be given. There were other restraints on the supply side of the market. Shortages of specific skills, of spare parts and of raw materials all conspired to produce under-utilization. The difficulties which were experienced in obtaining adequate and dependable supplies of local raw materials, and dislocations caused by the operation of import licences were especially serious, as the discussion of import controls in chapter 10 demonstrates. Whether the cause lay with demand or supply the implication was the same: that over time, as supply problems and/or market limitations were overcome, utilization would improve, costs would fall and the economy would obtain greater benefits from the investments of the past.

This latter type of argument is supported by evidence that there was much underutilization of capacity in the later sixties, summarized below:

(a) The government estimated that at the end of 1966 actual manufacturing output was only one-fifth of the single-shift capacity of installed plant,[19] and Steel also found much below-capacity production of manufactures later in the decade.[20]

(b) The 1965 *Annual Plan* presented data on state industrial enterprises showing that their actual production in 1963–4 was only 29 per cent of capacity.[21]

(c) The mines controlled by the State Gold Mining Corporation achieved in 1969 a level of output only 59 per cent of the output achieved in 1961, while the labour force decreased by only 11 per cent.[22]

(d) The large number of state farms set up in the first half of the period had a theoretical production potential vastly in excess of achieved output. Thus, 104,000 acres were planted on state farms in 1965 as compared with acreage available for cultivation of 1,026,000. It was estimated that in 1966 the total number of nearly 4,000 tractors in the country were only about 20 per cent utilized.[23]

(e) A transport study found that virtually all Ghana's roads were greatly underutilized and that, 'The road system presently in place can accommodate present traffic volumes and any projected volumes at an approximate six per cent annual growth rate at least until 1980 and in most instances well beyond 1980.'[24] This was partly due to an ageing fleet of commercial vehicles and to a deterioration during most of the sixties in the standard of road maintenance.[25]

(f) The same study estimated that the existing permanent way and rolling stock of Ghana Railways was sufficient for handling approximately twice as much freight as was actually being conveyed in the late sixties. In 1968 the railway handled about 20 per cent less cargo than in the early sixties even though it had a larger labour force at the end of the period.[26]

(g) A similar report on telecommunications concluded that, 'For the money expended in the past, Ghana could at the present time be providing much better service than it is now able to offer.'[27]

(h) Trawlers purchased for deep-sea fishing, in both the public and private sectors, were underutilized and some that achieved notoriety in Ghana were never used at all.[28]

These pieces of evidence are reinforced by the results of a macroeconomic study by Newman, although neither the data nor the methodology permit treating the results as more than illustrative.[29] Further details are given in Appendix B, which sets out national estimates of overall utilization (excluding agriculture). With 1960 = 100, overall utilization in 1965 is estimated at 55·0 and only 50·5 in 1969. These figures imply an apparently extreme fall in utilization levels in the first half of the decade but they are consistent with the independent evidence already presented.

The implication for the policy-makers who succeeded Nkrumah seemed clear: large increases in domestic production were obtainable simply by bringing existing resources into fuller use, by bringing the economy nearer to its production frontier. The figures in Appendix B suggest that non-agricultural output could have been more than doubled if utilization were restored to the 1960 level. On this reasoning Nkrumah's successors stood to be the main beneficiaries of his policies, and the strategy of the NLC was based precisely on this reasoning. Their attempts, while cutting investment, to maintain economic growth by improving utilization and completing the more promising of partly-completed projects, was not entirely without success. But the basic truth is that the economy was just as stagnant after Nkrumah as in the earlier part of the decade, with virtually no growth in total GDP during 1964–9.[30] More foreign exchange was allocated for the importation of industrial raw materials and spares, and controls were gradually removed from these items – but the rate of expansion of industrial value-added fell to only about half its former level.[31] Import liberalization was carried much further by the Busia government which also expanded domestic demand. This should have brought even more capacity into production but, so far as the data permit us to say, the economy continued to stagnate and the result was inflation and a balance of payments crisis rather than increased output. How can we explain the behaviour of an economy that is apparently functioning far below its production frontier but behaves as if fully employed?

First, not all the arguments deployed earlier are watertight. For example, the argument that capital formation in the first half of the sixties became more heavily biased towards infrastructural projects with long pay-off-periods is not borne out by figures on the composition of capital formation, given in the *Economic Surveys*. While there were admittedly substantial variations between individual years, overall the proportions of capital formation devoted to transport and other types of equipment rose between 1955–9 and 1960–5 from 27 per cent to 32 per cent and the share going to buildings (chiefly residential housing) fell from 52 per cent to 47 per cent.

This is not to deny that much investment in the later Nkrumah period was in infrastructure, but we should also consider the pattern of capital formation in the fifties. The strategy then was to build up infrastructure in the hope of inducing more directly productive investment. The sixties should have been, and presumably were, beneficiaries of these investments, which should have been raising the returns from past and current directly productive investments, through improved systems of distribution, communications, water and power. Given the shift in favour of directly productive investments in the first half of the sixties and the effects of earlier investments, the productivity of investment should have risen rather than fallen.

Arguments to the effect that physical capital formation outstripped the availability of skilled manpower similarly need substantial modification, for educational expansion began in the fifties and was already producing a larger flow of trained manpower by the earlier sixties. However, it failed to keep pace with physical capital formation in the first half of the decade, as is shown in Table 7.1 above. Fixed capital per 'high-level' worker is shown there as rising very substantially during the first five years. What is more noteworthy, though, is that by 1970 it seems more likely than not that the ratio was down to the 1960 level, perhaps even below it. This further increases the puzzle of why so little progress was made in raising productivity in the second half of the decade. No doubt, the rapid expansion of the school system resulted in lower standards, and the educationalists were not necessarily producing the types of skill most needed in the economy, for there remained many serious shortages of specific skills.[32] Moreover, the youthful age-structure of the trained labour force inevitably meant that much of it lacked practical experience. But despite these qualifications, it surely remains surprising that so little economic benefit appears to have been enjoyed in the latter part of the decade from Nkrumah's education drive. It appears that the barriers to improved utilization were rather deep-rooted ones and that we must look elsewhere for explanations of the paradox of modernization without growth.

This is especially so if we study other aspects of the pattern of factor proportions. There was no general shortage of land in the sixties, for large areas were virtually uncultivated and agricultural practices remained land-intensive.[33] There was similarly no general shortage of labour, for substantial unemployment and under-employment may be presumed to have persisted throughout the decade. Thus if we look at the total picture, the argument that capital formation in the late Nkrumah years failed to produce adequate returns in the short run because of shortages of co-operant factors is an unconvincing one.

In the search for alternative explanations, it is instructive to compare the record of the sixties with that of an earlier period in which the structure of the economy was also in transition, utilizing the results of Szereszewski's pioneering research on Ghana's economy from 1891–1911.[34]

A Historical Comparison

Szereszewski's thesis is as follows. Prior to about 1890 the economy was in a low-level equilibrium, with traditional production and consumption the predominant form of economic activity. Then in the last decade of the nineteenth and the first decade of the twentieth centuries major changes occurred in the structure of the economy. The share of traditional consumption began to fall as new activities came to the fore, much higher levels of investment were attained, the relative importance of international trade increased and the composition of exports was radically transformed. The most important change was the creation of the cocoa industry; exports of this product rose from nothing in 1891 to comprise almost half total export earnings twenty years later. There was a simultaneous growth in the output of gold following the establishment of Ashanti Goldfields' mine in 1897.

In this period, unlike the sixties, structural change was accompanied by rapid growth. Order-of-magnitude national accounts show an average growth rate (in constant prices) of 7·6 per cent p.a. in 1891–1911, rising as high as 9·4 per cent in the second decade.

What induced these changes? Szereszewski contends that the level of economic activity in 1891 was essentially constrained by the volume of labour services being offered. This, in turn, was a function of the 'terms of transformation', i.e. the efficiency with which marginal increases in work could be transformed into imported consumer goods and other desired items. The efficiency of transformation would depend upon the marginal productivity of labour in export activities and upon the terms of trade received by workers. The supply of labour in 1891 was only being partially utilized because the efficiency of transformation was such that much potential labour was actually devoted to leisure. Then came the reaslization that cocoa cultivation offered a much improved efficiency of transformation. The possibility of acquiring imported consumables, services and housing through the cultivation of cocoa caused the marginal utility of income to rise above the marginal disutility of work, leisure was forgone and the cocoa industry was created.[35]

The creation of this industry, based upon the capitalization of formerly idle labour, was the chief motive force of growth and structural change in this period, but supporting it was the development of the gold-mining industry and associated investments in a railway. By 1911 the value of gold exports was about two-thirds the value of cocoa exports but the direct impact of the gold industry on the national economy was less than this ratio might suggest, for it was an enclave development of the type usually associated with colonialism, imposing 'a factor combination which does not derive from the internal availabilities, and consequently does not offer a wide range of employment to local factors of production . . .' (Szeresewski, 1966, p. 105). Between them, however, these two new industries induced major increases in construction, service activities and government expenditures, which also, of course, stimulated economic expansion.

While precisely this pattern of development was not an available option at the beginning of the sixties, there are large and suggestive contrasts between the process described by Szereszewski and the developments of the 1960s, summarized in the following interconnected points:

(a) Development in 1891–1911 was export-oriented, firmly based upon demonstrated comparative advantage. Development in the sixties, on the other hand, was inward-looking, neglected exports and, as is ahown in the next chapter, was sometimes based upon activities in which Ghana apparently had large comparative disadvantages.

(b) The expansion of agricultural activities was at the heart of the earlier period of structural change, whereas agriculture remained stagnant in the sixties, with the emphasis very heavily on industrialization.

(c) In both periods there were major additions to the country's capital stock but the economic burdens these imposed on the national economy were far greater in the sixties. Much of the investment occurring in 1891–1911 took the form of the capitalization of labour which had formerly been enjoyed as leisure, and the social cost of this to the national economy was minimal. In contrast, the capital formation of the sixties used imported techniques and

equipment, and imposed large social costs in savings and foreign exchange.
(d) If the investments in cocoa are viewed as a capitalization of labour, the development of this industry was highly labour-intensive. It made little use of purchased producer goods, required virtually no imported inputs and only small amounts of managerial talent. It therefore led to relatively small 'leakages' from the national economy and produced large net benefits for the balance of payments. This compared favourably with the development of the mining industry in the same period, and with the sixties. Many of the industries created in the sixties were enclaves: based upon imported technology, capital- and management-intensive, making little use of domestically produced inputs and often making small or negative contributions to foreign exchange.[36]

We are now, perhaps, in a better position to understand the paradox of modernization without growth.

Technologies and Factor Proportions
An important lesson to be drawn from the Szereszewski period is the importance of the factor proportions embodied in the development of an industry in determining how much impact it has on the rest of the economy. As Szereszewski puts it, 'there is a strong presumption that long-run prospects of development are connected with a wide absorption of local factors of production.'[37] If we consider factor proportions in the first half of the sixties we come nearer to explaining the paradox, for it was development heavily biased towards imported technologies and imported factors, favouring industries and techniques requiring large inputs of (largely imported) capital and management, relative to local labour and natural resources.

The most important sources of bias were Nkrumah's sectoral priorities, especially his emphasis on industry, power (to facilitate industrialization) and the mechanization of agriculture. There is no industrial break-down of the capital stock to demonstrate this point (if any demonstration is necessary) but the national accounts do provide industrial estimates of capital consumption and when these are expressed as proportions of gross value-added, as a rough index of relative capital intensities, power, 'large-scale' manufacturing and the service industries are shown to be the most capital-intensive activities. Agriculture and traditional manufacturing are at the opposite end of the spectrum, but these activities were low in Nkrumah's list of priorities. Capital intensity was therefore built into his industrial priorities and this, plus the tendency for manufacturing to depend upon imported materials and components, necessarily lessened the impact of his policies on overall development. However, there were also capital-intensive biases *within* industries, partly because of relative factor prices.

Even in 1960 Ghana had what has become a characteristic set of factor price distortions in developing countries.[38] Legislation and banking regulations held down interest rates, although only in the modern part of the economy, with traditional money-lenders charging far higher interest.[39] The exchange rate of the cedi was over-valued, keeping the cost of imported capital equipment below its true social cost. At the same time, minimum wage legislation raised the incomes of unskilled labourers and probably had a general upward effect on wages.[40] With the opportunity-cost of unskilled labour probably well below money wage levels and with the actual cost of capital well below its social cost,[41] investors at the beginning of the sixties already had several inducements to use capital rather than labour.

These biases became stronger during the remainder of the Nkrumah period. Roemer has shown that indices of manufacturing wages relative to capital costs rose by 20 to 25 per cent between 1960 and 1965, although the situation became less unfavourable to labour in the latter half of the decade.[42] With the exchange rate and interest rates largely unchanged in the earlier years but with industrial money-wages rising, the incentive to use capital-intensive techniques increased, although the devaluations of 1967 and 1971 and an interest-rate reform in 1971 brought relative factor prices nearer to a social optimum.

It is often argued that for technological and other reasons the elasticity of substitution between factors is too low for relative factor prices to have much impact. However, the evidence gives little support to any extreme elasticity pessimism. It is suggestive, for example, that the modern sector of the economy, which has been faced with artificially low capital costs and artificially high wages, is capital-intensive, whereas the traditional sector, which pays higher capital costs and lower wages, is far more labour-intensive. There is also substantial evidence that Ghanaians are responsive to pecuniary incentives.[43] More specifically, Roemer investigated elasticities of substitution within various manufacturing industries and found elasticities of between 0.7 and 1.3, with a cluster around 1.0.[44]

While believing that for a number of reasons his results have an upward bias, he nevertheless concluded that, 'there is promise of enough labour-capital substitution in the aggregate to make a neo-classical factor price policy worthwhile.' This he illustrates with a calculation showing that a 25 per cent fall in the index of wages relative to capital costs would be capable of creating up to 30 per cent more jobs in manufacturing within five years than would otherwise have been the case.[45] The onus of proof is therefore upon those who argue that factor prices do not matter.

Another influence was the usual preference of politicians, managers and engineers for the shiniest, technologically most advanced production processes – a preference which the biases already discussed did not discourage them from indulging. Somehow, the unemployment problem was not seen to impinge upon the choice of techniques, as is neatly illustrated by what the manager of a sugar factory told a committee of the State Planning Commission in 1965:[46]

> The manager thought labour represented a problem. The large number of labourers engaged on the plantation (formerly 680 but now reduced to 500) would not have been necessary if there were enough machinery in good condition to work with, for the sort of plantation envisaged for the factory requires mechanization. But since the machines are not available for use, the labourers . . . have to be actively engaged. When the machines become available then the problem of redeploying the labourers [has] to be considered. Fortunately, since the labourers are employees of the State Farms Corporation, they could be transferred to work on other State Farms elsewhere.

Labour displaced by machines was someone else's problem.

What is suggested by these considerations – and this is a point taken up in the next chapter – is that Nkrumah's chosen development path had severe *dynamic* limitations. Factories were imported wholesale, embodying technologies and factors adapted to the circumstances of the industrial countries in which they were developed but ill-suited to Ghana. Nkrumah was rightly critical of the dualistic nature of the economy as it had developed under colonialism but the ironical result of his own policies was to emphasize this feature of Ghana's economy.[47] At the root of this was his rejection of a strategy that would build upon existing practices, improving them by the infusion of carefully adapted foreign technologies. The traditional sector was largely ignored and much of his 'modernization' consisted of introducing islands of advanced technology and a proliferation of economic enclaves, increasing the contrasts between the traditional and modern sectors. Inter-sectoral flows did increase, but not to the extent that they could have done.

If biases in investment decisions had an adverse effect on their potential for the development of Ghana's economy so, too, did a decline in the quality of investment decisions. As pointed out earlier, most investment decisions were made by the state in the earlier sixties but there is much evidence that many of these had little economic rationale. As is illustrated in following chapters, the absorptive capacity of the public sector to 'invest in soundly conceived development programmes and projects that can be carried out well and operated economically upon completion'[48] became severely over-strained. Berg has put the point vividly:[49]

> By 1965 Ghana was an administrative jungle. There were thirty-one ministries. Statutory corporations were scattered all over the place. It is not certain that at any one time anyone knew just how

many there were. Key operating Ministeries were cut up perio-
dically, their functions divided, then shuttled back and forth . . .
Now the absorption of these new administrative units and the
coordination of all the new functions of the public sector would have
been a Herculean job even if there were lots of trained people available, little politicization of decision-making and firmly-established
institutions for making considered economic decisions.

As Berg implies, there was much politicization of decision-making.
Omaboe complained that,[50]

In Ghana the politicians are always ahead of the civil servants and
planners in the general consideration and implementation of
economic and social projects. This has meant that almost all important projects have had to be initiated by politicians who on many
occasions have taken their decisions and committed the nation to a
certain course of action before the technicians were consulted.

Since they wanted quick results, it is not surprising that the politicians
were ahead of the civil servants, for when in later years government
investment was determined more by the rate at which the civil service
could prepare projects the tempo dropped to something of a snail's
pace. But the politicians were not only concerned with promoting
economic development; sometimes they had very different objectives
in mind. They were certainly impatient of the time consumed by
thorough project appraisals. The result was large inputs of human and
inanimate capital impotent to generate economic growth because
devoted to low-productivity projects. And once the money was misspent it was lost forever.

Several of the themes of this chapter are taken up again in the following one, which ends by drawing conclusions from both.

Appendix to Chapter 7

A Educated High-level Manpower Supplies, 1960–70

TABLE 7.A
Illustrative Estimates of Educated High-level Manpower Supplies, 1960–70

Output of Educational System	1960	1961	1962	1963	1964	1965	1966	1967	1968	1969	1970
1. Teachers											
a. post-middle schools	1,221	1,188	670	900	—	586	1,076	1,862	1,504	3,542	2,378
b. post-secondary schools	130	136	151	179	179	197	200	195	261	579	925
2. Secondary school graduates[a] (net)	666	884	934	1,226	1,533	2,123	2,876	3,303	3,187	3,901	4,357
3. Technical school and polytechnic graduates[b]	600	600	600	600	600	600	600	600	600	600	600
4. University graduates[c]	(150)[f]	(160)[f]	177	222	228	481	526	596	665	806	819
5. TOTAL OUTPUT	2,767	2,968	2,532	3,127	2,540	3,987	5,278	6,556	6,217	9,428	9,079
Wastage from Pre-existing Stock											
6. High estimate[d]	1,425	1,465	1,510	1,541	1,588	1,617	1,688	1,796	1,938	2,067	2,288
7. Low estimate[d]	660	723	791	843	911	960	1,051	1,178	1,339	1,485	1,724
Net Increase											
8. With large initial stock (5–6)[d]	1,342	1,503	1,022	1,586	952	2,370	3,590	4,760	4,279	7,361	6,791
9. With small initial stock (5–7)[d]	2,107	2,245	1,741	2,284	1,629	3,027	4,227	5,378	4,878	7,943	7,355
Total Stock at Year End											
10. With large initial stock[d]	48,829	50,332	51,354	52,940	53,892	56,262	59,852	64,612	68,891	76,252	83,043
11. With small initial stock[d]	24,107	26,352	28,093	30,377	32,006	35,033	39,260	44,638	49,516	57,459	64,814
12. Index of 10 (1960=100)	100	103	105	108	110	115	123	132	141	156	170
13. Index of 11 (1960=100)	100	109	117	126	133	145	163	185	205	238	269

Fixed Capital Stock

14. Fixed capital stock in 1960 prices[e] (¢ mn.)	1,684	1,959	2,183	2,460	2,727	3,034	3,232	3,312	3,363	3,420	(3500)[f]
15. Capital per high-level worker (¢ 000)											
a. with large initial stock	34·5	38·9	42·5	46·5	50·6	53·9	54·0	51·3	48·8	44·9	42·1
b. with small initial stock	69·9	74·3	77·7	81·0	85·2	86·6	82·3	74·2	67·9	59·5	54·0

Sources: Ministry of Education; *1960 Population Census*, Vol. IV, Table 8; *Survey of High-Level Manpower*, 1960; T. M. Brown, 1972, Table D–1. I should like to acknowledge the great assistance of Mr Peter Williams in devising this table.

NOTES:

[a] Output of Ghana government secondary school fifth form raised by 5 per cent to allow for returnees from foreign secondary schools and a further 10 per cent for output of private secondary schools in Ghana, *minus* 10 per cent allowance for graduates going overseas, 200 p.a. admission into polytechnics, admissions into universities and post-secondary teacher training courses, and an assumed 15 per cent examination failure rate.

[b] Would normally take up posts as artisans or technicians (rough estimate).

[c] Graduates with first degrees.

[d] The high estimate for the stock at the beginning of 1960 is taken from the census results (see sources) at 47,487; in the low estimate this figure is adjusted to 22,000 on the basis of detailed comparisons of the census results, and data contained in the 1960 *Survey of High-level Manpower* and in Jolly, 1969 Table 1–I. Wastage has been calculated throughout at the rate of 3 per cent of the stock at the beginning of the year.

[e] Gross capital stock.

[f] Approximate estimate.

Appendix to Chapter 7

B *On the Measurement of Excess Capacity*

The estimates set out below result from the application of improved data to a linear-logarithmic Cobb-Douglas type of production function derived by Newman from 1960 cross-section data on non-agricultural inputs and outputs in Ghana by region. The equation obtained was:

$$\log_{10}Y = -0 \cdot 44672 + 0 \cdot 61544 \log_{10}K + 0 \cdot 37129 \log_{10}L$$
$$(7.760) \qquad\qquad (3.235)$$

where

Y = gross domestic product excluding agriculture, ₵ millions, in 1960 prices;

K = non-agricultural capital stock, ₵ millions, 1960 prices;

L = non-agricultural employment, thousands of persons.

Fitting this to the cross-sectional data resulted in a coefficient of correlation of 0·99 and large t-values (in brackets above) for the independent variables. The sum of the two coefficients was very close to 1·0, indicating constant returns to scale outside agriculture. Newman also tested this function by fitting it to data on the later 1950s and obtained a fairly good predictive value.

The sources of data employed to obtain the results below were:

for gross fixed capital stock: T. M. Brown, 1972, Table D–1 (multiplied by 2 to convert his estimates to gross figures);

for non-agricultural employment: data from chapter 4, Table 4–4, with linear growth assumed between 1960 and 1970;

for gross non-agricultural value-added: Table 4–B and data on local food consumption and cocoa value-added in various *Economic Surveys,* Singal and Nartey, 1971, and other data supplied by the CBS.

The results were as follows:

TABLE 7.B
Trends in Non-agricultural Capacity Utilization, 1960–9 (as percentage of 1960 level)

1960	100·0	1965	55·0
1961	79·7	1966	48·3
1962	77·6	1967	48·4
1963	71·3	1968	47·7
1964	68·3	1969	50·5

NOTES

[1] *See* Table 4.1.

[2] Kuznets, 1966, *passim.*

[3] Calculated from *Industrial Statistics,* 1970 and Table 4–B.

[4] *See* Little *et al.,* 1970, Table 2.13, comparing manufacturing growth rates in domestic and world prices. The later are invariably smaller, but only modestly so.

[5] *See* Steel, 1970, Table V–4, showing that 78 per cent of his sample came into production during the sixties. CBS data suggest a somewhat lower proportion but this is likely to be at least partly attributable to a diminishing representativeness of their coverage.

[6] For the original tabulation *see* Killick, 1966, Table 14.3. 'Significant' was defined as domestic output in excess of 10 per cent of 1960 trade values. An even greater extent of import-substitution is indicated if plants coming into production after 1970 or established but not yet in production are included.

[7] From *Industrial Statistics,* 1970, and Table 4–4 above.

[8] *See* Table 4.3, items 1 and 2.

[9] Calculated from Szereszewski, 1966, Table 3.1, and an unpublished input:output table for 1968. These figures are calculated from tables reduced to eight sectors in order to achieve comparability. Intra-sectoral flows have been excluded. For a detailed discussion of the sectoral structure of the economy in 1960 and of the relationship between the complexity of inter-sectoral flows and the stage of development *see* Szereszewski, chapter 3.

[10] *See* p. 70.

[11] *See* chapter 9 on this subject.

[12] *See* pp. 147–8.

[13] The Auditor General's *Report* for 1966/67 lists government investments as at mid-1966 totalling ₵238 million, which figure rises to at least ₵400 million if conservative provision is made for the Volta River Authority (at least ₵100 million – see the VRA *Annual Report* for 1966), the Black Star Line (a shipping corporation), the Water and Sewerage Corporation, Ghana Housing Corporation, Tema Development Corporation, Ghana Commercial Bank, National Investment Bank and various other organizations not included in the Auditor General's figures. Direct investments by the government, excluding statutory corporations and public institutions, are recorded by Ahmad (1970, Table XII) as totalling rather more than a further ₵400 million in 1960–5, giving a grand total of at least ₵800 million. In the same period gross domestic fixed capital formation totalled ₵1,300 million (*see* chapter 4, Table 4–A), which makes the state's share a little over 60 per cent. However, of total domestic capital formation about ₵600 was attributable to buildings (*Statistical Year Book, 1965–1966,* Table 125), which is largely an estimate of house-building. If it were possible to subtract expenditures on house-building from the total and from state investments, the remaining share of the latter could scarcely be less than 80 per cent and could easily be more. Berg (1971, p. 201) suggests a proportion in the range of 70–80 per cent of the total.

[14] *See* Table 4.1.

[15] Examples of this type of argument include Genoud, 1969; Hymer, 1971; Scott, 1967, pp. 105–6; various issues of the CBS *Economic Survey;* and, with qualifications, the present writer (Killick, 1965, pp. 25–6).

[16] *Annual Plan for 1965,* page 10.

[17] Contracts were awarded in 1961 but construction of the dam was not completed until 1966 and the Valco smelter did not go into production until 1968.

[18] *Economic Survey, 1963,* paragraph 73.

[19] This estimate was contained in a submission to Ghana's aid donors in 1966.

[20] Steel, 1972, p. 230. *See* chapter 8 for a fuller discussion of this.

[21] *Annual Plan* for 1965, Appendix 3. The average of 42 per cent shown there is incorrect, apparently being an unweighted mean.

[22] *See* chapter 9.

[23] Dadson, 1970, Table B.2, p. 302, and p. 194.

[24] Nathan Consortium, *Transportation Development in Ghana,* 1970, Main Report, p. 55.

[25] ibid., and also Ewusi, 1971B, Appendix IV.

[26] Nathan Consortium, op. cit., p. vii.

[27] Page Engineering Consultants, 1969, p. v.

[28] *See Two-year Plan,* section VI.4, on excess capacity in the fisheries industry.

[29] *See* Newman, 1970.

[30] *See* Table 4.1.

[31] The *Industrial Statistics* show that gross output in manufacturing in constant prices grew at 10·1 per cent p.a. in 1962–6 and at 10·6 per cent p.a. in 1966–70, but the comparable figures for value-added were 11·3 per cent and 6·1 per cent.

[32] Various instances are provided in later chapters. A 1968 *High-level and Skilled Manpower Survey* revealed many key shortages, especially of technical and scientific workers.

[33] It was calculated that in 1963 there were about three acres of land in cultivated areas but under fallow or virgin vegetation for every acre actually under cultivation, although there were large regional variations (Killick, 1966, p. 223). See also chapter 1.

[34] *See* Szereszewski, 1966, upon which the following description is based.

[35] Cocoa is not indigenous to Ghana. It was introduced from abroad and began to be taken up by the local farmers in the 1880s. For an excellent treatment of the early development of this industry *see* Hill, 1963.

[36] Several of the points asserted here are taken up in the next chapter.

[37] Szereszewski, 1966, p. 106.

[38] *See* Little *et al.,* 1970, especially chapter 3.

[39] *See* Killick, 1966, pp. 303–6, and sources cited there. It is difficult to generalize about interest charged by money-lenders but without doubt it is far higher than in the organized capital market.

[40] *See* Isaac, 1962, for a good discussion of the effects of minimum wage legislation; also Killick, 1966, pp. 136–42.

[41] Newman estimated the opportunity cost of capital to be in the range of 10 to 15 per cent in the late sixties and the Ministry of Finance and Planning employed a shadow interest rate of 15 per cent at the beginning of the seventies. By contrast, bank lending rates on secured loans were generally in the range of 6 to 7 per cent in the first half of the decade and 7 to 9 per cent in the second half (*see* Bank of Ghana *Annual Report* for 1968/69, Statement 7).

[42] *See* Roemer, 1971, Table 1. Other calculations in his Table 3 show increases of between 8 and 23 per cent in 1965 and improvements thereafter.

[43] *See* chapter 12.

[44] Roemer, 1972, Table 3.

[45] ibid., p. 25.

[46] Extract from the minutes of a meeting held in April, 1965.

[47] *See* chapter 1 on the dualism of the economy at the beginning of the sixties.

[48] This is Waterston's definition of absorptive capacity – *see* Waterston, 1966, p. 300.

[49] Berg. 1971, p. 211.

[50] Omaboe, 1966, pp. 460–1.

8 *The Unbalanced Growth of Agriculture and Industry*

The Strategy and its Results

Industrialization equals development: that was the base of Nkrumah's economic strategy. We saw in chapter 3 how industrialization was expected to strengthen the balance of payments, and reduce unemployment and the economy's dependence on imports, but the central point was that Nkrumah and his colleagues made no intellectual distinction between industrialization and development. Virtually all today's rich countries are industrial, *ergo* development is industrialization.

That Nkrumah and those around him viewed the matter in this way carried important implications. One was a rejection of the criterion of comparative advantage, because its application would have resulted in a slower growth of manufacturing and a continued reliance on primary production for which, as we saw, Nkrumah had a considerable contempt. He was quite explicit about his rejection of the type of reasoning which the theory of comparative advantage is based upon:[1]

> There is an argument that contends that young nations emerging from colonialism are indulging in wasteful expenditures by duplicating industries and ventures which have already been perfected by the older industrialized nations of the world, whose products are available at lower cost than for which they can be manufactured by us. It may be true in some instances that our local products cost more, though by no means all of them, and then only in the initial period. But even if it were substantially the fact, it is not an argument that we can accept. It is precisely because we were, under colonialism, made the dumping-ground of other countries' manufactures and the providers merely of primary products, that we remained backward; and if we were to refrain from building, say, a soap factory simply because we might have to raise the price of soap to the community, we should be doing a disservice to the country.

He was, therefore, little concerned with the normal criteria of economic efficiency in his pursuit of industrialization; colleagues and advisers could expect an unsympathetic hearing if they were to urge caution on such grounds.

The equation of industrialization with development also implied an attitude towards technology which guided Nkrumah's attempts during his later years. At the beginning of the sixties Ghana's economy was markedly dualistic in structure, as was pointed out in chapter 1; the modern sector was dwarfed by the traditional one, and there were few flows between them. Agriculture was dominated by peasant farmers whose methods had changed little in a hundred years.[2] Traditional processes also remained important in manufacturing, and an industrial census found in 1962 that 99 per cent of all manufacturing establishments had five or fewer paid employees (in most cases none at all).[3] In both industry and agriculture, then, Nkrumah had a choice: to build upon what already existed, to help the traditional sector gradually improve its methods and productivity – or to break with the past and to introduce ready-made technologies from abroad. Again, Nkrumah's response was explicit. Addressing a pan-African conference of farmers Nkrumah argued that the major task 'is the creation of a complete revolution in agriculture on our continent – a total break with primitive methods and organisations and with the colonial past . . .'[4] Similarly, his industrialization drive meant the creation of many new factories, rather than the encouragement of the growth and improvement of existing enterprises.

Nkrumah had political reasons for providing little assistance to the peasant farmers and for discouraging the rise of an indigenous class of private industrialists,[5] but many who did not share his political position nevertheless thought very similarly as regards development strategies. Both the CPP and the opposition, remember, were advocating industrialization and the mechanization of agriculture in the fifties, and the civil service seemed to think along similar lines. Agriculturalists had consistently urged mechanization, a report by the Deputy Food and Agriculture Officer in 1960 concluding that farmers' living standards could not be improved by traditional methods,[6] and Nkrumah's chief planner was also advocating mechanization.[7] Also, of course, many economists believed that development entailed industrialization, especially the production of import-substituting manufactures. In these respects, then, Nkrumah was merely swimming with the intellectual tide.

This was less true of his drive to increase the participation of the state in the productive system. State participation was extended in various sectors of the economy, including agriculture. The United Ghana Farmers' Council (UGFC) was charged with organizing co-operatives and the provision of agricultural extension services. A State Farms Corporation was created which rapidly expanded the number of its farms and its total land holdings, and the Workers' Brigade and the Young Farmers' League also ran farms. A Food Marketing Board was set up 'to fix minimum prices for all foodstuffs' and to improve the efficiency of the distributive system. These, then, were the new institutions to achieve the 'total break with primitive methods and organisations . . .' which Nkrumah called for.

Industrialization, mechanization and socialization were the policies. Earlier chapters have shown the general nature of their achievements. There was substantial import-substitution and manufacturing output was greatly expanded. But industrialization was accompanied by slower growth, partly because the supply of food-stuffs failed to keep pace with demand, leading to inflation and pressures for large quantities of imported foods.[8]

By other criteria the achievements were also modest. Industrialization was expected to reduce unemployment, but despite industrial expansion, total recorded employment in 'large-scale' manufacturing in 1970 was only about 1·6 per cent of the total labour force, while it contributed about 10·0 per cent of GDP, indicating the capital-intensive nature of the developments which occurred.[9] Strengthening the balance of payments was another objective, but, despite import-substitution, this was not achieved either. Ghana's experience was typical of other countries in discovering that import-substitution worsened rather than improved shortages of foreign exchange, at least for some years. Steel found that in 1967–8 about a quarter of manufacturing output was undertaken at a net loss of foreign exchange, ie foreign exchange costs exceeded the amount of foreign exchange saved.[10] There were other examples of inefficiencies of this type. Reusse, for instance, found that productivities on Ghana's modern fishing fleet were so low that it also was a net loser of foreign exchange,[11] and evidence in chapter 5 showed that major export-processing industries were probably net users of foreign exchange. These factors, and the necessity to import substantial amounts of foods which might otherwise have been grown efficiently within Ghana seriously undermined the balance of payments.

Despite Nkrumah's explicit rejection of the relevance of comparative advantage, it is also illuminating to see for those industries which did save foreign exchange how economically they did so, in terms of their use of domestic resources. Steel calculated the domestic resource costs per unit of net foreign exchange saved and compared these with alternative foreign exchange rates. An equilibrium exchange rate can be interpreted as defining the break-even point for the transformation of domestic resources into foreign exchange; in the period he was studying the exchange rate was ₡1.02=$1.00 and, had this been an equilibrium rate, it would have indicated that production should proceed when the domestic resources costs (DRCs) of earning or saving a dollar's worth of foreign exchange were less than ₡1.02, but that it would be in the national interest to import goods whose DRCs were greater than ₵1.02. Of course, that exchange rate was not an equilibrium one, so as an alternative he took the rate ₵1.53 = $1.00, implying a 50 per cent devaluation in cedi terms. Firms whose DRCs were less than ₵1.02 he labelled as 'efficient' and those with DRCs in excess of ₵1.53 were categorized as 'inefficient'. His results, summarized in Table 8.1, showed that as at 1967–8 much of Ghana's manufacturing sector was inefficient – and the position then was probably better than at the end of the Nkrumah period. Moreover, this inefficiency was not offset by the generation of externalities, so far as can be judged, for Steel did not find any which justified the high DRCs.[12]

TABLE 8.1
Efficiency Ratings of Ghanaian Manufacturing, 1967–8[a]

	domestic resource costs per unit of foreign exchange	percentage of total output
Efficient net savers of foreign exchange	<1.02	13·5
Intermediate do.	1.02–1.53	19·2
Inefficient do.	>1.53	43·3
Net losers of foreign exchange	—	24·0
		100·0

Source: Steel, 1972, Table VI.
NOTE:
[a] These figures are based on 1967–8 utilization and include provision for depreciation and a 15 per cent return on assets.

Overall, then, Nkrumah's agricultural and industrial policies were fairly unambiguous failures, and the remainder of this chapter is devoted to an examination of possible causes of this lack of success.

The Industrialization of Agriculture
The inflation of local food prices had become a highly sensitive political issue by the mid-sixties, and the position of the government was that it was a problem of distribution rather than production. Thus, the Minister of Agriculture:[13] 'There is adequate food in the country. The problem has been the failure of food agencies to get them to the market. I intend setting up a separate body within the Ministry of Agriculture to take up the distribution of food . . .'
  In the same year a Commission of Enquiry was set up to enquire into 'trade malpractices', whose report duly placed responsibility for inflation upon the inadequacies of the distributive system.[14] Governmental agencies were established to undertake food distribution, including a Food Marketing Board and Ghana Groceries, and various others, such

as the state farms and Workers' Brigade, were also involved in transportation and marketing. Was the government right to emphasize the distributive aspect of the problem?

The evidence on this question is partial and mostly indirect, but there seems little doubt that there was a decline in the efficiency of the transportation system in 1960–5. The standard of road maintenance fell[15] and feeder road construction was curtailed. The shortage of foreign exchange and resulting import controls resulted in large reductions in the number of new goods vehicles brought into the country, so that the number of Ghanaians per licensed goods vehicle rose from 489 in 1960 to 553 in 1965 (and 645 in 1969), and the average age of the vehicle fleet rose sharply.[16] Even these figures tell only part of the story because in 1963–6 there were recurring shortages of vehicle tyres and other spares so that at any one time many vehicles were likely to be off the road.

The deterioration of the transportation system was, however, a direct consequence of policy failings which could have been remedied, so it was naturally not this that was emphasized by government spokesmen. They rather blamed the middlemen for raising prices, and there was much talk about profiteering and hoarding.[17] This type of defence is much more difficult to sustain, as the evidence shows the traditional distributive system to be competitive, successful in substituting labour for capital, and reasonably efficient in coping with the highly complex task of collecting a wide variety of often perishable food-stuffs from a multitude of small farmers and transporting them over often long distances to the consumer.[18] Lorry charges for local food-stuffs seem explicable by reference to economic considerations such as length of haul, loading times, weight, value and cleanliness,[19] and other researches show the distributive system as a highly competitive one.[20]

One can compare wholesale and retail price indices for local foods to gauge changes in the efficiency of the distributive system, on the assumptions that if the system were deteriorating (a) the correlation between the two would become weaker and (b) the retail index would rise relative to the wholesale index as retail costs and profit margins went up. Examination of CBS data from March 1963 to September 1970 yielded the conclusions (1) that the two series were closely correlated throughout, but (2) that the wholesale index was the more unstable, with the retail system providing greater stability by absorbing some of the movements in wholesale prices in both directions, (3) that there was no consistent divergence between the two series taking the whole period, suggesting that the efficiency of the retail system had not changed much, but (4) retail prices rose relative to wholesale (indicating deteriorating efficiency) in 1966–8 and 1970, but moved in the opposite direction in 1963–4 and 1969.

Not too much weight should be placed on indirect evidence of this kind but in combination with facts already mentioned it strongly suggests that at most, declining distributive efficiency provides only a very partial explanation of the inflation of food prices. The periods in which food prices rose most rapidly relative to other prices were 1963–6 and 1969–71 (Figure 4.1) and these correlate poorly with the years in which our indicators suggest the distributive system to have been under the greatest stress. This is especially the case with the later years, when a substantial feeder road programme was underway.[21] Following Ewusi, I regressed changes in food prices relative to other prices upon changes in the stock of goods vehicles and, while the resulting coefficient was negative, as was to be predicted, it was not statistically significant, again suggesting that other factors were of greater importance in explaining the relative inflation of food prices.[22] Thus, while deficiencies in transportation and storage facilities did contribute to the food price inflation,[23] arguments that they were solely responsible must be rejected as much too strong. The core of the problem, I suggest, was one of inadequate output.

The task, then, is to explain a failure of agricultural production, and to do this it might be useful to develop an informal model of food production in an economy such as Ghana's. It is necessary to recall first the nature of the rural economy at the beginning of the sixties, as briefly described in chapter 1. It was almost entirely based upon small-scale peasant farming, land-intensive, using negligible inputs of purchased capital goods, and based essentially on traditional cultivation techniques. How might such an industry meet an increasing demand for its output? If, for the time being, techniques are taken as given, and a completely elastic supply of cultivable land is assumed,[24] output will be a simple function of the number of workers and the average length of their working day. The supply of labour will, in turn, primarily be a function of three things: the differential between rural and urban real earnings (which, together with expectations about prospects for urban employment, would determine the rate of urbanization); the attractiveness of cultivating food crops relative to export crops such as cocoa; and the productivity of labour (determining the amount of leisure that must be forgone in order to achieve a given output). Disregarding variations in soil qualities, raising productivity would depend upon improved practices and/or larger inputs of capital relative to labour.

If, alternatively, we hold labour supply constant, the capacity to increase output depends exclusively upon larger inputs of capital and/or improved cultivation techniques. The use of capital and better techniques thus perform two purposes: raising the output of a given labour force and inducing a larger supply of labour by increasing the attractiveness of farm work relative to urban work, or leisure. Since traditional agriculture is generally very slow to modernize itself,[25] changes in techniques and associated uses of more capital will depend upon government policy, for example through the provision of extension services.

Considering the Ghanaian situation in the light of this model, it was clear at the beginning of the sixties that powerful socio-economic forces were reducing the supply of agricultural labour relative to the supply of non-agricultural labour. Urbanization was proceeding apace,[26] and expansion of the school system meant that many youngsters who had formerly helped out on the farms were now mostly unavailable for such work. Improvements in cultivation techniques and increased use of capital were thus essential if the expected increases in demand for food resulting from population growth and improvements in per capita incomes were to be met. On this model, government agricultural policies were crucial.[27]

Except for the cocoa industry, the British showed little interest in agricultural research and extension services, but during the fifties various endeavours by the Ministries of Agriculture and Community Development met with sufficient success to enable a national extension service to begin by the end of the decade.[28] Given good advice based on sound research, it was found that farmers responded well, so the development and support of research and extension work was a serious policy option for Nkrumah's government.[29]

In substance, if not in form, it was an option they rejected. In 1962 responsibility for extension work was transferred from the Ministry of Agriculture to the United Ghana Farmers' Council (UGFC), the farmers' wing of the CPP, whose economic activities had hitherto been confined to the marketing of cocoa. Among its new responsibilities were the provision of advice to farmers, the formation of agricultural co-operatives, and 'To accept the leadership of the CPP and its Government materially, financially and morally.'[30] Its legal form was obscure but in practice it did what the party and the government bade it do, and was in no way accountable to the farmers.[31] Many of the Ministry of Agriculture's extension staff were transferred to government farms and the remainder were absorbed by the United Ghana Farmers' Council.

The results were disastrous. The UGFC lacked the expertise, administrative capacity and motivation to operate an extension service. Its officials used their positions to cheat the farmers,[32] who became increasingly hostile to the organizaion which was supposed to help them. Extension work was further hamstrung by serious shortages of imported supplies such as matchets, fertilizers and seed. The result was that such extension service as had existed at the beginning of the sixties deteriorated drastically. An official enquiry concluded in 1966 that 'The effect . . . of the UGFCC on farmers has been sinister and the farmers' discontent and apparent hostility towards the UGFCC . . . is justified and hardly to be wondered at.'[33] Another observer concluded that:[34]

For farmers in Ghana the word 'co-operative' had come to be associated with the UGFCC, which was virtually a wing of the CPP, and with exploitation of farmers by petty party officials. On the Volta resettlements farmers regarded co-operative organisation not as voluntary but as a scheme imposed by authority and inferior to their traditional practices.

However, it was not on the extension service and the mobilization of the peasant farmers that Nkrumah pinned his hopes for his 'complete revolution in agriculture'. Given the paucity of past agricultural research, with no developments even remotely comparable with those that led in Asia to the 'green revolution' of improved hybrid varieties, a policy of depending upon improvements in traditional agriculture could promise only gradual results. Improved varieties of oil-palm, coconut and cotton did exist but there were few research results upon which to base an improvement programme for the major food crops. In short, the extension service did not have much to extend; concentration on research and extension could only offer large results in the longer term but Nkrumah was in too much of a hurry for that. He decided that the 'total break with primitive methods' would have to be achieved through the large-scale importation of foreign technology and his strategy might be described as the industrialization of agriculture. In essence, it was a strategy of *mechanization*, although plans also existed for many irrigation projects.

The politicians, agriculturalists and officials who were at one in advocating mechanization did so in the teeth of past experience, for an attempt at mechanized farming in the north of the country during the fifties had proved an expensive failure and an official summing-up on it concluded that, 'the fundamental lesson is, without doubt, that the new ways cannot at present compete with traditional methods of agriculture as practiced in that region.'[35] Considerable evidence was also accumulating elsewhere in Africa that mechanization was generally unsuccessful.[36] Nevertheless, that was the policy and four organizations were made responsible for executing it: the UGFC was responsible for mechanized 'co-operative' farms; the Young Farmers' League ran a few settlement farms; by 1965 the Workers' Brigade was running 10 mechanized farms; most important of all, the State Farms Corporation was by 1965 managing 105 farms, about half of which were new, most of the remainder being former demonstration and experimental stations hived off from the Ministry of Agriculture.

The UGFC's endeavours to establish mechanized co-operative farms met with little success, largely because they were unable to deliver the tractor-ploughing services and other technical supports which the farms needed.[37] So, to all intents, Nkrumah's agricultural strategy depended upon the performance of government farms. In agriculture, more than in any other sector, success or failure hinged

upon the performance of public enterprise. Performance, unfortunately, was lamentable. Assessing the achievements of public enterprises can be a difficult matter, as is demonstrated in the next chapter,
but no such difficulty presents itself in the case of Ghana's socialized
agriculture, for its performance was poor by almost any standard.
Although they were supposed to operate on a commercial basis, the
state farms absorbed ₡19·8 millions in subventions in 1963–5 but their
failure in terms of physical output was even more striking. Take, for
example, the comparisons set out in Table 8.2 between the results
achieved by state farms and peasant farmers.

TABLE 8.2
Comparative Performance of Peasants and State Farms[a]

	Peasants	State Farms
No. of workers (000s)	1791	18
Area cultivated (000 acres)	6361	49
Output (000 tons)[b]	5960	10·6
Yield (tons per acre)	0·94	0·21
Labour productivity (tons per worker)	3·33	0·59
Yields of specific food crops (tons per acre)		
Maize	0·49	0·26
Rice	0·49[c]	0·13
Yams	2·63	1·68
Groundnuts	0·40	0·18

Sources: 1970 Population Census, Vol. II, Table I; 1970 Sample Census of Agriculture,
    Vols. I and II; State Farms Corporation; Rourke, 1973A, Tables 1 and 2.
NOTES:
[a] Data on peasant farms relate to 1970. First five entries for State Farms are for 1964;
    the lower four entries, on yields, are averages for 1963–4. The six-year discrepancy
    between the reference dates probably only detracts from the comparison in a minor
    way because it is unlikely that major changes occurred in the yields and productivities
    shown for peasant farmers between 1964 and 1970.
[b] Census output data have been adjusted to economic yields using data in Rourke,
    1973A. For crops not included by Rourke I have assumed the same ratio of economic
    to biological yield as the average of those crops included in his estimates.
[c] Average yield obtained from unimproved local seeds without use of fertilizer (*see* 1970
    Census of Agriculture, Vol. II, Table II.5).

Bearing in mind that the State Farms Corporation had absorbed
many of the Ministry of Agriculture's professional officers, that it had
command over infinitely more capital assets and other modern inputs
than the peasants, and that it was receiving favourable treatment in the
way of financial support, the allocation of import licences and the
provision of technical assistance, it is little short of staggering that it
should have achieved lower yields and smaller outputs per man.[38] The
large-scale thefts of produce which occurred, being excluded from
production data, admittedly have the effect of exaggerating the con-

trasts, but that is an ambiguous defence of the state farms. The conclusion of the World Bank mission which stayed in Ghana towards the end of 1965 was that neither the state farms nor the Workers' Brigade,[39]

> has had success in achieving either its aim of significantly improving agricultural production or of attaining financial self-sufficiency. Indications are that workers of both agencies produce little more, if as much, as they and their families consume, and that if engaged in traditional agriculture they would produce significantly greater quantities of farm produce at a much lower cost.

The failure was not completely uniform; a few farms, planted chiefly to rubber and oil-palm, eventually became viable or showed promise of doing so, but the failures were far more evident than the successes. The state farms may be defended on the grounds that 1964 was too early to assess their performance, but post-Nkrumah experiences do not give this defence much support. The policy of the NLC and Busia governments was to retain farms which showed promise of viability, shedding only those which appeared hopeless. Between 1966 and mid-1971 the number of state farms was accordingly cut from 105 to 33 (in itself a telling commentary on the quality of the original investment decisions) but even this core did poorly. Only about a quarter of total available acreage was under cultivation in 1971 and the Corporation was still making large financial deficits, averaging ₵1·4 million in 1969 and 1970.[40]

Accounting for these results is deferred to the next chapter; suffice it to mention here that many of the farms were established with little prior planning, their managers were often political appointees knowing little of agriculture, that implements were ordered from many different sources with little thought for the organizational problems of a mechanization programme, and that there were many acute shortages of trained personnel and supplies. In consequence, a high proportion of their machines was usually out of service, and actual results were far below the Corporation's own targets.[41] The Workers' Brigade probably did worse – its failure to maintain even the most elementary records protects it from damaging statistical comparisons but does not speak well for the standard of its management. Irrigation did not get much beyond the drafting board during the Nkrumah period but schemes which were implemented, such as those associated with two sugar projects, also proved highly unsuccessful, as did the settlement schemes of the Young Farmers' League.[42]

The informal model of food production developed earlier drew attention to the critical role of government policy in the improvement of cultivation methods and greater use of modern inputs in agriculture. In view of the extreme limitations of Nkrumah's agricultural policies and the failure of government farms to contribute significantly to food production, it is perhaps not difficult to understand why agricultural output failed to keep pace with the expansion of demand. Nkrumah was as mistaken in believing that mechanization offered him a short-cut remedy for colonial neglect of the food producers as he was right to wish to introduce more modern techniques and a greater use of capital. As a Marxist he should have known that a revolution cannot succeed without careful preparation. He wanted an agricultural revolution but neglected such elementary pre-conditions as the creation of an administration to conduct it, research into the problems and possibilities of introducing improved techniques,[43] as well as the availability of adequate numbers of trained agriculturalists, and so on. In his contempt for 'primitive methods and organisations' he established new enclaves of technologies entirely alien to accumulated agricultural knowledge in Ghana and quite unrelated to Ghana's resources availabilities.[44] He wanted a revolution; instead he got a shambles. He introduced capital and modern technology; but the technology was inappropriate and much of the investment was money down the drain.[45]

In retrospect, we can see that the results would have been even worse had it not been for a number of factors which ameliorated the situation, but which were not considered desirable by the government. The inflation of food prices relative to the general price level called forth corrective responses. Besides slowing the expansion of demand, it probably slowed down the rate of urbanization and the associated drift to the towns;[46] improvements in the farmers' terms of trade probably induced a rise in the volume of female labour devoted to farming in the sixties;[47] these same price movements probably improved the utilization of rural labour by reducing the seasonality of employment,[48] and by inducing a greater work effort from the rural work force through marginal substitutions of work for leisure.[49]

The great rise in the attractiveness of food farming relative to the cultivation of cocoa[50] probably also had an effect in ameliorating the food supply position, albeit to the detriment of Ghana's chief source of foreign exchange, by inducing farmers to switch from cocoa to mixed or food farming.[51] Finally, the failure of Ghana's non-agricultural industries to grow as fast as had been planned also limited the pace at which the demand for food grew, and this too helped to avoid more severe shortages.

Explaining the Inefficacy of Industrial Expansion

We turn now to try to account for the inefficacy of Nkrumah's industrialization drive. Large investments in the creation of manufacturing plants, as shown earlier, resulted in an industrial structure which was inefficient in static terms and also apparently failed to generate longer-run dynamic effects on the rest of the economy to compensate for the short-run inefficiency. How may we explain this?

It may be useful to start by returning to one of the preoccupations of the previous chapter: the problem of underutilized capacity. It was mentioned there (p.171) that at the end of 1966 the government estimated actual manufacturing output to be only a fifth of single-shift production capacity. The allocation of import licences was radically changed after 1966 to favour larger imports of raw materials and spares and it is generally believed that this did improve utilization. Nevertheless, Steel's 1967–8 survey of manufacturing found firms still operating at an average of only 35 per cent of what they nominated as their 'maximum theoretical output', and the extent of utilization was a statistically significant explanation of domestic resource costs (DRCs) per unit of foreign exchange saved or earned.[52] The lower the rate of utilization, the higher the DRCs. Under-use of resources is a characteristic of low-income countries but what is surprising about the Ghanaian experience is the *extent* of underutilization for, while international comparisons present serious conceptual and practical difficulties, the evidence in Table 8.3 strongly suggests that underutilization in Ghana was abnormally severe. It is difficult to believe that the very large differences between Ghana and the other countries in the table could be explained just in terms of measurement discrepancies.

TABLE 8.3
Comparative Manufacturing Capacity Utilization: Ghana and other Developing Countries

Country	Year	Utilization as % of capacity
Argentina[a]	1964	64·6
India[b]	1964	65·4
West Pakistan[a]	1965	73·8
Taiwan[ac]	1965	62·3
Ghana	1967–8	34·8

Sources: Ghana: Steel, op cit. Other countries: Little *et al.*, 1970, Tables 3.4-7.
NOTES:
[a] Capacity in the cases of Argentina, West Pakistan and Taiwan was defined as 'full utilisation at the customary number of shifts'. The figure shown for Argentina is an unweighted mean of all industries shown by Little.
[b] The standard used in this case was 'estimated productive capacity'. The figure shown is an unweighted mean of all industries recorded in the lower half of Little's Table 3.5.
[c] A calculation of an unweighted mean estimated from grouped data in Little's Table 3.7. This figure can be regarded as no more than a rough order of magnitude.

Finding underutilization to be an important cause of high DRCs, Steel re-estimated firms' DRCs on the assumption that they were all operating at full capacity. The result was that at full capacity 50·6 of total output would be produced 'efficiently' (DRCs < 1·02), as against only 13·5 per cent at 1967–8 utilization levels. The proportion of 'inefficient' production (DRCs > 1·53) fell from 67·3 to 42·6 per cent.[53] Note that even in these extremely favourable circumstances more than two-fifths of output would have made inefficient use of Ghana's resources.

The explanation usually given for below-capacity use of Ghana's manufacturing plant is that foreign exchange shortages and the resulting import controls kept factories short of materials, components and spare parts, and this is an explanation which Steel emphasizes. Chapter 10 presents evidence indicating that this was indeed a powerful constraint upon industrial production and thus the policy of the NLC and Busia governments of increasing the allocations of foreign exchange to cover the needs of industry was an eminently sensible one. There are, however, strong reasons for believing that much underutilization stemmed from more fundamental causes.[54]

Ghana's industrial statistics show that between 1966 and 1970, when the quantity of imports of industrial raw materials went up by nearly half, gross output per manufacturing establishment actually declined in real terms by 9 per cent, and that constant-price value-added per establishment went down by a remarkable 24 per cent over the same period.[55] These figures are truly surprising, for improved capacity utilization would imply greater output per establishment. It is possible that this trend was partly due to a tendency for the newest establishments to be smaller than those existing in 1966, but there is no obvious reason why this should have been the case and the evidence for it is only rather weak.[56] Recalling the macro-economic evidence presented in the appendix to the last chapter that capacity utilization did not improve much in the later sixties, and the figures in Table 5.8 showing the rate of import substitution to have slowed down considerably, one must conclude that the evidence runs strongly counter to a belief that underutilization resulted largely from import shortages and could, therefore, easily be reduced by improved foreign exchange allocations.

This conclusion is reinforced by the results of an official survey conducted in 1968 of a sample of manufacturing firms. Respondents were asked, (a) If you were able to produce at full capacity in 1969 (while other firms in your industry remained at current levels of production) would you be able to sell your entire product in Ghana? and (b) If all firms in your industry were able to produce at full capacity in 1969 would the industry be able to sell its entire output in Ghana? The answers are summarized in Table 8.4.[57]

We naturally cannot tell how well informed the respondents were about the sizes of the market and their competitors. Maybe they were unrealistically pessimistic, although if they were seeking larger import licence allocations it would have been to their advantage to play down the existence of a demand constraint. The fact is that only 24 per cent

TABLE 8.4
Industrial Capacity and Market Size, 1969

	(percentages of total responses)	
Reply	Firm only	Whole industry
Yes, at current prices	46	24
Yes, if retail prices were reduced	17	13
No, capacity exceeds market	37	63

Source: Ministry of Finance and Planning

of them thought that the market was big enough to absorb the full capacity output of their industry at ruling prices and 63 per cent believed that industrial capacity exeeeded the market size at any feasible price. No less striking, 37 per cent of the respondents thought their own capacity exceeded the market. Why should so many plants have been built with capacities in excess of reasonable expectations of demand and market shares? Whatever the answer, the evidence of this paragraph points far more to market size as a constraint than to supply factors. It may well be that while the NLC's import policies were assisting improved use of industrial capacity their disinflationary fiscal and monetary policies were working in the opposite direction,[58] which perhaps helps to explain the decline in the volume of output per establishment. By this logic, the import liberalization and expansionist fiscal and monetary policies of the Busia administration should have sparked off a major industrial boom, but industrial statistics show only 7 per cent rise in total constant-price manufacturing value-added in 1969–70, and tax data fail to reveal much expansion during 1971.[59] Keynesian expansion of demand appeared as unable to achieve radical improvements in utilization as improved import policies. How, then, is the excess capacity to be explained? There are at least a few hypotheses to be offered.

Remember, first, that Ghana's economy had been quite a fast-growing one until the beginning of the sixties (chapter 4). It was only later that people began to realize that stagnation was not just a passing phase, and it is likely that factories were built in expectation of a faster growth of consumer demand than actually materialized. The expansion of the past, and the optimism induced by Nkrumah's big push and the *Seven-year Plan* may provide some explanaion of the apparent over-investment. As the 1962 *Economic Survey* put it:[60]

> The publication of the draft Seven-year Development Plan has also strengthened the confidence of the private business community in the future of the economy of Ghana and the prospects for a rapid economic growth in the coming years look exceedingly bright.

Associated with this was a deteriorating flow of economic information upon which to base investment decisions. As the government intervened more and more in the economy and as relative prices departed further and further from equilibrium, information provided by the interaction of supply and demand became increasingly misleading. Planning and controls were intended to provide an alternative but, as is shown in chapter 10, controls tended to be either ineffective or damaging and, as was shown in chapter 6, nothing could have been more misleading as a guide to the future than the *Seven-year Plan*. In these circumstances, a decline in the quality of investment decisions was probably inevitable.

As a special case of this, we may anticipate the next chapter to mention the several state enterprises which were set up with little economic rationale. Mention is made there of a factory for processing mangoes with a capacity said to be several times the size of total world trade in canned mango products; of tomato-canning factories without tomatoes; of sheet glass capacity far in excess of the domestic market, and so on. The rapid expansion of state involvement industry by a government which placed little weight on efficiency considerations and whose decision-making processes became increasingly chaotic, did nothing to rationalize industry. We are reminded of a point that has been made before – that some of the 'capacity' we are discussing is spurious, a purely statistical result of 'investments' which promised few, if any, future benefits.

Another reason sometimes given for the underutilization of capacity in developing countries is that industries are given protection so high as to permit them to operate well below capacity and yet still be highly profitable.[61] This is probably valid for Ghana. Despite their economic difficulties and high costs of operation, there is little evidence of a high mortality rate among manufacturing firms and substantial profits were probably made. However, this does not provide a very convincing explanation of excess capacity, for if firms are profitable even though underutilized, how much more so could they be if they were operating nearer to their limit? Protection and an associated lack of competitive pressures may help to explain low cost-consciousness and inattention to careful pre-investment appraisals but does not provide a convincing reason why there should have been a systematic tendency to build plants too large for the market.

Another possibility is that investors built plants larger than they would otherwise have chosen in order to obtain larger allocations of import licences for raw materials, on the basis that the scarcity-value of the licensed goods was large enough for it to pay to invest in useless plant in order to obtain more licences. This argument also fails to provide a convincing explanation of wide-spread and large-scale over-investment, for the more-or-less permanent creation of unusable plant in return for an uncertain and temporary possibility of obtaining more licences would seem a high-risk type of expenditure, compared, say, with investment in another country or the payment of bribes.

A final hypothesis that may be mentioned relates to economies of scale. There is some controversy about the importance of this factor in the industrialization of developing countries. Steel found DRCs to be positively correlated with size and concluded that there appeared to be dis-economies of scale in Ghanaian manufacturing,[62] and Kilby, using evidence drawn from Western African experiences, argues that only a minority of developing countries are likely to be hampered in the early stages of industrialization by inadequate markets.[63] He reaches this conclusion largely because he found in Nigeria that each region tended to be industrially self-sufficient, i.e. that manufacturing plants confined themselves to the local market rather than selling in the whole of the national economy. But this suggestive piece of information may tell us no more than that the high costs of transportation in a large country with a poor network of roads and railways were sufficient to outweigh potential economies of scale. After a careful survey of the available evidence, Sutcliffe concluded that 'there is a large number of industries . . . in which economies of scale can be obtained up to levels of output greatly in excess of those in most under-developed countries, and also greatly in excess of current consumption of those commodities in the same countries . . .'[64] and the present writer found scale economies to be an important explanation of industrial productivity differences in Ghana in 1959.[65]

The point can be demonstrated more strikingly by referring to the conclusions of an International Economic Association conference that, 'it seemed to be our general impression that most of the major industrial economies of scale could be achieved by a relatively high-income nation of 50 million; and that nations of 10–15 million were probably too small to get all the technical economies available . . .'[66] Now reduce this to values. We take $1400 as a representative per capita income of high-income countries at the beginning of the sixties.[67] This means that countries with gross products of about $14,000 million to $21,000 million were considered too small to get all available scale economies. Now compare with Ghana's GDP in 1965, of about $1,500 million at the official exchange rate, or, say, $1,000 million after adjusting for the over-valuation of the cedi. Ghana's economy, measured in this way, was only one-fourteenth of the countries identified at the lower end of the range of those too small to obtain full economies of scale. This understates the comparison, moreover, for, with relatively high income elasticities of demand for manufactured consumer goods, the relevant market size is proportionately greater in a high-income country than is indicated simply by comparing GDP values.

These considerations may help to explain the excess capacity. It may be that plants were constructed to catch scale economies, in the hope that somehow it would be possible to utilize them; if we link this possibility with demand optimism early in the sixties[68] we at least have a plausible hypothesis which would be worth further exploration by a future investigator. It may also be that some minimum plant sizes are determined by technological conditions and that, with assured protection and monopoly profits, it was worthwhile to undertake the investments despite the inadequacy of the market.[69]

Leaving the puzzle of excess capacity there, we turn to consider other causes of the inefficacy of Ghana's industrialization. One was the tendency towards capital-intensity. We might advance the obvious presumption that Ghana would be most efficient in processes requiring relatively large inputs of local factors of production and raw materials, and that she would be at a relative disadvantage in products using large amounts of imported capital goods and materials.[70] A variety of conditions were shown in the previous chapter to have resulted in a capital-intensive path of development, diminishing the impact of investment on the overall growth of the economy. Given that factor prices, import licensing policies, wage legislation and the government's own predilection for technologically advanced processes all operated in favour of the use of capital, we may conjecture that one of the reasons for the short-run inefficiency of Ghana's manufacturing sector and its limited spill-over effects on the remainder of the domestic economy was its capital-intensity, and we may recall that manufacturing contributed proportionately about six times as much to GDP as it did to total employment.[71] Steel's researches partially confirm this, for he found DRCs to be positively and significantly correlated with the capital-intensity of the firms he studied, consistent with the view that Ghana has a comparative advantage in relatively labour-intensive production.[72]

Mention has been made earlier of the heavy dependence of Ghanaian manufacturing upon imported raw materials and components. Two alternative statistical indicators of this are available. One is derived from an input:output table for 1968, which shows the direct imports of materials of the manufacturing sector to be 54 per cent of total inputs. The second is derived from data in the Bank of Ghana showing imported inputs to comprise a weighted average of 74 per cent of total inputs in 1968. The discrepancy between the proportions of 54 and 74 per cent may be attributed (a) to the fact that saw-milling (which uses local timbers) is excluded from the latter calculation and (b) to a tendency to declare as materials imports that are in fact finished goods, in order to evade taxation and import restrictions. On either score, the evidence demonstrates that Ghana's manufacturing sector makes limited use of local materials, especially if processed exports such as wood and cocoa products are excluded. Looking at the major industrial groups given in the Bank of Ghana data, the food, drinks and tobacco groups make the greatest use of local inputs; textiles (based on imported cloth and yarn), chemicals, petroleum, the various metal-based industries, and machinery-producing industries use scarcely any.

One of the main theoretical advantages advanced in favour of an industry-led strategy of economic development is that manufacturing is supposed to have greater linkages with other sectors and may thus be expected to induce investments and expansion elsewhere in the economy.[73] In Ghana's case, however, the linkages did not develop, which helps to explain why industrialization failed to galvanize the rest of the economy into more rapid growth. Comparison of figures in a 1968 input:output table with one prepared by Szereszewski for 1960 is most revealing in this respect:

TABLE 8.5
Linkages of Manufacturing Sector with Rest of Economy, 1960 and 1968

	1960	1968
1. Purchases from other sectors as percentage of total material inputs	65	46
2. Sales to other sectors as percentage of total sales	25	14

Sources: Szereszewski, 1966, Table 3.1; Central Bureau of Statistics (unpublished table for 1968). Both tables were consolidated to eight sectors in order to make them comparable. Intra-sector flows are excluded.

Both backwards and forwards, the linkages weakened quite markedly in relative terms. The implication of these *averages* is that the linkages of the factories set up *during the sixties* must have been appreciably weaker even than the proportions shown for 1968. Many industrial enclaves were created and it is therefore not surprising that Ghana's industry tended to have high costs and few dynamic effects. By the same token, industrialization could not contribute much, directly or indirectly, to the solution of the unemployment problem. Indeed, if we had data on the number of workers in Ghana's traditional processing industries displaced by the advent of protected, capital-intensive industries it could even be that the net impact of industrialization on total employment was negative.[74]

No survey of the causes of industrial inefficiency in Ghana would be complete without discussion of industrial protection which the government was very willing to provide to investors. Typically, protection was granted on an *ad hoc* basis or as a by-product of revenue-raising measures, and the results were irrational and arbitrary. Abban and Leith investigated the protection of Ghanaian manufacturing for 1968 and found nominal rates of between zero and 128 per cent, with no readily apparent rationale.[75] Leith also made calculations of *effective* protection and showed rates between −246 per cent and 116,993 per cent.[76] Both in the enormous variations in the effective rates and their lack of any system, effective protection was even more irrational than nominal protection.

The general prevalence of protection and the lack of system about it helped to produce the inefficiencies noted earlier; this was a cost of Nkrumah's rejection of comparative advantage. On the other hand, it would not be correct to label Ghana's economy as highly protectionist. By comparative standards Ghana is at the moderate end of the spectrum. Little *et al.* give rates of nominal protection of manufactures for six developing countries in 1962 with an unweighted mean of 72 per cent, against a median for Ghana in 1968 of 33 per cent. Similarly, they provide rates of effective protection of manufacturing in seven developing countries with an unweighted mean of 139 per cent, as against a median for Ghana in 1968 of 57 per cent.[77] It should also be remembered that overvaluation of the cedi, by holding down the relative price of imports, reduced the effect of duties and other protective devices. Alternatively, the protection could be seen as a necessary compensation for the over-valued currency.[78] It was, however, supplemented by other forms. As will be shown in chapter 10, import licensing was used to prohibit or restrict the supply of competing foreign goods, although Leith concluded that licensing provided an 'uncertain and erratic' source of protection.[79] Protection was also provided through tax holidays and similar investment incentives under a 1963 Capital Investments Act and earlier legislation, and the value of these concessions could be very substantial.[80] Many state enterprises were assisted with budgetary subsidies.

While there was little system in the structure of industrial protection, it did nevertheless have consistent biases; tariffs expressed as percentages of the value of imports were highest on consumer goods and lowest on intermediate and capital goods, as shown in Table 8.6.

TABLE 8.6
Import Duty Collections as Percentage of c.i.f. Imports, by End-use, Selected Years[a]

End-use category	1959	1966	1969
Non-durable consumer goods	—	47	21
Durable consumer goods	—	46	30
ALL CONSUMER GOODS	21	47	23
NON–DURABLE PRODUCER GOODS	5	24	13
Durable producer goods	—	11	10
Producers' equipment	—	4	6
ALL CAPITAL GOODS	4	—	—
TOTAL IMPORTS	15·5	29·9	18·9[b]

Sources: Scott, 1967, Table 12; Stern, 1971, Table 3; C.B.S. and customs data.
NOTES:
[a] A dash indicates data not available.
[b] Includes import surcharges.

Although there were large changes in the levels of duty collections between the years, the hierarchy consumer goods-intermediate goods-capital goods remained unchanged. The effect, of course, was a strong incentive towards 'finishing-touches' industries, since the largest protection was for producers of finished consumer goods, with much less for producers of materials and capital goods. Relief from import duties provided under the Capital Investments Act had similar effects, and the low taxation of capital goods also had the effect of encouraging capital-intensity.

There were other factors operating in favour of capital-intensity. Tax concessions granted under the Capital Investments Act, for example, provided for accelerated depreciation allowances, which reduced the effective cost of capital. Similarly, chapter 10 shows that the import licensing authorities gave preference to imported capital goods over intermediate and consumer goods during the Nkrumah period. This not only directly facilitated large capital investments but also placed a premium on processes which minimized the wastage of materials, which probably meant capital-intensive processes.[81] On the other hand, this same pattern of discrimination tended to undermine the bias towards finishing-touches industries mentioned above; there could scarcely have been stronger incentives to use local materials than the chronic shortages resulting from the administration of import controls.

A reference forward to the next chapter completes this survey of the reasons why Nkrumah's industrialization failed to impart much dynamism to the economy as a whole. The reference is to the sub-standard performance of many of the state manufacturing enterprises set up in the first half of the sixties. While assessment of their performance is not a simple matter, it is shown in chapter 9 that most state enterprises produced poor economic results, although the same was not necessarily true of enterprises run in collaboration with private partners. State enterprise was not as important to Nkrumah's industrial policies as to his agricultural policies, where we have shown the failure of government farms to have subverted his whole strategy. Nevertheless, the share of the output of enterprises wholly or partly owned by the state increased 70 per cent between 1962 and 1966 and by the latter year accounted for almost a third of gross manufacturing output (Table 5.7), so the deficiencies of these concerns had considerable implications for the overall impact of industrialization.

In sum, a wide-ranging set of conditions conspired to limit the efficacy of the industrialization drive. Over-optimism about the future growth of the economy and a search for economies of scale produced an underutilized and high-cost structure of industry. The unselective and arbitrary protection, a variety of biases favouring capital-intensity and processes with few linkages with other sectors, a deteriorating quality of investment decisions, and sub-standard performance on the part of state enterprises – when taken together provide a fairly powerful explanation of the failure of industrialization. There are, however, limitations to the approach so far adopted, of treating agricultural and industrial performance as independent of each other, and the next paragraphs explore the ways in which they interacted.

The Consequences of Unbalanced Growth

The well-known three-sector model of balanced growth developed by Professor Lewis is useful at this point.[82] Taking agricultural production for the home market, manufacturing production for the home market, and production for export, he argues that stagnation of any one of these sectors will tend to retard the growth of the others. The most successful development path is one which achieves a balance in the expansion of each of these sectors. It was a balance which Ghana failed to achieve in the sixties. Chapter 5 showed how government policies, especially the over-valuation of the cedi, discriminated against exports during the Nkrumah era, and that export earnings and volumes remained generally static. The stagnation of agricultural production for the home market has been mentioned on numerous occasions.

This unbalanced growth was a direct result of government priorities. Exports received low priority and agriculture played second fiddle to industry. It could be retorted that, far from neglecting agriculture, the Nkrumah government invested far more in agriculture in the first half of the sixties than any government had ever done before, but while this is true it is also misleading.[83] As we saw earlier, a very high proportion of government expenditure on agriculture was misspent in that it produced negligible results. Moreover, almost all of it went to government farms, while support for peasant farmers declined, and the cocoa industry was being milked to finance development in other sectors, on the Soviet model.[84]

This lack of balance was seriously inimical to the success of the development effort. The neglect of exports contributed in a major way to the constant shortages of foreign exchange. These, in turn, led to shortages of imported inputs for industry and even for agriculture,[85] and so held back both sectors. Similarly, the failure of agriculture affected industry in a number of negative ways. Since Ghana remained an essentially agricultural economy, most domestic demand for the products of the country's manufactures would have had to emanate from the rural economy but this source of demand remained largely static. Lagging output raised food prices relative to other prices and, on the reasonable assumption that the price elasticity of demand for local food was less than unity,[86] this means that an increasing proportion of total disposable incomes was being devoted to the purchase of foodstuffs, with correspondingly less for manufactures. With per capita private consumption declining and expenditure elasticities for food items less than unity,[87] the combined effect of these forces was to subtract in a serious way from the demand for Ghana's manufactures – which may help to explain the large underutilization of industrial capacity discussed earlier.

Agricultural stagnation hit industry in the supply side too. Industries processing local agricultural products, such as sugar, fruit canning and vegetable oils, encountered great difficulties in obtaining adequate and reliable supplies, and others which could have been based upon local agriculture, like the textile industry, fibre bags, meat canning and cigarettes, relied upon imported supplies – to the detriment of their production costs, their contribution to the balance of payments, and their spill-over effects on the rest of the economy. The incapacity of agriculture to keep pace with domestic demand for food maintained constant pressure for large allocations of foreign exchange for food, and such imports competed directly with foreign exchange for the needs of industry. Lastly, the inflation of food prices and its impact on the general price level helped to raise manufacturing production costs.[88] This trend coupled with the over-valued cedi and the inelasticity of supplies of agricultural raw materials, effectively foreclosed the possibility of profitable exporting for most industries and kept them to the narrow confines of the domestic market.

Some Conclusions

We can return now to the central issues with which this and the previous chapter were concerned: why did the investments and industrialization of the sixties fail to generate growth? And why in the later sixties did the economy behave like a fully employed one when it was operating well within its production frontier?

In some measure, the mistakes which Nkrumah made in his industrial and agricultural policies were the mistakes of many other underdeveloped countries. The limitations of an import-substituting strategy have by now become well known, and there are striking similarities between the Ghanaian experience and the conclusions of a major comparative study of other developing countries:[89]

> The main theses in this book are that industry has been over-encouraged in relation to agriculture, and that, although there are arguments for giving special encouragement to industry, this encouragement could be provided in forms which would not, as present policies do, discourage exports, including agricultural exports; which would promote greater efficiency in the use of resources; and which would create a less unequal distribution of income and higher levels of employment in both industry and agriculture.

This is not to say, however, that Ghana is just another case, for not many countries have achieved such abysmal results from so large an effort as that undertaken under Nkrumah. In truth, the uniqueness of Ghana is a matter of degree – but the degree of failure was extreme and will cast a shadow over the economy for many years.

One of the points to emerge from these two chapters is the great importance of the type of technology transfer undertaken during development. To some extent, this was determined by the sectoral and product choices which were made, but also by the economic inducements which existed for the employment of capital or labour, and the predilections of the government in its own investments. The general point can be put quite simply: that technology will result in the highest efficiency, the greatest net benefit to the balance of payments, and the greatest spill-over effects into the rest of the economy, which employs local materials and factors of production. This type of technology is, on the whole, unlikely to incorporate the most recent advances in scientific knowledge, and is therefore liable to be thought of as 'inferior'.[90] It is also unlikely to be a technology which may be applied without adaptation to local conditions. Much of what went wrong with industry and agriculture was a result of inappropriate technology choices, resulting in farming fiascos and in the creation of inefficient industrial enclaves.

The consequences of a deteriorating standard of investment decision-making are also seen to be of considerable importance, in that they neutralized much of Nkrumah's large investment effort. Returning to the figures on capacity utilization in the appendix to chapter 7, it is evident that there is much ambiguity about the concept of capacity, for much of the 'investment' of the first half of the sixties was actually a form of consumption, yielding few, if any, returns in the longer run. The large volume of 'investment' in the earlier sixties could not compensate for the low-productivity uses to which much of it was put and for the declining standard of economic management. This is reminiscent of the findings of Kuznets and others, that the quantum of factor inputs explains only a rather small part of the growth of the now-industrialized economies and that this growth was due primarily to improvements in the quality, not quantity, of inputs 'traceable to increases in useful knowledge and better institutional arrangements for its utilisation'.[91] In Ghana's case, quality and institutional arrangements probably deteriorated. Useful knowledge was there to be tapped but Western technology was aped rather than adapted to Ghana's own conditions. There is, in other words, no necessary connection between growth and structural change unless the changes are, in some relevant sense, efficient ones.

The foregoing also serves to draw attention to the pervasive importance of government policies and the importance, therefore, of getting them right. The failings of both agriculture and industry were due essentially to policy mistakes. Moreover, these interacted upon each other to produce circumstance in one sector which undermined the possibilities of success in the other. Though Ghana's economic structure remained a relatively simple one, the web of inter-relationships between its various parts was becoming sufficiently complex for policy measures directed at one part to have subtle but real consequences elsewhere in the system. Specifically, the failure to maintain some reasonable balance in sectoral expansion proved self-defeating. The priority placed on industry combined with stagnation elsewhere in the economy to undermine the industrialization itself.

Of course, the pervasive importance of policy was largely deliberate. The rapid spread of state intervention and participation in the economy, desired for its own sake because it was regarded as a necessary condition for the creation of socialism, naturally increased the potency of government actions for good or ill. The fact that government actions reviewed in this chapter had adverse effects, not only imposed a heavy economic penalty on the Ghanaian nation, but also undermined the objective of socialism itself. If it is true that socialism requires a large degree of state participation in economic transactions, it is surely no less true that the new, socialist forms should replace the old with tolerable efficiency, so that enjoyment of the material benefits of economic development are brought nearer or, at least, not pushed much further away.

Finally, the obstinate difficulties encountered in raising the low levels of capacity utilization signal a problem which is taken up in the concluding chapter. Professor Hirschman postulates his celebrated advocacy of unbalanced growth based on the notion that the disequilibria thereby created will tend to bring agents of change into action to correct the imbalances and keep the economy moving forward.[92] In Ghana's case, however, there were few signs that corrective responses were set in motion despite failings which were quite spectacular in their severity. Part of the answer, no doubt, is that Nkrumah's government was not allowed enough time for us to judge how it might have responded to the disequilibria, but the theme of chapter 11 is that even after the coup of 1966 there was more continuity than change in economic policy and the corrective responses remained inadequate. The problem remains, therefore. Why did the Nkrumah government disregard the lessons of earlier experiments in mechanized farming, for example, and why did it persevere in pouring ever-increasing amounts into state farms when the evidence could not have been plainer that some change of course was needed? By what tortured logic did it continue to starve existing industries of materials and spares in order to import the capital equipment needed to create yet more industries? In short, why did Ghana's economy and policy prove so inelastic in the face of shortcomings which clearly were having the gravest economic and political effects?

NOTES

[1] Nkrumah, 1963, pp. 111–12.

[2] The term 'peasant' is used in this book as a convenient shorthand to describe Ghana's many small farmers, although in several respects they differ substantially from the peasants of other parts of the world.

[3] *See* Killick, 1966, pp. 276–7.

[4] Nkrumah, *Africa Needs Her Farmers*, Government Printer, Accra, 1962 (cited by Apter, 1973).

[5] *See* above, pp 37 and 50.

[6] Uphoff, 1970, p. 602.

[7] Mensah was reported in the *Ghanaian Times*, 5 April 1962, as saying that the easiest ways of raising agricultural productivity were through mechanization, the development and application of technical science, and changes in the government's investment structure.

[8] Imports of food and live animals were generally 15 to 20 per cent of total imports throughout the sixties. Items on which substantial sums were spent and which Ghana probably could have produced at reasonable cost included rice, cattle and meat, sugar and tobacco.

[9] Estimated from data on the labour force in Table 4.4 and from the 1970 *Industrial Statistics*. These exclude establishments employing fewer than 30 people. The contibution to GDP is estimated from Singal and Nartey, Table 16.4, and more up-to-date industrial statistics.

[10] Steel, 1972, Table VI.

[11] Reusse, 1968, pp. 73 and 82.

[12] He found, for example, that high DRCs were not compensated by larger labour-training efforts or by a tendency to locate away from industrial centres (thus promoting a greater diffusion of industrial activities). On the assumption (a doubtful one for Ghana) that the government has a relatively high marginal propensity to save, firms' net contributions to government revenue might also be counted as a species of external economy. On examination of this, he found that firms with high DRCs were less likely to make positive net contributions to government revenue than the remainder, thus compounding the disservice they were rendering to the economy. *See* Steel, 1970, pp. 124–6.

[13] Reported in the *Ghanaian Times*, 13 July 1965.

[14] *Abrahams Report*, 1965.

[15] Nathan Associates, *Transportation Development in Ghana*, 1970, p. 48, found that 28 per cent of the mileage of black-top roads needed restoration going beyond normal maintenance work and that this was also the case with 42 per cent of the mileage of laterite roads.

[16] Calculated from Ewusi, 1971B, Appendix II, and population data in chapter 4, table 4.B. *See also* Stoces, 1966.

[17] *See Abrahams Report, passim.* The tendency to attribute shortages to the distributive system was not peculiar to the Nkrumah regime. The response to shortages and inflation of the Busia government and the National Redemption Council was very similar, including the creation by the former of a new state agency to handle food distribution (*see One-year Plan, 1970/71*, pp. 58–60).

[18] *See* Lawson, 1966A, *passim*; also Bauer, 1963.

[19] Lawson, 1966B, *passim*.

[20] Garlick, 1971, especially p. 73; also chapter 10 below.

[21] *See One-year Plan, 1970/71*, Tables 13.1 and 13.2.

[22] The regression was calculated on first differences for 1960–9 and yielded the correlation coefficient R= -0.4105 and the equation Y=1.474 - 0.359X where Y=food
$$(1.273)$$
prices relative to other consumer prices and X=number of goods vehicles. Ewusi, 1971B, Table 3, did a similar calculation, but without adjusting food prices for the general rate of inflation, obtaining similar but weaker results.

[23] Nyanteng and van Apeldoorn, 1971, chapters V and VI, found that the distributive system could be a problem, especially in placing the farmer in a price-taker position in villages with no usable road; and Okali and Kotey, 1971, p. 45, found that farm output was sometimes discouraged by poor communications.

[24] For much of rural Ghana this is a reasonable assumption but there are probably substantial areas now in which population growth is placing the traditional land-rotation system under more stress, reducing the fallow periods and diminishing the quality of the soil.

[25] Ghanaian agriculture conforms well to the view presented by Schultz, 1964 – fairly efficient in the static sense of maximizing returns from given inputs but with little endogenous capability of technical progress.

[26] Caldwell, 1967, chapter 3 and especially Table 3.13, showed that the urban population grew three times as fast as the rural population in 1948–60 and the results of the 1970 census showed that Accra's population went up about three times as fast as the rest of the population (73·2 per cent in 1960–70 against 23.6 per cent).

[27] Note that this view of the problem makes no explicit provision for the land tenure system as an important variable affecting agricultural performance. There are wide differences of opinion on whether tenure arrangements constitute a serious constraint in Ghana but, in my view, the balance of the evidence is in favour of those who argue that traditional arrangements have proved sufficiently flexible to accommodate large changes in land-use and farming patterns. *See* Hill, 1963, *passim*, and Dadson, 1970, pp. 62–3. The model also abstracts from the question of rural credit.

[28] *See* du Sautoy, 1958, chapter VIII, and Twum-Barima quoted by Uphoff, 1970, p. 580, on the early history of the extension service.

[29] Extension work in parts of the north had, for example, greatly increased the number of farmers using bullock-drawn ploughs (Dadson, p. 48), and various observers had testified to the responsiveness of farmers – *see* du Sautoy, *loc. cit.*, and Uphoff, pp. 334 and 581.

[30] UGFC, *General Secretary's Report*, 1964–5, quoted by Dadson, pp. 94–5. Much of the following is based upon Dadson's excellent study of the socialization of agriculture in the first half of the sixties.

[31] The *Report* of the Auditor-General, Parts II and III, 1964, p. 33, comments on the legal obscurity of the UGFC and records that at the end of 1963 the President's Office directed that it should abide by government decisions intended for state and para-statal organizations.

[32] The *de Graft-Johnson Report*, 1966, p. 9, documented a number of malpractices, and the *Abrahams Report*, 1965, paragraphs 67 and 68, revealed the operation of a thriving black market for matchets, which were supposed to be distributed at a controlled price by the UGFC. Beckman, 1972, p. 24, also comments on corruption and aggrandizement in the UGFC.

[33] *de Graft-Johnson Report*, p. 20.

[34] Chambers, 1970, p. 235.

[35] Agricultural Development Corporation, 1957, p. 9. *See also* Quansah, 1972. Interestingly, Hancock, 1942, p. 188, records that in the thirties the United Africa Company found that their attempts to grow cocoa in the Gold Coast on a plantation basis could not compete with the traditional peasant farming of this crop: another case where modernity did not equal efficiency.

[36] *See* Dumont, 1962, pp. 56–9, for a characteristically staccato statement of the pitfalls of early mechanization.

[37] Miracle and Seidman, 1968B, pp. 36–44.

[38] Miracle and Seidman, 1968A, pp. 19–20, have objected to similar comparisons on the grounds that data on the peasant farmers are unreliable, and that 'over half the state farms were planted with rubber and palm trees, a major share of which were not yet bearing.' The first objection is a *non sequitur*. The admitted unreliability of the data is reason for treating the comparisons as only revealing orders of mag-

nitude but, unless reasons are given for thinking the data to be systematically biased, the comparisons remain valid. The second point is more solid, although their own data (Appendix 1) show that the total acreage planted to all crops, including rubber and oil-palm, that had not come into bearing was less than two-fifths of the total acreage cultivated by the state farms in 1964 (38 per cent). Against this one would have to set a comparable figure for peasant farmers; how much would remain of their point after this adjustment is not clear. In any case, their conclusions on the relative efficiency of the state and peasant farms (pp. 44–5) also turn out to be in the favour of the latter.

[39] International Bank, 1966, Annex 8, p. i.

[40] *See* Table 9.1. Other information provided by Ministry of Finance and Planning. *See also* Due, 1969, pp. 648–9.

[41] *See* Dadson, chapter 7. In 1963–4, for example, the acreage cultivated by the state farms was an average of only 43 per cent of their own targets for those years.

[42] In 1965 the League was cultivating 1,215 acres with 1,040 settlers as against a target acreage of 31,000 acres.

[43] Dumont emphasizes the inadequate basis of research for mechanization in the conditions of tropical Africa, and Dadson demonstrates the seriousness of this deficiency in Ghana's case. He goes on (p. 279): 'But during this period, research and extension were casualties of politics, and little progress was made in the organised production of knowledge regarding the adaptation of imported and recommended but untried technologies. The situation was only worsened by control of technical services passing into the hands of technically untrained men.'

[44] Perhaps Nkrumah equated mechanization with socialism, in which case he should have noticed that the Chinese were placing little trust in state farms and tractors – *see* Chen and Galenson, 1969, pp. 121–2.

[45] The substantial but fruitless investments in several of the state farms is a good illustration of the point made in the discussion in chapter 7 of 'excess capacity', that much of what is conventionally recorded as capital formation was really a form of consumption yielding no future stream of benefits.

[46] The urbanization of employment proceeded less rapidly in the sixties than had been expected. Table 4.4 shows agricultural employment to have gone up by 1·4 per cent p.a. in 1960–70, against 3·4 per cent p.a. in the case of non-agricultural employment. By contrast, Stoces, writing in the mid-sixties, estimated the rate of increase of agricultural labour, before adjusting for the effects of greater school attendance, at about 0·8 per cent, with a correspondingly larger increase in the non-agricultural labour force (Stoces, 1966, Table 6, line 1). *See also* Mensah, 1962.

[47] *See* Table 4.4, item 3, which records that almost all the increase in agricultural employment was attributable to a 200,000 rise in the number of women workers.

[48] *See* Rourke and Obeng, 1973.

[49] Local observers believe that there was an increased tendency for the smaller-scale farmers also to hire their labour out to others in these years.

[50] *See* Table 4.D, line 13.

[51] Rourke, 1973B, shows for the Eastern Region that with a producer price of ₵10 per load for cocoa the returns from pure cocoa farming were substantially lower than from cocoa intercropped with food items, and from certain kinds of food farming.

[52] Steel, 1970, pp. 45 and 142. *See also* Steel, 1972, pp. 226–7. A survey conducted by the government in 1967 found industry to be operating at 40 per cent of single-shift capacity (report of a subcommittee on import requirements, January 1968) and, allowing for the different concepts of capacity, this finding is consistent with Steel's.

[53] Steel, 1972, Table VI.

[54] Leith, 1973, chapter 4, found that capacity utilization was significantly correlated with the value of import licence utilizations, but the explanatory value was low ($R^2 = 0.133$), emphasizing again the importance of other factors.

[55] Constant-price gross output per manufacturing establishment as recorded in the *Industrial Statistics*, was ₵466,700 in 1966 and ₵426,200 in 1970. Constant-price

value-added per establishment was ₵281,200 and ₵214,200 respectively. Imports of industrial intermediate goods (in post-1967 devaluation cedis) rose from ₵64·9 million to an estimated ₵97·4 million in the same period.

56 Average employment per establishment fell from 172 to 145, or by 16 per cent, but some of this decline may be attributable to older establishments who were known to have reduced inflated payrolls after 1966.

57 The number of establishments providing answers to these questions was 46. The sample was somewhat biased towards larger establishments, which probably influenced the answers to question (a).

58 *See* line 17 of Table 4.B, which shows a decline in constant-price per capita private consumption in 1965–9.

59 The indicator used here was government receipts from sales and purchase taxes, 40–50 per cent of which are derived from levies on domestic manufactures. After allowing for the inflation of consumer prices (other than local foods), there actually was a small decline – from ₵32·7 million to ₵31·8 million – from 1970 to 1971, although these figures can, at best, give only a rough indication of industrial trends.

60 *Economic Survey, 1962*, paragraph 34.
61 This argument is used by Little *et al.*, pp. 98–9, and also Steel, 1972, pp. 230–1.
62 Steel, 1970, p. 138.
63 Kilby, 1969, p. 351.
64 Sutcliffe, 1971, p. 226.
65 Killick, 1966, chapter 7.
66 EAG Robinson (ed.), 1963, p. xviii.
67 The UN, 1964B, Table 2.3, shows per capita GDP in 'developed market economies' to have been $1410 in 1960.
68 It is said that a state-owned shoe factory was built on a large scale in order to catch the pan-African market.
69 An implication of these arguments is that marginal costs in Ghanaian manufacturing are likely to be far below the previous average and Steel's calculations support this view. Were it not for a greatly over-valued currency and other artificial restraints, it is possible that firms could have escaped the confines of the domestic market by exporting, although in fact very little exporting was undertaken.
70 In support of this, Steel, 1972, p. 234, found a correlation, significant at the 99 per cent level, between high DRCs and assembly-type operations, which in Ghana are based almost exclusively on imported components.
71 *See* above, p. 187.
72 Steel, 1972, p. 234.
73 *See* chapter 2 and, especially, Hirschman, 1958, chapter 6.
74 A comparison with Japan's industrial history is instructive here. In her case industrialization took a fairly labour-intensive form because cottage industries, instead of being replaced, became absorbed into the new structure through subcontracting (*see* Fei and Ranis, 1964, p. 142). I am aware of very few comparable cases in Ghana. Generally, there are few transactions between traditional and modern manufacturing units and their relationship is competitive rather than complementary.
75 Abban and Leith, 1971, Table 1.
76 *See* Corden, 1971, Chapter 3, for an explanation of the concept of effective protection. Not too much weight should be placed on the extreme values, which result from small amounts of value-added at world prices (the denominator) as much as from excessive protection.
77 *See* Little *et al.*, Tables 5.1 and 5.2 The medians for Ghana were calculated after excluding mining activities and industries with negative value-added at world prices from Abban and Leith, 1973, Table 3.5.
78 Hence, various duty rates were lowered at the time of the 1967 devaluation.
79 Leith, 1973, chapter 3.
80 *See* Killick, 1966, pp. 402–4, for an extreme example, and the *One-Year Plan*,

[81] *1970/71*, pp. 92-3, for discussion of the operation of the Capital Investments Act.
Roemer, 1972.

[82] Lewis, 1955, pp. 277–8.

[83] Government capital expenditure on agriculture, forestry and fisheries went up from about ₵2·5 million in 1960/61 to a peak of ₵18·8 million in 1965.

[84] *See* Table 4.D, line 11 which shows an index of the real value of cocoa farmers' incomes declining by two-thirds between 1960 and 1965.

[85] Imports of Gammalin 20, an anti-capsid spray, effectively ceased in 1965 and at the same time a shortage of imported matchets, a widely used farming tool, developed (*see Abrahams Report*, paragraphs 67–8). The 1965 foreign exchange budget allocated only ₵2 million for agriculture, compared with ₵114 million for manufacturing and a total import programme of ₵312 million. *See The Budget, 1965*, p. 7.

[86] I do not know of any estimates of price elasticities of demand for food in Ghana but Weisskoff, 1971, shows various calculations for several developing countries virtually all of which are less than unity.

[87] The national expenditure elasticity of demand for food in 1961–2 was estimated by Ord *et al.*, 1964, Table V.1, at 0·64.

[88] *See* Table 4.D, line 3, which indicates that money earnings per man in industry rose by 35 per cent between 1960 and 1965.

[89] Little *et al.*, 1971, p. 1.

[90] The importance of the distinction between technical and economic efficiency emerged strikingly from a study by the author of diamond mining in Sierra Leone (Killick, 1973A), where the technically primitive but more nearly indigenous part of the industry was shown to have brought relatively greater developmental benefits to Sierra Leone's economy than a modern, capital-intensive, foreign mine.

[91] Kuznets, 1966, p. 491. *See also* Dennison, 1967.

[92] Hirschman, 1958, chapter 4.

9 The State as Entrepreneur

Increasing participation of the state in the productive and distributive systems was regarded by Nkrumah as being necessary for the creation of a socialist society and was central to his economic strategy. Large sums were invested in newly created state enterprises but, as suggested earlier,[1] these investments failed to yield the economic benefits expected of them. The task of this chapter, then, is to analyse the performance of the state in fulfilling an entrepreneurial role and the weaknesses to which public enterprises were prone.

It is an untidy task, for the topic forbids a simple, clear-cut treatment and there is a mass of factual evidence to attend to. The approach adopted has been to present a wide variety of illustrative evidence on state enterprises, mostly operating in the agricultural and industrial sectors, in order to give due weight to the complexity of the problems which they encountered and the various ways in which their performance may be assessed. Readers willing to take the evidence as read could proceed directly to the concluding section but are warned that in so doing they would miss startling information, and that the evidence is more than usually open to conflicting interpretations.[2]

The Objectives of State Participation

It was argued in chapter 3 that Nkrumah's policies could not be understood unless the creation of a socialist state was recognized as one of his primary objectives, and that he saw socialism as entailing an increasingly important role for the state in all spheres of economic activity. The *Seven-year Plan* was based on this premise, and on at least one occasion Nkrumah described his domestic policy as 'the complete ownership of the economy by the state.'[3] That the expansion of state participation could be regarded as an end in itself does not mean, however, that Nkrumah was uninterested in the enterprises which were created or in the way they performed. State participation was seen as a means to achieve several objectives, and in order to be able to make a sympathetic assessment of their performance and difficulties it is important to clarify the tasks which public enterprises were intended to carry out.

To start at a broad level of generality, state participation could be seen as a means of reconciling Nkrumah's desire to modernize and develop the economy on the one hand, and to increase the degree of economic independence on the other. In the absence of even the potential of a local entrepreneurial class to carry out industrialization at the speed Nkrumah wanted, reluctant as he was, in any case, to encourage the emergence of such a class, and deeply suspicious of foreign capital and other trappings of 'neo-colonialism', there was a vacuum which the state was starred to fill. It was this type of rationale which was most often given for state participation in the fifties[4] and which officials and the less ideologically committed of Nkrumah's Ministers emphasized throughout.[5] For example, a speech by one of Nkrumah's old-guard Ministers argued that the government would play a greater role in industrialization because:[6]

(1) Private enterprise, with its profit motive, feels willing to enter fields with high and quick returns only;
(2) Private enterprises do not want to plough back their profits but prefer to reduce our hard-won foreign currency by transferring a proportion of their profits abroad;
(3) Savings for investment could be most quickly and effectively generated only on a communal basis through creating surpluses in annual government budgets.

In agriculture, too, the state was seen as undertaking tasks which private enterprise could or would not do. This is well stated in Dadson's summary of the rationale for the socialization of agriculture:[7]

Firstly, the introduction of modern production techniques would be much easier and faster on state and collective farms than on peasant farms because the services and resources for improvement, including specialised management, would be centralised and distributed among fewer units. Instead of training and serving many widely scattered farmers, only a relatively few managers need be trained. Secondly, socialised agriculture would operate large-scale farms which would capture the economies of scale associated with the high-priced capital equipment and lumpy investments, such as irrigation, to be introduced. Thirdly, the risk associated with the recommended technical innovations would be assumed by the government in the case of the public sub-sector, and minimised, in the case of the co-operatives, by state assistance in capital, technical resources and marketing channelled through the UGFC [United Ghana Farmers' Council].

Socialized agriculture was also to play an educational role: 'the State

Farms Corporation should concern itself with the introduction of new crops and proven techniques . . . This would be an effective means of popularising new methods . . .'[8]

State enterprises, then, were to be instruments of modernization and sources of investible surpluses. This latter point was repeatedly stressed by Nkrumah and his colleagues. He re-emphasized it when launching the *Seven-year Plan*,[9] which was also very explicit:[10]

> The projects chosen for state investment must include a large proportion with high rates of return and short payoff periods . . . State enterprises will be expected to make a contribution to the public revenues within a reasonable time, and they should not be allowed to become a permanent liability to the economy: enterprises which make losses permanently represent a waste of both capital and current labour resources.

Any tendency to regard profit-making as inappropriate to a socialist economy was scorned, with the retort that the difference between socialism and capitalism 'does not lie in whether or not surplus or profits are made, it lies in who appropriates the surplus and how it is used.'[11] and at a dinner held for Premier Chou En-lai the generation of investment funds by state enterprises was singled out by Nkrumah as one of the chief lessons Ghana could learn from the People's Republic of China.[12] Even after he was deposed, when he might have wished to play down this aspect, Nkrumah still insisted that state enterprises were expected to make profits.[13]

Viewed in this way the role of the state was an entrepreneurial one and public enterprises were to be *development projects*, introducing improved techniques of production, capturing economies of scale, moving into areas which would be neglected by private capital as too risky or insufficiently profitable, and generating surpluses for re-investment (however, note the conflict between the latter two objectives). But the ambitions of the government for its creations did not stop there. We should recall that by the early sixties Nkrumah and his party felt under pressure to bolster their popularity by offering more tangible economic benefits and that he saw socialism as a way of securing these.[14] This provided very different purposes for state enterprises. What mattered most from this point of view was that the new factories and farms should be physically impressive, should be spread over the country, should create new jobs, and (although this was a minor theme) should benefit the consumer via lower prices. And, just as it was necessary to impress the electorate, it was also necessary to reward party activists, so these enterprises were used as sources of party patronage. State enterprise, on this view, was an *instrument of political power*.

Of the 'political' objectives, only the creation of employment received much public articulation. The Workers' Brigade has already been mentioned as an organization created to reduce unemployment and subsequently directed into large-scale farming. Another unit created largely because of governmental fears of unemployment was the State Gold Mining Corporation (SGMC), set up in 1961 to run several mines which private owners intended to close down as uneconomic. There was some reference in this case to the need to prevent export losses but it was the spectre of 15,000 unemployed miners which really haunted the government.[15] Dadson similarly notes that, beside the objectives quoted earlier, the state farms were seen as means of reducing rural unemployment.[16] The hapless state farms were burdened with yet another task: to help the fight against inflation by selling at less than market prices. The creation of an Agricultural Produce Marketing Board, and, later, of a Food Marketing Board were also intended to help keep food prices low.

It is scarcely necessary to mention the major potential conflicts between the developmental and political tasks of the public sector. There is an obvious short-run conflict in any enterprise between padding the payroll and maximizing the re-investible surplus. It is similarly difficult to reconcile job-creation with the use of modern technology if 'modern' is identified with the latest capital-intensive processes. Even more obvious is the conflict between requiring an enterprise simultaneously to sell at artificially low prices and to earn profits. What has been signalled here, then, is a problem of multiple, potentially inconsistent and unreconciled, objectives. For the time being, however, state enterprises will be discussed as if their primary tasks were economic.

The Economic Performance of the Public Sector
That Nkrumah's government succeeded in rapidly expanding the state sector has already been demonstrated. A high proportion of total investment was undertaken by the state, there was a sharp rise in the number of manufacturing concerns owned wholly or partly by the state (Table 5.7) and, if socialized agriculture contributed little by way of output, it absorbed the bulk of the incremental resources devoted to agriculture in the first half of the sixties. This expansion proliferated new public agencies, so that as of March 1966, 53 state enterprises, 12 joint state/private enterprises, and 23 public boards were reported.[17] That these and the central government itself bulked large relative to total economic activity, may be judged from a careful estimate, from admittedly imperfect data, that in 1968 the public sector generated 26 per cent of the GDP.[18] Thus, the performance of the public sector was crucial to Nkrumah's development strategy and could not fail to have an important influence on the overall behaviour of the economy.

How well or badly did public enterprises perform? Most public discussion of this question has centred around their profitability, which is a useful starting point. As Nkrumah perceived, an unprofitable enterprise subtracts from the resources available for new investment and (if we assume growth to result from investment) retards the growth of the economy. The profit record also provides some test of competitive efficiency. But perhaps the main reason for judging state concerns by their profitability is that this is the yardstick most emphasized by successive governments in Ghana. The NLC's policy was to transform existing state enterprises into 'viable' units, where viability was defined as 'securing a return above current and other additional costs involved in bringing the plants into operation.'[19] The Busia government went further and made the earning of a reasonable return on investment a statutory requirement.[20] In its turn, the NRC duly issued the stern enjoinders to make profits with which the managers of state enterprises had become thoroughly familiar.[21]

Those responsible for running state concerns, at least in the manufacturing sector, also used profitability as the test of success or failure. The Industrial Development Corporation (IDC), responsible for running a number of state industries in the fifties, judged performance largely by this measure.[22] So did the State Enterprises Secretariat, which took over responsibility in this area in 1964.[23] So did the Ghana Industrial Holdings Corporation (GIHOC) which, in its turn, took over responsibility for state manufacturing enterprises in 1968.[24]

Adopting this criterion for the time being, how profitable was the public sector? Looking at the overall picture, the answer is not at all. An attempt is made in Table 9.1 to summarize the available financial data on commercial-type public enterprises, where it can be seen that both in the middle and at the end of the decade large aggregate losses were recorded, although the trend was an improving one. The size of the deficit in 1964–5 may be compared with another estimate, namely that at mid–1966 the state had invested a total of ₡164 millions in these and a few other public enterprises.[25] The table shows that losses were incurred by the manufacturing concerns which came under GIHOC, but the largest deficits are recorded in the lower section of the table for the public corporations. It is evident, too, that the profit performance was a very mixed one as between different enterprises and also over time.

More revealing, perhaps, was the persistent co-existence within individual industries of loss-making public enterprises with private firms which may be assumed to have been profitable by virtue of their continued existence. Cases in point at the end of the decade (public enterprises in brackets) included fishing (State Fishing Corporation), construction (State Construction Corporation), distribution (Food Marketing Corporation), road transport (State Transportation Corporation), shoes (State Footwear Corporation), and housing (State Housing Corporation).[26]

TABLE 9.1

Profit and Loss Record of Selected State Enterprises, 1964–5 and 1969–70[a]

	(₵ thousands)	
	1964–5	1969–70
A. GIHOC ENTERPRISES		
1. Fibre bag factory	−318·8	+109·5
2. State boatyards	− 8·4	+ 90·4
3. Brick and tile factory	− 18·7	− 31·3
4. Tema steelworks	−295·4	−203·8
5. State cannery	+ 15·3	+548·2
6. Metal products	+ 24·4	− 67·7
7. Paper conversion	+ 2·1	+123·3
8. Sugar products – Asutsuare	−983·3	−1526·8
Komenda	−208·5	−1212·5
9. Cocoa products, Takoradi	−506·6	+1039·4
10. Paintworks	+117·9	+246·3
11. Vegetable oil mills	−323·8	−208·5
12. Marble works	+ 41·6	− 40·3
13. State distillery	+953·4	+857·5
14. Electronic products	+ 29·8	+100·3
15. SUBTOTAL of above (net)	−1,479·0	−176·0
B. PUBLIC CORPORATIONS, etc.		
16. National Trading Corp.	+6514·5	+2668·0
17. State Farms Corp.	−12,732·5	−1361·0
18. State Fishing Corp.	−239·5	−338·3
19. State Construction Corp.	+353·9[b]	−614·7
20. State Gold Mining Corp.	−2689·2	−6754·1
21. State Hotels and Tourist Corp.	−137·4	+ 51·5[c]
22. Ghana Airways	−3573·2	−2857·4
23. Food Marketing Corp.	−133·6	−237·9
24. SUBTOTAL items 16–23 (net)	−12,637·0	−9,443.9
25. GRAND TOTAL (net)	−14,116·0	−9,619·9

Source: Auditor General *Annual Reports* (various issues).

NOTES:

[a] All commercial-type public enterprises are recorded here for which financial data exist for both 1964–5 and 1969–70. The figures are 12-monthly averages of available data falling within the two-year periods. In most cases it is believed that the figures are for profits/losses before provision for depreciation and taxation. In some cases, however, the figures are after depreciation and/or taxation, and in others the figures are trading results only, i.e. before provision for overheads, etc. It is possible that some of the figures are after provision for government subsidies but subsidies have been netted out whenever possible.

[b] 1963 figure.

[c] Consolidated results of corporations responsible for hotels and tourism.

On this criterion, then, public projects failed to meet the requirements of the governments which created them. It is interesting to compare this record with the results of an IMF study of the financial performance of government-owned corporations in less developed countries. These show that, overall, the corporations in question earned a surplus before depreciation equivalent to eight per cent of the mean value of revenues and expenditures – a figure which would have been substantially larger, were it not for the proclivity of certain European and Latin American countries to run highly unprofitable railways for social reasons.[27] It is not possible to provide an equivalent estimate for Ghana's public sector but it is clear from Table 9.1 that the figure would be negative, indicating unprofitability. Comparatively as well as absolutely, then, the financial performance of Ghana's public sector was poor.

Confining the examination to the directly productive, i.e. agricultural and industrial, state enterprises, the performance is uneven. Mention was made in the previous chapter of the inadequacies of the State Farms Corporation, shown as a major loser in Table 9.1. The State Gold Mining Corporation (SGMC) was another substantial drain on government finances, it being estimated that in 1961 to 1971 subsidies to this corporation amounted to ₵33 million in addition to ₵11 million spent in acquiring the mines.[28] State-manufacturing also proved unprofitable in the Nkrumah years. Between 1950–1 and 1960–1 the IDC had an accumulated operating deficit of ₵4·0 million[29] and for the enterprises that subsequently became GIHOC subsidiaries Table 9.1 records an average deficit for 1964–5 of ₵1·5 million. However, GIHOC could boast improvement in the later sixties as shown in the table. GIHOC's best performers were a cocoa processing factory, a liquor distillery and a fruit cannery; two sugar factories made enormous losses. Finally and significantly, enterprises owned jointly by the state and private partners were consistently more profitable than concerns owned wholly by the state. All but one of the fourteen joint enterprises for which figures are available were making profits in 1966–67.[30]

Despite these exceptions, however, the overall financial performance of state enterprise was at best indifferent. But profitability, while it is the criterion most generally applied in Ghana, seems to this writer to be a poor indicator of public-sector performance, for a variety of reasons.

The elementary point is often overlooked that only in a competitive situation is profit a reasonably reliable indicator of efficiency; when this condition is not met, an inefficient producer may make profits because of monopoly power. In fact, many of Ghana's state enterprises were monopolies or were selling in highly imperfect markets. Industrial statistics indicate that, in 1969, 83 per cent of the total gross output of state enterprises was produced in industries in which state concerns contributed 75 per cent or more of the total output of the industry.[31] In six industries state enterprises accounted for the whole output. Bearing in mind protection from foreign competition,[32] profits earned in such monopolistic situations are an exceedingly unreliable guide to economic efficiency, with very limited competitive pressure to keep down costs. An absence of competition combined with the distortions in factor and product markets mentioned in preceding chapters implies very large potential divergences between private and social valuations – a point well illustrated by Fordwor's estimates, in which there was no correlation between the private and social rates of return for a variety of Ghana's state enterprises.[33]

Examination of specific cases also calls the usefulness of the profit criterion into question. For example, the distillery which contributed so handsomely to the surpluses of GIHOC (Table 9.1) did so on the basis of a very high level of protection and, far from its profits indicating social efficiency, its operations probably involved negative value-added when valued at world prices.[34] It was also buying sugar molasses for conversion into alcohol from one of the sugar factories at below cost. Again, a cocoa products factory was among the most profitable state enterprises in the late sixties,[35] but its surpluses were derived from the fact that the Cocoa Marketing Board was obliged to sell beans to the factory at less than world prices; in fact, this was another of the industries involving negative value-added at world prices.[36]

Finally, we might mention the Ghana National Trading Corporation (GNTC), which, despite having to observe price controls (chapter 10), made an annual profit of ₡6·5 million in 1964–5 (Table 9.1). That it should have done so tells us little about efficiency because much of its business consisted of the importation and distribution of consumer goods; not only was the cedi greatly overvalued in these years, placing a handsome scarcity premium on foreign goods, but the Corporation was favoured in the allocation of import licences. It was predictable, then, that by 1969–70 – by which time there had been a devaluation, a liberalization of imports and reduced discrimination in favour of GNTC in the allocation of licences – its annual profits had fallen, to about ₡2·7. That its surpluses were a poor performance indicator is further illustrated by this extract from a 1965 official report:[37]

The monopoly over the importation of essential goods accorded to the Ghana National Trading Corporation has also wrought its own havoc. We do not believe that GNTC possesses the logistic talent to move large quantities of goods at short notice over a wide area. Indeed, it could not even clear its imports from Tema harbour with despatch, while some smaller importers had some of their goods trapped under the ponderous GNTC consignments. In all such cases, consumers were the real victims. They suffered unnecessary deprivation and the additional charges involved in this clumsiness were passed on to the people.

These remarks on the limitations of the profitability criterion have so far been adverse to the public sector but other considerations pull in the opposite direction. Mention was made earlier of social objectives for the public sector which conflicted with short-run profit maximization. In consequence, some enterprises were forced to sell at below ruling market prices or to employ excess labour (the state farms were required to do both things), and they could not reasonably be condemned for making losses. As a more special case, the state gold mines could not have been expected to show profits, for they were unprofitable when taken over and were subjected to much inflation of costs which was not of their making, while for most of the sixties selling their output at a fixed world price. It is interesting to record, though, that there were cases in which state concerns sacrificed social objectives in order to maximize profits. Again, the state distillery provides an illustration. It was originally intended to provide a cheap and healthy substitute for a crude local spirit. However, it soon found that the upper end of the liquor market was more lucrative and turned to producing for the middle class.[38] Joint enterprises have probably been most prone to this type of action, for the state was usually a sleeping partner content to let the private shareholders determine policy and manage operations. Thus, in explicit defiance of government policy, the management of a jointly owned soap factory ceased production in 1970 of a popular brand of carbolic soap without notifying the government board members.

Another factor telling against the use of a profitability criterion is that a high proportion of state enterprises was set up during the first half of the sixties and, in some cases, did not begin production until 1966 or even later. Businesses can expect to make losses initially and it seems likely that the improved trend in GIHOC finances shown in Table 9.1 is at least partly due to the fact that more and more of its enterprises were overcoming their teething troubles.

For these and other reasons which will become apparent later, other tests must be applied in order to make a sensible assessment of economic efficiency. Put at its most general, indicators are sought of the efficiency with which the public sector has used the resources devoted to it, relative to the general efficiency of resource-use in the economy. The data are not good enough to permit direct estimates of the marginal productivities of capital and labour so we are forced to use indirect evidence, which is fortunately not lacking. Enough was said in chapter 8 about productivities on state farms, and to keep the task within manageable limits the following discussion will be confined to state industrial enterprises.

First, there are comparative data on labour productivities, where the term is used broadly to refer to output or value-added per man. A study of industrial labour productivity in 1959 found that productivities tended to be well below average in state concerns[39] and, while much happened after 1959, more up-to-date statistics suggest that the same remained true throughout the sixties. The results are summarized in Table 9.2.

Looking for the moment at the last sub-period, 1969–70, it can be seen that labour productivity in state concerns remained well below that in private concerns and even further below the rather exceptional figure for joint enterprises. These results are, of course, highly aggregated (the published data do not permit an industry-by-industry breakdown) and it could be that these adverse figures, although consistent with earlier findings, result from a different spread of state concerns across the manufacturing sector than in the other two categories. Examination of the evidence does not, however, support this explanation, for the industrial composition of state manufacturing is similar to that of private firms.[40] Furthermore, Odling-Smee examined statistics on value-added per head in manufacturing in 1968 in those industries in which both private and public establishments were substantially involved and found productivity in public enterprises to be an average of only 56 per cent of the levels attained in the private sector[41] – almost the same as the figure for 1969–70 in Table 9.2. The relatively poor showing of the state sector is all the more noteworthy because, as is mentioned later, state enterprises tended to be more capital intensive than their private competitors – which should have resulted in higher, not lower, labour productivities.

TABLE 9.2
Comparative Labour Productivities and Costs in Manufacturing Enterprises by Type of Ownership, Selected Periods (means of two-year periods)

	1962–3	1965–6	1969–70
Value-added per person engaged [a] *(₵)*			
1. Private enterprises	1,635	1,775	1,424
2. Joint state/private	4,503	4,415	2,871
3. State enterprises	748	690	784
4. State as % of private	45·7%	38·9%	55·1%
5. State as % of joint enterprises	16·6%	15·6%	27·3%
Total wages and salaries as percentage of total value-added [b] *(%)*			
6. Private enterprises	23·4%	23·4%	23·9%
7. Joint state/private	14·0%	13·5%	17·4%
8. State enterprises	51·0%	46·1%	30·6%

Source: *Industrial Statistics,* various issues.

NOTES
[a] Calculated in constant, 1962, prices.
[b] Calculated in current prices.

However, Table 9.2 does show an improvement in the relative performance of state enterprises during the later sixties (see lines 4 and 5). They remained less efficient, by this measure, than other manufacturing firms but were at least catching up. This presumably reflected the various steps taken after 1966 to improve management standards, although it may also have been helped by the once-for-all results of newer firms overcoming teething troubles.

The outstandingly high productivities in joint state-private firms should also be noted from the table, although there was a fall in the second half of the decade. This may partly result from a significantly different industry-structure in the case of these units (see footnote 40), but also from more efficient managements than those in wholly state-owned units and more favourable government treatment than typically enjoyed by wholly privately owned concerns.

No improvement can be reported in the case of the State Gold Mining Corporation (SGMC) comparable with that for state manufacturing. Table 9.3 sets out statistics on labour productivity in the SGMC mines and in the then privately owned Ashanti Goldfields, showing that while productivity in Ashanti was improving in the sixties, there was a sharp deterioration in the SGMC mines in the second half of the decade. Thus, while the number of tons of ore processed per man was greater in the three main SGMC mines in 1959 than it was in Ashanti, by 1968 (the latest year for which comparative data are available) the Ashanti figure was above all the others.[42]

Leaving aside the efficiency of the use of labour, the next step is to obtain an idea of the productivity of the capital employed. Only indirect and scrappy evidence is available, and we are forced to use measures of capacity utilization as a rough indicator of the efficiency of capital use. Mention was made on p. 171 of the estimate for 1963–4 showing actual output of state enterprises to be only 29 per cent of rated capacity. However, economic conditions at that time made under-utilization almost inevitable, and more recent data would be preferable. Unfortunately, it is only possible to report some specific examples, which probably give a somewhat biased impression, for the poor performers are the most likely to receive publicity. The information is nevertheless worth some attention:

(a) In 1967 and 1968 the state footwear factory achieved production levels averaging only 24 per cent of rated capacity – 480,000 pairs of shoes annually as against a capacity of two million.[43]

(b) In 1967 the state sugar factory at Komenda achieved an output of 21 per cent of capacity; another factory at Asutsuare managed a mere 3 per cent.[44]

(c) Between 1965 and 1968, six vessels of the State Fishing Corporation achieved annual average catches of 1,512 tons per vessel, against the opinion of an independent consultant that 'under reasonable management the productivity of this type of vessel in

Ghana should be somewhat above 3,000 tons a year.'[45]
(d) It has been stated of the state distillery that from the time of its commissioning it has only operated at about one-third capacity.[46]
(e) A study of a state copra oil mill shows that in 1962–6 the throughput of the factory averaged 69 per cent of milling capacity. Notwithstanding this, mill capacity was doubled in 1967, and utilization rates in 1967 and 1968 were 21·4 and 6·6 per cent.[47]
(f) The fibre bag factory is said to have operated at 25–30 per cent of one-shift capacity between 1964 and 1970.[48]

Tables 9.2 and 9.3 indicate a further performance criterion related to the two just discussed, namely unit costs of production. The bottom five lines of Table 9.3 contain the firmest information, showing that during the sixties SGMC unit working costs went up by about two-and-

TABLE 9.3
Comparative Productivities and Costs on State and Private Gold Mines, Selected Years

Mine	1951	1959	1965	1968	1971
SGMC Mines[a]	*Tons of ore milled per man*				
Tarkwa	141·5	130·6	90·0	76·7	72·9
Prestea	81·5	104·0	122·3	89·5	79·0
Konongo	24·9	66·6[c]	51·3	57·2	30·4
Ashanti Goldfields	27·3	60·1	98·4	93·2	—
	Indices of productivity per man; 1961=100[b]				
SGMC (consolidated)	78	102	102	80	65
Ashanti Goldfields	46	92	136	139	—
	Working costs per ounce of gold – cedis				
SGMC (weighted average)	—	18.4	31.4	45.5	64.3
of which:					
Tarkwa	15.6	20.2	59.8	69.6	87.0
Prestea	14.6	18.7	28.1	33.0	43.2
Konongo	7.5	16.4[c]	18.5	43.4	97.8
Ashanti Goldfields	—	10.5[d]	11.2	13.4	—

Sources: Killick, 1966, Table 11–2; State Gold Mining Corporation; Ashanti Goldfields, *Annual Reports;* Ghana Chamber of Mines, *Annual Reports.*
NOTES:
[a] These mines became the responsibility of SGMC in 1961, with exception of Konongo, which was taken over in February 1965.
[b] Indices of fine ounces of gold produced per man, adjusted to exclude the effect of changes in ore qualities.
[c] 1960 figure.
[d] 1961 figure.
A dash indicates data not available.

a-half times in 1959–68, while the Ashanti increase was much smaller. There was, moreover, a further 40 per cent increase in SGMC costs in 1968–71, so that in 1971 working costs alone averaged ₡64.3 against a realized price per ounce of ₡47.0.

Cost comparisons in the manufacturing sector unfortunately have to be derived by inference rather than from direct data. The last three lines of Table 9.2 do, however, give labour costs relative to value-added in manufacturing and show that wages absorbed substantially higher proportions of total value-added in state enterprises than in the other two categories shown. It may be inferred from these figures that unit costs tended to be higher in state manufacturing enterprises, although that admittedly is not the only possibility.[49] However, while over time the growth of earnings and productivity were about equal in the private sector, leading to stability in the proportion of the wage-bill to value-added, this proportion declined in the state sector, i.e. productivity rose more rapidly than average earnings.

As a concluding and related test of the relative performance of the public sector, we can enquire into its contributions to the balance of payments and the efficiency with which it converted domestic resources into foreign exchange. Calculations of domestic resource costs (DRCs) per unit of net foreign exchange saved or earned have been made for a few state enterprises with results ranging from ₡0.77 (fibre bags), to ₡1.36 (glassware), to ₡2.14 (footwear).[50] Some supposedly import-substituting or exporting state concerns actually involved negative value-added in world prices: the cases of the cocoa products factory and the liquor distillery have already been cited in this connection; a meat canning factory falls into a similar category by being a net loser of foreign exchange.[51]

Steel, whose research into the efficiency of Ghanaian manufacturing was cited extensively in chapter 8, concluded from regression analyses that publicly owned plants in 1967–8 were inefficient savers or earners of foreign exchange but no more so than the rest of Ghanaian industry.[52] This is the first substantial piece of evidence which we have seen in which state enterprises do not compare adversely with the private sector, but is a little misleading, for Steel also found that large and capital-intensive plants tended to have higher DRCs, and attention to his detailed results shows that state interprises tended to be somewhat larger and more capital-intensive than the overall average.[53] Moreover, his sample only included ten state enterprises.

Note finally the following estimates of the DRCs of the SGMC mines in 1970:[54]

	Cedis per unit of foreign exchange
Tarkwa mine	(Net foreign exchange loser)
Prestea mine	1.18
Konongo mine	1.44
Dunkwa mine	1.46
AVERAGE FOR ALL MINES	2.36

Overall, the mines were inefficient earners of foreign exchange, using ₵2.36 of local resources for every cedi's-worth of net foreign exchange earned, but this stemmed almost solely from the Tarkwa mine, which had sunk to such a remarkably low level of efficiency that it consumed more foreign exchange than the value of its output. No comparable calculation can be made for Ashanti Goldfields but there can be little doubt that their DRCs would not exceed some fraction of a cedi.

To sum up, this section has sought to appraise the economic performance of the public sector in carrying out the developmental and entrepreneurial functions which Nkrumah's government expected of it, neglecting for the time being any substantial discussion of its success in achieving the non-developmental objectives which the politicians also had in mind. In the end, it has proved harder to use a single criterion of comparative economic performance, which is analytically satisfying and amenable to empirical testing, than it has been to characterize the general standard of economic performance of Ghana's public sector. Despite measurement problems, the spotty nature of the evidence and substantial variations between specific enterprises, it may fairly be concluded that the comparative performance of the public sector was poor in the sixties.

State enterprises were unprofitable – absolutely, by comparison with public enterprise in other developing countries and by comparison with private enterprise in Ghana – and they were unprofitable despite considerable monopoly powers. While profitability is an unsatisfactory yard-stick, data on relative productivities, unit costs, and balance of payments effects also point fairly unambiguously in the direction of poor comparative performance. We should also remember the disastrous showing of government farms demonstrated in the previous chapter (Table 8.2). To this generally rather dismal account three qualifications should be mentioned, however. (a) Joint state-private enterprises have been doing far better than any others. (b) There was clear evidence of an improving trend among state manufacturing enterprises during the later sixties; whether they will eventually catch up or whether many of the improvements were of a once-for-all nature, only time will show. (c) It has not so far been possible to say much about spill-over effects on the remainder of the economy and any longer-run dynamic effects; a certain amount of evidence relevant to this is, however, presented below.

So far as the sixties are concerned, then, state enterprise failed to fill the entrepreneurial gap, to propel the economy forward, and to generate the surpluses which Nkrumah, however unrealistically, demanded of them. And, given the centrality of rapidly expanding state participation to Nkrumah's development efforts, their failure undermined his entire strategy. It is thus important to establish why the failure occurred, and the remainder of this chapter is devoted to a survey of the factors contributing to the poor economic performance of Ghana's public sector.

Reasons for Poor Performance: (a) Project Planning

The adequacy of the project planning process represents a logical starting-point, by which is meant the arrangements for the identification, design, appraisal, siting and construction of state enterprises. Beginning with a look at the factor proportions incorporated in the projects which were approved, mention has already been made of Steel's finding that state manufacturing enterprises tended to be somewhat more capital-intensive than the rest of his sample. Ministry of Finance and Planning data suggest a capital investment of about ₵5,000 per worker in the projects approved in the first half of the sixties.[55] That is to say, an investment of about one million cedis was needed in order to create an extra 200 jobs in state industries. In the absence of comparable data on the private sector, it is impossible to characterize such an investment per worker as either large or small, and in any case, it was argued in chapters 7 and 8 that there were considerable inducements for private investors also to opt for capital-intensive techniques. However, since the alleviation of unemployment was one of the principal reasons for industrialization given in the *Seven-year Plan,* a really huge investment bill would be implied for industrialization to absorb a significant number of unemployed, if each job were to cost ₵5,000.[56]

Evidence on individual projects supports other data in indicating the public sector to be particularly prone to capital-intensity. The sugar factories at Komenda and Asutsuare provide cases in point, in both their agricultural and industrial aspects. On the agricultural side, the intention was that all the sugar should be grown under irrigation – even though rain-fed sugar grows well in Ghana and subsequent experience showed that yields were not significantly higher in irrigated areas – and under mechanized plantation conditions – even though peasant farmers have since proved to be the lower-cost producers.[57] As far as the factories are concerned, Pickett *et al.* have not only shown that much more labour-intensive processes were technically possible than those actually installed but also that a variant of the labour-intensive alternative would have yielded larger private and social returns.[58]

The government farms provide a further example of a perverse mix of factors: in response to a plentiful supply of agricultural land and shortages of capital and foreign exchange, government farms were based upon the intensive cultivation of land by the use of imported tractors. Dadson has shown that in the first half of the sixties the number of tractors in the country was increased about 25-fold (admittedly from a very small base),[59] and that in a sample of 15 state farms a median of just over 35 acres was cultivated per tractor in 1965.[60] The ratio of capital to labour was almost infinitely greater than that on most peasant farms, notwithstanding the employment of excess labour on state farms.[61]

Two other examples may be mentioned. A report on the state footwear factory noted that it was installed with conveyors, reducing the number of workers to move shoes in process, although conveyors were little used elsewhere, even in the US; and the paper by Pickett *et al.* shows that it would have been feasible to build a commercially more promising shoe factory with a per-worker investment of only about one-sixth of the actually installed investment.[62] Secondly, a report on the State Fishing Corporation made a comparison between the value of per-worker investment in vessels by the Corporation with a small fishing port in the US and showed investment per worker about eight times as great in Ghana as in the American example.[63]

A rather consistent tendency for the government to opt for project designs emphasizing grandeur rather than economy reinforced the bias toward capital intensity. There were several examples of this. Uphoff cites a pharmaceutical factory, where a relatively modest design was turned down in favour of another which eventually cost nearly ten times as much and which included 'eleven bungalows for managers, a handsomely outfitted administration block, a large cafeteria with one of the biggest and most modern kitchens in Ghana, and housing for experimental animals better than that in which most Ghanaians lived.'[64] The footwear factory similarly included nineteen bungalows, a four-storey administrative block, six blocks of 'cloak-rooms,' a kitchen and a canteen; it is small wonder that a later evaluation of this project concluded that 'the overall size of all the buildings is much too big . . .'[65] These were almost the same words as the conclusion of a similar study of a fruit cannery: 'In general, the buildings are over-designed and over-built.'[66] Fruit canneries at two other locations revealed the same tendency to over-design; one of them had a capacity for the production of mango products, for which there was recognized to be no local market, which was said to exceed by some multiple the total world trade in such items.[67] There was also the case of a glass factory. Here the Minister of Industries had been faced with a clear choice between two designs, one providing for the production of both bottles and sheet glass and another which argued against installing a sheet glass capacity at that stage of Ghana's development. The Minister recommended the former alternative on the grounds that it was 'the most complete "turn-key" proposal for a really up-to-date and first class glass factory,' with the consequence that the sheet glass plant, with a capacity nearly three times the size of the local market, was never brought into production and has since had to be converted for bottle-making at an extra cost of about ₵2.5 million.[68] We might lastly cite the construction in different parts of the country of two tomato canneries, the capacities of either one of which would have met total domestic demand.[69]

The glass factory was one of a number of projects in which the technical design of plant was inappropriate. Thus, an early report on the construction of a steelworks utilizing scrap recommended the installation of blast furnaces rather than electric ones, on the grounds that the former were more economical in the production of the low-grade type of steel products needed in the local market. High-cost electric furnaces were nonetheless installed.[70] In the case of the footwear factory, equipment was installed for four different types of shoe construction but two of these were unfashionable and the equipment for them could not be used.[71] A last example relates to the fruit cannery, on which it was reported that 'The many food processing experts who have examined the pineapple and citrus canning facilities . . . have agreed that this plant is poorly designed for the situation existing in Ghana'.[72]

As can already be implied, arrangements for pre-investment feasibility studies were quite inadequate. In some cases it is doubtful whether any such studies were undertaken at all. This appears true of most of the new state farms, for, as the World Bank was to point out, 'the most simple calculations of costs and returns would have indicated the lack of viability inherent in many of the Corporation's projects prior to their implementation.'[73] It also appears true of at least one of the sugar projects.[74]

However, some type of feasibility study was undertaken in most cases – but mostly by the very companies who would sell the equipment for any factory which was subsequently built and who, in the words of the Ministry of Finance, were 'more interested in selling than in anything else.'[75] There were blatant examples of studies arriving at favourable conclusions only on the basis of quite unrealistic assumptions. Appraisals of fruit canning possibilities by a Jugoslav company were among the worst. It was they who failed so lamentably to consider the market for the output of the mango cannery; the same company based a study of the two tomato canning factories on an assumed price for tomatoes of one pesewa per pound when farmers were receiving from ordinary market traders $5\frac{1}{2}$ to 9 pesewas in one centre and up to 15 pesewas in the other.[76] In similar fashion, British consultants (who subsequently built and managed the project) based their analysis of the steelworks on an assumed price for electric power which was only about 30 per cent of the going rate for other industrial consumers.[77]

Using interested parties to undertake feasibility studies sometimes killed potentially sound projects as well as promoting unsound ones. A case in point was the use of companies who were supplying Ghana's cement industry with imported clinker to study the possibility of replacing the clinker with domestic limestone.[78] This was done twice and it can come as little surprise that both companies arrived at negative conclusions. The same mistake was made regarding the creation of an alumina plant, where the company studying the project had a clearly established interest in producing a negative result, and duly did so.[79] As a final item in this catalogue of errors, feasibility studies undertaken almost never went beyond a commercial appraisal and were therefore, unlikely to lead to socially efficient investment deci-

sions.[80] Since factor prices were distorted in favour of the use of capital, this concentration on commercial appraisals no doubt helps to
explain the tendency for projects to be excessively capital-intensive.

Locational planning proved another weakness, with several examples of enterprises whose viability was undermined by poor siting. The
manufacture of glass products, for example, is normally a market-
orientated industry because of high transportation costs but Ghana's
glass factory is located many miles from the two main points of
consumption, Accra and Kumasi, its location having apparently been
determined by the nearby existence of suitable sand.[81] Or take the
following description of a cattle-based industrial complex:[82]

> The footwear factory was to have been an example of balanced
> industrial growth in the country as one leg of a tripoid agro-industry
> complex. It would have linked the Meat Factory in the North
> through transportation of the hides to the South (for a distance of
> over 500 miles) to a tannery (now abandoned); the leather was to
> have been backhauled to the Footwear Factory in Kumasi, in the
> centre of the country and about 200 miles north of the tannery.
> Since the major footwear market is in the Accra metropolitan area,
> the shoes would then have to be transported an additional 200 miles
> back to the South.

The location of the meat factory has itself been severely criticized on
economic grounds.[83]

Some of this was undoubtedly motivated by the desire to disperse
industry over the country, and, especially, to politically sensitive or
favoured areas. The clearest example was the decision to establish a
state farm in every parliamentary constituency;[84] the siting of various
small vegetable oil mills also sacrificed economic for political
benefits;[85] it is also believed that a sugar factory was established at a
rather unfavourable site at Komenda for political motives.[86] There
were doubtless other examples which have not been documented.

Problems were encountered in the construction and equipment of
projects, with frequent delays in construction because of poor co-
ordination.[87] The six years it took to complete the footwear factory, for
example, was partly responsible for the obsolescence of much of its
plant by the time it was ready to go into production. In common with
other agriculture-based industries, the sugar factories were completed
before the associated plantations, and the Komenda factory stood idle
for more than a year because it lacked a water supply system.[88] There
were also problems with equipment. A parliamentary report alleged
that plant supplied for vegetable oil mills 'was of pre-war manufacture
and had been lying idle for more than 30 years' before being supplied.[89] The government farms also ran into insoluble shortages of
spare parts and ancillary equipment for their tractors, partly because

no less than twenty-two different makes and models of tractors were in use.[90]

Nowhere did the weaknesses of project planning reveal themselves more starkly than in the agro-industries. Some years ago I drew attention to the fact that most IDC projects based on local raw materials had run in to serious difficulties and concluded:[91]

> The lesson to be learned from these examples is not that local materials are inferior or inevitably unreliable but that when a project is planned on the basis of local raw material supplies the source of supply must, for planning purposes, be treated as part of the project itself. To treat these two aspects as even semi-independent of each other is to invite trouble . . .

That lesson was not learned in Nkrumah's time and trouble, having been invited, duly arrived.

One example was the meat processing factory established to produce corned beef at Bolgatanga in the far north of the country. Reusse has pointed out that the project was basically ill-conceived. Competitive production of corned beef either requires large supplies of scrap meat left over after the prime cuts have been removed, or a substantial exportable surplus of low-cost slaughter-stock which may be canned and sold abroad. Neither of these conditions existed, for Ghana imports much of her meat and cattle, and the whole carcass finds a ready demand as fresh meat. Thus, the factory was doomed to produce high-cost corned beef and to be a net loser of foreign exchange.[92] It is fortunate, therefore, that it has never been possible to supply cattle to the factory in the numbers needed for the production of corned beef, despite strenuous efforts to secure adequate supplies.[93] Mention might also be made here of an associated failure in the production of leather: it was originally planned that the state footwear factory would get about half its leather supplies locally but in fact had to rely wholly on imports.[94]

The sugar industry is another whose agricultural weaknesses have received publicity in Ghana. From their inception the two sugar factories operated at far below capacity for lack of cane. Both were intended to be largely supplied by their own plantations, under irrigation, but many and persistent difficulties were encountered. The plantations were not ready when the factories were completed, despite delays in the latter; the irrigation facilities were still not finished by the early seventies; and great difficulties were met in co-ordinating the programmes of the Ministry of Agriculture (and other agencies responsible for aspects of sugar cultivation) and of the factory managements.[95] In the end the difficulties were found too great and a fresh start had to be made; the World Bank provided a ₵20 million loan to 'rehabilitate' the industry with new equipment, an improved cultivation programme, and Dutch management.[96] A small factory producing copra oil similarly ran into serious and persistent supply problems with the result, already reported, that it consistently operated at well below its capacity output.[97]

But the saddest cases of all related to the factories built to can tomatoes and other fruits, the experiences of which are exemplified in the following extract from a Ministry of Agriculture memo written just over a year before the factories were to be commissioned:[98]

> *Project*   A factory is to be erected at Wenchi, Brong Ahafo, to pro-
> cess 7,000 tons of mangoes and 5,300 tons of tomatoes per annum.
> The factory is to be commissioned in November, 1966. If average
> yields of crops in that area will be 5 tons per acre per annum for
> mangoes and 5 tons per crop per acre for tomatoes, there should be
> 1,400 acres of mangoes and 1,060 acres of tomatoes in the field to
> supply the factory . . .

> *The Problem*   The present supply of mangoes in the area is from a
> few trees scattered in the bush and tomatoes are not grown on
> commercial scale, and so the production of these crops will have to
> start from scratch. Mangoes take 5–7 years from planting to start
> fruiting and tomatoes could produce two crops per annum. How to
> obtain sufficient planting materials and to organise production of
> raw materials quickly become the major problems in this project.

It is difficult to imagine a more damning commentary on the efficiency of project planning. Uphoff has recorded the ineptitude with which the industrial and agricultural phasing of another tomato canning factory was handled, leading at one point to the use of border guards and police to keep away private wholesalers while the management bought 30 tons of tomatoes needed to give the factory a trial run![99] The quality of local tomatoes and mangoes was also found to be unsuitable for industrial processing. At the time of writing it has not been possible to start production at either factory, although efforts are being made to bring them into use.[100]

It was, of course, entirely characteristic that crop production should prove to be the Achilles heel of these industries in the late Nkrumah years. The distrust of the peasant farmers, the deterioration of the extension services, the proliferation of largely un-coordinated and generally inefficient agencies responsible for various aspects of agricultural policy, and the generally chaotic nature of project plan-ning which were characteristic of the later Nkrumah years undermined the prospects of the agro-industries, even though, being based on local supplies, these were the ones which could have contibuted most to the development of Ghana's economy had they been soundly conceived and efficiently executed. There was also, it seemed, little comprehen-sion of the special complexity of agro-industries:[101]

The presence of a wild-growing variety of a particular crop (or the cultivation of a local variety by local farmers) seemed often to be taken as a sufficient indication that conditions were favourable for the growing of a commercial crop. That economical processing of the quality of the end product will often demand cultivation of specially bred varieties with different soil or climatical requirements or different susceptibility to diseases and pests, was a point which – understandably enough for us – was not always fully appreciated. The same applied to the special character and skill requirements of agricultural operations which are closely geared to large-scale processing units, which for the optimal utilisation of expensive capital installations demand close integration of agricultural and processing operations during the stage of implementation as well as during actual operations.

With a very severely limited managerial and administrative capacity to co-ordinate complex projects of this kind, and a political climate which placed little premium on careful, cost-conscious planning it is perhaps not surprising that the agro-industries were among the least successful of all the experiments in state participation.

Reasons for Poor Performance: (b) Financial
Shortages of working capital and other financial hinderances have been a common complaint of state enterprises. To give an early illustration, the management of the IDC complained bitterly about a 'general curtailment of development funds' in the mid- and later fifties, and for a time was forced to abandon their expansion programme. Several subsidiary companies got into financial difficulties and the IDC was forced to make its profitable enterprises subsidize those in the red.[102] Ten years later almost exactly the same could be written of GIHOC. It too was complaining, probably justly so, that it has been funded with inadequate working capital, and was resorting to cross-subsidization.[103] The state gold mines ran into even graver difficulties. For a time in the mid-sixties and (to a reduced extent) later, the SGMC was unable to obtain fuel, explosives and other essential materials partly because it could not pay its bills and was being denied further credit, and this caused work stoppages. There were delays in paying wages, with predictable effects on morale and labour relations, and the management found itself preoccupied with the day-to-day task of scraping enough money together to keep the mines going; naturally the longer-term planning and development of the mines suffered.[104]

However, closer examination raises the question of whether shortages of funds are rightly to be seen as a cause or an effect of the poor performance of state enterprises. Reasons sometimes given for financial difficulties do not have much substance. One such example is that several of the industrial enterprises were initially over-valued and that the inflated asset values were a financial millstone around the necks of the enterprises in question. In the case of the footwear enterprise, for example, it was found that the actual cost of the factory and its equipment was about 50 per cent greater than a 'prudent investor' cost of a factory of about the same capacity;[105] a comparable estimate for the Pwalugu and Wenchi fruit factories showed their cost to have been 85 per cent greater than a 'prudent investor' cost;[106] there were probably other cases which have not been documented. While this certainly points to poor investment decisions, it does not offer an explanation of enterprises running into current financial difficulties, for depreciation provisions in these concerns were purely notional and did not involve locked-up depreciation reserves.[107]

Another complaint was that enterprises ran into difficulties because they were forced to sell at sub-market prices. The state farms were required to sell their produce at below current market prices,[108] and the sugar factories sometimes found themselves competing with imported supplies the prices of which were artifically and unsustainably low.[109] In general, however, it is surprising how little political pressure was applied on the pricing policies of state concerns. The *Abrahams Report* stated in 1965 that 'In the case of State Industrial Corporations, the Management of each Enterprise has, in the past been solely responsible for determining pricing . . .'[110] and this remained generally the case through to the early seventies.

One reason for the recurring complaints about shortages of capital funds was unprofitability. To revert to the IDC case, it was found on investigation that the period in which the organization was complaining most strongly about shortages of money was one in which the government was increasing its financial support of the Corporation on an unprecedented scale.[111] Why the complaints? Because at the same time the operating deficits of IDC were also expanding very sharply, absorbing a good deal of the money voted to it by parliament. Similarly, shortages of funds experienced in the sixties by such concerns as SGMC, the sugar projects, and the Esiama oil mill were directly related to their operating losses and consequent inability to generate working capital.

Furthermore, the less successful enterprises often had much of their capital tied up in unsaleable stocks of finished products and, perhaps, raw materials.[112] This was true, for example, of the footwear and (for a time) glass factories. The case of the SGMC was more complicated, as two factors interacted to keep the Corporation chronically short of liquidity. The first was a reluctance on the part of successive governments to face up to the high financial cost of keeping the mines open, causing the complaint that 'Governments have never fully accepted the costs of maintaining the Corporation as an employment-creating device but at the same time have never been prepared to allow it to operate on sound commercial and mining principles.'[113] The second was the fault of the Corporation's management: a tendency to base budget estimates upon unrealistic assumptions of improvements in its own performance, causing actual deficits to be larger than planned, which added further to financial stringency. The case of the IDC parallels that of the gold mines, for too much of its capital was locked up in projects wished upon it by politicians, and it too tended systematically to underestimate the losses of its subsidiaries, which then absorbed funds intended for other purposes. Yet another factor affecting the liquidity of state industries was a tendency for the gestation phase of projects to be substantially longer than planned, absorbing funds which had been earmarked as working capital.[114] Further difficulties were created by the tardiness of other public bodies and the central government in paying their bills – a factor, for example, which seriously reduced the liquidity of the state construction corporation.

It is, then, difficult to disentangle cause from effect in this discussion. Poor economic performance as often as not led to shortages of finance, which made performance even worse. This became a vicious circle, but in the general case there was a 'capital shortage illusion'[115] at work and finance was not the root cause of sub-standard performance. To revert to the IDC, its real difficulty was not shortages of money but its inability to find paying investments and to administer its projects. As these managerial weaknesses became increasingly evident, government confidence in the IDC diminished and Ministers were increasingly tempted to interfere with its day-to-day working, which made matters worse. Poor performance, shortages of funds and deteriorating relationships with government became mutually reinforcing. All in all, it would be much easier to accept the 'shortage of funds' argument if there were reasonable grounds for thinking that additional funds would have been more wisely invested than those actually received.

Reasons for Poor Performance: (c) Over-manning

A tendency for state enterprises to retain surplus labour helps to explain their lower labour productivities, higher unit labour costs and generally poor economic performance. 'Overstaffing,' lamented the State Enterprise Secretariat, 'is one of the major problems of state corporations. There is hardly any enterprise which is not overloaded with redundant staff'.[116] However, it is useful to distinguish between the special cases of units maintained primarily to create (or prevent a reduction in) employment, and other more commercially oriented concerns which were nevertheless over-manned. We have already noted that the SGMC was set up to protect the jobs of miners threatened with unemployment,[117] and one might thus take the whole SGMC operation as essentially an employment-creating device – which did not prevent governments from judging SGMC by its profitability. There is one unambiguous example of using the SGMC to maintain employment, at its mine at Bibiani. This ran out of ore in 1968 but was nevertheless not closed, so that in mid-1973 it was still maintaining a labour force of several hundreds even though it had not produced an ounce of gold for several years. The Workers' Brigade is another example of an agency set up specifically to create jobs, and to a substantial extent the Nkrumah government used the state construction and housing corporations for the same purpose.[118]

But apart from these special cases, there is considerable evidence to support the Secretariat's complaint of general over-manning. Documentary evidence – relating to a state-owned boatyard, vegetable oil mills, the footwear factory, a match factory, the state farms and others – would be too tedious to present here.[119] Suffice it to give two (admittedly extreme) examples. There was first the case of a bamboo processing factory which was found in 1966–7 to have spent just ₵219 on raw materials whereas wages and salaries amounted to ₵16,184.[120] Then there was the State Fishing Corporation:[121]

As of October 1, 1968 the corporation had on its payroll 435 sea-going personnel, despite the fact that for months it had no vessel fishing. In addition, since there is surplus labour within the corporation it should at least be possible to get the work done. Why the personnel department needs 53 people on the payroll is hard to imagine and why books cannot be kept up-to-date with 37 people in the accounts department is unbelievable.

With the disciplinary and morale problems which invariably attend over-manning, it is not surprising that some state enterprises ran into industrial relations problems. The state gold mines were, on occasion, seriously affected. A long and convincing memorandum from a mine manager explaining the failure of the mine to achieve its targets summed it all us as, 'Complacency being allowed to develop through feeling over-secure on the job,' and in 1965 the SGMC Chairman, a life-long trade unionist and President of the Ghana Trades Union Congress at the time of his appointment as Chairman, complained that strikes were becoming 'rampant' and called for more effective action against them.[122] Dadson has recorded similar disciplinary problems on the state farms, with workers turning up late, going early and not working very hard between times. In his opinion, 'Possibly, the greatest problem of socialised farming was how to extract effort from workers,'[123] and a government Minister accused state farm workers of 'sitting down and drinking palm wine when they should be working'.[124] The problem was not, however, confined to these examples and in 1966 the Ministry of Finance listed 'over-staffing and indiscipline' as one of the major factors militating against the efficiency of public enterprises.[125]

Most of the blatant cases of over-manning were the result of political decisions. This was, of course, true of the Workers' Brigade and SGMC, and presumably of the redundant pool of labour in the construction corporation. There is little doubt that other concerns also came under political pressure to keep on more workers than they needed. In September 1965, for example, the Nkrumah government decided that no state agency should make any large-scale retrenchment of labour without the approval of Cabinet and in the previous year Nkrumah had asked state enterprise to provide part-time jobs for members of parliament without independent sources of income.[126] After the 1966 coup it took a major decision by the NLC to lay off nearly 40,000 redundant workers in various state agencies.[127] However, political priorities did not change after 1966 as much as might be thought, for in June 1966 the SGMC found it necessary to seek the permission of the NLC to 'lay off any redundant worker who refuses to accept an alternative job' (no reply to this request is on file), and it was first the NLC, then the Busia administration, and subsequently the NRC which refused to close the Bibiani mine. The Amamoo Report had some strong things to say about this case:[128]

> In many ways the recent history of the Bibiani mine exemplifies the weaknesses that have existed within the Corporation and in its relationships with successive Governments. Already in 1965 the mine was making losses equal to nearly 50% of the value of the gold recovered and it was known at the end of that year that ore reserves equivalent to only one year's operations were available. It is surprising, therefore, that the first recorded mention of the need to close the mine is dated June, 1966. Since then the story has been one of repeated prevarication on the part of successive Boards and Governments. It is natural that a decision that would take away the livelihood of over a thousand workers and take away the main source of income from a whole township should be taken only reluctantly but the harsh fact is that between the beginning of 1966 and June, 1971 it is estimated that keeping the mine open will have cost the Corporation a total of *C4·4 million* and it would be hard to justify to the tax-payer that this was money well spent.

What is hinted at in this quotation, however, is that responsibility for the state of affairs described was shared by the politicians and the managements, and this was probably rather general. In Ghana to hide behind the politicians (especially discredited politicians) must have been a temptation to managements too weak to put their own houses in order. Thus, the State Enterprises Secretariat suggested that over-staffing was a political matter but later in the same document attributed over-staffing in a match factory to high absenteeism, poor labour training and a low labour effort![129] Or take these comments on the causes of over-staffing in the fishing corporation:[130]

> The only cause given beyond the responsibility of management, for the poor performance is excess labour caused by a ruling by the NLC

that more than 10 workers cannot be laid off at one time without special permission. Nevertheless, people could have been laid off in smaller numbers over time . . . The reason is that the management is rather unqualified for the job.

Similarly, the management of the state construction corporation continued to take on new labour when it had a large pool of redundant workers,[131] and Dadson blames the State Farms Corporation's own 'inability to devise and operate effective supervisory and disciplinary systems' for low morale in that organization.[132] We should, in other words, distinguish between politically motivated employment creation and the inefficient utilization of labour by project managements.

Whether the social gains of using the public sector as an employment-creating device were sufficient to outweigh the economic costs does not permit an unambiguous answer. What is fairly clear, though, is that it represented a high-cost way of providing what were, in effect, unemployment benefits. Consider again the extreme case of the Bibiani mine. Taking the figures of the *Amamoo Report*, it can be estimated that the per-worker cost of keeping the mine 'open' was well in excess of ₵800 annually, which figure may be compared with a statutory minimum wage worth less than ₵200 a year in the first half of the sixties, rising to about ₵230 by the end of the sixties. It would have been financially possible to close the mine and pay about four times as many unemployed the minimum wage with no net cost to the budget. More positively, it would have been possible to invest money spent on the mine in new activities providing jobs on a permanent basis and contributing to the development of the economy. Much the same could be said of the Workers Brigade, whose per-worker costs in 1960–5 were well over double the value of the minimum wage.[133] Only on the most short-term or parochial political grounds might these costs have been worthwhile; even as a social policy to alleviate unemployment over-manning the public sector was probably an unnecessarily costly policy. If so, it was also inequitable, for the devotion of large resources to a small number of workers absorbed finances which could have provided relief to a far larger number of people.

Reasons for Poor Performance: (d) Shortages of Technical and Managerial Skills
Mention was made in chapter 1 of the scarcity of skilled manpower at the beginning of the sixties, and shortages of this kind contributed their share to the problems of the public sector. Specific shortages of trained manpower reduced the efficiency of government farms for, even though they had access to most of the relevant expertise available, they were still critically short of agriculturalists and agricultural engineers.[134] In 1964 Ghana had just three such engineers, with one each in the Ministry of Agriculture, the state farms, and the farmers'

cooperatives – at a time when mechanization was proceeding rapidly.[135] There were problems at lower levels of skill too, as indicated by this vivid passage from the remarks of a machinery salesman:[136]

> We sell a bull-dozer [for] ₡50–60,000. The chap turns up and says I am a driver. Ten days later he is on top of that machine, another week later he has slashed it to pieces; ₡50,000 down the drain just for the fact that somebody... did not ask... a few questions and find out whether he is an operator.

The state gold mines also suffered from 'a serious erosion of senior personnel, especially in technical occupations' which undermined its efficiency.[137] The 1971 *Amamoo Report* referred to this as a 'critical' problem and suggested it was due to over-rapid Ghanaianization:[138]

> whereas in 1960–61 there were about 500 expatriates working on the mines, the number was down to 158 in 1965 and stands currently at a mere 56. While the mines were probably overmanned at the senior levels ten years ago and there was much scope for Ghanaianisation, the number of qualified and experienced Ghanaians was (and remains) strictly limited . . .

In the manufacturing sector, the State Enterprises Secretariat complained of shortages of skilled and supervisory personnel resulting in haphazard planning and budgetary control, and the Auditor-General lamented the dearth of accountants.[139]

Nowhere did shortages of qualified personnel have a more critical impact than in the agencies responsible for the selection, creation and overall management of state manufacturing enterprises. In the fifties responsibility rested with the IDC but, although it was set up in 1951, it was not until 1953 that its first projects officer was appointed and he did not remain long in office. Throughout its history, the IDC was under great pressure to process a large number of potential state projects and was inadequately staffed to do the job.[140] Precisely the same could be said of the Ministry of Industries (subsequently the State Enterprises Secretariat) which was responsible for the rapid expansion of state industry in the first half of the sixties. The *Industrial Statistics* shows there to have been a total of 53 manufacturing enterprises wholly or partly owned by the state in 1966, most of which had been created during the earlier sixties, but during most of these years there were fewer than twenty senior officers in the Ministry to plan and oversee this expansion[141] as well as undertaking all the other responsibilities of the Ministry. Doubtless, most of them had administrative rather than technical or economic qualifications. Similar shortages of senior staff were later experienced in the headquarters of GIHOC.

Of all the skill shortages in Ghana's public enterprises, the ones most often mentioned by observers were the inadequacies of their management. The most fully documented case is that of the IDC, where this was serious both in individual subsidiary companies and at headquarters.[142] The headquarters organization lacked a clear chain of command, hence, inevitably, the issuance of conflicting instructions and the emergence of friction at high levels. The management repeatedly failed to maintain the most rudimentary standards in the administration of small loans. And when in 1958 Nkrumah laid down new and relatively clear policy guidance for the corporation the management almost entirely failed to implement it.

A confused authority structure was likewise a characteristic of the State Farms Corporation, with much friction, especially between the administrative and technical officers, and there was little attention to the collection of essential data for the proper management of the farms.[143] Over-centralization was another weakness of the state farms, with farm managers wielding little real authority. This was also true of the SGMC, which was intended as a holding company, leaving each mine to be run by its own management, but which very rapidly took over their direct management.[144] The same could also be said of GIHOC, whose very first directive forbade enterprise managers from incurring capital expenditures in excess of ₡1,000 and from changing product lines without the prior permission of headquarters. Since the headquarters were inadequately staffed by qualified personnel, the effect of centralization was generally negative as I was able to observe and as van der Wel has noted with regard to the sugar projects.[145] However, some enterprises have enjoyed good management. The SGMC, after surviving a disastrous appointment in its early years and against heavy odds, managed to sustain a competent management at most mines and at the centre.[146]

In general, however, the overall standard of management in the public sector was poor, symptomatic of which was the conclusion of the Auditor-General that, 'Generally, the accounts of the Corporations, with but few exceptions, were improperly kept and there was undue delay in the production of final accounts.'[147] There is ample evidence of this in his reports and, since properly kept financial records are an essential tool of management, the implication is that management was doing its job poorly.

A substantial part of this problem stemmed from a politicalization of managements. To quote the Auditor-General again:[148]

the primary consideration for the selection of a Chairman of a Corporation was his party affiliation and even where the need for technical know-how necessitated the employment of an expatriate or qualified Ghanaian as Managing Director there was constant friction between him and the Chairman.

The State Enterprises Secretariat similarly complained that in the

Nkrumah period public enterprises 'became the dumping ground of unskilled and unqualified personnel,'[149] and Dadson has shown that most of the management cadres of the state farms and Workers Brigade were unqualified save in their party affiliation.[150] Political favouritism of this kind did not cease with the 1966 coup, although it undoubtedly diminished.[151]

Even if there had been no politicization, however, the basic truth is that, to quote the State Enterprises Secretariat again, 'Ghana as a developing country, lacks the men with the requisite knowledge and experience in industry and therefore the level of management is generally relatively low.'[152] The obvious medium-term remedy was to look abroad for men competent both to manage the enterprises and to train Ghanaians to take over later, and extensive use was indeed made of expatriate managements. Mixed results were obtained, however. While there were many cases in which the foreigners did a good job, there were others in which this was not true. The 1966–7 *Report* of the Auditor-General lists six enterprises in which the foreign companies who sold or supplied the equipment for the factories were subsequently appointed managing agents and he notes that all but one of these were performing poorly.[153]

Some of these failures could be attributed to management contracts which were (a) costly to the enterprise and (b) failed to give the managements a pecuniary interest in efficient and profitable operation. The management agreement for the glass factory was fairly typical. The agents were to be paid a fixed percentage of total sales, irrespective of the number of personnel required, which provided an incentive to keep the provision of personnel to a minimum and, while it gave them an incentive to maximize sales, it did not link the rewards to the costs or profitability of the enterprise.[154] Similar arrangements were negotiated for the cocoa products factory, where it was at one time estimated that, in relative terms, the management was about ten times as expensive as in another, jointly owned, concern producing a similar output. Recourse to expatriates offers no assurance of improved performance unless sensible terms are agreed with conscientious managing agents.

Reasons for Poor Performance: (e) Corruption
Another potential explanation of poor performance is that corruption distorted the project planning process and day-to-day operations. The plausibility of this line of defence is strengthened by the rich variety of malpractices which occurred in the Nkrumah period, as revealed by judicial enquiries after the 1966 coup. The corruption of the Nkrumah government is a factor much stressed by Ghanaians. Probably the most damaging way in which dishonesty in high circles could have penalized state enterprises would have been for unviable projects to be established as a result of bribery. It is not clear whether this happened in

more than a very small number of cases. It does seem that it was common for Ministers to require firms to pay commissions of 5 to 10 per cent of the value of government contracts awarded. This was supposed to go to the CPP but no clear distinction was observed between the finances of the party and of members of the government.[155] One major contractor admitted making payments of this kind and there is no doubt that others also did so. There is, on the other hand, little evidence that practices of this kind had much impact on state enterprises (although to ask for evidence is admittedly to ask for a lot). It appears that the circumstances surrounding the purchase by the government of the private trading company which subsequently became the National Trading Corporation were murky and that in this case an illicit payment as large as ₵2 million may have been involved;[156] inducing the government to take over a firm which was in some financial difficulties on terms unfavourable to the state, was clearly prejudicial to that Corporation's subsequent chances of commercial success. It also appears that the activities of the Workers' Brigade were riddled with malpractices which could only have adversely affected its efficiency, although this was probably more a matter of dishonest officials than of corruption within the government.[157] Finally, there were allegations that unfavourable contracts were foisted on to the state distillery as a quid pro quo for the contractors' contributions to the CPP.[158]

It would be possible to take a 'tip of the iceberg' view of these examples and to argue that corruption had a serious impact on the performance of the public sector, but the examples themselves are rather insignificant in relation to the whole sector. For what it is worth, the author's view is that corruption in the Nkrumah period (and thereafter) was only a minor reason for the poor performance of state enterprises.

Reasons for Poor Performance: (f) The Trivialization of Political Control

To what extent were state concerns at a disadvantage because of their accountability to the government and Parliament? Almost all the enterprises discussed in this chapter were constituted as public corporations, a British concept which embodies a distinction between overall policy, which is supposed to be a matter for the government, and day-to-day operations, in which the corporations are supposed to have a high degree of autonomy. Rather obviously, this distinction is likely to be a difficult one to maintain in practice, for day-to-day actions may have considerable implications for general policy, and general policy directives have to be translated into detailed operational practices. Public enterprises in most countries complain about the adverse effects of 'political interference' and there have been many complaints along these lines in Ghana.[159] This section, then, explores the relationships which grew up between public enterprises and their political masters.

It is, in fact, quite easy to generalize this relationship, using the words of the Amamoo Committee regarding the SGMC:[160]

> Governments have made poor use of their control over the policies of the SGMC. In principle, governments should exercise overall control over the general lines of policy of public corporations and leave the corporations free to take the day-to-day decisions necessary to implement these policies. In the case of the SGMC it has been the other way around: a good deal of detailed interference and very little by way of general policy guidance.

Indeed, files of the SGMC fail to reveal a single written policy directive from the relevant Minister in 1961–5, although it is likely that he did give verbal instructions. It is similarly reported that officials of GIHOC (a post-Nkrumah creation) stated that their Minister had not handed down any directives on the policies of the GIHOC enterprises, as he was empowered to do,[161] and it was noted earlier that, for the most part, enterprises have been left free to determine their own pricing policies. Even less attempt seems to have been made to exert control over the policies of government farms. Dadson shows that the government had virtually no control over the Workers' Brigade or the State Farms Corporation, both of which were largely removed from the formal accountability and control normal for other state agencies.[162] Governments similarly proved disinterested in the joint state-private enterprises and did not use their board representation to influence the policies of these firms.[163]

Most interesting of all, perhaps, is the history of the IDC in the fifties.[164] There was an almost complete lack of clarity about what the government wanted IDC to do. When the corporation was reconstituted in 1951 the government had few ideas, if any, about the differences between the new and old organizations and the policies which should be pursued. Similarly, when in 1952 the government became dissatisfied with the Corporation and wished to change its policies, it was left to the IDC itself and an outside expert to formulate the new policy. The government seemed to have nothing to contribute and when a 'new' policy was submitted which scarcely differed on any point of substance from the old, it was accepted by the government just the same. When in 1958 Nkrumah finally announced a specific and substantially new policy statement, the Ministers in question so failed to follow this up that the policy was simply not implemented. When during 1960 the government's view changed once more, no policy directive was issued and the Corporation was left to define its own role as best it could.

Ministerial uninterest in general policy, a reluctance to apply disciplinary sanctions to those who failed in their duties, and a situation in which ministerial responsibility to parliament at best functioned poorly were circumstances which scarcely made for a high degree of public accountability on the part of state enterprises, although it did not prevent parliament from being vigorously critical from time to time.[165] The lack of accountability showed up in various ways. Few corporations submitted annual reports and accounts within the statutory time limits, and attempts to integrate them more fully into national economic planning were frustrated by their tardiness in supplying information.[166] Returning again to the IDC, we may cite a 1958 report by Professor W. Arthur Lewis:[167]

> The IDC has suffered greatly from outside interference, in the shape of members of Parliament and other influential persons expecting staff appointments to be made irrespective of merit, redundant staff to be kept on the pay-roll, disciplinary measures to be relaxed in favour of constituents, businesses to be purchased at inflated prices, loans to be made irrespective of security, etc.

The opposition frequently charged that the IDC was being made a dumping-ground for party supporters during the fifties and, while the usual government response was to deny it, one Minister admitted more than he ought to have done when he replied, *'But that is proper: and the honourable Member too would do it if he were there.'*[168] Indeed, the IDC suffered from much detailed political interference and various projects, including the CPP's printing house, were wished upon it by political pressures.[169]

Detailed political interference continued to trouble state enterprises in the sixties. An enquiry into a state furniture factory said of the behaviour of members of Nkrumah's government:[170]

> They interfered with the administration of the Corporation; they forced the Management to engage unqualified people; they purchased large quantities of furniture on credit from the Corporation and deliberately refused to pay . . . In some cases the ex-CPP politicians forced the Management to reduce their accounts and also the accounts of their favourites without any assignable cause or reason.

Even early in the seventies budget hearings were told of similar examples, including pressures as to whom Ghana Airways should hire as air hostesses. Dependence on budgetary subventions involved several state concerns in a different kind of complication, for civil service budgetary procedures were ill-adapted to the requirements of commercial operations. The IDC was very explicit about this, complaining that tortuous procedures for securing governmental approval for new projects, shuttling between ministries and other bodies, undermined its ability to do its job when business dealings required reasonable despatch. On one occasion its budget allocation was cut substantially without warning, causing a severe drop in morale and bringing the Corporation near to what its Chairman termed an organization collapse.[171]

More than a decade later GIHOC's sugar factories found themselves in similar difficulties with the civil service. The author was involved in attempts to ensure that these factories received sufficient funds from the budget for them to do what the government seemed to want them to do, and that in itself was a time-consuming and unsatisfactory process. But having been voted roughly adequate amounts in the budgets was not the end of their problems, for they still had to get the money released when they needed it and this proved even harder, so that delays in the release of budgeted funds played a significant part in holding up the progress of these factories in 1969–70.[172] The SGMC encountered similar problems. From the first few months of its operation it was placed in unnecessary financial difficulties by the failure of the Ministry of Finance to release monies voted to it and much of the time of the top management was devoted to frantic money-raising trips to Accra.[173] Its experience in the 1963–4 budget provides the sharpest example of the difficulties of depending on the government's budget: (a) in deciding how much subsidy to ask for, the board decided to pare its estimated needs of ₵4·2 million down to ₵3·2 ('in the hope that the Ministry of Health would take over the mines' hospitals'); (b) in the course of budget hearings with Ministry of Finance officials this was further reduced, to ₵2·6 million, which was recommended for acceptance to the Minister of Finance; (c) arbitrarily and without warning the Minister cut the figure again to ₵1·0 million, which he mentioned in his budget speech as a sign of 'the determination of the Government to make the mines of the Corporation stand on their own feet' (naturally, though, the Corporation was not to be allowed to close mines or lay off workers).

What emerges is that there was a trivialization of political control, meaning a general disinterest of ministers in matters of general policy combined with frequent, often ill-judged and sometimes self-seeking, interferences with the everyday operations of state enterprises. This was scarcely the model of behaviour upon which the concept of the public corporation was based and could scarcely fail to be detrimental to efficiency, although it was an experience by no means unique to Ghana.[174]

Reasons for Poor Performance: (g) The Economic Environment
As a concluding item in this catalogue of factors affecting the efficiency of state enterprises, it is salutary to note that the fact of their public ownership by no means insulated them from circumstances making for general inefficiency in the economy, discussed in earlier chapters. For example, chapter 10 will show that although the import licensing

authorities discriminated in favour of the public sector they neverthe-less experienced difficulties in obtaining adequate foreign exchange allocations at the right times, and in the first half of 1965 state indust-rial concerns were subjected to 'frequent and prolonged' stoppages of work for this reason. Various import-substituting enterprises, including the sugar and steel industries, were also adversely affected by the over-valued exchange rate.

The disintegration of economic organization and decision-making which was apparent in the first half of the decade perhaps had the most pervasive influence. A good deal has already been said about this under the heading of project planning, and the discussion at this point will be confined to giving just one example of how incompetence in one state agency undermined efficiency in others. One of the new agencies established after Independence was a State Supply Commission to be the agent of government and para-statal organizations in their over-seas procurements. The Supply Commission rapidly earned itself a reputation for inefficiency (which it still had in the early seventies), the effect of which was to aggravate the already acute problems associated with the shortage of foreign exchange and the deficiencies of the import licensing system. The SGMC, for example, expressed severe dissatisfaction with the Supply Commission and eventually obtained permission to handle its own needs. In the meantime supply shortages forced mines to stop production on occasion and retarded develop-ment work. The Supply Commission blamed the SGMC's inability to pay its bills but there is much evidence that the Commission suffered from acute internal problems, often failed to reply to correspondence, and did not establish a satisfactory system of progress-chasing and reporting.

These deficiencies were symptomatic of a more general problem in the agencies responsible for the public sector, in which shortages of staff, weak organization structures, and inappropriate operating rules and procedures combined to prevent them from offering needed ser-vices at more than a low level of efficiency.[175]

Multiple Objectives and The Special Case of The Volta Project
'Lack of clarity about objectives has been a prime cause of muddle, friction and deficit in the past.' This judgement was made about public enterprise not in Ghana, but in Britain,[176] but it is an appropriate text for Ghana's experience. The first section of this chapter elaborated on the multiplicity of objectives which governments have expected the public sector to satisfy, and on the unresolved conflicts between economic and political objectives. But having noted them we avoided the complications they created by assessing state enterprise as if its role was primarily entrepreneurial. This issue should no longer be evaded, for it stands at the centre of many of the difficulties discussed above.

For one thing, the introduction of non-economic objectives greatly increases the difficulty of arriving at an 'objective' assessment of the performance of the public sector. It is not hard to show that the state farms and state industries performed poorly by comparative economic standards but it is much more difficult to arrive at an objective conclusion if there is a possibility that governments were compensated for the economic failings by political benefits accruing from the erection of impressive-looking factories, the spending of money, the creation of jobs, the avoidance of foreign domination of the economy, and the financing of party activities. Indeed, it would be idle to pretend that any objective assessment is feasible in the face of this difficulty: all an economist can do is to point out the economic costs associated with the non-economic benefits.

Looking back at the several 'explanations' of the poor *economic* performance of state enterprises on earlier pages, a few stand out as particularly important. Poor project planning, especially for the agro-industries, was among the most serious: most of the real disasters in the public sector were projects whose original conception or planning was thoroughly mistaken. In fact, the weaknesses of project planning make it surprising that there was not a higher proportion of disasters.[177] The generally low standard of management and interference by politicians in the tasks of management also contributed in a major way to poor economic results. But the enquiry can be pushed deeper by asking why the creation of new state enterprises was allowed to outstrip the resources devoted to project planning, why incompetent managements were tolerated, and why interfering politicians were not disciplined. The answer to each question, it is suggested, is to be found in unresolved tensions between the economic and political motives of the Nkrumah and, to a lesser extent, successor governments. The following judgment has a much wider application than the SGMC, about which it was written:[178]

> *the basic cause of the present weaknesses of the Corporation is political in nature.* Since it was formed in 1961 no Government has provided the Corporation with the conditions necessary for its success. One reason for this is that Governments have tried to pursue contradictory objectives. Governments have tended to speak with two voices about the duties of the Corporation. With one voice they justify the necessity for the Corporation on social, non-commercial grounds i.e. on the need to prevent unemployment (and perhaps to earn foreign exchange). With the other voice, however, they talk of the Corporation in *commercial* terms, stressing the need to obtain profits and criticising the management for having to depend on budgetary subsidies.

The supervention of political motives permits a quite different view of the public sector than that given on earlier pages. 'Political interference' emerges as a logical result of the use of state enterprises to reward party activists and to extend the area of political control.[179] And inattention to economic efficiency in the planning and operation of enterprises becomes explicable if the creation of such enterprises is accepted as an end in itself and as an ostentatious display to impress the electorate. This does not mean that the economist must remain agnostic; he can still urge that an efficient enterprise is more likely to impress than one which cannot produce at more than a fraction of its capacity, and he can point out, as was done earlier in this chapter, the apparent irrationality of using state enterprise as a form of unemployment relief. It does mean, however, that the genesis of the problems he identifies lies outside his own professional domain.

The importance of the political dimension is further illustrated by the Volta River Authority (VRA), an important public corporation which we have so far neglected. The VRA was set up in 1961 as part of the Volta river project with the tasks of supervising the construction of the Volta dam, the subsequent generation and transmission of hydroelectric power, the development of fishing and transportation on the lake, and development of the lakeside area.[180] The dam and associated works, which cost a total of ₵142 million, were financed by equity investments by the Ghana government (₵59 million), and loans from the World Bank (₵48 million) and the US and UK governments (₵35 million).[181] The Authority was a public corporation, similar to other state enterprises, except that it was responsible directly to the President.

What makes the VRA of particular interest here, and what sets it apart from most other state concerns, is that, in terms of its main duties, it was a success story.[182] It is true that its attempts to resettle the former residents of inundated areas ran into serious difficulties, especially (and characteristically for Ghana) the creation of an improved agriculture,[183] but in its main functions of building and operating the hydro-electric project the record is clearly favourable. The dam was finished ahead of schedule (which was one of the sources of difficulty of the resettlement programme) and at well below the original estimated cost. And since the turbines began generating the VRA has generally out-performed the initial World Bank projections, as is shown in Table 9.4. The power sold and profitability in the first five years of operation both exceeded original projections, and, more generally, the reputation of the VRA has remained high – high enough for it to attract additional World Bank and bilateral aid loans.

The question this example poses is, to what exceptional conditions may the superior record of the VRA be attributed? Three obvious, if essentially superficial, explanations offer themselves.

First, unlike so many other state investments, the Volta project was exhaustively prepared and evaluated before work was commenced. An initial evaluation was prepared at the beginning of the fifties and a Preparatory Commission was then set up which presented a large,

TABLE 9.4
Volta River Authority: Comparison of Planned with Actual Performance, 1966–70

	1966	1967	1968	1969	1970
1. *Power Sales* (Gwh)					
a. Projected	384	884	1753	2257	2402
b. Actual	450	1455	2473	2674	2806
2. *Net earnings* (₡mn.)					
a. Projected	2·29[a]	−3·06	−0·83	0.78	1.84
b. Actual	1·33[a]	−3·08	0·35	1·55	1·82
3. Net earnings (as % of Ghana investment)					
a. Projected	—	—	—	0·97	2·29
b. Actual	1·8	−5·28	0·60	2·60	3·10

Sources: World Bank, *Appraisal of Volta River Hydroelectric Project*, Annex 6.
Volta River Authority, *Annual Reports* (various issues).
NOTE:
[a] There was no provision for depreciation in 1966.

favourable report in 1956. For reasons which need not concern us, the project hung fire for a while until a 'Reassessment Report' prepared by another team of consultants breathed new life into it. Finally, when the possibility of a World Bank loan was mooted the Bank itself undertook two meticulous appraisals.

A second contrast is that the act creating the VRA was unambiguous about the objectives it was to pursue. It established that the principal duties of the Authority were economic in character, enjoining it 'to conduct its affairs on sound commercial lines' and to fix its power rates so as to earn profits.[184] A third and related contrast is that the VRA has not been plagued with the 'political interference' from which so many other state concerns suffered. This may be partly attributable to the nature of the project itself[185] and to the greater degree of legal autonomy accorded to the Authority,[186] but the absence of 'political' objectives was even more important.

However, these explanations are superficial because they provide no clue as to *why* the government was willing to behave towards the Authority in a markedly different manner from the treatment of other state concerns. The answer, of course, is to be found in the external financing of the project, especially the involvement of the World Bank. In order to secure the participation of the Bank (without which it may not have been possible to get the project underway at that time) the Nkrumah government found itself required to comply with conditions designed by the Bank to ensure that the project would be operated to its satisfaction. Thus, its prior approval was required for the appointment of the Authority's Chief Executive, the power rates were to be set in consultation with the Bank, an accounting firm acceptable to the Bank was to advise on the Authority's financial records. In an additional agreement in 1969, the Authority agreed to review its operations, organizational structure, staffing policies and accounting system in a manner acceptable to the Bank, and to take appropriate measures. That the Bank proved a hard-nosed lender is surely a major explanation of the hands-off policy adopted by the politicians towards the VRA. Of course, agreements can be broken; that they were not in this case may be attributable to the emergence after 1966 of governments less inclined to politicize the public sector, and to the importance of the World Bank as a major potential source of new aid funds, directly and through its influence on other donors.

The agreements into which his government entered on the Volta project clearly fell within Nkrumah's own definition of 'neo-colonialism',[187] and this example illustrates the trade-off between the economic benefits to be derived from foreign capital on the one hand and the loss of freedom of political action on the other. Nkrumah was subsequently to cite the Volta project against detractors' charges of bribery and corruption,[188] but this laid him open to the charge the that the Volta project was 'the exception that proved the rule' and that it would have been a different matter had the World Bank not been watching so closely.

Two final pieces of evidence may be mentioned in support of the thesis that many of the problems of the public sector were political. It may be recalled that the profitability and productivity of joint state-private enterprises, in which the government tended to be a sleeping partner, were shown to be much better than those of units owned wholly by the state. This strongly suggests that superior economic performance was attributable to the unambiguously commercial objectives of these firms, to the care which the private partners may be assumed to have taken in their pre-investment appraisals, and to their relative insulation from overt political interference. Secondly, a comparative study dealing with public enterprise in Uganda, Nigeria and Ghana concludes that wide differences in commercial performance are largely to be explained by variations in the 'political milieu in which state enterprises operate . . .'[189] It is shown, for example, that in the period under study, public enterprise in Uganda had not been politicized and had performed well commercially, whereas comparable agencies in Nigeria and Ghana had produced abysmal commercial results and had been the victims of extensive politicking.

Conclusions

What conclusions might be drawn from all this about the future role of state enterprise in the development of Ghana's economy? Some, at least, remain optimistic:[190]

The classical socialist strategy of public ownership and management of business enterprises has been tried in Ghana perhaps as extensively as it has been tried anywhere in Africa. I do not subscribe to the view that our experience proves the inability of publicly-owned capital to function as one of the major engines for economic development.

A number of questions emerge. Were the weaknesses discussed in this chapter peculiar to the Nkrumah period? Does the capacity exist radically to improve public sector performance? Above all, are there grounds for believing that state enterprises will in future be allowed by the politicians (civilian or military) to function primarily as 'engines for economic development'?

The first of these questions is the easiest to answer. It is clear that while the worst excesses did occur during the first half of the sixties, the problems and sources of weakness were much in evidence before the distinctively socialist phase of Nkrumah's period of office and after he was deposed. For example, the IDC was first created in 1947 and after it had done poorly the legislation reconstituting it in 1951 was a classic example of muddled thinking at governmental level. Yet the responsibility for these failings lies firmly with the colonial administration rather than with Nkrumah and his party. The poor performance and many unresolved problems of the IDC occurred essentially during the fifties while the government was still pursuing quasi-'colonial' economic policies. Similarly, the use of state enterprises for non-developmental purposes continued after 1966. It was in the post-Nkrumah years that governments refused to close the Bibiani mine and continued to display unresolved ambiguities about priorities for state concerns. Moreover – and this brings us to the second question – the economic performance of the public sector remained patchy after the 1966 coup. An improvement was observable in the productivities and costs of state manufacturing concerns in the later sixties (Tables 9.1 and 9.2), although this may prove to be mainly a one-for-all effect of overcoming teething troubles. No comparable improvement was recorded for the SGMC (Table 9.3); and various other important agencies, such as the state farms (chapter 8), state shipping, construction, housing and fishing corporations, the Timber Marketing Board, and the Omnibus Services Authority, have continued to perform poorly or worse. It would, in other words, be more convincing to attribute the failings of the state sector to the Nkrumah regime if more marked improvements had been achieved thereafter.

The truth, one feels, is that Ghana's human, managerial and organizational resources are not yet sufficient for governments to be capable of responding effectively to the problems of state enterprises. Many of the reasons for poor performance discussed in the course of this chapter relate to the limited capacity of the state for efficient participation in the productive and distributive systems, and it takes much more than a change of government to improve this – a point argued more fully in chapter 12. Indeed, frequent changes may merely add to organizational confusion and low morale. Van der Wel's study of the sugar projects contains interesting observations which are relevant here. He points out that over the years these projects were the subject of several investigations by independent consultants, who between them had identified all the major problems and had suggested various curative measures. But little was done. The managerial and decision-making machinery was incapable of digesting this advice and acting upon it. Reports were lost or 'seemed to lead a hidden life unknown to those who would have benefitted most from their factual contents.'

> There are – to put it in plain words – things that cannot be done, and of which it would be unrealistic to assume that they can be done. All the reforms and changes in the machinery of government, which were outlined in the Seven Year Development Plan as prerequisities for its successful implementation, at the same time condemned that plan as being unrealistic or overambitious. The fact that problems are identified or foreseen, does not mean that they can be corrected or prevented.[191]

To one who had the experience of working within Ghana's planning machinery those words ring terribly true.

This is not to say that no lessons have been learned. There exists in GIHOC an organizational structure with a potential for achieving real improvements in both the performance and accountability of state industries. The worst of the state farms have been abandoned and after it assumed office the NRC made real attempts to use budget procedures to clarify and solve the problems of a number of public corporations. After protracted resistance, the principle of World Bank participation in the two sugar projects had been accepted, with all that implied.

It is tempting to think that changes in the legal framework of public enterprise might bring further improvements. Pozen, for example, suggests that the delicate balance between political accountability and managerial autonomy built into the concept of the public corporation is unsuitable for commercial undertakings and that a limited liability status would be better.[192] However, he is not sanguine about the effectiveness of legislative changes: 'Compared to the influence of non-legal factors, the statutory framework is relatively unimportant . . .' In this judgement he is echoed by other authorities, one of whom is particularly to the point:[193]

> True autonomy is out of the question . . . government can always and should always be able to intervene in any matter really important to the government. Advocacy of autonomy simply highlights the need to educate responsible top organs of government in the

ordinances of self-denial which would restrict their intervention to really important concerns.

So we are led inexorably back to the role and preferences of the politicians, who in the past demonstrated a willingness to sacrifice economic benefits for short-term party, constituency and personal advantage. In a way, Mensah was wrong to suggest that state enterprise has been extensively tried as an instrument for Ghana's economic development, for politicians declined to give consistent priority to the developmental objective in running the public sector. Moreover, in so declining they acted in the tradition of other countries, it being almost a defining characteristic of public enterprises that they are required to pursue multiple but unclearly specified objectives. Thus, despite the improvements achieved, if we conclude that Ghana's future governments will continue to behave within this tradition we are bound to be sceptical about the contribution which public enterprise might make to the development of the economy. The question thus boils down to the nature of Ghanaian politics.

It is to be hoped that Ghanaian public opinion will gradually adopt a longer-sighted view of the roles of their representatives, for to some extent the politicians acted under pressure from their constituents. Perhaps, too, politics in Ghana will become more concerned with issues of principle and policy, because the trivialization of political control stemmed to a large extent from the fact that Ministers did not perceive theirs as a policy-making role. But one thing which will remain detrimental to the developmental contribution of state enterprise is that while the beneficiaries of non-developmental activities tend to be easily identified, organized and vocal, the losers of economic benefits forgone are diffused, inarticulate, unorganized. The high risks and uncertainties of political life in Ghana will similarly make for short-time horizons and discourage the sacrifice of immediate political advantage for longer-term benefits. On balance, one fears there are stronger grounds for expecting more of the same than for anticipating radical improvements.

NOTES

[1] *See* p. 204.

[2] This chapter ranges fairly freely in time, forward and backward. Material is presented which relates to the fifties and the later sixties, to the extent that it contributes to an understanding of the entrepreneurial role of the state. The enterprises I know best are an Industrial Development Corporation which operated during the fifties (*see* Killick, 1972–3, for extensive discussion of this corporation) and the State Gold Mining Corporation. The State Farms Corporation and Workers' Brigade have been thoroughly researched by John Dadson (*see* Dadson, 1970), and I am grateful for his permission to call extensively upon his results. In addition to these cases, there is much, admittedly less systematic, information on other public corporations which is also utilized.

[3] *See* p. 38.

[4] *See Africa Digest,* Vol. V, No. 4, January-February, 1958, p. 156, (cited by Folson, 1971, p. 7), for a statement by Nkrumah along these lines.

[5] The 1966 *Report* of the State Enterprises Secretariat (pp. 1–2) provides a useful illustration of a civil service view of the state as filling an entrepreneurial gap. As an example of the view of state involvement as increasing economic independence, note the explanation of its new chairman for the creation of the Ghana National Trading Corporation: 'The idea is to end a situation in which 95 per cent of our retail and wholesale trade is in foreign hands' (cited by Fitch and Oppenheimer, 1966, p. 113).

[6] Krobo Edusei as reported in the *Ghanain Times,* 10 February 1962.

[7] Dadson, pp. 80–81.

[8] *Seven-year Plan,* p. 79. *See also* the Deputy Minister of Agriculture: 'In both co-operatives and state farms modern scientific methods will be applied. By observing and applying these methods the ordinary farmer will improve his methods and increase his yield' (*Parliamentary Debates,* 27 February 1963).

[9] 'I must make clear that these State Enteprises were not set up to lose money at the expense of the taxpayers. Like all business undertakings, they are expected to maintain themselves efficiently, and to show profits' (*Parliamentary Debates,* 11 March 1964). On this occasion he went so far as to say that, besides permitting greater investment, their profits 'will allow the government to lessen steadily the burden of taxation.'

[10] *Seven-year Plan,* p. 4.

[11] Victor Peslo in the party journal *The Spark,* 27 November 1964. *See also* S. G. Ikoku in the *Daily Graphic,* 24 September 1965.

[12] *Ghanain Times,* 16 January 1964.

[13] Nkrumah, 1968, p. 79.

[14] *See* pp. 34 and 42.

[15] The SGMC files record statements by the Chairman of the Corporation of 20 July 1962 and by the Minister of Industries of 20 September 1963 both of which only mention the employment aspect, although an earlier explanation to the IMF referred also to the need to conserve foreign exchange as a motive for buying up the mines. For an account of the creation of the SGMC and its early performance *see* Killick, 1966, Chapter 11.

[16] Dadson, pp. 214–15.

[17] Auditor-General's *Report* for 1964, Part II, p. 2. *See also* the Appendix to chapter 11.

[18] Odling-Smee, 1972, Table 1.

[19] *Two-year Plan,* p. 59.

[20] Pozen, 1972, p. 828.

[21] Col. I. K. Acheampong, Chairman of the NRC, as reported in the *Daily Graphic,* 15 April 1972.

[22] *See* Killick, 1972–3, *passim.*

[23] 'Looking back at the past two and a half years during which the secretariat has been in existence, one can say with some degree of satisfaction that the Secretariat has endeavoured to justify its existence. Whereas at the end of 1963 only four state corporations had made profits, and eleven had incurred losses, at the end of 1965, 11 corporations made profits while 6 made losses . . .', State Enterprise Secretariat, *Report,* 1966, p. 3.

[24] *See* article by GIHOC public relations officer in *Daily Graphic,* 13 March 1972.

[25] Auditor-General's *Report* for 1966–7, pp. 37–8.

[26] I am indebted to John Odling-Smee and David Forsyth for these examples.

[27] *See* Gantt and Dutto, 1968, Table 3.

[28] *Amamoo Report,* 1971, p. 4.

[29] Killick, 1972–3, Table 2.

[30] Auditor-General's *Report* for 1966–7, Annexure VII. *See also* his *Report* for 1969/70–1970/71, and the *One-year Plan, 1970/71,* p. 89.

[31] Calculated from *Industrial Statistics, 1969,* Table 27. 'Industry' is here defined as an ISIC four-digit sub-group. Joint enterprises were excluded from the calculation.

[32] The median level of effective protection, as calculated by Abban and Leith for 1968, in those industries dominated by state enterprises was 45 per cent, about the same as the overall median of 43 per cent (negative value-added cases excluded throughout).

[33] *See* Fordwor, 1971, Table 10.1. His calculations, based on assumptions including full-capacity output, used a 15 per cent rate of discount.

[34] Abban and Leith show a rate of *nominal* protection of 85 per cent for the distillery industry in 1968, when 81 per cent of the total industry output was contributed by the state enterprise. Leith shows negative value-added for the industry, and a rate of effective protection of −277 per cent (the figure is negative because of the negative value-added). Steel's data, however, do not indicate negative value-added.

[35] *See* Table 9.1, and *One-year Plan, 1970/71,* Table 11–4.

[36] Leith, 1973, Table 3.5.

[37] *Abrahams Report,* 1965, paragraph 40.

[38] Pozen, 1973.

[39] Killick, 1966, p. 170.

[40] The end-use classification of manufacturing value-added in 1969 was as follows (percentages):

	State	Joint	Private
Investment and related goods	11·0	21·6	6·9
Intermediate goods	14·8	26·3	14·6
Consumer Goods	74·1	52·1	78·5
	100·0	100·0	100·0

(I followed Steel's grouping of industries into end-use categories for this purpose.) The state sector is slightly more weighted towards capital goods and away from consumer goods than private firms but this does not explain their poor productivity ratings because one would expect higher value-added per man in this relatively capital-intensive sector, as achieved by joint enterprises, which are most heavily involved in the production of capital goods.

[41] Odling-Smee, 1972, Table 4. The two specific and recent productivity comparisons of which I am aware are also greatly to the disadvantage of Ghana's state industries. The *One-year Plan, 1970/71* (p. 87) mentions the average quantity of sugar cane cut per man during harvesting in Ghana's sugar plantations to be about 0·5 tons per day, compared with 2·0 to 2·5 tons in Malawi and Kenya. Calculations by the management of the output of shoes per worker in Ghana's State Footwear Corporation in 1968 showed productivity to be less than one-fifth of the levels attained in Nigeria and Jamaica.

[42] In terms of gold produced per man, Ashanti has always had far higher labour productivities but this is largely because it mines a much better grade of ore. Productivity is measured in terms of tons of ore in the first four lines of Table 9.3 in order to abstract from the differential ore qualities.

[43] Ministry of Finance and Planning.

[44] Data kindly supplied by David Forsyth.

[45] Report by Fishing Consultants, 1969, p. 7.

[46] Pozen, 1973, p. 15.

[47] Bartels, 1970, Appendix I.

[48] Grayson, 1973A.

[49] The lower profitability of state concerns would create a tendency in this direction, and it would be theoretically possible for compensating savings to exist elsewhere in the cost structure, although I know of no evidence to indicate that this happened.

[50] These estimates relate to the late sixties and are based upon Ministry of Finance and Planning data.

[51] Reusse, 1968, p. 18, shows that corned beef produced at the meat processing factory at Bolgatanga would have foreign exchange costs 33 to 50 per cent greater than the c.i.f. cost of imported canned corned beef.

[52] Steel, 1970, p. 146, and also Steel, 1972, p. 232.

[53] Steel, 1970, Table C-III.

[54] Calculated from data provided by SGMC.

[55] The data related to a total of twenty projects completed in 1964 and 1965, or due to be completed in 1966. Including provision for working capital, the mean estimated investment per worker was ₵4,963 (₵4,161 excluding working capital).

[56] To illustrate, assume state industries were to absorb a quarter of 1960 unemployment plus 10 per cent of the net additions to the non-agricultural labour force in 1963–70, as projected in the *Seven-year Plan* (table 7.1). This would have involved the creation of about 80,000 new jobs and, at ₵5,000 per worker, an investment bill of ₵400 million. The total of ₵400 million may be compared with a planned total of all types of capital expenditure by the government of ₵888 million over the plan period (*see Plan,* Table 13.9).

[57] Reusse, 1968, Chapter 3.

[58] Pickett *et al.,* 1973, Table 2, give the following illustration of the actual nature of one of the Ghanaian factories and a labour-intensive alternative employing a Khand-sari process:

	Actual	Alternative
Numbers employed:		
Full time	476	700
Seasonal	219	3,000
Internal Rate of Return:		
Private	6·5	12·0
Social	8·0	13·0

The rates of return assume a far better standard of performance than actually achieved at the factory. (*See also* the quotation on p. 178.)

[59] The number of tractors in Ghana went up from about 140 in 1960/61 (Dadson, p. 181) to over 3,500 in 1966 (Dadson, Table 7.6).

[60] Dadson, Table 7.13. I have used medians because his means are biased by one or two extreme values.

[61] The acreage cultivated per man on the state farms averaged about 3·0 in 1964–5, which was not much more than the average acreage cultivated by the peasant farmers.

[62] The *NIB Footwear Report,* p. 45, notes as 'advantages' of the use of conveyors that 'they reduce the number of shoes in process, give the factory a neater appearance and no service help is required to move shoes in process'. *See also* Pickett, *et al.,* pp. 7–8.

[63] Fishing Consultants, 1969, p. 13.

[64] Uphoff, 1970, p. 562.

[65] NIB Footwear Report, p. 43.

[66] NIB Cannery Report, Chapter 7. [67] Ministry of Finance and Planning.

[68] Ministry of Finance an Planning; *see also One-year Plan, 1970/71,* p. 85.

[69] Ministry of Finance and Planning.

[70] ibid.

[71] NIB Footwear Report, p. 42. This points out that one of the redundant lines was for the manufacture of a 'heavy, cumbersome shoe' which is 'used in some coid countries'.

[72] NIB *Cannery Report,* Chapter 7, p. 1.

[73] World Bank, 1966, Vol. II, Annex 8, p. 6.

[74] Miracle and Seidman, 1968(A), p. 40.

[75] *The Budget, 1966/67,* Report on State Enterprises, p. 3. Soviet project studies appear

to have been more scrupulous than most, and Stevens, 1972, cites examples where the Russians declined to go ahead with unviable projects being urged upon them by the Ghana government.

[76] Data provided by Ministry of Finance and Planning.

[77] ibid.

[78] Uphoff, 1970, pp. 576–7.

[79] The study was undertaken by the majority shareholder of the Valco consortium that had already made it quite clear that it did not at that stage wish to invest in an alumina plant. *See* Killick, 1966, pp. 402–7.

[80] van der Wel, 1972, p. 8. *See also* footnote 33.

[81] Tyner, 1969.

[82] Grayson, 1973A.

[83] Reusse, 1968, p. 21.

[84] Dadson, 1970, p. 265.

[85] Public Accounts Committee, 1965, pp. 9 and 24–6.

[86] Uphoff, 1970, pp. 539–40.

[87] *See* p. 170–1.

[88] van der Wel, p. 27.

[89] Public Accounts Committee, 1965, p. 9.

[90] *See* Dadson, Table 7.6, pp. 129–30 and 185–200.

[91] Killick, 1966, p. 291.

[92] Reusse, 1968, Chapter 1.

[93] These included the creation of specially simplified foreign exchange procedures at the northern border with Upper Volta to facilitate the importation of cattle, although few of these found their way to the factory. Shortly after the 1972 coup the Chairman of the NRC ordered GIHOC to commence production of corned beef and this resulted in some frenzied efforts by the management to comply with the order. A few tins were produced and the Chairman was duly shown in the press eating from one of them with relish, but efforts to maintain a supply of cattle proved unavailing and production was soon discontinued.

[94] NIB *Footwear Report*, p. 36.

[95] *See One-year Plan, 1970/71*, p. 87, and Uphoff, pp. 541–3. As an adviser to the government the author attended budget hearings in 1970 at which, as had been the normal practice, the mechanization section and the irrigation section of the Ministry of Agriculture, and GIHOC on behalf of the management of the sugar factories, each submitted separate and conflicting programmes relating to sugar cultivation. On this occasion, it was eventually arranged to get these agencies to sit around the same table to reconcile their plans, although the gap between intention and performance was so large that there could be little confidence that actions were co-ordinated in actual practice.

[96] *West Africa*, 8 January 1973, p. 49.

[97] *See* Bartels, op. cit.

[98] From a memo by the Ministry of Agriculture to the Committee on the Supply of Raw Materials, dated August 1965.

[99] Uphoff, pp. 498–501.

[100] The argument usually employed is that the cost of creating the factories should be treated as sunk and therefore that they should be opened, although estimates that excluded capital costs and incorporated appropriate shadow prices showed that, even on this basis, to open the factories would be pouring good money after bad. Nevertheless, GIHOC announced at the beginning of 1973 that it was going into the large-scale farming of tomatoes to supply the factories (*West Africa*, 1 January 1973).

[101] van der Wel, pp. 6–7.

[102] Killick, 1972–3, Part II, and same author, 1966, pp. 291–2.

[103] *One-year Plan, 1970/71*, p. 83, and *Daily Graphic*, 13 March 1972.

[104] A memo from the Corporation to the Ministry of Finance of 28 May 1970 sum-

marized the position accurately: 'Problems of foreign exchange and local liquidity have had a very serious effect on production over the last few years. More recently management on each mine has been concerned almost on a day-to-day basis over cash requirements to meet wages and such essential stores as petrol, diesoline, explosives, etc.; so much so that more important mine planning operations have had to take second place.'

105 NIB *Footwear Report,* Chapter IX.
106 Information from Ministry of Finance and Planning.
107 Auditor-General's *Report* for 1965-6, paragraph 159.
108 Dadson, pp. 172-6.
109 Reusse, p. 55.
110 *Abrahams Report,* p. 37.
111 Killick, 1972-3, Part II, especially Table 1.
112 Auditor-General, *Report* for 1965-6, paragraph 159.
113 *Amamoo Report,* p. 8. The author was secretary to the Amamoo Committee.
114 *Annual Plan, 1965,* p. 24.
115 The expression is borrowed from Schatz. This paragraph summarizes an argument deployed more fully in Killick, 1972-3, Part II.
116 State Enterprises Secretariat *Report,* 1966, p. 9. Peil, 1972, p. 36, also found that state enterprises employed, on average, at least twice as many clerical workers as other firms of the same size and type.
117 Consistent with this, most of the 619 workers laid off by one of the mines shortly before they were acquired by the government were substantially re-employed by the SGMC. However, apart from Bibiani, it does not appear that the SGMC mines normally carried a large number of unnecessary workers. In 1970 the management estimated it had 220 redundant workers, out of a total labour force of over 10,000 (Bibiani excluded from both figures).
118 An unpublished survey by T. K. Kumekpor revealed that the Ghana National Construction Corporation (GNCC) had operated a 'Central Redundant Pool' since 1962 which grew in size over time. Some 16,000 GNCC workers (out of a total labour force of 45,000) were laid off after the change of government in 1966. Some of these were found to have already taken up other employment.
119 *See* 1966 State Enterprises Secretariat *Report, passim;* Larbi-Odam, 1970, p. 5; NIB *Boatyards Report,* 1968, p. 1, for examples.
120 Auditor-General's *Report* for 1966-7, p. 39.
121 Report by Fishing Consultants, 1969, p. 3.
122 These references are from SGMC sources.
123 Dadson, pp. 232-3.
124 Reported by Uphoff, 1970, p. 522.
125 *The Budget, 1966/67,* p. 4.
126 Pozen, 1973.
127 The following lay-offs were reported in *West Africa,* 25 February, 1967:
  16,000 National Construction Corporation
  9,600 Workers Brigade
  9,000 State Farms Corporation
  2,300 State Housing Corporation
  1,200 Cocoa Division of Ministry of Agriculture.
128 *Amamoo Report,* p. 22.
129 State Enterprises Secretariat *Report,* 1966, pp. 9 and 56.
130 Report of Fishing Consultant, p. 3.
131 Source as for footnote 118.
132 Dadson, p. 235.
133 Calculated from data in Godfrey, 1971, Table 7.2.
134 Dadson, pp. 27, 130-1 and *passim.*
135 ibid., p. 187. According to an official report, the Workers' Brigade's Chief Mechanical Engineer was 'a stark illiterate'. The entire technical staff of the Brigade con-

sisted of one agricultural officer, eight technical officers, and four agricultural assistants (p. 225).

[136] Quoted by Dadson, p. 188.

[137] *One-year Plan, 1970/71*, p. 104.

[138] *Amamoo Report*, p. 8.

[139] State Enterprises Secretariat *Report*, 1966, p. 8; Auditor-General's *Report* for 1964, Part II, p. 3.

[140] *See* Killick, 1966, p. 290; and 1972–3, Part II.

[141] Annual budget estimates made provision for 26 officers in the administrative class (or equivalent) in 1962/63 and for all years thereafter up to 1968 the provision was for 17 or 18 such officers.

[142] Killick, 1972–3.

[143] Dadson, pp. 218–32.

[144] A government press release of 7 March 1961 stated that it would not be the object of the SGMC to run directly any of the gold mines which would remain separate companies, but the records of the Corporation suggest that direct running was the actual practice almost from the start. By July 1962 it had initiated the winding-up of the separate companies. In 1973, however, the Corporation reverted to giving its major mines semi-autonomous status.

[145] *See* Pozen, 1973; van der Wel, 1972, pp. 17–18; and *One-year Plan, 1970/71*, p. 84, which talks of the future p olicy of GIHOC being 'to achieve some measure of decentralization'. That decentralization did not go very far is suggested by an allegation reported in *West Africa* (29 January 1973) that the Komenda sugar factory had been forced to cease production because of delays at GIHOC headquarters.

[146] *Amamoo Report*, p. 9, stated in 1971 that the existing management of the Corporation had the capability of greatly improving economic performance if only it was given sufficient authority and resources, although it did criticize the management for an insufficiently commercial approach to some of its decision-making (p. 13).

[147] Auditor-General's *Report* for 1964, Part II, p. 3.

[148] ibid., p. 3.

[149] State Enterprises Secretariat *Report*, 1966, p. 7.

[150] *See* footnote 143.

[151] *See* Uphoff, 1970, p. 619, n. 248.

[152] State Enterprises Secretariat *Report*, 1966, p. 7.

[153] Auditor-General's *Report* for 1966–7, p. 36.

[154] This paragraph is based on Ministry of Finance data.

[155] *See Apaloo Report*, 1966, especially pp. 12–16. Among the other enquiries conducted after the 1966 coup *see* the *Kom Report*, 1967, and the *Tsegah Report*, 1967.

[156] *Apaloo Report*, pp. 30–9.

[157] *Kom Report, passim.*

[158] Pozen, 1973.

[159] For an opposite view, relating to the British experience, *see* C. D. Foster, 1971, *passim*. He argues that boards of public corporations have achieved a high degree of autonomy and that the ability of Ministers to influence corporation policies depends on their success in persuading the boards to heed their advice.

[160] *Amamoo Report*, 1971, p. 9.

[161] Pozen, 1973.

[162] Dadson, pp. 101–2, 248–56. *See also Kom Report*.

[163] *See Reports* of the Auditor-General for 1964 (Part II, p. 17) and 1966/67 (p. 52); and *One-year Plan, 1970/71*, p. 89.

[164] The following summarizes some of the conclusions in Killick, 1972–3, Part II.

[165] ibid., and also Kraus, 1971, pp. 49–50.

[166] 'As a general drive to assess the level of Government investment in the enterprises and as a means of controlling their performance, a new form of financial and

production plan covering investment, income, expenditure, and profit as well as requirements for credit and foreign exchange was introduced in 1965. Unfortunately, of the 54 corporations only 32 submitted financial plans for 1966,' *The Budget, 1966/67,* Report on State Enterprises, p. 4. On delays in the preparation of accounts *see* the annual *Reports* of the Auditor-General.

[167] Cited in Killick, 1972–3, Part II.

[168] Minister of Works, N. A. Welbeck, in *Legislative Assembly Debates,* 1955, No. 1, cols. 301–310 (my italics). Welbeck subsequently became General Secretary of the CPP and was for a time an important political figure.

[169] Killick, 1972–3, Part II and also *Quist Report,* 1969, pp. 5–6.

[170] *Tsegah Report,* p. 67. That the distinction between political accountability and managerial autonomy has remained a difficult one to draw is suggested by a report early in 1973 that the NRC was preventing the Cocoa Marketing Board from re-establishing a sales office in London, as the Board wished to do – *see West Africa,* 20 January 1973.

[171] Killick, 1972–3, *passim.*

[172] *One-year Plan, 1970/71,* p. 87.

[173] As early as November 1961 the reluctance of the Ministry of Finance to release funds was causing the Corporation acute liquidity problems and this type of problem continued spasmodically throughout the sixties.

[174] The conclusion of a recent comparative study of state enterprise was that 'The most important of the many problems with which every country under study struggles, mostly with indifferent success, is that of the proper balance of managerial autonomy and political responsibility, which latter involves a measure of public direction' (Friedmann and Garner (eds.), 1970, p. 335). *See* Pozen, 1972, for a valuable study of the appropriateness of the public corporation concept to Ghanaian conditions.

[175] *See* van der Wel, 1972, p. 17.

[176] C. D. Foster, 1971, p. 19. Coombes, 1971, pp. 212–3, also draws attention to the reluctance of British governments to articulate their objectives for nationalized industries.

[177] Cost-benefit studies by Fordwor of 14 state enterprises found private and social rates of return in excess of 15 per cent in all but two of them, although it must be added that these were hypothetical calculations based on some strong assumptions, including full capacity utilization (Fordwor, 1971, *passim*).

[178] *Amamoo Report,* p. 8 (italics in original).

[179] Dadson draws attention to the use which was made of the units of socialized agriculture to extend the area of political control – *see* p. 278 and *passim. See* also Beckman, 1973A.

[180] For the history and economics of the Volta project see Killick, 1966 chapter 16, and the references cited there; also, King, 1967, pp. 128–55. The Volta lake is said to be the world's largest man-made lake.

[181] From VRA *Annual Report, 1970,* financial statements C and D.

[182] I have elsewhere drawn attention to the limitations of the Volta scheme as a development project, especially to its enclave characteristics (Killick, 1966, chapter 16), and would still argue along those lines. The Volta River *Authority* is a success story in the sense of its proven capacity to carry out its statutory duties efficiently.

[183] Chambers, 1970, especially chapter 12, shows that the agricultural programme for the resettled communities, which envisaged relatively intensive, mechanized cultivation, was probably the least successful aspect of the Volta project. Community development endeavours also ran into considerable difficulties. He also suggests (p. 260) that the agricultural aspect was less carefully appraised than the rest of the project.

[184] Volta River Development Act, 1961, section 21.

[185] Hirschman, 1967, pp. 53 and 110 suggests reasons for believing power generation projects to be 'less malpractice-prone' than many others.

186 The Act (section 20) empowers the President to give the VRA directions of a general character but only in matters of 'exceptional public importance', which are not inconsistent with the other provisions of the Act, e.g. with the obligation to operate on commercial lines.

187 'Still another neo-colonialist trap on the economics front has come to be known as "multilateral aid" through international organizations: the International Monetary Fund, the International Bank for Reconstruction and Development (known as the World Bank) . . . These agencies have the habit of forcing would-be borrowers to submit to various offensive conditions, such as supplying information about their economies, submitting their policy and plans to review by the World Bank and accepting agency supervision of their use of loans,' Nkrumah, 1963, pp. 242–3.

188 'At a time when our detractors talk much of bribery and corruption in the developing countries, it is noteworthy that not a single penny went astray or was misappropriated in the entire Volta undertaking, which involved countless contracts over many years,' Nkrumah, 1968, p. 84.

189 Frank in Ranis (ed.), 1971, especially p. 117.

190 Mensah, 1971. The National Redemption Council, while confining Mensah to jail, appears to have accepted his point of view on this matter, for it soon moved to extend the area of state participation.

191 van der Wel, 1972, p. 34.

192 Pozen, 1972, p. 844.

193 P. H. Appleby quoted approvingly by Hanson, 1965, p. 351. *See also* Coombes, 1971, p. 210 ('We are rather sceptical of the value of reforms to the statutory relationships of Ministers with boards, considering the real solution to be in the organization of the undertakings and the policies of governments towards them.'), and Friedmann in Friedmann and Garner (eds.), 1970, p. 335 ('Ultimately this is a matter of political practice and tradition which no written law can satisfactorily solve . . .').

10   *The State as Controller*

Having reviewed the performance of the state as an entrepreneur, we turn to examine its achievements in the administration of direct controls. The urge to control was powerful in Nkrumah's Ghana and re-emerged in full strength after the 1972 coup. It was shown in chapter 2 that a large body of economists looked with scepticism at the efficacy of the market mechanism as an agent for economic progress in low-income countries; chapter 3 showed that Nkrumah fully shared this scepticism, and expressed unbounded faith in the superiority of economic planning and control. It was also shown that, although Nkrumah and his colleagues affected to see colonialism as embodying the quintessence of laissez-faire, colonial administrations had themselves been markedly interventionist in a number of areas, having enacted legislation to control prices (during the Second World War), rents, and interest rates (*see* pp. 23–4).

In the early sixties, a far larger edifice than they could have intended, was built upon the foundations which they had laid, so that by 1962 there was in existence an extensive range of regulations covering imports, foreign exchange transactions, prices, bank lending, wages, and so on. So long as the state could undertake these tasks efficiently – and it should be stressed again that in the buoyant first years after Independence the politicians believed the power of the state to be almost unlimited – there was, after all, a persuasive case to be made in favour of controls. Take the example of import controls.[1] Faced with the emergence of a balance of payments problem, controls promised a more certain way of keeping the volume of imports within the availability of foreign exchange to pay for them, while at the same time permitting the government to discriminate between alternative goods to reflect its own priorities. Given the volatility of Ghana's main export crop, controls could impose a smaller resource cost than the alternative of maintaining a large buffer of foreign exchange reserves; they could be used to protect Ghana's fledgling industries and to promote the objective of economic independence.[2]

Inevitably, a gap emerged between the hypothetical and the actual, and this chapter assesses the efficiency of controls, traces their consequences for the performance of the economy, and identifies the sources of the weaknesses which emerged. Arguably, the most important controls imposed in the early sixties were those regulating imports, and much of this chapter is taken up with a detailed study of these. This is followed by a briefer examination of the operation of price controls, and an attempt to draw some more general conclusions. As in the previous chapter, the focus will be on the Nkrumah period but the discussion will also range forward in time to include the experiences of the later sixties.

I   Import Controls

A Brief History

When in December 1961 it was announced that existing 'open general' (i.e. non-restrictive) import licences would not be renewed for 1962 and that importers would henceforth require specific licences, this was a decision which had been forced upon the government at short notice by a rapidly deteriorating balance of payments.[3] There had been current account deficits in four out of the five previous years and these had caused increasing concern, but as late as July 1961 the Minister of Finance said, 'I do not believe that the imposition of quantitative import controls will serve our objectives; such controls are expensive in terms of man-power, and often lead to corrupt practices which we must avoid at all costs.[4] The country, it should be remembered, was heading towards a deficit of record size. Imports were rising sharply, partly because of speculation against the possible introduction of controls,[5] and in the course of 1961 the coutry's international liquidity slumped from ₵544 million at the end of 1960 to ₵325 million twelve months later (Table 5.1). The imposition of import controls was the government's response.

The haste with which it had to be improvised ruled out a carefully worked out scheme and it must be presumed that in 1962 licences were issued on an *ad hoc* and arbitrary basis. During the course of that year, however, a register of importers was developed, classified according to scale of business, and the Ministry of Trade began to work out specified procedures for processing licence applications.[6] In his 1963 budget speech the Minister of Finance and Trade announced that a foreign exchange budget would be drawn up (although it was not until 1965 that this was actually done) and during that year the procedures were further improved. However, the appointment in late 1963 of a new Minister of Trade aborted these procedures for reasons discussed later.

From 1963 until the coup in 1966, there was increasing criticism of the manner in which the controls were operated. Shortages emerged and rumours of corruption at the Ministry of Trade resulted in the appointment of a commission of enquiry at the end of 1962.[7] Public dissatisfaction continued, however, and in 1965 another investigation was conducted.[8] The publication in 1965 of the first foreign exchange budget represented, at least on paper, a major step towards the rational planning of the country's external transactions. Prepared under K. Amoako-Atta (who had become Minister of Finance) in consultation with the Ministry of Trade, the Bank of Ghana, and Import and Export Advisory Board, and representatives of 'strategic' industries'[9] it attempted to forecast the foreign exchange which would be available to finance imports in 1965 and to allocate these between the public and private sectors, and to different end-uses. A similar document was prepared for 1966,[10] but was immediately overtaken by the change of government.

Following the 1966 coup, licences already issued for that year were revoked,[11] a new programme drawn up, and yet another commission of enquiry instituted.[12] Procedures were adopted by the NLC, similar to those worked out in 1963; the register of importers was revised and licence allocations were published in the official *Commercial and Industrial Bulletin.* A special committee was formed to prepare annual import programmes, operating from the Bank of Ghana and including representatives of the Ministries of Agriculture, Industries and Trade, and the Ghana Industrial Holding Corporation.

A further refinement introduced in 1968 was the preparation of two alternative import programmes: a 'desirable' and an 'operational' programme. The latter was based on expected foreign exchange availabilities, including already committed foreign aid, whereas the former was an assessment of the imports the economy would need to achieve stated improvements in economic performance. The difference between these two programmes was then presented at meetings with foreign aid donors in support of Ghana's case for more aid.[13]

Simultaneously with the attempts to improve the control system, the NLC began to reduce its coverage. Beginning in 1967, the range of goods on non-restrictive 'open general' licences (OGLs) was progressively expanded and a process of liberalization was begun which was markedly accelerated by J. H. Mensah as Finance Minister of the Busia administration. The growth of the share of total imports covered by OGLs is indicated by the following figures:

	Percentage of total imports on OGL
1967	3%
1968	17%
1969	37%
1970	57%

A further liberalization announced in mid-1971 was estimated to raise the proportion to 75 per cent[14] and, allowing for other minor categories, to leave only 20 per cent still covered by specific licences. These figures may be compared with an IMF estimate that in 1962–3 only 7 per cent of imports were *not* covered by specific, restrictive licences.

Liberalization had gone so far by 1970 that the import programming developed earlier was virtually redundant. With a large and growing proportion of imports outside the administrative control of the government, the preparation of more or less elaborate schemes for those imports still controlled became an unreal exercise and, although foreign exchange budgets continued to be prepared, even for 1971, 1969 was the last year in which a serious attempt was made to implement a detailed programme. For this reason, the 1970 and 1971 programmes are not studied in any detail here. Even in 1969 liberalization had gone far enough to cause considerable problems for those in charge. The return to comprehensive specific import licensing announced by the NRC in February 1972 was thus a reversion to a degree of control that had not been experienced during the previous four or five years.

The Purposes of Import Controls
Although controls were first introduced for balance of payments reasons, they were also used to achieve other objectives. A memorandum by the Bank of Ghana came as near to a comprehensive statement as it has been possible to find. It distinguished between the primary and secondary purposes which the controls were expected to achieve.[15] The primary purposes were to 'bring about a balance between total imports and total exports of goods as a means of halting the drain on the reserves' and to 'regulate the flow of imports into the country with a view to excluding the importation of non-essentials'. The subsidiary objectives were to increase the volume of imports from socialist countries with which Ghana had signed bilateral trade and payments agreements, and to 'discourage the importation of certain goods which were or could be produced locally . . .'[16]

The Nkrumah government used the controls for the further purpose of transferring foreign exchange and import capacity from the private to the public sector. The foreign exchange budgets for 1965 and 1966 were quite explicit about this. The latter, for example, allocated no less than 74 per cent of total imports to the state sector, a policy which would have necessitated a transfer of foreign exchange from the private sector equivalent to 47 per cent of its anticipated foreign exchange receipts.[17] Finally, the Nkrumah government was using the controls to change the composition of imports so as to facilitate a high level of industrial investment.

Thus, the objectives the planners were expected to achieve during the Nkrumah period could be summarized as:
(a) To protect the overall balance of payments by keeping the total

value of imports within the estimated availability of foreign exchange available to pay for them.[18]

(b) Within this total, to provide an efficient allocation according to the stated priorities of the government. During the Nkrumah period these priorities included:

   (i) increased imports from bilateral trade pact countries;

  (ii) restructuring the composition of imports in favour of capital equipment, at the expense of inessential consumer goods;

 (iii) transfers of foreign exchange from the private to public sector; and

 (iv) protection of local import-substituting industries.

The defence of the balance of payments remained a major objective of the governments which succeeded Nkrumah's but their allocational priorities were different. The main plank of the NLC's strategy was to maintain economic growth while cutting back on investment by improving industrial capacity utilization.[19] The government thus looked to the import planners to give higher priority to imported raw materials and spare parts, with less emphasis on capital goods. Bilateral trade and payments agreements were cancelled or allowed to lapse.[20] Expansion of the number of state enterprises in the directly productive sectors of the economy was brought to a halt and a greater stress placed upon making foreign exchange available to the private sector.

Two further objectives which took on importance after 1966 were (a) to use the import licensing system to maximize the utilization of foreign aid, and (b) to discriminate in favour of private Ghanaian importers. These desiderata do not receive further attention here but it seems that, in 1968 at least, the system actually operated to the *disadvantage* of Ghanaian importers,[21] although the logistics of import liberalization in 1969 and 1970 were used to reduce the business of smaller foreign import firms, typically owned by Lebanese. That some success was achieved with the aid objective is negatively suggested by the fact that aid utilization became more difficult as liberalization proceeded.

Thus throughout the sixties the import planners were expected simultaneously to satisfy a number of objectives, and it is by these criteria that their performance should be assessed.

Assessment: (a) The Balance of Payments

The need to preserve the country's foreign exchange reserves was a recurring theme throughout the sixties. Nkrumah asserted that 'We shall not allow our savings to run down in order to get into a position where we have to beg for money . . .'[22] and the *Seven-year Plan* argued that,[23]

As fluctuations in foreign exchange earnings are recurrent because of the reliance on a few export items, it is essential that the reserves should be maintained during the plan period at a level which contains a cushion to meet unforseen and sudden deficits in the balance of payments. During the plan period, it should be a matter of policy not to draw the reserves significantly below the end of 1963 levels.

Similarly, in 1965 the Finance Minister spoke of the need to 'save a further drain on our reserves' as 'one of the most important tasks we have set ourselves for this year.'[24] The NLC went further and predicated the operational import programmes for 1967, 1968 and 1969 on increased gross reserves and reduced current arrears (see Table 10.1 below).

What happened to Ghana's external reserves and liquidity thus provides a first approximate reading of the success of import controls in achieving the balance of payments objective. Referring back to Table 5.1 it can be seen that they were unable to prevent a precipitate decline in international liquidity during the Nkrumah period and were unable to achieve the replenishment which was desired by the NLC from 1966 to 1969. This is not to say that controls had no effect on the size of payments deficits. Other things being equal, the balance of payments would have been in an even worse condition in the absence of controls. From 1958 until the imposition of controls at the beginning of 1962, imports were on a steeply rising trend, but throughout the remainder of the sixties (with the exception of 1965) annual imports were kept below the 1961 level, despite buoyant demand conditions. While the 1961 figure was artificially large because of speculation against import restrictions, and thus does not provide an ideal basis for comparison, there was nevertheless a considerable achievement in restraining the volume of imports.[25] But while the authorities did reduce the import bill, they were unable to achieve fully the balance of payments objectives of successive governments.

In seeking an explanation of this it is useful to examine separately two possible causes of failure: (1) an inability to forecast the balance of payments with the necessary degree of accuracy, and (2) an inability to limit imports to the intended levels. Table 10.1 presents a comparison of annual forecasts of how much foreign exchange would be available to finance imports with the recorded balance of payments figures. It is clear from this that there were in each year significant item-by-item differences between forecast and actual values. Line 11 of the table provides a measure of forecasting errors by expressing the sum of each year's 'difference' column as a percentage of the sum of the 'forecast' column (ignoring signs throughout) and shows that the mean deviation ranged between 16 per cent and 41 per cent, with an average for the whole period of 30 per cent. That the deviations should be substantial is not at all surprising, given the volatility of the world cocoa market, but differences between forecast and actual export earnings were by no means the only source of error, nor always the main ones. In value terms, errors in forecasting the invisibles and private capital receipt items were almost as large as errors in export forecasts and, relative to their forecast values, the errors for the former two items were much larger than those for exports.[26]

Taking 1965–9 as a whole, the failure of the authorities to protect the external reserves to the desired extent could not be attributed to forecasting difficulties, for the planners generally erred on the side of pessimism in their estimates of import capacity. This is clear from the last column of Table 10.1, which displays the mean differences for each item over the period as a whole. It will be seen (lines 8 and 10) that actual imports exceeded the total forecast of import capacity by an annual average of ₵27 million and, had total imports achieved the targets which were set, the reserve position would have been better than planned, by an average of ₵7 million p.a. Failure to hold imports to planned levels explains the authorities' inability to conserve the external reserves, and also the accumulation of a larger than intended volume of medium- and short-term debt (see line 5).

Referring back to Figure 5.1(A), it is apparent that from 1961 to 1966 a year of reduced imports alternated with a year of increased imports. This behaviour resulted from something similar to a stock-building cycle. In 1962, the first year of controls, it was easy to reduce imports because there was a substantial cushion of stocks to fall back upon. Monthly import data indicate, however, that as stocks were run down, imports tended to revert to pre-control levels, towards the end of 1962.[27] Thus, *under the pressure of demand,* imports went up again in 1963 to the second-highest level ever recorded and presumably permitted some replenishment of stocks. When, early in 1964, the authorities became alarmed at the deteriorating payments position and revoked all licences[28] they were able in that year to reduce the level of imports because once again there were stocks to fall back upon.

From the oscillations of previous years larger imports could have been predicted for 1965, but not the enormous increase which actually occurred (see Fig 5.1). It was recorded earlier that in his 1965 budget speech the Minister of Finance described the maintenance of the external reserves as 'one of the most important tasks we have set ourselves for this year'; as late as September 1965 he assured the National Assembly that the foreign exchange plan 'will be substantially fulfilled' and that 'gross reserves willl stand at virtually the same level' as they had been at the end of 1964.[29] The truth was, however, that, for reasons given in chapters 5 and 6, imports were quite out of control; licences were issued in that year to the value of ₵406 million as compared with the planned level of ₵312 million.[30] Fortunately, not all the licences were utilized but, even so, imports rose to a new record level – a record which still stood seven years later.

Substantially greater success in restraining imports was achieved after the 1966 coup but the tendency for actual imports to exceed

TABLE 10.1
Balance of Payments Forecasts and Actuals (in millions of pre-1967 devaluation cedis)

	1965			1966			1967		
	Forecast	Actual	Difference	Forecast	Actual	Difference	Forecast	Actual	Difference
1. Exports f.o.b.									
(a) Cocoa	144	148	+4	144	116	−28	158	128	−30
(b) Other	91	82	−9	88	84	−4	86	75	−11
2. Net invisibles and transfers	−41	−45	−4	−55	−39	+16	−63	−53	+10
3. Net private long-term capital receipts	15	26	+11	10	42	+32	23	25	+2
4. Net public long-term capital receipts	−5	2	+7	3	1	−2	25	1	−24
5. Net suppliers' credits and trade credits[b]	91	71	−20	39	30	−9	−25	10	+35
6. Net IMF position	—	−8	−8	—	33	+33	9	13	+4
7. Changes in bilateral balances	+17	+25	+8	—	−4	−4	−4	−16	−12
8. Changes in external reserves[c]	—	+38	+38	−16	−12	+4	−8	+24	+32
9. Errors and omissions	—	+5	+5	−1	+3	+4	—	+3	+3
10. Total resources available for imports C.I.F. (net balance on above)	312	344	+32	213	254	+41	201	210	+9
11. Total of deviations from forecast as % of total forecast (ignoring signs throughout)		28%			38%			41%	

	1968[d]			1969[d]			Mean of 1965-69		
	Forecast	Actual	Difference	Forecast	Actual	Difference	Forecast	Actual	Difference
1. *Exports f.o.b.*									
(a) Cocoa	162	151	−11	176	174	−2	157	143	−14
(b) Other	85	86	+1	80	106	+26	86	87	+1
2. Net invisibles and transfers	−60	−52	+8	−55	−68	−13	−55	−51	+4
3. Net private long-term capital receipts	16	16	0	15	8	−7	16	23	+7
4. Net public long-term capital receipts	35[a]	29	−6	38[a]	34	−4	19	13	−6
5. Net suppliers' credits and trade credits[b]	−38	−16	+22	−8	−2	+6	12	19	+7
6. Net IMF position	—	8	+8	−9	−4	+5	0	+8	+8
7. Changes in bilateral balances	—	−1	−1	—	+8	+8	+3	+2	−1
8. Changes in external reserves[c]	−5	−4	+1	−20	+2	+22	−10	+10	+20
9. Errors and omissions	−1	+4	+5	—	−12	−12	0	+1	+1
10. Total resources available for imports c.i.f. (net balance on above)	195	220	+27	216	246	+29	228	255	+27
11. Total of deviations from forecast as% of total forecast (ignoring signs throughout)			16%			26%			30%[e]

NOTES:

[a] This figure refers to aid already committed and makes no provision for the disbursement of newly committed aid funds.

[b] Includes changes in trade and payments arrears.

[c] Includes changes in assets and liabilities of commercial banks. A plus sign indicates a reduction of reserves.

[d] Export and import figures include Valco. For these two years I have presented the forecasts that were prepared in conjunction with the 'operational' import programmes rather than those that were presented to the aid donors.

[e] Calculated reading horizontally along line 11.

Sources: *The Budget, 1965* (Accra, 1965); The Foreign Exchange Budget 1966 (Accra, 1966); *Statistical Year Book, 1965–66* (Central Bureau of Statistics, Accra, 1969); *Annual Report* of Bank of Ghana for 1970–71 (Bank of Ghana, 1971); unpublished data provided by Bank of Ghana.

planned levels persisted, as can be seen from line 10 of Table 10.1. Moreover, there is evidence that disinflationary fiscal and monetary policies pursued by the NLC had as much to do with the generally modest level of imports in their years as did import controls. In 1968, for example, there was another very large over-issue of licences: issues totalled ₵440 million against an operational programme of only ₵279 million, and that a high proportion of the licences were not utilized may be at least partly explained by the depressed state of domestic demand. The oscillations of earlier years had already demonstrated the sensitivity of imports to domestic demand conditions – a finding corroborated by Leith's researches.[31] The tendency to issue licences in excess of import capacity continued throughout, and during the liberalization of 1969–71 imports which had not been liberalized increased even more rapidly than those which had been freed of 'controls':[32]

Increase between 1st Quarters	OGL Imports	Other Imports
1969–70	9·5%	22·7%
1970–71	33·9%	44·5%
1969–71	46·7%	77·3%

In short, while there is little doubt that controls reduced the volume of imports, it is also evident that they were unable to do so to the extent consistent with successive governments' desire to conserve and strengthen the external reserves. The excess of actual over planned imports was chronic to the system, which was apparently unable to resist the excess demand which existed throughout most of the decade.[33]

The consequence was that in all years covered by Table 10.1 there was either a reduction in reserves (1963–5, 1967, 1969) or a smaller increase than intended (1966, 1968). Arrears on current payments and on profit remittances increased in the same period and this was another residual element which had to absorb the cost of excess imports (e.g. in 1965, 1966 and 1968).

The control system may have imposed an additional cost to the balance of payments over and above the factors already considered. The introduction and maintenance of controls involved, at least until 1967, a more or less explicit rejection of policies which operated through the price mechanism. As the national currency became increasingly over-valued, the incentives to export and for foreign firms to invest in Ghana became weaker. Since the real villain of Ghana's balance of payments problem was the stagnation of her export sector, it could be that the heaviest cost of import controls was that they distracted attention from the need to boost exports and were associated with policies which actually discouraged them. A scheme of export subsidies was not seriously tried until 1971.

Assessment: (b) Allocative Efficiency

Besides protecting the balance of payments, the planners were supposed to allocate imports according to government priorities. As
described earlier, the priorities of the Nkrumah government included
increased trade with socialist and other bilateral trade pact countries, a
restructuring of imports away from 'non-essential' consumer goods in
favour of capital equipment, a transfer of foreign exchange from the
private to public sectors, and the protection of local industries. To what
extent were these objectives achieved?

A good deal of progress was made in shifting the *geographical origin*
of Ghana's imports in favour of the socialist countries during the first
half of the sixties. The share of imports from centrally planned countries rose from an average of 4 per cent of the total in 1959–61 to 20
per cent in 1964–6. Between 1960 and 1964 imports from bilateral
partners increased by 170 per cent while imports from other sources
fell by 9 per cent. There probably would have been some tendency for
the share to grow even under a liberal regime – there having been some
increase during the fifties – but there is no doubt that it was greatly
accelerated by the discriminating use of the licensing system. Even in
1962 it appears that attempts were made to direct importers to
specified countries of supply[34] and, although this was abandoned in
1963, it was restored again in 1964, when 35 commodities were identified which could only be imported from trade pact countries unless
they were unable to supply.[35] When the licensing authorities ceased
this discrimination in 1966, the share of imports emanating from these
countries went down markedly (from 20 per cent in 1964–6 to 8 per
cent in 1967–9), although this change was reinforced by the cessation
of new credits from them and the emergence of Western countries as
major aid donors.

It is true that the reorientation of Ghana's import trade could not be
achieved overnight. There were various complaints that licences were
not issued early enough for compliance with the rather rigid procedures of the central planning authorities[36] but, even so, the authorities
were successful in achieving a rapid shift in the desired direction. They
were, however, less successful in expanding bilateral trade with neighbouring African countries, which remained small.

There is equally persuasive evidence that the import planners were
successful in changing the *end-use composition* of imports in the
general directions desired by successive governments. The remarkable
shift which occurred in the composition of imports during the
Nkrumah period, away from consumer goods and in a favour of capital
equipment was already noticed in chapter 5 (see Table 5.2); while it is
likely that some change in these directions would have occurred
anyway, as import-substituting industrialisation got under way, the
licensing system accelerated the process and facilitated the
industrialization of the first half of the sixties. Table 5.2 also shows that

after the overthrow of Nkrumah the authorities were successful in implementing the new preferences for a shift away from new investment and an improved availability of industrial raw materials.

The planners did not get it all their own way, however. Although their achievements were real, they often found it difficult to impose their desires on the actual pattern of imports, both during and after the Nkrumah period. The *Annual Plan* for 1965, for example, complained that shortages of capital equipment, raw materials and spare parts had resulted from an undesirably high level of consumer good imports in 1964,[37] and in his 'mini-budget' of September 1965 the Finance Minister produced data showing that actual imports licensed were weighted much more heavily towards consumer goods than was intended in the foreign exchange budget for that year.[38] More comprehensive information is available for 1968 and 1969, and Table 10.2 presents a comparison of the end-use composition of the operational import programmes for those years with actual imports.

TABLE 10.2
Programmed and Actual End-use Composition of Imports, 1968–9[a]

	(percentages of total)			
	1968		1969	
	Programme	Actual	Programme	Actual
1. Non-durable consumers' goods	21·0	24·2	19·6	24·7
(of which, food)	(10·4)	(10·9)	(11·9)	(10·3)
2. Durable consumers' goods	4·5	4·7	2·5	5·4
3. Fuels & lubricants	7·4	6·8	6·6	6·4
4. Non-durable producers' materials	34·4	30·8	39·8	29·6
5. Durable producers' materials	8·3	8·7	5·1	10·4
6. Producers' equipment	24·3	24·9	26·5	23·3
7. TOTAL	100·0	100·0	100·0	100·0

Sources: Bank of Ghana; *Economic Surveys* (various issues).
NOTE:
[a] Includes Valco imports.

In both years consumer goods (durable and non-durable) took a larger share of the total than intended, whereas raw material imports were well below expectations. At the single commodity level there were also large discrepancies between what the planners intended and what actually happened, as will be shown later. In fairness, it should be added that to some extent in 1968 and more so in 1969, import liberalization had gone far enough for it to be especially difficult for the planners to perform their job with precision.

At the rather broad level of aggregation presented so far the planners had considerable success in changing the composition of imports in the desired directions, but were they able to do so *efficiently*? Were they as successful at the micro-economic level as they were overall? Although the evidence is not systematic, it seems that here there is a different story to tell.

First, the increase in the share of capital equipment in the Nkrumah years, was accompanied by detailed licensing failures which either delayed the completion of investment projects or caused them to cease operations because of materials shortages. Thus, the *Abrahams Report* alleged that completion of a sugar factory was unnecessarily delayed because the Ministry of Trade 'would not issue licences to import paint to protect steel structures,'[39] and there were several instances when firms had to close down temporarily for want of crucial spare parts. The 1965 *Annual Plan* expressed serious dissatisfaction with this:[40]

A particularly unfavourable aspect of this situation has been the waste of capital and the loss of potential output when major pieces of capital equipment have been unable to operate owing to the absence of small but vital spare parts. All sectors of the economy seem to exhibit this feature. The use of construction equipment in both the public and private sectors has been considerably below optimum. Many industries have had periods of slowdown or even complete stoppage in production.

Even more serious, however, were the consequences of shortages of industrial raw materials which developed in 1963–6. Ghana was starving her existing industries in order to build new ones and there was much criticism of this. The 1964 *Economic Survey* complained that industrial output had been held back by inadequate supplies of raw materials, and went on,[41]

This is one of the major problems hindering the rapid industrial advancement of the country. It has not been possible yet for those responsible for the issue of licences to evolve a machinery that will enable the industrial sector of the economy to be provided with its allocation of foreign currency at the appropriate times. As a result of this, establishments have had to run at less than optimum capacity.

The following year's *Survey* echoed the same theme,[42] and alleged inefficiency and corruption in the Ministry of Trade came under attack in *The Spark* , the ideological organ of Nkrumah's own party.[43] The *Abrahams Report* gave a particularly poignant example of the adverse effects of materials shortages:[44]

In the case of the State Paints Corporation, it applied for import licences for raw materials in September of last year, and the licences were issued in May of this year. It had to abandon operations altogether between May and July. At the same time, licences were issued for the importaton of paint at an expenditure of foreign currency running at an average pro rata rate four times that of raw materials. The Corporation has furthermore been prevented by an inadequacy of raw materials from following up export enquiries

from other African countries. On account of its stoppage, private
retailers have been selling the Corporation's paint at £G4 per gallon
when it could have been sold without loss at £G1.5s.

Problems of this kind were not confined to manufacturing. Even
agriculture, which uses few imported supplies, suffered from shortages
of fertilizers, insecticides and matchets; and the transportation system
was also adversely affected.[45]

It should be added, finally, that there were instances in which the
timing of licensed imports weakened the position of local producers.
One example was the importation of a large quantity of bottles from
Czechoslovakia and China in 1965 just before a new glass factory was
commissioned, so that the factory was for a time unable to sell its bottles. Other examples include the importation of a large quantity of
maize in the middle of the 1967 season, and of fish in mid-1970,
causing local catches to be left rotting on the shoreside. It appears,
then, that the success of the planners in manipulating the overall end-
use composition of imports was achieved at a high cost to allocative
efficiency.

Their other main achievement in this area was a major reduction in
the share of consumer goods. To what extent were they able to achieve
this efficiently, in the sense of discriminating between 'essential' and
'luxurious' consumer goods? The answer is that there were recurring
shortages of what are conventionally regarded in Ghana as essential
consumer goods. In the second half of 1963, for example, shortages
developed of sugar, salt and other items, and the position became
worse in 1964:[46]

> It has not . . . been possible yet to draw up a priority list of import
> items with the complete elimination, for the time being, of luxurious
> commodities. The result is that at times when very essential com-
> modities are in short supply, the counters of certain shops have on
> them unessential items like canned potatoes, etc. from trade and
> payments agreements countries.

Drugs were among the items which became scarce in 1964.[47] Even
1965, when licence issues for consumer goods exceeded the import
plan by 43 per cent,[48] did not see an end to the scarcities. In the view of
the *Economic Survey*, 'the country had to cope with the most acute
shortages of basic commodities since import licensing was introduced'
in 1965, [49] and there is good reason to believe that these shortages
were a major reason for the popularity of the coup which brought
down the Nkrumah government.[50]

Improvements in the licensing system after the coup resulted in a
more rational flow of consumer good imports but did not put an end to
the anomalies. In April 1968 the Bank of Ghana noted that,

fairly large quantities of consumer goods of a luxury or semi-luxury nature can now be found in the big stores. It is not clear whether these are being brought in because of the importers are taking advantage of the 'omnibus' character of certain licences or whether there are other loopholes. At any rate, the appearance of these commodities in the market coupled with the reported shortages of raw materials is a matter that has already elicited adverse comment.

By 1969 Dr Busia's Progress Party had come to the conclusion that direct trade controls 'have harmed the welfare of the consumer and prevented an orderly growth of the economy.'[51]

To sum up, evidence leaves little doubt that, although the authorities achieved desired changed in the overall composition of imports, they were unable to combine this with detailed licensing according to a coherent and well-ordered set of priorities. The result at the microeconomic level was an inefficiency which served to intensify the damage done to the economy by the overall scarcity of foreign exchange.

The reasons for this will be explored shortly but the point should be made here that not all the shortcomings described above could be laid at the doors of the programmers. Specifically, it appears that in 1963–5 Nkrumah was willing to keep factories short of materials and spares if that was necessary to sustain his plans for industrial expansion. This questionable policy was not the responsibility of the officials, who should be assessed according to their success in implementing the political instructions handed down to them. Thus, in some measure the allocative distortions which marked this period were the result of apparently irrational political priorities rather than a failure of the licensing system as such.

There remain for discussion two other objectives, which can be dealt with briefly. The first of these was the transfer of foreign exchange from the private to the public sector, or the *socialization of imports.*

As noted earlier, the foreign exchange budgets for 1965 and 1966 envisaged a massive transfer of foreign exchange earnings from the private to the state sector, and, while it is impossible to measure the extent to which this was achieved, there is no doubt that a substantial socialization of imports did occur in the last years of the Nkrumah period. The industrial expansion which the import programmes were tailored to accommodate was very largely generated by the public sector and this was a period when consumption was also being socialized.[52] Trade statistics indicate that direct government imports rose as a percentage of the total from 7·0 per cent in 1961–2 to 11·6 per cent in 1964–5,[53] but this does not include the imports of state enterprises and similar para-statal agencies. That licensing discriminated in their favour is confirmed by the 1965 *Economic Survey* (para. 282), which noted that:

.... most manufacturers were unable to satisfy their requirements of raw materials and spare parts. The sectors most severely hit were the private sector, followed by the co-operative sector. The advance in the State and Joint State/Private Sectors, on the other hand, was remarkable.

But even state enterprises had supply problems. The difficulties of the State Paints Corporation have already been mentioned; a report by the State Enterprises Secretariat referred to difficulties in 1964 because licences were delayed or inadequate. It went on, 'The first half of 1965 was characterized by frequent and prolonged stoppages of work in almost all the enterprises due to acute shortage of raw materials and spare parts'[54] (licences were issued later that year). Once again, then, it seems that *overall* the licensing authorities were able to carry out the political requirements of the Nkrumah government but that the record was less satisfactory when it came to detailed operation.

The remaining principle by which the import planners were required to allocate licences was that of *protecting local industries.* This was emphasized to parliament when licensing was first introduced and it was acted upon to some extent. Nkrumah's desires to give priority to capital goods imports and to transfer foreign exchange to the public sector were themselves part of the industrialization drive, but the licensing system was also operated as an explicit device of domestic protection. In October 1963, for example, imports of footwear, matches, toilet paper, nails and plastic utensils were prohibited,[55] and the *Economic Survey* for that year noted that the rapid growth in the number of manufacturing plants was 'helped partly by the introduction of import licensing...'[56] In the following year the authors of the *Survey* were less confident on this score, arguing that the erratic functioning of the licensing system made it difficult for businessmen to plan ahead and that the resulting uncertainty 'was reflected partly in the reluctance of business enterprises to increase investment...'[57] Leith concluded from his studies that import licensing provided only an 'uncertain and erratic' source of protection.[58] What is abundantly clear is that the manner in which the licensing system was operated provided a distorted and arbitrary set of investment incentives which was unlikely to result in efficient import-substitution.[59]

Problems and Weaknesses
The conclusion emerges that, while import controls were by no means completely ineffective, they were inefficient. What, then, were the sources of weakness?

One – a point made familiar by the previous chapter – was that single policy instrument was being used to achieve a multiplicity of objectives. Had the programmers been able to concentrate, for example, on controlling the total value of imports they might have done well, but to do this while at the same time shifting importers to bilateral pact suppliers, changing the composition of imports in favour of industrial investment, giving preference to public sector imports, protecting local industry *and* doing all these things in a smoothly functioning manner, would have taxed the best informed, most efficient planning agency in the world. Tinbergen has, of course, demonstrated formally that each government target should employ a separate policy instrument, and that more instruments are needed when governments are pursuing policies intended to be discriminating in their effects.[60] Less formally, while a single policy instrument can help to achieve more than one objective, it is unlikely to be able to do so with precision. Too many different things were being asked of the planners; to some extent failure was written into their terms of reference.

Another source of difficulty implicit in what has already been written was that the planners did not receive sufficient political support. It is to be presumed that every major departure from previously agreed import programmes required ministerial sanction, and there were a number of such departures. The most spectacular of these was in 1965. On this occasion the Minister of Finance apparently did not receive the support of his President, because his carefully devised import programme was simply swept aside by a President insisting on completing an enormous new conference building and on filling the shops for a meeting of the Organisation of African Unity.[61] It was, however, a more general problem. If the licensing system was not to come under internal pressure and if there was not to be domestic inflation, it was necessary that restraint be exercised on domestic demand, but the Nkrumah government pursued strongly expansionary policies and ran an especially large budget deficit in 1965. There was as a result much domestic inflation, which lowered the relative price of imports and yet further intensified the pressure to license an unsustainably large volume of imports.[62]

Moreover, this problem did not disappear with Nkrumah. The NLC also proved unable or unwilling to restrain consumption, private and public, to the levels upon which their own import programmes were based. For example, the operational import programme for 1969 was based upon assumed increases in private and government consumption of ₵30 million and ₵15 million but the actual increases were ₵75 million and ₵21 million.[63] In consequence, consumer goods imports in that year were well above the planned level. In fact, throughout much of the sixties, buoyant domestic demand created intense pressures on the licensing system. It is also worth noticing that import programmes were normally prepared for calendar years but that, with the exception of 1965, fiscal years covered different twelve-month periods. This situation could scarcely have assisted the co-ordination of fiscal and balance of payments policies.

In all years the import programme was exceeded and a reasonable conclusion to draw is that when they came under strong pressure to grant more licences the responsible Ministers gave way – both in the Nkrumah period and after. Hence, the committee responsible for the import programme noted in a memo of March 1970 that for 'essential' food items, 'the licensing authorities are always under pressure to issue licenses whenever it is felt that stocks were low. Imports of these items could therefore be deemed to be as close to actual demand as possible allowing for changes in stocks.' Not only were governments asking too much of the import programmers; they were also failing to give them the support they needed.

In the popular mind, however, there was one overwhelming cause of the deficiencies of the licensing system: *corruption*. There was good evidence for regarding this as serious. The *Akainyah Report* found substantiated allegations of bribery and the forging of licences against fairly junior officers of the Ministry of Trade and against the chief of the Criminal Investigations Department of the police. The *Abrahams Report* also hinted heavily at malpractices in the same Ministry.[64] If what those enquiries brought to light seemed relatively minor illegalities, the same cannot be said of the findings of the *Ollent Report*. This found that Nkrumah's last two Ministers of Trade had set aside carefully devised procedures for the allocation of licences in order to obtain bribes. Under A.Y.K. Djin, it said:[65]

> licences were issued solely at his discretion, capriciously exercised with the consequent development of a crisis in the import trade . . . He embarked upon irregularities in the issue of licences and fraudulently exploited the situation created by himself for his own benefit to the advantage of members of his family and personal friends . . .

Under Kwasi Armah there were:[66]

> open corruption and malpractices . . . licences were issued on the basis of a commission corruptly demanded and payable by importer on the face value of the import licenses issued. The commission was fixed at 10%, but was in special cases reduced to $7\frac{1}{2}$% or 5%. The corruption was not spasmodic but organized and systematically operated through agents . . . so that decent importers were compelled to accept the improper methods of obtaining licences as the only means of survival.

These enquiries also discovered various other forms of illegality. Akainyah found that businesses had been illegally selling their licences or had mis-declared the goods imported, and the *Abrahams Report* (para. 120) talked of 'importers of straw who would be unable to finance the imports, and who, we think, made over to others more substantial than themselves the use of licences which they had obtained.'[67] Again, it appears that this problem outlived Nkrumah. After it took over in 1972 the NRC set up yet another commission of enquiry charged, *inter alia*, with investigating the allocation of import licences under the Busia government, and this heard some apparently damaging evidence from senior civil servants and others to the effect that Ministers varied the normal procedures for allocating licences to favour specific individuals and companies who were financing the ruling party.[68]

It is nevertheless difficult to believe that these illegalities offer more than a partial explanation of the defects of the licensing system.[69] Serious allegations of large-scale corruption are confined to the tenures in office of Ministers Djin and Armah, i.e. roughly 1964 and 1965, and yet neither before nor after this period did the system work smoothly. Things did improve from 1966 but the *Economic Survey* for 1967 (para. 236) still found the system highly defective:

> Even though there was some improvement in the issue of licences, it still needs to be emphasised that the selective allocation of import licences itself is a non-market mechanism which leaves much to be desired from the standpoint of efficiency. Shortage of raw materials and spares continued to hamper rapid progress generally in nearly all the industry groups . . .

Doubtless, considerations such as these, plus the influence of the IMF and external aid donors, induced the NLC to make a beginning with the liberalization of imports which was accelerated by the Busia government.

Examination of the details of the various annual import programmes shows that some of the difficulties were inherent in the manner in which these programmes were prepared. They had to be implemented and monitored by the government departments directly responsible for the import trade – the Ministries of Trade and Industries, and the Department of Customs and Excise. But, for the most part, the programmes were not set out according to the Standard International Trade Classification (SITC) employed by these agencies. Only in 1966 was the foreign exchange budget expressed in SITC categories, and then only at the single-digit level. In all other years the programmes were chiefly specified according to a curious mixture of end-use, industry-of-use, and specific commodity categories. Before they could be given operational content, the programmes had to be converted into SITC classes which, at best, created a major additional burden of work for the Ministries and, at worst, resulted in a substantially different pattern of licensing from that intended. A further consequence was that it was impossible to monitor the programmes as drawn up, for the trade statistics follow the SITC, and the end-use composition of imports is only estimated annually after long delays.

Available evidence suggests that mis-specification of the programmes seriously undermined their effectiveness, for it appears that the Ministries did not always convert the programmes into SITC equivalents with much accuracy. Take 1968, for example. This year, and 1969, represented the high point in the sophistication of the import planning process. A vast amount of information (or quasi-information) was collected from industrial concerns and others, and a co-ordinated attempt was made to draw up a detailed plan which reflected national needs and priorities.[70] But of the total of ₵210 million licences issued in 1968, no fewer than ₵89 million were for 'various goods', covering all kinds of imports. Most of the hard work which was put into the 1968 programme was rendered futile by subsequent failures to implement it. It is not surprising that the figures of Table 10.2 show differences between what the planners intended and what actually happened.

By no means the entire problem arose from the failure to specify the programmes by the SITC, however. The programmes did list some commodities which could be unambiguously converted into an SITC code and, again, it seems that the Ministries adhered to the programmes only in the most approximate manner. Table 10.3 lists all the commodities shown in the 1968 and 1969 operational programmes which can be directly compared with actual imports in those years. Taking the commodities as a group, it shows that actual imports differed from the planned amount by an average of plus or minus 38 per cent and 39 per cent respectively.

To be fair to the implementing Ministries, it does appear that in some cases the programmers were not very successful in gauging the country's detailed needs: see, for example, the very large shortfalls between planned the actual imports of butter (1968 and 1969) tobacco (1969), tallow (1968) and maize (1969). Another reason for differences was the considerable spill-over into each year of goods licensed in the previous year.[71] The import programmes were not adjusted to take account of these spill-overs. Furthermore, many licences were not fully utilized and, in the absence of advance knowledge of under-utilization, this was also bound to result in detailed discrepancies between the plans and what actually happened. The Ministry of Trade over-issued licences expecting some to be unutilized but, in the absence of accurate information, tended to exaggerate the extent of under-use. In some years this was a major factor, for example in 1965 and 1968.

Granted all this and granted also that the licensing system ought to remain flexible, sensitive to planning errors and changing circumstances, the suspicion remains that the Ministries of Trade and Industries paid rather little attention to the details of the import programme when they came to prepare specific licences. This, at least, was the view

TABLE 10.3
Comparison of Programmed and Actual Imports of Selected Commodities, 1968–9 (millions of cedis)

Item	1968			1969		
	Programme	Actual	Difference (%)	Programme	Actual	Difference (%)
Rice	5·7	6·8	+19%	n.a.	–	–
Maize	n.a.	–	–	1·0	0·3	–70%
Milk and cream	8·5	6·3	–26%	7·6	7·9	+ 4%
Butter	0·9	0·1	–89%	1·0	0·25	–75%
Sugar	6·6	8·2	+24%	7·3	8·3	+14%
Fish and fish preparations	2·0	4·5	+125%	3·3	4·9	+48%
Meat and meat preparations	5·7	2·8	–51%	2·3	3·4	+48%
Crude petroleum	12·6	13·6	+ 8%	11·0	14·5	+32%
Lubricants and other fuels	8·4	7·5	–11%	9·0	8·1	–10%
Tobacco (unprocessed)	4·4	3·8	–14%	4·6	0·3	–93%
Tallow	5·1	3·0	–41%	4·4	4·6	+ 5%
Wheat flour	6·3	7·2	+14%	6·8[a]	4·5[a]	–34%
Mean difference			±38%			±39%

Sources: CBS Annual Report on External Trade, Vol. 1, 1966–8; CBS External Trade Statistics, December 1969; Bank of Ghana.
NOTE:
[a] Unprocessed wheat.

of an inter-departmental committee in charge of the formulation of the annual programmes, which complained in a memo of March 1970 that,

> the licensing procedures are diffused and the authorities do not always go strictly according to the details of the programme. In addition, records of licenses issued often lack the necessary details to enable a reclassification on a comparable basis with the programme. Large amounts of licenses issued for instance are classified 'various' and no customs item numbers are given so that it is impossible to ascertain the degree to which the programme is actually being followed in detail by the licensing authorities.

The committee went on to discuss whether detailed planning ought not to be abandoned altogether but preferred the alternative, 'to encourage the licensing authorities to follow the programmes in some detail or . . . give sufficient details of licences issued to enable us to integrate our efforts on all fronts.'[72] However, co-ordination proved an insoluble problem, with poor co-operation persisting to the end of the sixties.[73]

Moreover, mere possession of a valid licence did not assure the would-be importer that foreign exchange would be released by the Bank of Ghana to enable him to use it. Many classes of imports were subject to mandatory 180-day credit arrangements from abroad and not a few importers had difficulty in meeting these requirements. The State Gold Mining Corporation, for example – one of Ghana's larger export earners – was seriously affected by its inability to establish the requisite letters of credit for materials and spares, even though they generally had adequate licences. Delays in satisfying the Bank's requirements were sometimes such that by the time credits had been arranged the validity of the licences had lapsed.

A fundamental difficulty in the way of achieving a practical import programme reflecting national needs was the enormous volume of accurate, up-to-date information that it would require. Data would be needed, commodity-by-commodity, on anticipated demand for the coming year, on inventory levels, on local production, and on the input requirements of local producers. Information would be necessary on the financial and managerial capacities of importers to utilize their licence allocations, and on the imports that would spill over from the previous year's licences. More than this: the civil service would have to be able to process this information intelligently and promptly to produce a carefully balanced programme. In practice, the quantity and quality of information, and the capacity to absorb it, fell drastically short of the ideal.[74]

Attempts were made to overcome these weaknesses. Applicants were required to submit detailed information but the preparation and processing of it became a source of weakness, not of strength. According to the *Abrahams Report* (paras. 102–103):

Administrative bottle-necks have bedevilled the issue of import licences to the injury not only of commercial houses but also of the consuming public. These bottle-necks have arisen from a number of causes which, in our opinion, include the sheer volume of documentation demanded by the former Ministry of Trade, an unwieldy method of validation severally involving the consent and counter-signature of the Minister of Trade, the Minister of Finance and the Governor of the Bank of Ghana – a virtual odyssey . . . The administrative congestion has resulted in avoidable delays in the issue of import licenses . . . which usually mean delays in the importation of commodities which may already be scarce, and some-times a total impossibility in importing them.

There were improvements after 1966. A major effort was made in the preparation of the 1968 and 1969 programmes to obtain detailed information from a large number of industrial establishments. Esti-mates of import requirements were derived (a) on a macro-economic basis from national accounts projections, (b) from detailed sectoral projections which took account of such matters as expected demand conditions, the desirability of protecting local producers, the raw materials required to produce a given volume of output and the degree of capacity utilization, and (c) were then reconciled with each other and with expected foreign exchange availabilities.[75] In fact, the files are a monument to the vast amount of work done. But, quite apart from the failure to implement the programmes, the exercise was sub-ject to a basic difficulty: the very existence of import restrictions and an over-valued currency provide a strong incentive for licence applicants to present false or exaggerated information in the hope of getting large allocations. It was well known that local producers often applied for raw materials greatly in excess of their real needs, naturally presenting supporting 'information' to reinforce their case. This helps to explain why in 1968 approved licences for industrial materials averaged a mere 24 per cent of the applications received.[76] Similarly, importers of final goods were constantly striving, by fair means or foul, to increase their own share of the market and thus reap the monopoly profits to be earned from the sale of imports.[77] Far from being a scientific attempt to calculate national needs, licence allocations had to be made on the basis of bluff and counter-bluff.

That the reforms produced some effect is suggested by line 11 of Table 10.1, where it will be seen that the mean deviations of actual results from the forecast balance of payments in 1968 and 1969 were smaller than for the three previous years, although the deviations of imports from their planned levels (+27 per cent and +29 per cent) remained large. But that the system made heavy demands upon the time and resources of importers is amusingly conveyed by a suggestion of the National Chamber of Commerce that 'the import licensing duties between the Ministry of Industries and the Ministry of Trade should be centralised. This would eliminate the necessity of walking to and from the two Ministries when a manufacturer is arranging for a licence.'[78]

First Conclusions
Only partial success could be claimed for import controls in the nineteen-sixties. They were successful in reducing the absolute level of imports, thus protecting the balance of payments, but the influence of domestic demand remained too strong for the controls to be able to conserve the external reserves in the manner desired. And, by focusing attention on the limitation of imports, they encouraged a neglect of export incentives that was fatal to any basic solution of the payments problem. Controls, on this view, merely postponed the introduction of measures to act on the fundamental sources of weakness.

It is a similarly mixed picture when one turns to the allocative efficiency of the system. Controls achieved substantial changes in the geographical origin and end-use composition of imports, in the directions desired by the governments of the day, and brought about a significant socialization of imports during the Nkrumah period. Whether they were as successful in systematically providing protection for local industries is more doubtful, but if one looks at broad trends it could well be said that the controls did what was required of them. When one looks at the system as it operated at the micro-economic level, however, it becomes clear that the programmers failed to evolve a system for an efficient commodity-by-commodity allocation of imports – a defect only partly due to the non-economic priorities of politicians. This failure imposed a major cost on the economy, in output and welfare forgone, and also, from time to time, generated a political climate which was certainly not intended. One reason for this failure, it is suggested, was that governments were seeking to achieve multiple objectives with a single policy weapon.

That the system failed at the micro-economic level is therefore not surprising, especially in view of the administrative problems described in a previous sub-section.[79] For a variety of reasons, detailed implementation of the programmes was carried out very loosely, which with other factors resulted in an actual composition of imports which bore only the most approximate relationship to the intentions of the planners. It was not so much that the micro-economic programmes failed; in a real sense there were no programmes at that level.

II Price Controls

The system of price controls which operated in Ghana throughout the remainder of the sixties was introduced in 1962 to complement the import restrictions which came into effect at the beginning of that year.

The price list as promulgated then, and as developed during the sixties, was largely confined to imported consumer goods and local manufactures with high import contents. The controls could thus be seen as an instrument of social policy to protect consumers by preventing importers and local manufacturers from earning monopoly rents arising from import restrictions (and other forms of industrial protection). However, successive governments thought of the price controls as going beyond this and as an *egalitarian* device for safeguarding the interests of the poor. When he introduced the second reading of the 1962 Control of Prices Act, the Minister of Finance and Trade talked of the need to 'bring the prices of the commodities needed by the masses within the reach of everybody,' and commended the Act because it would ensure that 'the people are not deprived of decent and inexpensive living by any privileged class.'[80] The following paragraphs are a condensation of the results of a study of the affects of these controls, which are more fully presented in an article in the *Journal of Modern African Studies*. Interested readers are referred to that source for fuller details of the nature of the study, the evidence collected and the results obtained.[81]

The Price List

As at the end of 1969 the government was seeking to administer a complex set of price controls. The number of separately specified items totalled 725 and, for many of these, several prices were given, according to quantity and locality of sale. In all, 5,920 separate prices were itemized. The smooth operation of so ambitious a scheme would demand extensive information on costs, quantities and qualities, and large inputs of administrative resources, so it is not surprising that, even though price controls had by then been in operation for about seven years, the 1969 list contained a considerable number of anomalies.

One was that it was not appropriately designed to have the egalitarian effects desired by the government. Among the more obvious high-income luxury goods included in the list were butter, instant tea, instant coffee, spirits and aerosol insecticides. The poor can afford to buy few imported consumer goods, or locally manufactured import-substitutes; it is the well-to-do (especially the expatriate community) who spend the greatest proportion of their incomes on such goods,[82] and who, therefore, would be the most able to benefit from the price control scheme. Trying to reduce income inequalities in Ghana by holding down the prices of a wide range of imported and locally manufactured consumer goods, *while leaving local food prices unaffected*, was a doubtful tactic. Controls on some local food prices plus a smaller list of imported wage goods (e.g. milk, sardines, corned beef) would have been more likely to have an egalitarian effect, although the inclusion of local foods would have presented formidable practical problems.

Observance and Evasion

Comparison of control prices with 145 observations of actual prices in March 1970, as recorded by CBS price enumerators, yielded the result that in only 17 per cent of the cases was the control price being observed and in 72 per cent it was being exceeded.[83] Since the extent of control observance was probably overstated in the CBS returns, it is evident that at that time price controls were not an effective economic policy. The mean value of all the observations was 16 per cent above the control.

There were, however, some systematic patterns in the degrees of observance and evasion. First, the extent of non-observance was higher in rural centres of population than in the cities and towns. In only one of the 69 observations relating to rural centres was the control reported as being observed and in 90 per cent of these cases the legal limit was being exceeded. Urban localities were more law-abiding, with a 30 per cent observance rate, which is of some importance since a fairly high proportion of sales of the commodities in question was likely to occur in the towns.

Second, the data indicated that control evasion was, as might have been expected, considerably greater on the traditional markets (rural and urban) than in the larger stores. Large government or expatriate-owned concerns are too conspicuous and too vulnerable to break the controls with impunity but the market-women are not so inhibited. It may also be that large stores are the only types of outlet with a range of goods wide enough to be able to recoup losses (or subnormal profits) by raising the prices of non-controlled items for which the demand is inelastic. Thus, the mean value of prices charged in stores was 117 per cent of the control price whereas in the markets the mean was 125 per cent. A breakdown of all the cases in which the controls were being observed indicated that they were to all intents ignored (a) in the rural areas and (b) on the urban markets. Practically all the cases in which the controls were being observed were in urban stores or in urban locations in which the type of outlet was not specified. It seems probable that most of these unspecified observations actually related to stores, and that the main control-observers were the government-owned Ghana National Trading Corporation (GNTC) and the larger expatriate trading concerns, such as the United Africa Company.[84]

Even though control observance on the traditional markets was insignificant, this does not necessarily mean that prices there were unrelated to those in the stores, for when the stores observe the controls this may either reduce the extent to which the market traders exceed the legal limit or indicate that the control price is near to the equilibrium price. Effective competition within the distributive system would keep the prices in the shops and on the markets from moving too far apart. The data suggest that competition may have been quite effective, because there was a clear correlation between prices charged in the shops and on the markets.[85] The market-women were able to charge a premium above the stores equivalent to about six and a half percentage points of the control price but, apart from this premium, any variation from the control price on the market was likely to be matched by virtually the same percentage variation by the stores.

Since the market-women often obtain their supplies from the very stores with which they are competing, it is possible that the close correlation between the two sets of prices arose from the application of a fixed cost-plus mark-up by the women. If the mark-up was inflexible it would be inconsistent with an interpretation of the data as indicating a competitive system. The data do not resolve this issue but the competitive interpretation is more consistent with the general view of the market mammies as shrewd and flexible profit maximizers.

If the competitive interpretation is accepted, the regression results imply that the stores were only likely to observe the control if the free market price was within or not far above the normal premium of the market traders. The mean value of observations on the markets in cases where a store in the same town was observing the controls was 110 per cent. When *all* retailers were exceeding the legal limit, the mean value of the store price was 126 per cent of the control price and on the markets was 133 per cent, i.e. only seven percentage points greater. When they did decide to break the law the storekeepers appeared to take the attitude that it is as good to be hanged for a sheep as for a lamb and raised their prices well above the control levels, while the market-women obtained a rather smaller premium. So long as the controls were observed in the stores they had an effect on the traditional markets, but there is little to indicate that the controls exerted a restraining influence in those cases where they were exceeded both in the stores and on the markets. The impression is gained of a rather competitive distributive system and a successful assertion of the power of market forces over government attempts to suppress them. This is reinforced by a further finding that the controls were most likely to be observed when there was a plentiful supply of the goods in question; supply shortages were associated with large evasions of the control prices.[86]

Were the controls more effective in the case of low-income wage-goods and did they therefore tend to be egalitarian? The data were limited but appeared to show that, far from protecting the prices of wage-goods, the controls had most effect on less essential items, especially in the urban areas. This was probably due to political pressure to peg the prices of essentials at unenforceably low levels, whereas more realistic control levels were acceptable for politically less sensitive items.[87]

Trends Over Time

An index of control prices of food items showed them to have risen at about 3·7 per cent annually between March 1963 and April 1972. Even had they been perfectly enforced, therefore, the controls would have been unable to prevent price increases, although the rate of inflation would probably have been more rapid in their absence. Comparison of the index just quoted with a CBS index of urban prices of imported foods shows the latter to have risen about twice as fast over the same period. It was in 1963–6 that the two indices moved apart; thereafter they moved roughly together. Given that in early 1970 the controls were largely ignored and that the index of control prices stood in a historically normal relationship to the index of actual prices, the most plausible explanation is that the controls were mostly ineffectual from their inception. The tendency for control prices to rise nearly as fast as actual prices from about 1966 resulted from periodic upward adjustments by the controllers, perhaps under pressure from the larger trading companies, in response to changing market conditions. The controllers thus acknowledged their impotence.

Effects on Wage Inflation

Controls are more likely to have a significant economic impact when they form part of an anti-inflationary prices and incomes policy. In Ghana, however, no formal attempt was made to link the introduction of price controls to wage restraint and, although the growth of money earnings did slow down in 1962 and 1963, neither statistics nor logic indicate that price controls could have had more than a temporary dampening effect on wage increases.[88]

Effects on Income Distribution

Price controls, because they were generally unenforced, proved in practice to be largely irrelevant to the distribution of income. However, they were most likely to be observed in the shops of the larger towns and cities, where the wealthy élite are more likely to reside and to buy the controlled goods, whereas the poor are most likely to do their shopping in the markets. It follows that controls tended to increase inequalities in real living standards, rather than diminishing them, Since the objective was to reduce inequalities, the price controls, insofar as they had any impact, were socially retrogressive.

Sources of Weakness

The ineffectuality of the controls is partly explained by the weaknesses of the enforcement mechanism. Between 1962 and 1964 reliance was placed upon reports from unpaid price inspectors but in the latter year the Ministry of Trade employed twenty full-time price inspectors. By 1966 the number had risen to 48.[89]. According to the *Abrahams Report*, the experience with both paid and voluntary inspectors was unhappy. They were alleged to be generally 'in the pay of profiteers' and to be engaged in buying at control prices and selling at a premium.[90] Indeed, the *Report* argued that because the cost of bribing them was passed on to the consumer, 'if there were no voluntary price inspectors, the prices of commodities could be expected to be just that much lower.'[91]

Presumably for these reasons, it was decided to discontinue the employment of inspectors, and by 1969–70 the nominal provision for 100 Price Inspection Superintendents had been dropped. Thereafter the price inspectorate was confined to one Chief Price Inspector and the task of enforcement was left to the police (and, from 1972, the army). The police apparently gave this work low priority, for the controls were more honoured in the breach than in the observance. Only in the urban shops were the controls being observed to any significant extent, as a result of socio-political pressures on GNTC and the larger expatriate trading companies. The market-women were sufficiently powerful to make it politically difficult to enforce at all strictly their observance of the controls.

III Conclusions

It is evident from these two studies that Ghana's experience with import and price controls in the sixties was unhappy, and casual observations suggests this to have been also true of other types of control.[92] At a broad level of aggregation, import controls had some effect in protecting the balance of payments and changing the composition of imports in desired directions but these results were obtained at such a high cost in micro-economic misallocations that other means might have been preferable. Price controls were largely ineffective and any impact they had was in the opposite direction to that intended. Neither type of control could claim to have overcome the pressures of supply and demand. It was shown, moreover, that results were still poor at the end of the sixties or early seventies, after seven or eight years' experience. We saw, for example, that a major effort was made in 1968–9 to improve import licensing, but while real progress was recorded many problems remained and, at the micro-economic level, the import programmes were scarcely implemented. Seemingly, the resources of governments and their civil servants were no match for the difficulties encountered. We might, therefore, revert to a theme taken up at the end of the last chapter, to ask whether the shortcomings were remediable or so fundamental as to rule out the successful operation of control systems at this stage of Ghana's development.

One theme common to both cases was that corruption had seriously detrimental effects, which is an intrinsic disadvantage of controls. Corruption and controls are bed-fellows in many countries,[93] and Ghana's own history has shown that it takes more than changes in governments, civil servants and procedures to overcome the powerful inducements to offer and accept bribes which are created by controls.

What must be re-emphasized, however, is that the elimination of corruption would not get rid of many of the problems which emerged in the sixties. It was shown, for example, that the price control list was quite inappropriate to achieve the objectives assigned to it, so that poor implementation may have been a blessing in disguise. As regards import controls, it was shown that for two years or so corruption had a serious effect on the efficiency of the system but even in periods when there were no allegations of large-scale corruption the controls did not allocate foreign exchange efficiently. There were various other major sources of difficulty, as was put clearly by the committee preparing the 1968 import programme. In a memo dated April 1968 they said, 'It is evident . . . that the successful organisation and implementation of the import programme in the present situation *is no longer merely a question of seeking integrity and orderliness in the issue of licenses.* It is a highly complex economic exercise requiring continuous review and coordination between the various agencies of the Government and great flexibility in execution' (my emphasis). The need was stressed in Part I for effective co-ordination (a) between the import programmers and those responsible for overall macro-economic policies, and (b) between the various agencies involved in the preparation and implementation of the programmes. There seems no intrinsic reason why this should not have been achieved, but co-ordination implies an administrative capacity which may not be realizable within the limitations of Ghana's public administration.

A further source of difficulty intrinsic to controls is the impossible demands which they make for information – a point emerging in both cases. It is not merely that in practice only limited data are available; it seems rather that the binding constraint is the capacity of the civil service to absorb and promptly utilize such information as is already available. Worse still, with import licensing, the very situation which necessitates controls also creates incentives for affected parties to supply false information, in support of inflated licence requests. These informational problems not only reduce the chances of being able to design appropriate control systems, they also hamper co-ordination and flexibility, and the task of monitoring the controls.

We have also noted more specifically administrative shortcomings, including an apparent unwillingness or inability to implement import programmes and enforce price controls. To overcome these deficiencies would, at best, be a slow task. Smoothly operating control systems demand large inputs of skilled administrative talent which at Ghana's stage of development are in very short supply. Thus, in the later sixties there was just one senior civil servant responsible for price control enforcement and, at the end of March 1969, the General Administration section of the Ministry of Trade had a total of only 45 officers in the administrative class to carry out an extremely wide range of function in addition to the administration of controls.[94]

In brief, there was in the sixties, and will be in the seventies, no realistic prospect of operating comprehensive systems of economic controls at more than a low level of efficiency. But this does not dispose of the case for controls. We live in a world of the second-best, so the relevant question is whether the real-resource cost of controls is greater or smaller than the cost of permitting imperfect market forces to operate more freely. This question will be raised in the final chapter. The next task, however, is to interpret what happened to economic policies after the overthrow of Nkrumah.

NOTES:
[1] *See* Meade, 1955, chapter XII–XVIII, for a discussion of the merits and demerits of trade controls.
[2] A political case for controls was expressed in an article by 'Julius Sago' in *The Spark*, 17 September 1965, arguing, *inter alia*, that controls represented the socialist means of tackling the country's economic dilemmas and were the only alternative consistent with Ghana's economic independence. Julius Sago was the pen-name for the editorial group of *The Spark*, the ideological journal of the CPP.
[3] *See* Killick, 1962, Pt. I, p. 16.
[4] *Parliamentary Debates*, Vol. 24, 7 July 1961, col. 121.
[5] *Economic Survey, 1961*, para. 353.
[6] Leith, 1973, chapter 2.
[7] *See* Akainyah Report, 1964.
[8] *See* Abrahams Report, 1965.
[9] *See The Budget, 1965*. This includes a section on the foreign exchange budget for 1965 and the page references refer to that section.
[10] *The Foreign Exchange Budget, 1966*.
[11] *Economic Survey, 1966*, para. 73.
[12] *Ollenu Report*, 1967.
[13] For published examples, *see* NLC, *Ghana's Economy and Aid Requirements in 1968*, and a similarly titled document covering January 1969 to June 1970.
[14] Calculated by J. J. Stern by assuming the same composition of imports as in 1970.
[15] *Akainyah Report*, pp. 4–5.
[16] Krobo Edusei, Nkrumah's Minister of Industries, elaborated the protectionist policy to parliament with characteristic panache:

> 'Since December last year, Ghana has for the first time decided to exercise one of the weapons of economic sovereignty – import control! So long as this weapon is carefully and wisely wielded, our young and infant industries which are facing ruthless competition from long established and giant monopoly industries overseas, will be protected against dumping . . . Where the government are of the opinion that the locally manufactured product can meet the entire home demand, and that its price and quality are up to satisfaction then a decision will be taken that in the interest of saving Ghana's precious foreign exchange earnings to finance the importation of INVESTMENT GOODS, no import licenses will be awarded to permit the importation of the commodity which is already being produced excellently in Ghana.'
> (*Parliamentary Debates*, 6 February 1962, cols. 198–9 – emphasis is original.)

[17] Ministry of Finance, *Foreign Exchange Budget*, 1966, pp. 6–7.
[18] In order to estimate the amount of foreign exchange available for imports it was, of course, necessary to specify policies or targets with respect to changes in external assets and liabilities, as will be shown shortly.

[19] *See* chapter 11.

[20] *Economic Survey, 1969*, para. 93.

[21] *See* Hakam, 1972, especially Table 7, where he shows that whilst in 1968 foreigner received licences equal to 30 per cent of their applications, the comparable propor tion for Ghanaian applicants was only 13 per cent.

[22] *Parliamentary Debates*, 4 July 1961.

[23] *Seven-year Plan*, p. 220.

[24] *The Budget, 1965*, para. 37.

[25] It has, for example, been estimated that in real terms imports declined by 30 per cen between 1961 and 1968.

[26] Expressed as a percentage of forecast values, the deviations from forecast (ignoring signs) averaged as follows over the five years:

Cocoa exports	9·6%
Other exports	11·9%
Invisibles and transfers	18·6%
Private long-term capital	65·8%

[27] *See Economic Survey, 1962*, para, 328, and *Annual Report* of the Bank of Ghana fc 1963–4, p. 20.

[28] ibid. *See also* Leith, op. cit.

[29] *Supplementary Budget Statement, 1965* p. 6.

[30] *Foreign Exchange Budget 1966*, p. 6.

[31] Leith, 1973, chapter 2.

[32] These figures were calculated from monthly trade statistics by J. J. Stern.

[33] It seems that the oscillating pattern of 1961–6 was being resumed in the seventie Following the reimposition of comprehensive import licensing early in the yea there was a large reduction in imports in 1972, in contrast with the boom of 1971 In 1973, however, the Commissioner of Trade announced an import programme c ₵483 million which, after adjusting for exchange rate changes, was even larger tha actual imports in 1971 (*see Daily Graphic*, 26 May 1973).

[34] This would appear to be the implication of the statement in the 1962–3 budget speec that the import licensing system would be reviewed 'to ensure that importers ar allowed some flexibility in choosing sources of supply', *Parliamentary Debates*, October 1962, col. 160.

[35] *See* Leith, 1973, chapter 2.

[36] *Economic Survey*, 1964, para. 112, and the *Abrahams Report*, 1965, p. 18.

[37] *Annual Plan for 1965*, p. 30.

[38] *1965 Supplementary Budget Statement*, pp. 5–6.

[39] *Abrahams Report*, p. 21.

[40] *Annual Plan for 1965*, p. 30.

[41] *Economic Survey, 1964*, para. 285.

[42] *Economic Survey, 1965*, para. 282.

[43] Article by Julius Sago in *The Spark*, 4 February 1966.

[44] *Abrahams Report*, p. 14.

[45] The generally chaotic conditions of the later Nkrumah period are nicely illustrated b this account of conditions in the first half of 1964: 'Much of the improvement in th import position is fictitious, in the sense that it cannot be maintained. Impo licences cut off in February [1964] were not restored until early May, and the large reductions in the original allocations were made. With the exception of flou sugar, milk, rice and some motor spare parts it seems no licences were issued in th period. Stocks were run right down. In early June there was an acute shortage of a types of imported foodstuffs and, more serious for the economy as a whole, ⟨ vehicles, tyres, spare parts, machinery and raw materials for local industries . . . Th effects of the crisis on the economy are likely to be more lasting. So many loc firms laid off labour that the Trade Union Congress set up a committee to whic employers must report their intention of laying off workers and their reasons fc this. It is reported that by early June over 3,000 workers had been laid off; the par

newspapers alleged that this was part of a conspiracy to sabotage Ghana.' (Economist Intelligence Unit, *Quarterly Economic Review – Ghana, Nigeria, Sierra Leone, Gambia*, No. 46, June 1964, pp. 2–3.)

[46] *Economic Survey, 1964,* para. 112. The author, who was then a lecturer at the University of Ghana, recalls that at this time, when many basic items were simply not to be had, there was a plentiful supply of Russian caviar and – in a country which grows excellent pineapples – Chinese tinned pineapples.

[47] *Parliamentary Debates,* 13 March 1964, col. 210.

[48] *1965 Supplementary Budget Statement,* p. 5.

[49] *Economic Survey,* 1965, para. 122.

[50] Uphoff conducted a public opinion poll after the coup and found that 'shortages of food, clothing, etc., and inflation of prices' were the most frequent reasons given why Ghanaians were happy about President Nkrumah's overthrow (pp. 715–6).

[51] *The Progress Party Manifesto,* 1969, p. 5.

[52] *See* pp. 72–6

[53] Calculated from the *Annual Trade Reports,* various issues

[54] Report by State Enterprises Secretariat on Programmes by State Manufacturing Enterprises, December 1965 (mimeo). *The Abrahams Report* (p. 18) documents that for 1965 the Secretariat obtained licences for ₵7.6 million against a request for ₵33.6 million.

[55] *See* Leith, op. cit. The list of items banned for apparently protectionist reasons grew over the years and at the end of 1971 included flour and bakery products, beer, certain petroleum products, bottles, radios, furniture, cigarettes, sausages and rubber stamps (*see Commercial and Industrial Bulletin*, Accra, Nos. 51A and 70). Ball-point pens and paper clips were added in 1972 (*see West Africa,* 4 August 1972, p. 1022).

[56] *Economic Survey, 1963,* para. 280.

[57] *Economic Survey, 1964,* para. 67.

[58] Leith, 1973, chapter 3.

[59] *See* Steel, 1970, p. 50 and *passim. See* chapter 8 for a fuller discussion of industrial protection.

[60] *See* Tinbergen, 1955, especially p. 70.

[61] *See* p. 106

[62] *See* chapter 6, Part III.

[63] *See* Bhatia, 1973, Table 4.

[64] *Abrahams Report,* paras. 106–108 and *passim.*

[65] *White Paper on Ollenu Report,* p. 3.

[66] ibid., pp. 4 and 6. It is amusing to find in this period that Armah was of the opinion that it was 'generally accepted' that the amount of corruption in Ghana had reduced to 'some way below the average for developing countries.' (*Daily Graphic,* 21 May 1964).

[67] The *Ollenu Report* (p. 24) found that Justice Akainyah's own wife had acted as an agent of Kwasi Armah to collect bribes, and the Justice subsequently resigned from the judiciary.

[68] *See* for example, the *Daily Graphic* issues of 2nd and 5th May, and 13th June 1972, and *Ghanaian Times* of 3rd May 1972.

[69] It is sometimes argued, e.g. by Professor Harry Johnson in a public lecture at the University of Ghana in 1971, that bribery is beneficial because it produces an allocation of resources more nearly approximating a free market allocation. The examples given here lend no support to this view. On the contrary, the evidence suggests strongly that the alleged corrupt practices of the two Ministers seriously aggravated the distortions created by licensing and prevented the application of procedures which would have helped to rationalize the system. The corruption also, of course, gave a strong incentive for the over-issue of licences, weakening the balance of payments.

[70] *See* Bhatia, 1973, *passim.*

[71] For example, according to Ministry of Trade data 25 per cent of all 1969 import under specific licences were covered by licences issued in respect of 1968.

[72] From Bank of Ghana.

[73] Bhatia, p. 24.

[74] The well-known existence of a good deal of smuggling across Ghana's northern and eastern borders was a major source of difficulty in this repect: Berg, 1964, p. 56 emphasizes that smuggling is boosted by, and undermines the effectiveness of, con trols. Even Ghana's statistics of recorded trade are unreliable, partly because o simple mistakes. For example, the *External Trade Statistics* for December 1969 (p 120) record that in 1969 Ghana imported 25 nuclear reactors from Italy at a uni cost of ₵3.68.

[75] *See* Bhatia, *passim.*

[76] *See* Hakam, 1972, Table 7.

[77] Price controls were established on imported consumer goods to prevent importer from earning monopoly profits but part II of this chapter shows that these wer little observed.

[78] Memo to Government, 11 May 1968.

[79] Predictably, micro-economic allocational problems were encountered soon after th return to comprehensive licensing in 1972. *See* the editorial of *The Spokesman*, 1 May 1973, complaining that the government was lurching from crisis to crisis in thi respect and complaining of a 'lack of cohesive planning.'

[80] *Parliamentary Debates*, First Series, Vol. 26, 12 February 1962, cols. 300–301.

[81] *See* Killick, 'Price Controls in Africa: the Ghanaian Experience,' *Journal of Moder African Studies*, September 1973. I am grateful to the editors for permission t reproduce here material originally published in the article.

[82] It has been estimated on the basis of a 1962 national household expenditure surve that the expenditure elasticity of demand for local foods was $0 \cdot 64$, as compare with $1 \cdot 30$ for imported food and $1 \cdot 24$ for drink and tobacco (Ord. 1964, Tabl V.1). The R^2s associated with these results were $0 \cdot 95$ and above. To give a specifi example, it was found that urban households with total weekly expenditure of 50 t 100 pesewas per person spent 70 per cent of the total on local foods whereas urba households with weekly per capita expenditures of 350 pesewas or more spent onl 46 per cent on local foods (ibid., Table C.2).

[83] In the other 11 per cent actual prices were below control levels.

[84] In his report to an annual general meeting of Kingsway Stores of Ghana, Ltd. (subsidiary of the United Africa Company) on 7 June 1972 the Chairman said that,

> Prices will continue to rise and unless a realistic view is taken on those com modities subject to price control, profit margins are likely to fall . . . too rigi an approach to price control can result in a severe reduction in the revenu which we pay to Government, uncertain employment prospects for our sta and a reduction in the ability of the business to provide for future developmer and to provide an adequate return to shareholders. (*The Echo*, 11 June 1972)

[85] A linear regression of all pairs of observations of store and market prices gave th following equation, where Y is an index of the price charged on the markets and) an index of the price charged in the stores, with the control price = 100:

$$Y = 6 \cdot 58 + 1 \cdot 012X$$

This gave an R^2 of $0 \cdot 79$, significant at the $0 \cdot 1$ per cent level. The standard error of) was $0 \cdot 265$, with a t-value of $3 \cdot 823$, also significant at the $0 \cdot 1$ per cent level.

[86] Classifying goods into three categories, according to availability, the mean values c actual prices, expressed as a percentage of control prices, were as follows:

	Mean value of actual prices as % of control prices
Plentiful supply	104
Intermediate	119
Supply shortage	138

[87] A regression of actual prices upon an index of control prices was consistent with the hypothesis that the extent of price control evasion would be inversely correlated with the extent to which control prices had been allowed to rise between 1962 and the reference date. The results have an $R^2 = 0.785$, with a statistical significance approaching the 0·1 per cent level. The equation was $Y = -45·14 + 1·092X$, with a t-value for X of 2·546, significant at the 5 per cent level. In other words, when the March 1970 control price had been held at, or not far above, the initial 1962 level, actual prices were well above the control, but in cases where the control price had been allowed to rise substantially above the original level, the actual prices exceeded the control by more modest proportions.

[88] Price, rent, profit and wage restraint were, however, put together as a policy package by the NRC in 1973, when legislation was adopted forbidding the increase of any price or rent without prior written consent, and limiting wage and dividend increases to a maximum of 2½ per cent annually (Prices and Incomes Regulations, 1973; L. I. 805).

[89] *Abrahams Report*, 1965, p. 55; *Annual Estimates for Ministry of Trade, 1966/67*, Ministry of Finance, 1966.

[90] *Abrahams Report*, p. 56.

[91] *Abrahams Report*, p. 56. On behalf of the Opposition Mr Jatoe Kaleo made what proved to be a very perceptive contribution to the debate on the 1962 Act. He asked for assurances that 'Unemployed ex-convicts' would not be employed as voluntary price inspectors adding, 'I suspect that if these people are going to work voluntarily and not be paid they will find a way somehow to meet their expenses.' In reply the Minister of Finance and Trade assured him that, 'we shall try as much as is possible within the realm of human capability to see that the best men are recruited for this job' (*Parliamentary Debates*, 12 February 1962, cols. 307–8). However, it seems that the 'realms of human capability' proved too restrictive, for the *Abrahams Report* (p. 55) has this to say:

> The procedure for appointment of price inspectors initially included public advertisements. Subsequently, however, A. Y. K. Djin, when he was Minister of Trade, assumed personal responsibility for engaging them. It is known that he made it possible, no doubt inadvertently, for even ex-convicts to be so appointed. Indeed, one of them had nineteen previous convictions for various breaches of the law when he was made price inspector.

[92] While no attempt can be made here at a systematic assessment of the efficacy of the *foreign exchange* controls, it could probably be said with accuracy (a) that they were only very partially effective because businessmen and others found extra-legal means of effecting transfers, e.g. through the manipulation of import and export invoices, but (b) that they nonetheless had the effect of discouraging new would-be foreign investors concerned about their future ability to transfer profits. These controls probably hit hardest at firms too visible, vulnerable or scrupulous to use extra-legal means. For example, the chairman of the supermarket subsidiary of the United Africa Company stated in June 1972 that only ₵43,000 had been paid to overseas shareholders since 1963, or 7 per cent of the total then due to them (*The Echo*, 11 June 1972). That others were less inhibited is suggested by the fact that when exchange controls were imposed in 1961 an estimated ₵86 million was outstanding in respect of payments for imports from the Sterling Area. No provision for the payments of these debts was ever made by the Bank of Ghana but by September 1971 outstanding applications for payment in respect of these items were less than ₵2 million, and the Bank assumed the remainder to have been paid by 'other means'.

Statutory controls over *house rents* have a long history in Ghana and a major attempt was made in the Rent Act, 1963 to make them more effective. An article by Gordon Woodman (*Legon Observer*, 6 October 1972) points out that under this law 'it has generally speaking been illegal since 1960 to increase the rents of any premises. (Indeed, taking the effect of earlier, repealed enactments together with the Act, it has in many cases been illegal to raise them since 1939.) . . . However, the most cursory acquaintance with relations between landlords and tenants will indicate that many of the provisions are frequently disregarded . . . The trouble is that [the laws] are disregarded.' In 1973 the NRC sought to improve matters with new legislation, the Rent (Amendment) Decree 1973 (NRCD 158), but another carefully reasoned article by Woodman (*Legon Observer*, 4 May 1973) suggested that this too was likely to prove unenforceable.

[93] *See* Myrdal, 1968, pp. 932–3 and Little *et al.*, 1970, pp. 213–15.

[94] Twenty-six of the forty-five were in the most junior grade of the administrative class of commercial officers – see *Annual Estimates for Ministry of Trade, 1969/70,* Ministry of Finance, 1969. Page 5 of this document describes the responsibilities of the 'General Administration' section as including the following: commercial policy; trade relations, including negotiation and implementation of trade agreements; correspondence on trade matters with foreign governments and firms; status reports on Ghanaian and foreign firms; handling of trade complaints; direction of Ghana's overseas trade missions; servicing of international organizations; administration of import controls; administration of price controls; preparation of monthly reports on regional supply and price trends; regulation of or liaison with a variety of para-statal and private organizations; provision of a secretariat to deal with immigration quotas.

11 After Nkrumah: Interpretations of Policies, 1966–72

Soon after a coup d'état in January 1972 had removed Dr Busia's civilian administration from office, the leader of the new military goverment addressed the staff of the Ministry of Finance and Planning on what the change meant for the framework of economic policy:[1]

> The political frame of reference which has guided your actions and your advice especially in the past two years, must be cast into the rubbish heap of history. This means a departure from the 'laissez-faire', so-called free market economy and the institution of effective planning in the allocation and utilization of resources . . .

This statement provides a useful starting point for an examination of the policies of the NLC and Busia governments, for it reflects an interpretation of that period which is widely held within Ghana and beyond.[2]

To elaborate this interpretation a little, economic policies in the sixties are seen as a clash of economic ideologies. First, at the beginning of the decade Nkrumah broke out of the 'colonial' mould and switched decisively to a socialistic strategy, rejecting an open, market-orientated economy and instituting a planned, regulated and centralized economy, in which the state was to become the predominant economic agent and the pursuit of development was to be given priority. Then, on this view, the overthrow of Nkrumah in 1966 brought into power military and civilian governments which were reactionary in the literal sense of rejecting what Nkrumah had sought to do and systematically reversing his policies. Spurning socialism, planning and controls, the NLC and Busia governments turned to a strategy which put stability above growth, reopened the economy, and returned to a private-enterprise, market-orientated and decentralized system. The state was increasingly disengaged from direct participation and control, and instead regulated the economy indirectly through the medium of the market. Finally, the argument concludes, the experiment with a 'so-called free market economy' failed, leading the second military goverment to return to the instrumentalities of a command economy.

The reader can judge from earlier chapters how far this interpretation provides an adequate representation of Nkrumah's policies; the question here is whether the view just summarized is a valid description of Ghana's experiences between the two coups. What is offered, then, is an essay in interpretation. No attempt is made to provide a comprehensive account of events and policies after 1966. Earlier chapters have already said a good deal about the post-Nkrumah years and it would be going beyond the purposes of this book to attempt a comprehensive survey. What is of interest to our theme is to examine the extent to which there were significant changes in economic policies, as the economics profession became more distrustful of the grand theorizing of earlier development economics, and to prepare the way for an examination in the concluding chapter of the problems which stood in the way of a successful transition from the stagnant and distorted economy which Nkrumah left behind him.

How should we understand the economic policies of the NLC and Busia governments? The thesis of this chapter is that the view of them as replacing Nkrumah's command economy by the reinstatement of the market is essentially a misleading one and that continuity rather than change was the outstanding characteristic of policies from 1966 onwards. What follows examines the elements of continuity and change in various aspects of economic policy beginning with that in which policies seemed to change most markedly – the balance of payments.

External Policy

Nkrumah, we have seen, pursued a policy which stressed the internalization of economic activity. The exchange rate was left unaltered and emphasis was placed upon import substitution reinforced by import and exchange controls. We saw, too, that he was suspicious of foreign capital and that, while claiming that he wanted both long-term aid and private capital, he pursued policies and made utterances which effectively ruled out the receipt of either on any scale. Ostensibly, large changes occurred after 1965. Both the NLC and Busia governments claimed to pursue more open policies, making more serious endeavours to secure inflows of long-term public and private capital and embarking upon what has been called 'an experiment with import liberalization.'[3] The main features of this experiment were the decontrol of imports,[4] and devaluations of the cedi in 1967 and 1971. Here apparently was a decisive substitution of the market for controls.

That this was a real and important shift is beyond dispute but is subject to substantial qualifications. Take, first, the position of the NLC. On a number of occasions they stated that they wanted to get rid of import and exchange controls, as when the Commissioner for Finance stated that it was 'the firm objective of the NLC to free our foreign trade and payments from all artificial restrictions and controls.'[5] At the same time, though, they seemed to realize from the outset that the new 1967 exchange rate did not go far enough by itself to establish an equilibrium which would permit liberalization to be achieved. Import and exchange controls were left almost unaltered and, in an official statement further elaborating government policy shortly after the devaluation, Omaboe, chairman of the National Economic Committee and the dominant figure in the formulation of the NLC's economic policies until 1969, referred to the devaluation as having 'cut down', rather than having eliminated, the difference between the black market and official rates of exchange.[6] He was in fact only in favour of decontrolling those items which even under licensing had to be imported in sufficient quantities to satisfy domestic demand, such as items of low-income consumption, spare parts and some industrial raw materials.[7] The plan published in 1968 made no reference to liberalization, stating rather that import licensing would be 'further improved'.[8]

Various pieces of evidence are consistent with this view of the NLC as holding only a limited belief in liberalization. They were, as described in chapter 3, pragmatic in their approach to government, more concerned with 'efficiency' than with the pursuit of a carefully worked out economic philosophy.[9] In pursuit of efficiency they wanted to get rid of import controls *where they were redundant,* and to improve the control system for those items which still needed to be restricted. Thus, the period of really rapid liberalization was during the Busia administration, and from 1967 to 1969 a major effort was made to improve the administration of import programming. It should be noted, too, that the 1967 devaluation was accompanied by substantial reductions in import duties on a variety of consumer goods, which, of course, had the result of reducing the effect of the devaluation on imports. Reference to Table 8.6 (p. 203) shows the extent to which import duty collections declined relative to the landed value of imports.[10] In fact, one suspects that the NLC's public commitment to complete liberalization was intended chiefly to mollify the IMF and aid donors.[11]

A further point of continuity was an abiding emphasis on import substitution rather than exporting. Given that the devaluation had not gone far enough to establish an equilibrium rate, export activities continued to be penalized by the structure of relative prices, although much less so than at the old rate. Exporters still stood in need of further incentives but it was not until as late as 1971 that a major export incentive scheme was finally implemented. The main thrust of the NLC's production policies was rather to utilize the country's import-substitution capacity more fully: a sensible strategy but an essentially inward-looking one nevertheless.

On examination, the position of the Busia administration was scarcely less ambiguous. Upon election the Progress Party was committed to move away from direct trade controls; they accelerated the rate of liberalization; when faced with a massive balance of payments crisis in 1971 they explicitly rejected a return to import licensing, opting instead for devaluation; and with the devaluation they abolished the remaining import controls. Leaving the devaluation aside for the moment, are the liberalization measures of 1970 and 1971 best understood as an attempt to substitute rationing by the market for rationing by fiat? When the question is put this way ambiguity is revealed, for while the government wanted to get rid of rationing by controls, it was reluctant to substitute any other allocative device.

If an unsustainably large import bill were to be avoided, liberalization was only viable if accompanied by tax increases which would contain the demand for imports to levels within the country's import capacity, for by 1970 the cedi was manifestly over-valued again, with an effective exchange rate for imports well below that of the early sixties (see Table 5.5). Some token taxation was included in the 1970 budget, with the imposition of temporary import surcharges, which were carried a little further in the 1971 budget (when a new tax was also levied on external payments for various invisibles). But even if the surcharges had been completely collected they would only have been equivalent to 13 per cent of the total landed value of imports in 1970 and 15 per cent in 1971, and demand elasticities were surely not large enough for these modest measures to contain the demand for imports. To make matters worse, various importers were exempted from the surcharges and others were allowed to defer payment of this tax, so that actual collections of the surcharge in 1970 and 1971 were equivalent only to 2·7 and 6·2 per cent of total imports respectively.[12] Superimposed on an erosion of the import duty base, the result of these measures was to leave the burden of import taxes (duties plus surcharges) in 1971 below the level of 1967 or of any earlier year since 1961.[13] In short, the tax effort was totally inadequate for liberalization to have been viable in the face of an over-valued currency. It was clear to economists working within the government that this was the case and that a major balance of payments crisis was inevitable unless further action was taken. Despite ever more urgent warnings of the impending crisis, the government did not use its powers to increase surcharge rates and declined to use the 1971 budget to deal with the problem in any other way. The result was a massive but short-lived import boom (see p. 307). So, while it is true that the Busia administration liberalized they did not substitute market restraints on demand;

not until the 1971 devaluation, that is.

That devaluation, which would have increased the average landed cedi price of imports by about 90 per cent, was the most decisive break with the past of any action since the 1966 coup. Had it been adequately reinforced by measures at home (and had the 1972 coup not supervened), it would, on reasonable assumptions, have brought market forces into play to keep imports within the country's spending capacity, stimulate exports and permit import and (eventually) exchange controls to be dismantled. But even that measure was a little ambiguous, for it was taken in desperation rather than as the culmination of a systematic programme of decentralization; and the key figure behind the liberalization, Minister of Finance Mensah, was most vigorously opposed to the devaluation, accepting it only when he saw that he could not prevent it. The economic philosophy of the chief architect of liberalization remained unclear; his actions were certainly not those of an adherent to the neo-classical verities.

What of the claim that the post-Nkrumah governments were more favourably disposed to foreign private investors? Here again, the record is mixed. They were both undoubtedly more concerned to create a favourable investment climate than Nkrumah had been and to allow the fiscal and other inducements of Nkrumah's Capital Investment Act a better chance to work. In the same period, however, certain types of activities were reserved exclusively for Ghanaians, a point to be taken up later. More importantly, the exchange controls (which remained intact throughout the period) were still operated to discriminate against the remittance of profits abroad, thus undermining the other attempts to encourage investors. In 1966 and 1967 transfers of profits and dividends, which had been severely restricted in the Nkrumah years, were virtually suspended. In 1968, under some pressure from aid donors, a scheme was announced which allowed industrial and agricultural firms to remit profits accumulated up to June 1964, with smaller concessions for companies operating in other sectors; a further relaxation was announced in 1969.[14] In 1970, however, despite abnormally large cocoa earnings, a virtual freeze was imposed on profit transfers and, although another tranche of remittances was announced for 1971,[15] this was not honoured and very little was allowed out. Recalling the conclusion of the previous chapter that actual imports always exceeded planned levels and that much of the excess was of consumer goods, it seems that the revealed preferences of the policy-makers favoured consumption rather than the use of foreign exchange for profit remittances. This draws attention once again to the ambivalence of external policies after 1966, for it must surely have been clear to the governments that they stood little chance of attracting much new foreign capital unless investors believed they would be able to repatriate their profits. The result was predictable: aside from a large new investment in the Valco aluminium smelter (whose profit remittances were strongly guaranteed under an agreement negotiated in 1960), only small amounts of private capital were received.

Domestic Economic Management

The 'popular' view of the NLC, as giving high priority to orthodox, disinflationary stabilization measures is surely correct. They saw a stronger balance of payments and reduced inflation as the chief objectives of domestic policies and as necessary pre-conditions for a resumption of the development effort. Fiscal policy, which fell into disuse as an instrument of stabilization earlier in the sixties, was rehabilitated as the chief component of the NLC's attempts to improve the standard of economic management.

Here, then, was a sharp break with the Nkrumah period. His emphasis was on sustaining a high level of investment but the NLC revealed quite different priorities. In the short run, restoring some balance to the economy meant cutting imports and reducing domestic demand relative to available supplies, necessitating a choice between reduced consumption or reduced investment (or a mixture of the two). Both externally and domestically, the choice was unambiguously to try to protect the consumer from yet further reductions in his living standards by placing the main burden on capital formation. We saw in the last chapter how the import licensing system was used in the NLC period to cut down on capital goods and to allocate more foreign exchange for the importation of raw materials and spares (almost entirely for use by industries producing consumer goods), and that actual consumer good imports exceeded planned levels. And we saw in chapter 4 how the domestic saving-investment gap was first reduced and then eliminated largely as a result of cuts in investment, with fixed capital formation declining from 23 per cent of GDP in 1964–5 to 13 per cent in 1968–9 (*see* Tables 4.1, 4.A and 4.B).[16]

It was largely through fiscal and monetary measures that this change was effected so it is worth looking a little more closely at what was achieved in these areas. The reader is referred to Tables 6.1, 6.2 6.3 (see pp. 000, 000, and 000) which present relevant data. Looking first at Table 6.2, column (5), it can be seen that the overall budget deficit was substantially reduced from the amounts experienced in the later Nkrumah years and that in 1966 and 1967 this was achieved in the face of substantially reduced tax receipts. Even more important for the purpose of stabilization was the fact that after 1966 the government borrowed only rather small amounts from the banking system, as can be observed from the first column of Table 6.5 above (p. 157).

One clear indication of the different approach of the NLC was in their attitude to taxation. Nkrumah, we saw in chapter 6, increased taxation substantially in his last years of office, so that by 1965 Ghana's tax effort was well above the average for comparable developing countries. The NLC took the view that taxes had become too high and talked of 'reducing the tax burden on the majority of our people'.[17] They were as good as their word and between 1966 and 1968 various taxes were either abolished or reduced, having the effect, as shown in Table 6.1, of significantly lowering the national tax effort.[18] Non-cocoa tax revenues fell sharply relative to the GDP – partly because of reduced import volumes but also as a result of a lower incidence of taxation (see Table 8.6 and Table 6.1, column 3).

At the same time, the NLC seems (this time in Nkrumah's tradition) to have decided that recurrent expenditures, which essentially meant the size of the civil service, could not be cut.[19] Indeed, salary increases, new recurrent obligations arising from past capital projects and larger public debt charges meant that current expenditures went up by about 9 per cent annually from 1965 to 1969.[20] Tax cuts and higher current expenditures, in combination with increased cocoa producer prices and a general relaxation of wage restraint, placed an extremely heavy burden of cuts on government capital spending if economic stabilization was to be achieved. Table 6.2 shows that this category of spending went down from about ₵142 million in 1965 to a trough of ₵56 million four years later.[21] A less alarming impression is given by the alternative classification in Table 6.3 but even this shows developmental spending falling relative to consumption from 107 per cent in 1965 to 53 per cent in 1969. The shares of capital and developmental spending, moreover, declined continuously from 1965 to 1969, although from 1968 the NLC professed to be moving to more growth-orientated policies.[22]

It has already been noticed from Table 6.5 that the NLC's fiscal measures sharply reduced government borrowing from the banking system after 1966. More generally, these figures show a greatly decelerated rate of bank credit expansion in 1967 and 1968. With money supply declining relative to domestic economic activity (Table 4.C, column 3), the monetary system exerted a restraining effect during the NLC period – another contrast with the later Nkrumah years.

But there were similarites as well, for in both periods monetary policies were rather ineffective.[23] In 1966, for example, the Bank of Ghana instructed the commercial banks to reduce non-government lending but it actually went up a little.[24] In 1967 and 1968 bank credit went up only moderately; in fact, the commercial banks did not increase their lending even to the amount permitted by the central bank's policies. The reverse became true in 1969, however, when commercial bank lending to the non-government sector went up by two-and-a-half times as much as was desired by the central bank.[25]

The poor co-ordination of fiscal, monetary and balance of payments policies which characterized the Nkrumah years was another weakness which continued after the coup. The previous chapter noted that import programming and budgetary policies were formulated for different twelve-monthly periods; the same was true of fiscal and monetary policies, each being formulated at different times. Thus, even when the whole thrust of government economic policy was upon improved short-term management, some of the serious defects which had appeared in earlier years could not be eradicated.

In consequence, the stabilization effort could claim substantial but incomplete success in bringing the domestic economy into equilibrium. Trends in bank credit were rather faithfully reflected in changes in the general price level: consumer prices (other than those of local foods) went up by nearly 11 per cent in 1966, rose between 1966 and 1968 by an average of only about $2\frac{1}{2}$ per cent, and then went up by another $7\frac{1}{2}$ per cent during 1969. [26] Private and public consumption rose by amounts greater than those planned,[27] and excess demand caused larger import bills than intended, spilling over into domestic inflation. The effects of the inflation, coupled with reduced taxation of imports, were to undermine the 1967 devaluation and to leave a price-deflated exchange rate for imports below what it had been, for example, in 1964 (see Table 5.5).

However, it would be unfair to conclude on a negative note. The NLC inherited enormous economic probems which were bound to take time to bring under control. Their achievements were substantial and economic management was greatly improved during their period of office.

If economic management in the NLC years marked a clear break with the policies of the later Nkrumah period, the same cannot be said of the Busia administration. That government, and especially Mensah, the Finance Minister, were determined to improve the growth record of the economy and embarked, therefore, upon expansionary policies. In doing so they inherited major advantages. Abnormally high world cocoa prices resulted in a windfall gain of foreign exchange earnings from cocoa, estimated by Leith at about ₵110 million in 1970 alone.[28] This also meant a gain for the budget, because the cocoa export duty was structured to capture 100 per cent of any increase above a certain minimum price level.[29] There was admittedly no reason to expect that cocoa prices would remain so high (they duly returned to lower, historically more normal, levels in 1971)[30] but in the short run the foreign exchange and saving constraints were less oppressive than usual. Thus, the 1969 budget statement could express the belief that the civilian government about to be elected 'can at least start from a situation that could form the basis for steady economic advance without constant crises.'[31]

That budget made only minor adjustments to the tax structure but began what was to be a major thrust of the two succeeding budgets for larger capital formation by the state. Government capital expenditures are recorded in Table 6.2 as rising from ₵56 million in 1969 to ₵109

million in 1970/71. Rapid though it was, even this expansion under-
states the true position, for in the 1970 and 1971 budgets a variety of
capital items which had formerly been financed through the budget
were placed 'below the line' for financing out of government reserves
or by bank credits. These items were substantial and it was estimated
after the 1971 budget that they would amount to nearly ₵60 million
additional to the expenditures recorded in the usual budgetary statistics.

Current expenditures also continued to grow rather rapidly and at
accelerating rates,[32] so that there was a very large growth in overall
state spending. However, tax revenues were also buoyant (Table 6.2),
with the result that the overall budgetary balance from 1969/70 to
1970/71 was much improved, even disinflationary, and the government was able to accumulate substantial cedi reserves. In consequence, net government indebtedness to the banking system was reduced
by about ₵40 million between June 1969 and June 1971. But much of
this apparent disinflation was spurious, because of the 'below-the-line'
spending already mentioned and other fiscal pressures for increased
bank lending to para-statal organizations.[33] So while the central
government was reducing its dependence on the banking system, total
bank credit was showing large increases – of about ₵130 million between June 1969 and June 1971.

Other factors were simultaneously at work generating further additions to domestic demand. The money incomes of cocoa farmers rose
to a new record in 1969/70 and were sustained there in the next
season;[34] import data suggest that private investment was also on the
increase.[35] In addition, it seemed that the acceleration of import
liberalization during 1969 and 1970 was releasing a demand for
imported goods formerly suppressed by licensing restrictions.

The buoyancy of domestic demand, an accelerated programme of
liberalization which failed to substitute market rationing for
administrative restrictions, and large increases in licence allocations
for those imports still supposed to be restricted led to a massive import
boom in 1970 and into 1971, as indicated by the following statistics of
total imports:[36]

	₵ million			₵ million
1965	457		1969	354
1966	356		1970	419
1967	308		1971	443
1968	314			

A good case could be made out in 1969 for taking advantage of the
cocoa windfall by increasing imports of more strategic items of capital
equipment, raw materials and spares, as well as, perhaps, a few of the
more essential consumer goods; but, in fact, the largest increases were

concentrated on consumer goods, many of which were scarcely essential. For example, registrations of private motor cars went up no less than 73 per cent between 1968 and 1970 and were still rising in the first half of 1971.[37] Thus the cocoa windfall was dissipated.

Large though it was, the import boom did not absorb all the surplus demand in the economy and during 1971 the rate of inflation bagan to go up again after a year of relative stability.[38] Seasonally corrected, the national consumer price index in June 1971 stood nearly 16 per cent higher than at the end of 1970 – mainly due to a poor minor food crop in the first half of the year but also reflecting a 7 per cent increase in the prices of non-food items.

The Minister of Finance thus had much to ponder as he began in mid-1971 to prepare the budget. Buoyant domestic demand was sustaining very high imports and domestic inflation but the cocoa boom was over, with all that held for the balance of payments and the budget. In fact, the prospect of large deficits on the balance of payments and the budget was already clear. Every indicator pointed to a need to take heat out of the economy and restore some kind of equilibrium. For the first time the Minister was forced to choose between continued expansion of government spending and a policy of stabilization. His response could not have been more explicit:[39]

> In the face of unfavourable trends which are forecast for tax revenues and the balance of payments, should Government cut back on development and even undertake measures of retrenchment in its current operations? Or should Government through its budget seek to support, maintain and perhaps increase the momentum towards accelerated development which had begun to show in the economy? The decision of our Government is that it is necessary and possible to maintain expansion.

To be fair, the budget did raise more revenues, largely through a new tax on external service payments and a National Development Levy which was effectively a supplement to the income tax. Moreover, one must sympathize with the desire to avoid reducing government capital formation as the NLC had done, given the economic stagnation experienced throughout the sixties. The fact was, however, that the Minister was proposing larger expenditures in the face of reduced tax revenues and an already large excess of domestic demand. What he was proposing, in other words, was a return to the deficit financing of the late Nkrumah period with no more prospect that this would induce sustained economic growth than in the mid-sixties. Analysis of the budget predicted that it would worsen an already grave balance of payments situation, would cause a major expansion of bank credit and a substantial rate of inflation – predictions which proved substantially correct.[40] So within two years of the cocoa boom the country was facing a balance of payments deficit exceeded only in 1965, with negative net foreign exchange reserves, many unpaid import bills and accelerating inflation at home.

Fiscal mismanagement was compounded by an absence of effective credit control, as indicated by the enormous increase in credit to non-government borrowers during 1971, shown in Table 6.5. The Bank of Ghana sought to exercise restraint behind the scenes but was faced by a Minister determined to pursue expansionary policies and by a breakdown in bank discipline. The central bank sought to hold down the expansion of commercial bank lending by directives and by large mandatory liquidity ratios but its injunctions were ignored. By mid-1971 all the commercial banks were failing to meet the minimum reserve ratios, and the expansion of credit permitted for 1971/72 was exceeded by a multiple of between two and three.[41] To make matters worse, a good deal of the credit expansion was being used to finance imports, thus directly facilitating the deterioration in the balance of payments.[42] There was effectively no monetary control in 1971.

To this crisis of its own making the government finally responded with the desperately large devaluation of December 1971, an event which, however, was quickly followed by the military take-over and the introduction of a different set of economic policy instruments. It was 1965 all over again:[43] an expansion of demand fuelled by fiscal and monetary policies with no parallel increase in import capacity or domestic output (food prices were again setting the inflationary pace), leading to an erosion of external reserves, an accumulation of short-term foreign debts and domestic inflation. The result in both cases was the military overthrow of a civilian government. The similarities were neither superficial nor coincidental, stemming from the same cause: a refusal to acknowledge the necessity to work within the foreign exchange and domestic saving constraints. Mensah in 1971, like Nkrumah in 1965, seemed to think that if only he could continue with expansionary policies the constraints would somehow melt away. (One difference, though, was that Nkrumah had no pretensions as an economist and his Minister of Finance was trying to restrain him; Mensah was both an economist and Minister of Finance.) Here was a specific illustration of the theme announced earlier, of the pronounced degree of continuity between the policies pursued in the first half of the sixties and those which came later.

Growth and Development Policies
A general description of the strategies of the NLC and Busia governments was provided in the concluding section of chapter 3, and the purpose of this section is again to focus on the extent of change in the style and observable content of policies directed towards the growth and development of the economy after the 1966 coup.

One important change was an abrupt halt to undiscriminating

industrialization and this, if only negatively, meant a better balance between industry and agriculture in government policies. The NLC sought to compensate for the reduced volume of industrial investment by measures intended to improve capacity utilization. In practice, the approach of the Busia government, while it rejected the view that past industrialization had been too fast, was essentially the same. In the long run, new industries were needed, they argued, but in the short run improving plant use remained the most urgent task.[44]

The post-Nkrumah emphasis on improved utilization might be seen as reflecting a greater stress on industrial efficiency – and it was shown in chapter 8 that Ghana's manufacturing industries were exceedingly inefficient at that time. Greater use of existing plant would help raise efficiency but even full capacity operation would leave many factories which, in social cost-benefit terms, were pauperizing the economy.[45] To pursue the efficiency objectives further would have meant rationalization of the system of industrial protection and a willingness to see at least some of the worst factories close down.[46] But these ingredients were notably absent from industrial policy. The emphasis was upon increasing the quantum of output rather than the efficiency with which it was achieved.

For example, an industrial policy statement issued in 1968 was almost entirely silent on industrial protection, confining itself to an assurance that the government would 'continue to provide a fair degree of protection to existing and new industrial undertakings to enable them to survive and to establish a foothold in a market in which consumers are wedded to imported competitive brands.'[47] The *Two-year Plan* (p. 56) did promise a review of the protective system, but nothing was done. The civilian rulers were no more receptive to the notion of industrial restructuring than the military. Mensah's reaction to recommendations for a more rational structure of tariffs and a uniform import surcharge was to introduce many detailed variations in duty rates, highly differentiated import surcharges and a list of 77 banned imports.[48] Beyond the rather painless provision of more adequate materials and spares, there was little in the record of either government to suggest that they were much more concerned with competition and comparative advantage than Nkrumah had been.

There was, on the other hand, a potentially very important change of policy towards food protection. Both administrations pursued a policy of disengaging the state from agricultural production and of transferring resources to programmes assisting private farmers.[49] Both governments promised to remedy Nkrumah's neglect of the private sector and 'rural development' was placed at the very heart of the Busia government's development strategy.[50] Power was returned to the Ministry of Agriculture; the extension services, credit facilities and rural infrastructure were to be improved; and research was to be intensified.

This was a shift of great potential importance qualifying the degree
of policy continuity after the deposition of Nkrumah. Yet, inevitably,
the reality fell some way short of the intentions. Under the NLC political leadership in the Ministry of Agriculture was poor. The extension
services remained weak, partly because of the past neglect of agricultural research, partly because the farmers had been made reluctant to
respond to government programmes by their experiences with the Farmers' Council,[51] and because the services were not concentrated on a
few realizable objectives. Thus, a survey in 1970–1 of two farming
districts known in advance to have received special attention from
government agricultural agencies revealed that 62 per cent of the farmers surveyed had never received help from the Ministry of Agriculture and half the remainder said that help was hard to get, especially
when most needed.[52] Of the agencies of socialized agriculture, only the
Farmers' Council was abolished; despite recommendations to disband
them, the State Farms Corporation, Workers' Brigade, and the settlement farms all lingered on, although on a generally reduced scale. On
the whole, Dadson's verdict on the NLC period is a just one:[53]

> over the three-year period of NLC rule, apart from pulling down the
> structures of socialized agriculture . . ., it was not clear that any
> substantial advance was being made in approaches towards farm
> modernization, although fundamentally different policies seemed
> to be favoured.

The Busia administration was not given enough time to assess its
agricultural policies, although it did seem that the stress on rural
development was beginning to effect a real transfer of resources. Progress was being recorded in the production of dry-rice in the northern
part of the country, and the feeder road system was improved and
extended.[54]

Given the generally poor performance of state enterprises, as shown
in chapter 9, reductions in the degree of state participation in production and distribution was an obvious option for the post-Nkrumah
governments, especially since both the NLC and Busia regimes
rejected Nkrumah's socialism and made various pro-private enterprise
statements. The NLC stated that the encouragement of private enterprise was one of its basic objectives,[55] and the election manifesto of
Busia's Progress Party affirmed its 'support for and confidence in private enterprise'.[56] At the same time, however, both promised to
increase the efficiency of state enterprises, although the NLC placed
some emphasis on the conversion of enterprises owned wholly by the
state into joint concerns as a potentially effective way of raising
management standards.[57]

Both governments, of course, stated that they wanted more foreign
private investment but the major theme was the nationalist one of

assisting Ghanaian business – a theme which emerged during the NLC period and received greater emphasis under the Progress Party.[58] The NLC passed a decree setting out a time-table of Ghanaianization, and the Busia government supplemented this with further legislation which accelerated the programme.[59] Under the 1970 Market Trading Act retail businesses with an annual turnover of ₵500,000 or less, and the operation of taxis and other minor service activities were immediately reserved for Ghanaians; commercial land transportation, bakeries, printing, manufacture of cement blocks and a variety of service activities were to be reserved a year later. The Busia government had already expelled some tens of thousands of people from other African countries who did not possess valid residence permits, an action which, especially because of the haste with which it was conducted, opened up many favourable opportunities for business and employment formerly held by non-Ghanaians (although it also led to some disruption, especially in the rural economy.)[60] Various types of special financial assistance were also provided for small-scale Ghanaian businesses.

Here again, it seems that there was a clear and significant break with the policies of Nkrumah, for it was shown earlier that he acted to restrain the growth of private Ghanaian business.[61] But how clear and how significant? Compare the following two statements:

> any small scale enterprise in the field of extractive, processing or manufacturing industry or transportation, employing thirty persons or less, which requires unsophisticated production or operational techniques or the value of whose fixed assets is ₵100,000 or less should be reserved for Ghanaians; no new foreign enterprise will be licensed to operate in these fields. Foreign private enterprise already operating in these categories of industry will be permitted to continue their operations provided they satisfy [certain] conditions . . .

and:

> In future the private small-scale personal enterprise sector will be exclusively reserved for Ghanaians. Foreign concerns already established in this sector will be allowed to contine operation, on condition that they do not expand their present establishment and scale of operations. In future, therefore, there will be no room for overseas interests in the small-scale enterprises sector in Ghana.

The first is from an NLC policy statement . . . the second from a 1962 speech by Nkrumah.[62] Post-Nkrumah governments were implementing a policy first announced, but not acted upon, by Nkrumah himself. Indeed the similarities are so close as to suggest that the NLC simply enacted legislation originally drafted for Nkrumah. All three governments restricted their Ghanaianization proposals to small-scale activities, which was a sensible way of going about it but which was bound to limit their shorter-term economic significance.

Of apparently more immediate importance was the announced intention of the NLC to reduce the state's involvement in industry and agriculture by closing down or selling off various state enterprises and converting others into joint state/private concerns. Mention has already been made of the disengagement from agriculture. Early in 1967 the NLC listed twenty state manufacturing and service enterprises, seven of which were to be offered for complete sale to private interests, with the remainder becoming joint enterprises. A few – laundry, furniture and bakery concerns – were successfully sold to Ghanaian businessmen but it was not long before this policy ran into a severe political storm.

The NLC had negotiated an agreement with an American company, Abbott Laboratories, for the sale of the state pharmaceutical factory on terms which came under strong public attack, especially from faculty members of the University of Ghana.[63] Ostensibly, the controversy was about the terms of the agreement, it being alleged that the government had sold the factory too cheaply,[64] but it was the fact that the sale represented a transfer of assets from Ghanaian to foreign ownership which gave heat to the controversy. In the trade-off between national control and economic efficiency the most vocal segment of public opinion appeared to discount the latter. In the face of this storm Abbott Laboratories withdrew and afterwards little more was heard of selling state enterprises. So in the end this policy did not amount to much. As recorded in the Appendix to this chapter, four state enterprises (most of them very small) were transferred to private ownership and a further four were converted into joint concerns. The Appendix also shows that another two para-statal organizations – a diamond mining company, which had never operated on a significant scale, and the Farmers' Council – were dissolved but that at least five new organizations were set up in the post-Nkrumah period and were operating in 1971. Out of the total of 53 public enterprises and corporations existing at the end of 1965, 43 remained wholly state-owned at the end of 1971 to which number should be added the five new ones.[65] The implication, of course, is that there was little change in the degree of state participation in economic activities after 1966.[66]

There is a substantial amount of other evidence for this. Looking back at Table 5.7 (p. 126), it may be seen that the share of manufacturing gross output originating in enterprises owned wholly by the state fell only from 19·5 per cent in 1966 to 15·6 per cent in 1970 and that this was more than offset by a growth in the importance of joint state/foreign enterprises. While the rapid growth in the relative importance of state enterprises of 1960–5 was halted, the share of output from firms under wholly private ownership remained unchanged at about 67 per cent between 1966 and 1970.[67] What does come out very

strongly is the effect of the Ghanaianization drive, with the share of
foreign-owned firms declining and joint Ghanaian/foreign private
enterprises growing.

The impression of a relatively unchanged importance of the state is
further strengthened by estimates that in 1968 26 per cent of the GDP
had originated in the public sector and that this was about the same as
the public sector's share in 1965.[68] Lastly, it can be calculated from
official statistics of recorded employment that the ratio of public sector
employees to private sector employees in 1969–70 was virtually identical with that of 1965 and well above the 1964 figure:[69]

1964	1·84	1968	2·65
1965	2·35	1969	2·36
1966	2·69	1970	2·34
1967	2·49		

All in all, then, the contention that the post-Nkrumah period wit-
nessed a significant shift to private enterprise is not borne out by the
evidence. In some areas, such as agriculture, there was a real change
and, across the board, the *expansion* of the state was brought to an end.
But there was little reversion from public to private ownership. The
effects of the Ghanaianization drive were still small by the beginning of
the seventies, and had taken the form of transfers from one (foreign)
set of private entrepreneurs to another.

It is interesting to ask what might have been expected to happen to
patterns of expenditure and debt-holding if there had been a shift
towards a more decentralized, private enterprise economy, and to
compare this with what actually happened. We could have expected:
(a) a de-collectivization of consumption decisions, reflected in a
growth of private relative to public consumption:
(b) the release of a greater share of investible resources for the privare
sector; implying
(c) a relatively smaller public sector claim on available bank credit.
It is not clear that any of these things happened.

As regards private versus collective consumption, reference back to
Table 4.1 (p. 68) shows that, while the rapid socialization of consumption of the earlier sixties was almost halted, public consumption still
grew a little relative to private consumption between 1964–5 and
1968–9. Though the national accounts are not very reliable, it seems
that one can fairly confidently rule out that there was any de-
collectivization of consumption in this period. Information was presented earlier on government saving after 1966, showing (a) that the
NLC substantially reduced the tax effort, (b) that recurrent expenditures expanded rather rapidly, perhaps on an accelerating trend, under
both post-Nkrumah administrations, (c) that the NLC closed the
budgetary gap only by very large reductions in government capital

formation, and (d) that, while the 1969/70 and 1970/71 budgets benefited greatly from the cocoa boom, when it was over a large budgetary
gap re-emerged, to be filled by deficit financing.

One way of gauging these factors is to examine what happened to
domestically held public debt in relation to government capital
spending. The rate of government borrowing from the rest of the
economy did slow down in absolute terms after 1965 but, relative to
the magnitude of capital expenditures, the government actually
became a little more dependent on domestic borrowing, despite the
much more favourable cocoa tax position during most of the post-
Nkrumah period.[70]

Finally, Table 11.1 compares the sectoral disposition of bank credit
as between 1965 and the beginning of the seventies, showing that the
central government was claiming a smaller proportion of total credit in
1970–1. However, it was explained earlier that this was partly a statistical illusion because expenditures which had formerly been a charge
on the government budget were shifted 'below the line' and were
financed instead by government-guaranteed bank borrowing. This
illusion disappears if the public sector is taken as a whole, and Table
11.1 suggests that the public sector not only continued to obtain the
lion's share of bank credit but even increased its claim. The private
sector, upon which governments said they were placing greater
reliance and which was contributing three-quarters of the GDP, was
only getting about 14 per cent of bank credit.[71] According to revealed
preferences, the private sector was not receiving priority. It was not
surprising, therefore, that the Bank of Ghana's proposals for credit
policies in 1971 should have treated lending to the private sector as the
residual after deducting the government's own credit needs from the
total allowable credit expansion.

We might finally revert to the extent to which post-Nkrumah
governments exhibited a preference for the use of market signals over
direct state intervention in economic transactions. The ambiguous case
of import liberalization has already been discussed; ambiguity was the
pervading characteristic of this whole question. One potentially
important move towards a market-orientation was an interest-rate
reform which more than doubled the returns to savings with the
commercial banks and led to a roughly comparable rise in bank lending
rates. Taking effect only in September 1971, it came too late to have
any impact during the brief remaining term of the Busia administration
but did nevertheless constitute a major loosening of state interest-rate
restrictions.[72]

But against this action must be set others which pulled in the opposite direction. Exchange, price, rent and wage controls were retained
intact throughout almost the entire period[73] and in some areas the reg-
ulatory powers of the state were further extended. The most startling
example was a Manufacturing Industries Act foreshadowed in the

TABLE 11.1
Estimated Public and Private Sector Shares of Total Bank Credit [a]
(₵ million and percentages)

	1965 [b]		1970–1 [c]	
	₵ Mn	%	₵ Mn	%
Central government	192	68	249	51
Other public sector	42	15	174	35
Total public sector	(234)	(83)	(423)	(86)
Private sector	49	17	67	14
Grand Total	283	100	490	100

Sources: Scott, 1967, Tables D–3 and D–4; Bank of Ghana, *Annual Reports* (various issues).

NOTES:
[a] Total credit by central and commercial banks, excluding cocoa finance and government use of IMF resources.
[b] Position as at year-end.
[c] Bank of Ghana data on credit to the public and private sectors are misleading. Their category 'credit to public institutions' covers only credit to the Cocoa Marketing Board and Ghana Supply Commission; their category 'credit to private sector' includes all credit to the public sector other than these two institutions and the central government. Their data on 'credit to the private sector' in 1970–1 has been allocated on the assumptions (1) that Ghana Commercial Bank was responsible for 65 per cent of commercial bank lending to what the Bank of Ghana wrongly classifies as the 'private sector' during this period (it was responsible for 68 per cent of total commercial bank assets and liabilities in mid-1968 – see p. 126), (2) that 75 per cent of this bank's lending in this category was actually to public sector borrowers (most public enterprises and corporations were required to do their banking with Ghana Commercial Bank and many of them were borrowing heavily in this period – often backed by government guarantees), and (3) that all 35 per cent of lending assumed to be done by the expatriate-owned banks was to genuinely private borrowers. Data are averages of monthly figures for the two years.

NLC's industrial policy statement but enacted in 1971.[74] This forbade the establishment or expansion of any manufacturing concern without the permission of the Minister responsible for industry, who could give permission 'on such terms and conditions as he may think fit', and was empowered to 'issue directions relating to the quality, quantity and prices of products of any manufacturing industry.'[75] If further evidence was still needed, nothing could have been more indicative than this of the absence of a consistent liberalizing philosophy in the Busia administration (although some members of the government were opposed to the Act). It was scarcely surprising, then, that the Busia administration's response to the inflation of food prices was to blame it on exploitative middlemen and to establish yet another government agency – the Task Force for Food Distribution – to try (with notable lack of success) to put matters to rights.[76]

A Note on the Policies of the NRC
Given all this evidence to the contrary, it is rather astonishing that the

policies of the NLC and Busia governments could have been interpreted as a return to laissez faire. Yet the NRC, which took over
responsibility for ruling the country at the beginning of 1972, was per-
suaded that this was the case, and it is worth describing briefly some of
its own policy actions during its first eighteen months of office.

It is easy to characterize these: a return to the task of creating a
command economy and a resumed expansion of the participation of
the state in economic activities. Among the first actions was a revaluation which undid about two-thirds of the effect of the December 1971
devaluation.[77] This action in the face of a grave payments crisis left the
NRC no alternative but to return to comprehensive import controls,
accompanied later by the reinstatement of an export bonus scheme
which had been ended with the 1971 devaluation. The coverage of
price controls was extended by the inclusion of a large number of
motor vehicle components, and the increase of any price was later for-
bidden except with the written permission of a newly created Prices
and Incomes Board.[78] Rents were similarly frozen and restrictions
placed upon increases in wages and dividends. 'Hoarding' and other
economic misdemeanours became subject to a mandatory minimum
sentence of fifteen years' imprisonment.[79]

The government announced its intention to reactivate various state
enterprises left uncompleted or abandoned after the overthrow of
Nkrumah[80] but of far greater significance for the role of the state was
the compulsory acquisition of a 55 per cent shareholding in the timber,
mining and oil industries, and certain others such as those producing
salt and fertilizers.[81] There was talk of reviving the Workers' Brigade
and State Farms but the government had second thoughts on this and
continued to support the private farmers. Regional Development
Corporations were established in each of the nine regions.

It seemed, then, that economic policy had come full circle. The
expansion of state control and participation begun under Nkrumah
was resumed. A few qualifications are in order, however. First, the
actions of the NRC were carried out largely in the spirit of nationalism,
with the Council collectively showing limited interest in Nkrumah-
style socialism – a significant fact because it suggested that they might
be more pragmatic than Nkrumah had been. Second, the NRC seemed
likely to avoid the worst mistakes of Nkrumah's agricultural policies,
and, in reinstating an export bonus scheme, showed an awareness of
the need for special export incentives in the face of an over-valued
currency. But, third, the NRC were going further than Nkrumah had
ever chosen to in taking control of foreign-owned industries. What is
clear is that they shared with him a continuing faith in the ability of the
state to participate effectively and extensively in the nation's economy.

Statement of a Problem

Perhaps one of the reasons why people see the NLC/Busia era as a return to a market economy approach is that such a response might have been predicted from the Nkrumah experience. Under him the economy lost its dynamic impetus, per capita incomes and living standards declined, apparent modernization was not accompanied by the benefits which it was expected to bring – results which coincided rather exactly with the switch to controls and extensive state participation. Without attempting to summarize them here, it seems a fair conclusion from earlier chapters to say that the combination of poor economic performance and increased involvement of the state were more than a coincidence. The state in the first half of the sixties recorded little success in medium- and short-term planning; artificial price distortions produced a highly inefficient industrial structure and other malign effects; state enterprises failed to fill the entrepreneurial gap and performed poorly, and the experience with administrative controls was generally an unhappy one.

What is more, the causes of these deficiencies went deeper than the obvious weaknesses of the Nkrumah regime, and the machinery of state revealed little capacity to respond to the challenge posed by poor performance. Shortages of personnel, institutional problems of administration and co-ordination, corruption, and politicization persisted beyond Nkrumah, together with the problems which they generated. In view of Nkrumah's inability to effect radical improvements under the system which he created, it is puzzling to understand why governments maintained so much continuity with this system after 1966. For what emerges from this chapter is that there was throughout the sixties and into the seventies an abiding faith in the efficacy of the state as an economic agent, despite much evidence of its inefficiency. Always excepting the aborted 1971 devaluation, it is a fundamental misreading of the NLC/Busia period to say that the market was tried and found wanting. It did not fail because it was not tried, except in the most ad hoc and half-hearted manner. The state emerged to dominate much of the economy in the first half of the sixties and remained dominant thereafter. That NLC/Busia policies were nevertheless misinterpreted as an experiment in liberalization helps to explain the subsequent actions of the NRC. Had they had a more accurate perception of the policies of their immediate predecessors they might have been less likely to begin enlarging the role of the state once more.

Be that as it may, how might we explain the continuity after 1966, the failure to attempt a more systematic decentralization of decision-making?

The political and economic philosophies of those responsible for policy under the NLC and Busia provide a superficial answer. The NLC were pragmatists, responding to felt economic needs, eclectic in their choice of policy responses and perceiving themselves as a caretaker administration laying the ground for a restoration of democracy. These were not the men nor the circumstances for the systematic application of a market-economy or any other economic philosophy.

The case of the Busia administration might have been different. They presumably had a longer time horizon, having been elected for five years on a base of tribal support which could be eroded only with difficulty. They had the reputation of being a government of intellectuals. And the last three-and-a-half years had shown that the difficulties of planning, control and participation had not disappeared with Nkrumah. Yet even before their election their attitude regarding the respective roles of the market and the state[82] had been highly ambivalent. In this administration there were four potentially important actors who were in a position to shape government economic policies. The Prime Minister and Minister of Finance J. H. Mensah were the most important, but Minister of Trade and Industries Richard Quarshie carried some weight. So did Jones Ofori-Atta, junior Minister responsible for planning, a trained economist and chief author of the parts of the Progress Party election manifesto dealing with economic policy.

The Prime Minister was for most of the time content to leave economic policy to his Ministers; only at a very late stage did he try to impose his own will, and it is very doubtful whether his thinking on economic matters was informed by carefully thought-out general principles. Quarshie, and ex-civil servant and businessman, might have been expected to want to reduce the involvement of the public administration but, in fact, (unsuccessfully) resisted the liberalization of imports and was the man responsible for the Manufacturing Industries Act described above. Ofori-Atta's powers as a junior Minister under Mensah were severely restricted but it is, in any case, doubtful whether he would have adopted the standpoint of a liberal economist:[83]

> the so-called open policies pursued in Ghana between 1957 and 1961 created more problems for the country than they solved. What is more they proved incapable of exacting the degree of sacrifice necessary for rapid structural transformation. The temporal coincidence between the imposition of controls and the shift in the ideological basis of policy was largely accidental. The attempt to associate the two and the general tendency to explain the controls in terms of the politics of socialism is, in my view, erroneous. The two can be separated from each other. A change in the orientation of fiscal and monetary policies towards the pursuit of more domestic savings, more capital formation and more investment in the strategic sectors of the economy, or towards granting the government greater control over the resources of the economy does not necessarily imply committing the government to authoritarian socialism. *Appreciation of the commonsense of economics is not a question of ideology.*

Of the four actors, Mensah was by far the most important and enough has already been written in this study to indicate that he, too, was no liberal economist, notwithstanding his decontrol of imports. He had, after all, been Nkrumah's chief planner and, even though he fell out with the more extreme wing of the CPP, there is nothing to suggest that he was in fundamental disagreement with most of the plan he wrote. Indeed, much of the 1969–71 experience falls into place if we see it as stemming from attitudes which had shaped economic policies under Nkrumah. In 1971 Mensah was calling himself a 'pragmatic socialist' and, while this term was not given a precise definition, it explicitly included a continuing belief in the ability of 'publicly-owned capital to function as one of the major engines for economic development.'[84] It also included faith in the efficacy of other state interventions, and one of the grounds on which he opposed the 1971 devaluation was that it would remove the discretion of economic management from the government.

But to demonstrate that neither the NLC nor the Busia governments were philosophically inclined towards much reduction in the economic role of the state is to provide only a proximate answer to the question of why there was so much continuity after 1966. Political philosophies are social phenomena and what has to be explained is why the experiences of 1960–9 did not throw up social forces which would have made a more radically liberalizing approach politically advantageous. To answer this question analysis of the interaction between politics, social change and economics is needed, one which will illuminate a wider range of queries than the one just posed. The next chapter includes an attempt to answer these questions.

Appendix to Chapter 11

Ownership Status of Public Enterprises and Corporations Existing at end-1965

	Status at end-1971	*Observations*
A *Directly Productive Enterprises*		
1. Fibre Bag Corpn.	Public	GIHOC controlled
2. Glass Manufacturing Corpn.	do.	do.
3. Paper Conversion Corpn.	do.	do.
4. State Pharmaceutical Corpn.	do.	do.
5. Brick & Tile Corpn.	do.	do.
6. State Cannery Corpn.	do.	do.

7. State Distilleries	do.	do.
8. State Electronics Corpn.	do.	do.
9. State Footwear Corpn.	do.	do.
10. Marble Works Corpn.	do.	do.
11. Meat Products Corpn.	do.	do.
12. Metal Industries Corpn.	do.	do.
13. State Paints Corpn.	do.	do.
14. Sugar Products Corpn.	do.	do. (converted into autonomous state enterprise in 1973)
15. Tema Steel Works Corpn.	do.	do.
16. Vegetable Oil Mills Corpn.	do.	do.
17. Cocoa Products Corpn.	do.	Controlled by Cocoa Marketing Board
18. Furniture and Joinery Corpn.	Private	Sold by NLC
19. State Laundries Corpn.	do.	do.
20. Tyre Service Corpn.	do.	do.
21. State Bakery Corpn.	do.	do.
22. State Match Corpn.	Joint state/private	Part share sold by NLC
23. Textile Manufacturing Corpn.	do.	do.
24. Cement Works Corpn.	do.	do.
25. State Farms Corpn.	Public	Much reduced in size after 1965
26. State Gold Mining Corpn.	do.	
27. Diamond Mining Corpn.	Dissolved	
28. National Construction Corpn.	Public	Now styled State Construction Corpn.
29. State Fishing Corpn.	do.	
30. State Publishing Corpn.	do.	
31. Tobacco Produce Corpn.	Joint state/private	Part share sold by NLC

B *Distribution and Transportation*

32. State Shipping Corpn. (Black Star Line)	Public	
33. State Transport Corpn.	do.	
34. Cocoa Marketing Board	do.	
35. Timber Marketing Board	do.	
36. Diamond Marketing Board	do.	
37. Omnibus Services Authority	do.	
38. United Ghana Farmers' Council	Dissolved	Formerly had monopoly as Cocoa Marketing Board buying agent
39. Ghana Airways Corpn.	Public	
40. Food Marketing Corpn.	do.	
41. National Trading Corpn.	do.	

C *Public Utilities and Other Service Activities*

42. Volta River Authority	do.	
43. Electricity Corpn.	do.	
44. Water & Sewerage Corpn.	do.	
45. State Housing Corpn.	do.	
46. Tema Development Corpn.	do.	
47. State Hotels Corpn.	do.	
48. State Insurance Corpn.	do.	

49. Ghana Commercial Bank	do.	
50. National Investment Bank	do.	
51. Agricultural Development Bank	do.	
52. Graphic Corpn.	do.	
53. State Boat Yard Corpn.	do.	GIHOC controlled

Public Enterprises and Corporation Created after 1965

a. Task Force for Food Distribution	Established 1970
b. Grains Development Board	Established 1969
c. Cotton Development Board	Established 1968
d. Bast Fibres Development Board	Established 1969
e. Export Promotion Company	Established ca. 1968

Source. *Annual Reports* of the Auditor-General supplemented by a variety of other sources.

NOTES

[1] From speech to staff of Ministry of Finance and Planning, 7 February 1972, by Col. I. K. Acheampong, Chairman of the National Redemption Council, reproduced in Acheampong, 1973, p. 31.

[2] Thus a few days after the coup *The Spokesman*, a newspaper which had always been opposed to the Busia government, stated 'The Busia Government were committed to devalue by 92 per cent because they were tied ideologically to the creation of a "free market economy" in Ghana, in a word, to the building of a capitalist State in Ghana.' (21 January 1972, p. 2). It may assist the reader to recapitulate government changes after 1966:
  (a) Nkrumah is overthrown by a military-police coup in February 1966. The new Government is styled the National Liberation Council (NLC).
  (b) Power is transferred to an elected civilian government headed by Dr Kofi Busia, leader of the Progress Party, in October 1969.
  (c) A second military coup in January 1972 brings the National Redemption Council (NRC) to power, headed by Col. I. K. Acheampong.

[3] Leith, 1973, chapter 5. This source contains an excellent account and analysis of the import liberalization, and the devaluations of 1967 and 1971, although Leith's interpretation of this period differs somewhat from mine.

[4] *See* p. 265 which shows that by mid-1971 about three-quarters of total imports were estimated to be freed from restriction.

[5] NLC, *New Deal for Ghana's Economy*, p. 4.

[6] ibid., p. 10.

[7] In an interview with the writer.

[8] *Two-year Plan*, p. 4.

[9] *See* pp. 54-6 for a brief outline of the strategy and policies of the NLC.

[10] The NLC also failed to raise specific duty rates which, therefore, diminished relative to the cedi landed value of the goods after the devaluation. A substantial part of the drop after 1966 was attributable to this factor.

[11] Between 1967 and 1969 I attended meetings between Ghana and her aid donors and can attest to the latter's desire for more rapid liberalization.

[12] Calculated from customs and trade data.

[13] It can be calculated from customs and trade data that collections of import duties and surcharges in 1971 were equivalent to 24·9 per cent of the c.i.f. value of total imports – a lower proportion than existed for all years from 1962 to 1967. *See also* Table 8.6.

[14] *See* Bank of Ghana *Annual Report, 1968–9*, pp. 2–3.

[15] Bank of Ghana *Annual Report, 1970–2*, p. 1.

[16] The rationale for this apparent sacrifice of the future for the sake of the present was (1) that much of Nkrumah's 'investment' had been unproductive so that the actual reduction was less than the figures seem to indicate (*see* chapters 7 to 9); (2) that lower investment could be offset by improved capacity utilization, which would increase output and reinforce the disinflationary effort; and (3) that in the short run, and given the squeeze that had already been exerted on the private consumer, there was no feasible political alternative to reduced investment. For a discussion of some of these points *see* Frimpong-Ansah, 1971.

[17] *See* 1966–7 *Budget Statement.*

[18] Between 1966 and 1968 there were reductions in import duties, sales taxes and income taxes, and some minor taxes were abolished. The cocoa producer price was raised, having the effect of reducing the incidence of the cocoa export duty. For details see NLC, *Rebuilding the National Economy*, pp. 4–5, and the annual budgets. Although the national tax effort did go down in these years, it is fair to recall the results of international comparisons of the tax efforts of various developing countries reported in chapter 6, which found Ghana's tax effort to be slightly above average in 1966–8 – *see* p. 147.

[19] It has been estimated that more than 50 per cent of the recurrent budget is absorbed by the cost of personal emoluments, including the emoluments of para-statal organizations dependent upon budgetary subventions. There were, it is true, reductions in public sector employment during 1966 but this appears to have been only rather temporary. About 38,000 public sector employees were laid off in 1966, mostly from para-statal organizations, equivalent to about 14 per cent of total public sector employment at the end of 1965 (see p. 259 for details). It appears, though, that some workers were taken on in other parts of the public sector, for official statistics record a net reduction of only 14,300 (or 5 per cent) between end-1965 and end-1966; by 1968 public sector employment was above the 1965 level (*see Labour Statistics*). *See* chapter 4, especially Table 4.D, on wage trends; and the *Mills-Odoi Report* on civil service wages and salaries.

[20] Calculated from Table 6.2. If public debt charges, the expenditure effects of the 1967 devaluation and other special items are netted out, the increase was about 6·7 per cent p.a.

[21] The actual cut was probably even larger than shown in Table 6.2, for various government capital investments were not recorded in the 1965 budget figures, as explained in chapter 6.

[22] *See Two-year Plan, 1968.* It should also be mentioned that in 1965–9 defence spending more than doubled, both absolutely and as a share of total government expenditures (calculated from *Economic Survey, 1969,* Table 11). The military claimed that increases were necessary because of Nkrumah's previous neglect of the armed services. No doubt this was true to some extent, although fiscal data for the earlier sixties do not entirely bear it out. In any case, it is not clear that this provided justification for the large increases in defence spending that occurred as late as 1968 and 1969 in a country with no obvious external or domestic security problems (for the Busia administration the army itself was the security problem!). By 1969 spending on defence was equivalent to 14·5 per cent of total (current + capital) government expenditures, compared with 7·0 per cent in 1965.

[23] *See* Frimpong-Ansah, 1971, on monetary policies in this period, although he goes too far in claiming that they 'succeeded in restoring conditions of financial stability'.

[24] The remainder of this paragraph is based upon information and data in various issues of the Bank of Ghana's *Annual Reports.* It would seem from a careful reading of the record that the Bank intended commercial bank loans and advances to be reduced by at least ₵14 million during 1966; they actually went up by ₵4 million.

[25] The Bank of Ghana stipulated that commercial bank lending to the private sector (excluding cocoa financing) should not go up by more than ₵10 million during 1969 but it actually increased by ₵25 million.

[26] *See* Table 4.D, line 6. An index which excludes local food prices is a better indicator of

the underlying inflationary trend in this period, for local food prices were strongly affected by an abnormally good harvest in 1966–7, and a particularly poor one in 1968 as a result of unusually heavy rains in that year.

[27] *See* Bhatia, 1973, Table 4.

[28] Leith, 1973, chapter 5.

[29] In the eight preceding fiscal years the cocoa export duty had brought an annual average of ₵39.5 million of tax revenues to the budget; in 1969–70 the average was ₵133.7 million. These figures are, however, partly affected by the 1967 devaluation.

[30] The third position c.i.f. London price of cocoa averaged ₵537 per ton in 1958–67, rose to an average of ₵863 per ton in 1968–70, fell back to ₵555 per ton in 1971.

[31] *Budget Statement, 1969–70*, p. 5. J. H. Mensah became Commissioner of Finance of the NLC early in 1969 and was subsequently Minister of Finance in the Busia administration. He was thus responsible for the 1969, 1970 and 1971 budgets, and a clear continuity of approach can be traced through these.

[32] Excluding debt servicing expenditures, the annual growth rates of recurrent expenditures from 1967–8 to 1970–1 were 5·4 per cent, 9·0 per cent and 11·0 per cent respectively.

[33] Among these were a rate of taxation of cocoa which the Cocoa Marketing Board could only pay by borrowing substantially from the banks (the Board also had to borrow because private produce buying agencies were indebted to it by large amounts – ₵41 million in August 1971); and the non-payment of bills to the Supply Commission, which also was forced to borrow. Bank borrowing by these two institutions went up by ₵62 million between June 1969 and June 1971.

[34] Payments to cocoa farmers were slightly above ₵120 million in both the 1969–70 and the 1970–1 crop years, as compared with an average of ₵84 million in the three preceding years.

[35] Capital good imports went up by 35 per cent between 1968 and 1970, an increase which is larger than can be explained by the growth of government capital expenditures.

[36] Total imports c.i.f. The figures have been calculated in the exchange rate established by the July 1967 devaluation. Source: *External Trade Statistics*, December 1971.

[37] Calculated from CBS *Statistical Newsletters* (various issues).

[38] *See* Table 4.D, line 7.

[39] *Budget Statement, 1971–2*, p. 28. Note how in this passage the Minister equates the growth prospects of the economy with the level of 'development' (i.e. capital) spending by the government.

[40] Besides a balance of payments crisis, papers prepared for the government on the likely consequences of the 1971–2 budget predicted a credit expansion of about ₵145 million and a rate of inflation of about 12½ per cent during the fiscal year. In the event total bank credit went up by ₵215 million and the consumer price index rose by 11·8 per cent.

[41] According to the Bank of Ghana, commercial bank lending to borrowers other than the central government was regulated by a formula which implied a net increase of ₵10 to ₵15 million. The actual increase during the fiscal year was ₵34 million.

[42] Commercial bank credit to finance imports expanded by 150 per cent between the beginning of 1970 and the beginning of 1972 (*see* Bank of Ghana *Annual Report, 1971*, Statement 6). Credit for the manufacturing sector went up 120 per cent in the same period and it is likely that much of this increase was also to finance enlarged stocks of imported supplies.

[43] *See* p. 154 for an account of the 1965 budget and the ensuing crisis.

[44] In a *Sessional Address* of 2 October 1969 setting out the policies that it would pursue, the government (p. 6) criticized the 'mistaken notion that industrial expansion has been too fast' but identified the greater use of industrial capacity as first priority.

[45] *See* Steel, 1972, who shows (Table VI) that raising output to full capacity would reduce the proportion of gross output produced 'inefficiently' (i.e. at a domestic resource cost in excess of 1·53), but only from 67 to 43 per cent.

[46] *See* pp. 202–3 on the arbitrary array of protective devices.

[47] NLC, *Industrial Policy Statement*, 1968, p. 6.

[48] *See Financial Statements* for 1970–1 and 1971–2 for details of duty changes. The Temporary Surcharge on Imported Goods Act, 1970, placed a large number of items into various categories, with surcharge rates of 5, 10, 25, 40, 75, 100, 125 and 150 per cent. This legislation caused many anomalies, a stream of petitions to the Ministry of Finance, and a large number of *ad hoc* waivers for successful complainants. The list of banned imports issued in August 1971 included some items that were already prohibited. Examinations of the list makes it clear that it was largely intended to give protection to local industries.

[49] The NLC's *Outline of Government Economic Policy*, 1967, p. 5, stated explicitly that the government's main contribution to agriculture would be to assist private producers. *See also Two-year Plan*, chapter VI.

[50] This theme is strongly expressed in the 1969 *Sessional Address*, pp. 1–4, and most fully intellectualized by Mensah, 1971, *passim. See also* the *One-year Plan, 1970–1* for a clear statement of the agricultural problem and of government intentions.

[51] Uphoff, p. 581.

[52] C. K. Brown, 1972, pp. 39–41. Farmers who had received help found it valuable.

[53] Dadson, 1970, p. 288.

[54] *See* 1971 *Budget Statement*, p. 35, and the *One-year Plan*, chapter 13, on the feeder roads programmes. The economic benefits from these were probably reduced, however, by highly politicized methods of deciding where the roads should be constructed.

[55] *Industrial Policy Statement*, 1968, p. 2.

[56] Progress Party, 1969, p. 7.

[57] *ibid.* and *Industrial Policy Statement*, 1968, pp. 3–4.

[58] *ibid.*, pp. 4–6, and Progress Party, 1969, p. 2. and *passim*.

[59] Ghanaian Enterprises Decree, No. 322 of 1968, and the Ghanaian Business (Promotion) Act of 1970. *See One-year Plan*, pp. 151–3, for a statement of Ghanaianization policy, and Grayson, 1972, for an appraisal of it.

[60] The expulsions were effected under the Aliens Compliance Order of 18 November 1969. Addo, 1972, p. 39, found that the resulting flight of aliens worsened an already existing shortage of agricultural labour.

[61] *See* pp. 36–7.

[62] From *Industrial Policy Statement*, 1968, p. 5, and Nkrumah in March 1962, quoted in Friedland and Rosberg, 1964, p. 272.

[63] The attack was led by Jones Ofori-Atta, who subsequently became junior minister of planning in the Busia administration, and was publicized by the *Legon Observer* before being taken up by the national press. For a brief account *see* Grayson, 1973A.

[64] Fordwor, 1971, presents data suggesting that there may well have been substance to this allegation.

[65] The list in the Appendix does not include agencies like the Workers' Brigade, State Films Industry, State Lotteries and the Tourist Corporation. It is possible that a few of the multitude of state agencies created during the Nkrumah period have been missed in compling the list but probably none of much importance.

[66] There was also a good deal of continuity in government policies towards the operation of state enterprises, as discussed in chapter 9, especially p. 217.

[67] One important development which should be mentioned, however, was the dissolution of the Farmers' Council and the subsequent emergence of private firms which competed with the Marketing Board to buy cocoa from the farmers. On the other hand, the state domination of the financial system increased, for the Ghana Commercial Bank reported that its share of total commercial bank business rose from 40 per cent in 1963 to over 60 per cent ten years later (*Ghanaian Times*, 21 May 1973).

[68] Odling-Smee, 1972, and later calculations.

[69] Calculated from the *Labour Statistics*. It should be borne in mind that the official

statistics of recorded employment cover only a modest part of total employment.
[70] Between end-1959 and end-1965 the domestic public debt rose by ₵374 million but during the succeeding six years the increase was down to ₵257 million. However, when expressed as proportions of total government capital spending in these periods, the increases in domestic debt were 58 per cent and 61 per cent of capital spending respectively. (Calculated from 1964 and 1969 *Economic Surveys*, various issues of the *Ghana Gazette*, and Table 6.2 above.)

[71] Admittedly the shares of the public and private sectors in 1970–1 are only estimated and are subject to substantial margins of error. On the other hand, no reasonable alteration of the estimating assumptions would alter the fact that the share of the private sector was small: we can be confident that their share lay in the range of 10 to 20 per cent of the total. There was a shift in the lending policies of the National Investment Bank in favour of the private sector after 1965, but the amounts were small. Their lending to the private sector went up by about ₵1.5 million in 1965–7 (*see* Harlander and Mezger, 1971, pp. 78–9).

[72] Table 4.C records (column 12) that real interest rates were generally negative, often rather severely so, during the sixties and this could be expected to have had a depressing effect on private saving. A preliminary analysis of data up to the first quarter of 1973 indicates that the interest reform was having some success, even though accelerated inflation meant that real interest rates on savings remained negative in 1971 and 1972. The rate of increase of the money value of time and savings deposits with the commercial banks (net of offsetting reductions in Treasury Bill holdings) had tripled – from 2·1 per cent per quarter to 6·6 per cent – and a catastrophic fall in the demand for bank loans predicted by the banking community had not occurred – the money value of bank lending 18 months after the reform was a little higher than the pre-reform rate. The reform was nevertheless unpopular with the NRC and in mid-1973 the Bank of Ghana was under considerable pressure to lower the structure of interest rates once more.

[73] It seemed at the time, though, that the 1971 devaluation would induce the government to abandon price controls, gradually relax the exchange controls and allow minimum wage legislation to become inoperative – further examples of how decisive this action would have been had it been allowed to take effect.

[74] The 1968 *Industrial Policy Statement*, pp. 9–10, proposed legislation along the lines enacted in the 1971 Act. The following quotations are from clauses 1 and 8 of the Act.

[75] Introducing the second reading of this Act, the Minister of Trade, Industries and Tourism could scarcely have been more explicit about his belief in the superior decision-making capacity of the state: 'the Bill is intended to enable the Government to regulate and direct the country's industrialisation programme. Such regulation is necessary not only to ensure the even distribution of industries throughout the country but also to ensure that our scarce resources are carefully husbanded . . . The object of the Bill is to guide the investor by assuring first, that he will not dissipate his investment on a manufacturing enterprise which we cannot support or accommodate; and, secondly, in the interests of the country generally, to ensure that the siting of the enterprise and its size accord with our development policy . . .' (*Parliamentary Debates*, 12 March 1971, col. 496).

[76] See *One-year Plan*, pp. 59–60.

[77] The revalued exchange rate established on 7 February 1972 left the cedi price of foreign exchange higher by a weighted average of 34 per cent than the exchange rate prevailing before the 27 December 1971 devaluation (which introduced a 90 per cent increase).

[78] Prices and Incomes Board Decree, 1972 (NRCD 119) and Prices and Income Regulations, 1973 (LI 805).

[79] Subversion Decree, 1972 (NRCD 90), clause 1(n). This law also made the smuggling or theft of various goods subject to a mandatory death penalty. Trial was to be by a military tribunal and there was no right of appeal. During its first year, however, this

law had not been much enforced.

[80] *See Daily Graphic*, 21 September 1972.

[81] NRC, *Ghana's Investment Policy*, 1973, *passim. See also* Decrees No. 132 and 139 of 1972.

[82] Recall that on the same page the party manifesto promised to de-control imports and to make price controls more effective – Progress Party, 1969 p. 5.

[83] Ofori-Atta, 1967, pp. 40–1 (my emphasis).

[84] Mensah, 1971.

12 *Lessons*

It is time to change tenses, from the past to the future. So far this study has been concerned to analyse the years gone by: now it asks what lessons can be learned for the future from 'the rubbish heap of history'. The chief aim of this concluding chapter, then, is to show what practical conclusions might be drawn for Ghana and countries like her. No attempt is made to provide a systematic summary of what has gone before, but the discussion does bring out some of the major points which have been established and tries to tie some of the loose ends together. A final section returns to the theme of this as a case study in applied development economics, to indicate some ways in which Ghana's experiences suggest the literature may need revision.

National Objectives, Economic Prospects, Strategy Choices
First, what kind of choices confront Ghana with regard to objectives, and economic strategies? The assumption upon which much earlier development literature was based, that the principal objective of economic policy in low-income countries should be the long-run maximization of the growth of per capita national income, is now widely questioned. Much concern is expressed for the need to attend also to the distribution of income and creation of employment. Especially during the Busia period, a similar shift of emphasis was discernible in Ghana. Another serious conflict of national objectives in Ghana was between growth and the pursuit of economic independence. Observers have contrasted the 'neo-colonial' but booming economy of the Ivory Coast with the more 'independent' but stagnant Ghana, dramatizing this choice between objectives.[1] And there are real trade-offs. The pursuit of an import-substitution strategy which ignored comparative advantage would deprive Ghana of benefits from international trade, as occurred during the sixties. Similarly, policies which discriminated severely against foreign private capital, management and skilled manpower might be expected to promote economic independence at the expense of efficiency and growth. Again, Rimmer

may be right to claim that the chief concern of policy-makers in Ghana is to redistribute income and employment in favour of themselves and their supporters, and that economic development is only 'an incidental outcome of human activity.'[2]

The tendency to over-dramatize policy options should not pass without challenge, however. For example, the recent stress on conflicts between social justice and economic growth has been exaggerated. The evidence that income distribution is worsening in developing countries is confined to a very small number of countries and the evidence that growth is actually detrimental to equity is weaker still.[3] More positively, redistributive policies are more likely to be politically feasible in the context of a growing economy than in a more static situation, especially given the well-known weaknesses of redistributive fiscal and other policy instruments. The trick, it seems to this writer, is to devise a growth-oriented strategy which has an assurance built into it that the benefits of growth will not be confined to the already well-to-do. A strategy which achieved 'redistribution through growth' would be even better.[4] There is, of course, a danger that growth would be accompanied by changes in political power in favour of the élite but there is no obvious reason to this writer why this should be a lesser danger in a more stagnant economy; in Ghana the trends in income distribution in the sixties were rather complex, defying neat classification into 'egalitarian' or 'inegalitarian' *and to a substantial extent were independent of movements in the locus of political power.* All of which is to say that we should not be too pessimistic about the possibilities of reconciling growth with equity, for an appropriately devised growth strategy provides the only feasible long-term approach to the problem of poverty.[5]

Much the same could be said of employment creation – an objective which will assume increasing urgency in Ghana. There is certainly no guarantee that economic growth will reduce unemployment to a socially acceptable level, but there is little evidence that the pursuit of growth is detrimental to employment creation, rather to the contrary.[6] It is easy to demonstrate that to forgo a long-run growth rate of GNP of one or two per cent in order to maximize employment in the short run would worsen rather than improve the employment situation after a few years.[7] Once more, the constructive response is to devise a growth strategy which discriminates in favour of (or at least stops discriminating against) the utilization of labour.

The apparent conflict between growth and economic independence has also been considerably overstated, for a number of reasons:

(a) The seeming economic costs of policies which descriminate against foreign trade, capital and personnel are smaller than they seem if viewed as necessary to weld a rather fragile, heterogeneous collection of tribes into an entity which thinks of itself as a nation, for it has been argued that the 'symbolic definition of the nation' may be an essential preliminary to the successful pursuit of economic modernization.[8] Whatever might be placed on the debit side, Nkrumah's successes in bringing the Ghanaian nation together were real and of potentially large *economic* value.[9] That the nation has survived hardships, disillusionments, political instability, and the re-emergence under Busia of a more tribalistic government is a tribute to the cohesion of what Nkrumah built.

(b) As a more specific aspect of (a), the Ghanaianization introduced by the NLC and accelerated by Busia, while it undoubtedly imposed short-run economic costs, may in the long term prove the only practical means of fostering the emergence of a modernizing, productively oriented class of Ghanaian entrepreneurs.[10]

(c) The policies of the sixties were not, on the other hand, optimal means of promoting nationhood and economic independence. On balance, Nkrumah's policies advanced independence in the sense of providing greater Ghanaian control over the economy, but in some ways dependence was increased.[11] Industrial policies created a manufacturing sector heavily reliant upon foreign supplies, and neglect of exports forced the country to depend upon foreign credits. Improved policies in these areas would have been good both for the country's economic development and its independence.

(d) For all Nkrumah's fears of the danger of neo-colonialism, it is not at all clear that Ghana has the option to leave much of her development to foreign capital and management. Far from waiting for the chance to pounce upon and exploit Ghana's resources, foreign investors have shown limited interest in Ghana during the last thirty years. Throughout the sixties, government attitudes and policies discouraged potential foreign investors and little investment was forthcoming from these sources. But the record of the nineteen-fifties is also instructive, for then the investment climate was favourable, there were no exchange controls to prevent the repatriation of profits, and there were liberal immigration quotas for skilled foreign workers. Yet, if the figures can be relied upon, from 1950 to 1959 the net inflow of private long-term capital over the whole period was just ₵4.0 million.[12] It seems that for Ghana, neo-colonialism is a paper tiger, and that the large role of foreign capital in the Ivory Coast results from an historical experience which Ghana could not reproduce even in the unlikely event that she should wish to. Of course, major new discoveries of mineral resources would revive the interest of foreign capital.[13] Failing that, Ghana has little choice but to depend essentially upon her own resources.

All in all, then, growth and independence do not seem as irreconcilable as is often supposed. Of course, undiscriminatingly autarchic policies would impose large and persisting penalties on the growth of national income, but it is suggested later than moderate nationalism and economic development may be mutually reinforcing.

The reader will be rightly suspicious of bland assertions that all apparent conflicts between policy objectives are easily reconciled, which is not the argument here. The point rather is that the choices discussed do not get to the heart of the matter. The central issue is the conflict of interest between the present generation and future ones. What has been argued, in effect, is that the objectives are reconcilable so long as a relatively long-term view is taken. In the short run one may maximize utility, for example, by using the public sector as a repository for the unemployed but only at a heavy cost to the longer-term solution of the same problems of poverty, unemployment and the viability of the national economy.

The first-order policy decision, then, is about time horizons, and its outcome cannot be taken for granted. Wallich's illuminating essay on 'derived development'[14] points out that one of the most important differences between today's low-income countries and those of Western Europe prior to their industrial revolutions is that today the impulse for development comes from the consumer rather than the producer. And while supply may create its own demand, the obverse is not true, if associated with a consumptionist bias which holds down saving and regards entrepreneurial profit-making with hostility. Bear in mind, too, the conclusion of chapter 4 that most Ghanaians today enjoy poorer living standards than they did ten or fifteen years ago – a situation in which there is likely to be a low propensity to save and it is politically most difficult to enforce saving through taxation. These facts and the riskiness of a political career in Ghana, may well induce decisions which sacrifice the future to the present, no matter how short-sighted such decisions may be, although Ghanaians have in the past demonstrated a willingness to take a long-term view, for example in their attitudes to education and in the development of the cocoa industry.

If the temporal choice is made in favour of the present, the development economist has little to contribute to economic policies. But he can perhaps influence that choice by pointing out a viable alternative, so the remainder of this section is devoted to an elucidation of the policy options available for the *long-term* development of Ghana's economy.

In going about this task it is convenient to identify three alternatives:
(1) An 'Nkrumah strategy' – a reversion to the strategy adopted during the first half of the sixties;
(2) A 'modified Nkrumah strategy' – one which retains the essentials of his strategy but avoids its worst excesses and mistakes, and pays more attention to implementation;
(3) A 'market strategy' – an approach which really tries what the Busia administration is wrongly thought to have done, namely to

disengage the state from control and participation, to reduce and eventually remove price distortions, and to allow resources to be allocated through the market mechanism, with government policies operating indirectly through markets.

The first of these can be dismissed. Earlier chapters, besides showing the dismal performance of Ghana's economy in the sixties, have emphasized the responsiblity of domestic policy failures. Adverse movements in the commodity terms of trade in the first half of the sixties made matters worse but did no more than precipitate a crisis which had anyway become inevitable. We have seen the failure of Nkrumah's large and in some ways impressive investment effort, how policy weaknesses helped to perpetuate the foreign exchange constraint and aggravate its effects on the economy, and undermined the industrialization drive, and the serious (in the case of agriculture, critical) effects of the poor economic performance of state-owned farms, factories and service activities. Furthermore, the policy failings reinforced each other to make the overall impact on the economy even graver than the sum of the individual defects. A case in point was the way in which unbalanced growth of agriculture and industry was self-defeating, with agricultural failure undermining the industrialization effort. It would obviously be absurd to repeat these mistakes. An 'Nkrumah strategy' would only be worth serious consideration if the more major policy failings could be rectified.

The need for change is all the clearer from contemplation of Ghana's economic prospects unless decisive actions are taken to improve them. Population will continue growing at $2\frac{1}{2}$ to 3 per cent annually and the unemployment problem can be expected to worsen. Net investment, which was negligible at the end of the sixties, will have to be raised if there is to be any serious prospect of adequate and sustained economic growth. This, in turn, implies a big increase in domestic saving, much of which would surely have to come from major fiscal reforms.[15] And improved export performance is quite essential for any sustained removal of the foreign exchange constraint.[16] Growth cannot be expected to occur autonomously; Ghana needs a policy revolution – either major policy changes or radically improved operation of past policies. The alternative is more stagnation, with all that means for the loss of human happiness.

Between the serious alternatives, the question is whether to remain within the tradition of Nkrumah's policies but try to make them work better, or to go for a more market-oriented strategy.

Continuing in Nkrumah's Tradition

The argument to be made out in favour of a 'modified Nkrumah strategy' may run as follows.[17] Nkrumah's development strategy was a basically sound one but it suffered from an unfavourable colonial heritage,[18] defects of leadership, poor implementation and adverse external circumstances. His large investments in physical and human capital built a foundation for future dynamic growth; that this growth has not yet materialized is due to inevitable time lags and the advent after 1966 of governments which were unsympathetic to the structural transformation intended by Nkrumah. The vastly expanded educational system will not only provide a larger flow of skilled personnel but will also widen horizons and heighten ambitions, thus increasing receptivity to modernization.[19] The large underutilization of productive capacity at the end of the sixties demonstrates the dynamic potential of the investments of earlier years, just as the deplorably poor experiences with planning, controls and state enterprises show how much scope there is for improvement. Nkrumah's critics have concentrated excessively on short-term questions of allocative efficiency, neglecting more dynamic considerations.

However (the argument may continue), weaknesses in Nkrumah's leadership would need to be remedied if this type of strategy were ever to work. Specifically, the constraints on the development of the economy would have to be accepted as such and priority given to their removal. Nkrumah's refusal to acknowledge the financial and foreign exchange constraints was foolish.[20] The government's economic objectives and priorities would have to be clarified, and the quality of policy-making improved. Failures in these areas had serious consequences in the sixties, especially for the balance of payments and short-term economic management. Lastly, there would have to be a greater willingness to impose political discipline; failure to do this led to corruption, lowered morale in the civil service and undermined economic planning.[21] None of these changes (the argument might conclude) would be overwhelmingly difficult; with them Nkrumah's strategy would succeed and the economy would move forward again.

Evaluation of this argument poses two questions, logically distinct but tending in practice to blend into each other: is it correct to say that Nkrumah's strategy was intrinsically sound? and what capacity do Ghana's systems of politics and public administration possess for radically improving the implementation of past policies?

We might begin to answer the first of these by asking about the soundness of Nkrumah's analysis of Ghana's economic situation, of which his strategy was a logical outcome. Was Ghana really caught in a 'vicious circle of poverty, which keeps us in our rut of impoverishment. . . [and] can only be broken by a massively planned industrial undertaking'? Was the economic structure left behind by the British and improved upon during the fifties so inadequate that development could only be achieved if it was radically transformed? Certainly, the structure left much to be desired, being excessively dependent on cocoa, dualistic in character and largely based upon pre-modern techniques of production (especially in agriculture). We should note, on the other hand, that economic performance in the fifties provides little suppport for the notion that Ghana was caught in a low-level trap. Growth during that decade was of the order of 5 per cent annually, or about 2½ per cent per capita, and its benefits were not confined to a foreign or an urban élite. The country was already relatively rich in human and physical capital, saving and investment ratios were rather high, and the population was responsive to economic incentives (*see* below). The infrastructure had been much improved during the fifties and, even if the human and institutional base remained fragile, there is no obvious reason why a strategy of building upon and improving what was already at hand could not have been viable.

It is suggested, then, that Nkrumah's perception of Ghana's economic problem was excessively dramatic, unduly pessimistic. If the diagnosis was wrong could the prescription have been right?

The chosen prescription was one which created many disequilibria, setting out to transform the economic structure, to introduce many changes of a discontinuous nature rather than building upon what already existed, especially to industrialize the economy. In this sense it may be called a *disequilibrium* strategy. Based on the seductive notion that a big push could propel the economy forward into self-sustaining growth, and that the rate of growth is essentially a function of the rate of capital formation, this strategy must have held enormous attractions for a politician in a hurry and under pressure to produce quick results. Attractive too was the emphasis on change and the relegation of short-term efficiency. So the big push was undertaken, the investment rate forced up, the economic structure changed. But the growth rate slumped, and structural transformation was accompanied by stagnation.

Without recapitulating all the reasons for these failures, it is worth drawing from earlier chapters what seem to have been the most fundamental errors. Firstly, we should recall the basic rationale of a disequilibrium strategy: that the opportunities, felt needs and tensions created by emerging disequilibria will call forth agents of change seeking to satisfy the new needs, thereby moving the economy forward.[22] The potential of a disequilibrium strategy, on this view, depends upon the capacity to respond to the emergence of newly felt needs; it depends, to put it differently, on an awakening of a latent decision-making potential. We will have a good deal more to say about this, but one dimension of responsiveness in which Ghana's public sector clearly failed was in its capacity to handle a greatly expanded volume of investment without disastrous declines in its productivity; the big investment push failed because of a drastic decline in the productivity of capital. This was partly because physical capital formation outstripped the supply of skilled labour during the earlier sixties, but restoration of an improved balance between physical and human capital later failed to bring with it comparable improvements in the productivity (or utilization) of capital. Besides skill shortages, there were deep-seated social and institutional obstacles to improved responsiveness to felt needs. A disequilibrium strategy was adopted which fatally failed to attend to the social conditions which could have made it succeed.

Its neglect of efficiency was another of the strategy's serious defects. Comparative advantage considerations, for example, were explicitly rejected by Nkrumah. This and his general disregard of conventional investment criteria, which he regarded as at best conservative and at worst obstructionist, resulted in highly arbitrary and dysfunctional provisions of industrial protection, a neglect of project planning in the public sector, and the waste of capital resources. Similar attitudes mistakenly placed short-term macro-economic management at a discount in favour of maximum public sector spending. These faults, it should be stressed, were not merely defects of implementation; they flowed directly from the intellectual frame of mind which embraced a disequilibrium approach to development and saw a conflict between short-run efficiency and long-run growth.

Perhaps the most fundamental criticism of Nkrumah's strategy concerns its view of modernization. It was essentially a strategy of *historical replication*: reproduce the sectoral sequences of the industrial revolutions of the nineteenth century; transfer the technologies developed during the advance of the industrial nations. Several observers have commented that Nkrumah, for all that he did to emancipate the people of Africa, lacked confidence in his fellow-countrymen – a view which is consistent with a strategy which, in the case of agriculture, most explicitly rejected the potential of improving traditional techniques in favour of Western techniques. This was a contradiction in Nkrumah the nationalist.

Influenced, perhaps, by a deterministic view of economic history, Nkrumah saw development as consisting of industrialization, including the industrialization of agriculture. This meant taking the techniques of production developed in industrial countries and implanting them in the domestic economy. It implied, therefore, a high degree of capital-intensity, because of the priority on industry and the unmodified use of technologies developed in countries characterized by an ample supply of capital. This bias towards large capital inputs was reflected in the choice of public sector projects, in the attempted mechanization of agriculture, in the bias of import duties in favour of capital goods, and, more generally, in relative factor prices.

This strategy could scarcely have made heavier demands upon an economy still possessing few modern skills, few domestic capital goods industries, a limited savings base, and a fragile export sector reliant upon a volatile world market. It could only make a limited contribution to the unemployment problem, leading to the absurdity of deliberately over-manning public enterprises designed for capital-intensive production techniques. Predictably for any who retained even the most qualified belief in comparative advantage, the outcome was a highly inefficient industrialization effort, which reduced real incomes in the short run but also had very limited dynamic potential, because many of the 'development projects' had few roots in the natural and labour resources of the economy. Symbolically, the most technologically advanced plant in the country – the Valco aluminium smelter – was a near-perfect example of an enclave, with electrical power its only significant domestic input.[23] There could be little spill-over from industries such as these, just as there was nothing the peasants could usefully learn from mechanized state farms.

In effect, Nkrumah mistook the appearances of modernization for the reality. Much effort and many resources were devoted to acquiring the symbols of modernity – the institutions, the machinery, the factories, the apparatus of state. The results were modernization without growth, occurring, I submit, because the strategy overlooked that past industrial revolutions have drawn their dynamism from innovation and adaptation. There was little of either in the many changes introduced by Nkrumah. Most 'innovations' were copied unchanged from some Western or Eastern model. They worked out differently, but the differences were not to Ghana's advantage.[24]

The strategy may finally be criticized for its closed economy approach: emphasizing import substitution and neglecting, indeed penalizing, exports. Ghana was not alone in making this mistake but the result was that her leaders lost sight of the elementary truism that a small country at an early state of development can only hope to achieve sustained growth if it has an expanding import capacity and, hence, a growing export sector.[25] The result was to create and then perpetuate a foreign exchange constraint which, more than anything, held back the growth which Nkrumah so wanted and needed.

On balance, then, this study does not show that Nkrumah's strategy was basically sound, nor that he laid a foundation from which dynamic growth can be expected in the future. On the contrary, it suggests that his strategy was based upon a misconception of Ghana's economic problem; that Ghana did not possess enough capacity to respond to new needs for a disequilibrium strategy to be appropriate; that the neglect of efficiency had serious consequences; that in reaching for the appearances of modernization the strategy neglected the innovation and adaptation which were the mainsprings of earlier industrial revolutions; and that it was an error to opt for a closed economy model.

This brings us to the second argument of those who would follow in the tradition of Nkrumah by maintaining that much better results could be obtained from improving the implementation of chosen policies. How much capacity has been shown for radically improving the execution of past policies?

During the Nkrumah period itself very little of this capacity was shown. In fact, the opposite was in evidence. Earlier chapters have recorded the deterioration of economic planning and short-term management during the last years of Nkrumah's administration; the failure of his government to adjust itself to the manifest weaknesses of its agricultural and industrial policies; and the disintegration of import programming in 1964 and 1965. On the other hand, it would be neither convincing nor fair to emphasize these facts, for Nkrumah was not given enough time to show how his administration would have responded to the failings which were becoming more and more evident towards the end of his rule.

Far greater significance may be placed on the record of the post-Nkrumah administrations. It was argued in the last chapter that the NLC and Busia governments continued many of the policies which they inherited but that – especially during the NLC years – a major effort was made to improve upon policy execution. However, an analysis of the later sixties showed that many difficulties were encountered in this endeavour and the achievements were limited, which led to the conclusion that the obstacles to improve execution must have been rather deep-rooted. Thus, efforts to improve economic planning and the administration of import controls were shown still to have left much to be desired in the late sixties and early seventies. Much the same was true of the performance of public enterprises; there were genuine improvements by the late sixties but many weaknesses remained and overall performance was still sub-standard. Co-ordination of domestic and external policies was a weakness which persisted throughout the sixties and into the seventies.

In a sense, this modesty of achievement supports the idea that improved policy implementation would yield large dividends, on the principle that the worse things are, the greater the benefit from improving them. But one suspects that the converse is true: things are so bad because improving them is so difficult. This brings us back to a point raised earlier, that the socio-economic system revealed a low capacity to respond to emerging disequilibria, in the manner postulated by challenge-and-response models of economic development and of the interaction of economic and political forces. Hirschman suggests, for example, that economic stagnation tends to generate social forces to overcome the obstacles to further progress, and a 'principle of the hiding hand', in which people respond with previously unsuspected degrees of creativity to unforseen problems of development projects.[26] Responses of this kind were conspicuously absent in the Ghana of the sixties; if this can be explained it will be easier to assess the validity of the 'improve implementation' school of thought.

In seeking an explanation, it is natural to look first at the civil service. There were, as has been shown, serious shortages of senior personnel. A tiny number of officers were responsible in the Ministry of Industries for the execution and oversight of the industrialization thrust, and there was an equally drastic paucity of personnel to administer import and price controls. There were serious personnel weaknesses in the planning ministry and in the agricultural extension services. Other examples could be given, such as the existence in 1970 of only nineteen senior staff in the administration responsible for the upkeep of the national road system,[27] leading consultants to conclude that 'maintenance of P.W.D. roads has almost collapsed . . .'[28]

Part of the explanation, then, is that too much was being asked of a small number of people. But this was only part of the problem, for the number of senior civil servants did increase over the sixties, as the output of the higher educational system expanded, to the point where fears were being expressed by 1973 about the future capacity of the public service to absorb university graduates at the rates of earlier years.[29] By the early seventies the number of Ghanaian economists in the Planning Ministry was far larger than in the earlier sixties but performance remained indifferent because of poor leadership, inadequate personnel policies, low morale and weak motivation. Observations also revealed that this malaise was rather general in the public service. Successive governments expressed dissatisfaction with their administrators. Prime Minister Busia called for greater discipline in a campaign which hit the right target with the minimum of practical effect. In his turn, the Chairman of the NRC complained that 'our past predilections are laziness, apathy and embezzlement,' and for a while the military was rather drastic with unpunctual office workers.[30] The problem of motivation and morale is elaborated in a most interesting study by the political scientist, Robert M. Price.[31] His surveys revealed strong family pressures for civil servants to behave in ways making for inefficiency and worse, and showed that officials had a low opinion of and a weak commitment to a civil service career, seeing the service largely as a source of security.[32] His conclusions differ sharply from the view that a strong civil service had been created during the colonial period. The British, he argues, failed to transfer a commitment to organizational roles characteristic of their own civil service. Theoretically, a system of rewards and sanctions could play upon the desire for security to command improved performance but in practice promotion is almost exclusively determined by seniority and the disciplinary system is ineffectual.

The conclusion offers itself, then, that deficiencies in the civil service prevented major improvements in policy execution after the downfall of Nkrumah. On the basis of his own dealings with the service, Finance Minister J. H. Mensah had reached a similar conclusion by 1970:[33]

Ghanaians have all been so used to think of themselves, with the encouragement of foreign admirers, as possessing a very capable ruling class. Fortunately, the foreign commentators always add the rider, 'in comparison with other African countries'. This of course robs the compliment of most of its meaning. The comfortable national self-delusion that Ghanaians are already a very competent and efficient people must be eliminated. When one watches the cruel ineffectiveness with which so much expensively-acquired equipment is operated in Ghana, when one realises the inability of most parts of our administrative and managerial machinery to deliver the high quality performance which is required for a more rapid pace of national progress, then one realises that Ghana may possess an articulate and polished élite in comparison with other African countries but she does not yet possess the managerial resources for running a fully modernised country.

Perhaps the weaknesses will be recognized and remedied but Price, for one, is pessimistic about the ability of the service to improve itself.[34]

However, it would be wrong to suggest that low responsiveness to felt needs was all attributable to the civil service. It would be especially wrong to portray the politicians as blameless sufferers from the inadequacies of their administrators. Ghana's political leaders bear a very heavy degree of responsibility for the things which went wrong in the sixties. The question here is whether the country's political processes, such as they have become through a succession of upheavals, possess more capacity for self-improvement than the civil service. This point is discussed briefly in the context of public enterprise performance on the last pages of chapter 9, where a rather negative conclusion is reached: politicians appear to have been little more 'efficiency-oriented' than their civil servants; and the continuing pressures and uncertainties of political life will tend to induce decisions based upon immediate rather than long-term advantage.[35] Moreover, the mechanisms for publicizing the need for reforms remain poorly developed. Currently, there is no parliament nor any comparable institution; even when a legislature existed it was not always effective. Under Nkrumah and Busia most of the national press was – and still is under the NRC – government-controlled, and few of the traditions which make the press an effective channel of criticism, information and advice have emerged. Most obviously under Nkrumah but also under Busia, civilian politicians revealed themselves to be excessively sensitive to whatever criticism did struggle to the surface and showed little recognition of the practical value which it could have had.

No less dulling to the capacity to respond to the challenge of past failings is a special tendency to agree with Henry Ford that history is bunk and to treat recurring problems as if they are new. This view was stated very explicitly after the 1972 coup, when the country's most widely read newspaper seemed to speak no less than the truth when it claimed that, 'For some obvious reasons it seems it is the consensus in the country that no more time and energy be expended on diagnosing "what went wrong" in the Busia regime.' The problems left behind, it went on, were so enormous 'that it would not profit anyone to spend further time in pointing out mistakes of the past from which no lesson is learned anyway.'[36] This also seemed to be the view of the NRC which reinstated various policy measures first introduced by Nkrumah in ways which did nothing to safeguard against a reappearance of the weaknesses which became evident under him.[37]

Clearly, then, any who wished to operate within Nkrumah's policy framework but improve its execution would find severe, deep-rooted obstacles to their endeavours. The large scope for improvement provides no assurance that improvements will be forthcoming; rather, the prospects would be better if the gap between the potential and the reality were smaller.

This section began by asking whether the poor results of Nkrumah's strategy were because of intrinsic defects in the strategy or because it was poorly executed. Green takes the latter view, arguing that 'The failures of planning in Ghana stem not from over-comprehensiveness or too much control but from massive lacunae and quite inadequate implementational control.'[38] But this is to oversimplify. Given the massive informational and administrative appetites of planning and controls, and the dearth of these types of resource in Ghana, no clear distinction can be drawn between the decision to establish a command economy and the subsequent deficiencies of this endeavour. *Poor implementation was implicit in the strategy itself.* A big push, concentrated in the public sector, highly politicized, and imposed upon a public administration of severely limited capabilities *entailed* a low standard of execution. Some of the ideas were bad, some good, but scarcely ever were they tailored to the practical limitations imposed by a social and institutional framework still, after all, at an early stage of development.

A Market Alternative

The major alternative posed earlier in this chapter to a 'modified Nkrumah strategy' was a market strategy, disengaging the state from control and participation, reducing and eventually eliminating price distortions, and allowing resources to be allocated through the market mechanism. To be taken seriously, this approach could not be one of laissez faire but would concentrate more on government policies which operate indirectly through the markets. Following the pattern adopted in the previous section, I first state the arguments in favour of this alternative and then its weaknesses.

To a large extent, of course, the case in favour follows from the negative conclusion of the previous section. It could be argued that the numerous efforts made in the sixties to provide superior substitutes for market signals manifestly failed. There was an almost perfect vacuum between the theoretical case for medium-term planning and what was achieved under the *Seven-year Plan*, the misleading investment signals of which contributed to over-investment in manufacturing capacity during the first half of the sixties. The various devices of protection

contributed to the emergence of a highly inefficient industrial structure. No serious attempt was made in the public sector to adjust for
discrepancies between private and social valuations of inputs and outputs; and the substitution of controls for the market place, when it was
not ineffectual, led to major allocational inefficiencies and perverse
consequences.

If it is accepted that radical changes are needed to shake Ghana out
of her stagnation and that the non-market alternative has small chance
of greater success in the future than in the past, a strategy which would
operate through the market commends itself almost by default.

However, there are also positive things to be said in its favour. It is
worth repeating that the policies of the fifties, which had a greater
market orientation, led to markedly better growth rates than those of
the following decade (although they also left many structural weaknesses in the economy). More importantly, there is much evidence that
the Ghanaian public is receptive to modernization and responsive to
economic incentives. As Arthur Lewis observed in the mid-sixties,
'Nobody has to be pushed into modernisation; on the contrary, the
demand for education exceeds the capacity of the government to
supply teachers.'[39] The élite in Ghana is essentially modern and educated, not traditionalist, averse neither to new ideas nor to a business
career.[40]

The view of Ghanaians as being 'economic men', although generally
resisted by the country's intelligentsia, is supported, for instance, by
migrations in response to regional income differentials,[41] and by their
attitudes to education. Thus, Foster concluded from his study of
education and social change that when one 'examines attitudes vis-à-
vis different types of formal education, one is impressed by the shrewd-
ness and the economic sagacity of the citizens of Ghana.'[42] He showed
school graduates to be well informed about employment prospects,
and realistic and flexible in their aspirations, a result which found
independent support in a study by Peil.[43] Corruption and smuggling,
widely and frequently deplored in Ghana, may be seen as further evidence of willingness to exploit newly created opportunites for private
gain, albeit with anti-social results.

The best-known example of responsiveness to new economic opportunities in Ghana is the creation at the turn of the century of the cocoa
industry, almost entirely on the basis of indigenous enterprise.[44] That
this industry remains responsive is demonstrated by studies which have
shown cocoa planting to be positively correlated with the cocoa producer price.[45] There is a good deal of other evidence that, *within the
limits of their knowledge of techniques,* other farmers in Ghana have
positive supply elasticities and are likely to be quite well informed
about the alternatives available to them.[46] The same holds for the
country's small-scale diamond miners.[47] Domestic trading activity is
not only vigorous but highly sensitive to changing opportunities.[49]

Positive and significant elasticities of substitution in response to changing relative factor prices were reported earlier. Finally, there was a considerable response to the opportunities created by the 1970 Ghanaian Business Promotion Act. There is, in short, no evidence of backward-sloping supply curves or other perverse reactions.

However, to demonstrate that Ghanaians are responsive to pecuniary incentives is not sufficient to establish the case for a market-oriented development path. Some critical questions should be asked. Were there not major market imperfections before the distortions introduced during the sixties? Is there a sufficient entrepreneurial potential for such a strategy to be viable? Does Ghana's social system have the capacity to accommodate the enormous societal changes which accompany economic development, or would it require a transformation too radical to be accomplished through the price system?

To take the last of these questions first, criticism of the modernizing potential of traditional African society has often centred upon the effects of extended family obligations, but the evidence on this is inconclusive. Price's negative findings on morale and motivation in the civil service have already been mentioned. His study goes on to emphasize the dysfunctional effects of family obligations, and Garlick's researches on Ghanaian businessmen indicated to him that 'family responsibilities tended to reduce a trader's power to undertake effective business enterprise.'[49] Others would dispute the generality of this finding,[50] or would regard it as a rather ethnocentric point of view.[51] The modernizing potential of Ghana's peasant agriculture is similarly disputed, especially as regards the effects of the land tenure and inheritance systems,[52] but the conclusion of one interesting study was that,[53]

> there may not be a choice between increasing production within peasant households and transforming the system since the transformation of peasants into capitalists is likely to require an initial substantial increase in some income, and since growth in peasant incomes also encourages the transformation of that system.

Of far greater importance, perhaps, are doubts about the innovative capacity of Ghanaian society – a capacity which stands at the heart of the development process. Owusu has put the point strongly:[54]

> Ghanaians at all levels of society are committed to achieving economic mobility, a rising social status, and the personal satisfaction of having the wherewithal to meet one's extended family obligations. Fathers achieve high status vicariously and even realistically through the economic mobility of their sons and daughters.
> But it is a 'conservative' modernity that hardly aspires to creative innovation. It is a modernity that aspires to privilege through high-

status seeking and is desirous of well-paid and materially comfortable, mostly white-collar, occupations.

Perhaps we should ask again what lessons can be drawn from the history of the cocoa industry. That the farmers responded to new opportunities? That the social structure was flexible enough to accommodate large changes? That the farmers were willing to take risks, to take a long view, and to reinvest their profits? Yes, all those things, but also that they were not innovative entrepreneurs, transforming traditional cultivation techniques.

Garlick similarly observed a weak innovative impulse among Ghanaian businessmen. He distinguished between business acumen, which Ghanaian traders possess in abundance, and the view of the entrepreneur as innovator, concluding that 'the entrepreneurial flame (in Schumpter's sense) burned low in Ghanaian traders.'[55] To remain in the Schumpeterian framework, one possible reason for the country's deficiencies of enterprise (or is it effect rather than cause?) is that business does not enjoy high prestige. Peil's investigations showed businessmen to enjoy a status rank only fourteenth out of thirty-five occupations, below soldiers, secondary school teachers and senior clerks[56] and Foster's researches similarly underlined the relatively humble prestige attaching to business.[57] It seems that the typical Ghanaian businessman does not plough back his profits to create a dynamically expanding enterprise which outlives its creator:[58]

A trader's business activities, it seemed, could be thought of as a series of short periods in each of which profit maximisation was sought. At the end of each period came a siphoning off of all that could be spared, for only when a business was new and still being built up would profits be ploughed back. Profits were for investment elsewhere, perhaps in other types of business enterprise, but especially in farming and housing ... the businessman was not displaying improvident behaviour; on the contrary, he was making a calculated, planned effort to meet the needs of himself and family ... in the total social context, this particular pattern of diversification enabled the businessman in general to make the most of his economic opportunities in the long run.

The general argument from these studies is that, with few exceptions, the size of private African business, including enterprises outside trade, was unlikely to increase ...

If these studies were of typical, relatively large businesses, then a business rarely survived into a second generation ... The tendency for a business enterprise to depend upon one individual, and the consciousness that a business would most likely die when its creator chose to retire, were obstacles to development.

Partly for reasons of this kind, past attempts to provide assistance to Ghanaian businessmen have achieved small results at high costs,[59] and Garlick is not alone in expressing doubts about the cost-efficiency of extension services to West African businessmen.[60] Hakam, on the other hand, argues that the most serious obstacles in the way of would-be Ghanaian industrial entrepreneurs were avoidable biases in the allocation of foreign exchange and loan finance.[61] We should remember, too, that a few sizeable Ghanaian entrepreneurs have emerged[62] – the beginning, perhaps, of something bigger.

Neither can the question of market imperfections be glossed over. Chapter 1 showed that at the beginning of the sixties, before the emergence of the grosser distortions which grew up during that decade, the economy was markedly dualistic in character. If we take dualism to refer to the co-existence of a traditional labour-intensive sector and a modern, capital-intensive sector, this was evident in many types of activity – in manufacturing, agriculture, trade, construction, mining and fishing. But dualism implies a failure to equalise at the margin, resulting from imperfect markets for labour and capital, and imperfect information flows. To be more specific, there was the usual three-tiered market for capital, comprising an unofficial 'kerb' market, an official market serviced by financial institutions, and access to foreign capital. The case was similar with labour, with minimum wage legislation probably at that time leaving a substantial gap between the official price of unskilled labour and its opportunity cost.[63]

Competition was also unsatisfactory in product markets. Competition between traditional and modern suppliers of similar products was probably not great and within the modern sector the number of units in a given industry was typically small, often amounting to just one producer.[64] That is less true today than it was at the beginning of the sixties but the average number of firms in a given industry remains small.[65] Moreover, the small domestic market and the search for economies of scale is likely to keep things that way. Lastly, transport and communications still leave a great deal to be desired, disseminating the information and incentives of the market system with low efficiency.

These considerations obviously weaken the argument for a market-oriented development strategy, for market imperfections and a dearth of innovative skills will tend to reduce supply elasticities,[66] distort the effects of policy inducements and induce only a sluggish pace of modernization. The entrepreneurial gap appears the most difficult, for we have suggested that foreign capital is unlikely to be very interested in Ghana (even if it were wanted), a modern indigenous entrepreneurial class is only just beginning to emerge, and the state has demonstrated severe limitations in trying to fill the gap.

To move towards a workable market strategy, then, would mean reducing the imperfections and distortions of the past, and the extent of state intervention in the operation of market forces. The next step, therefore, is to examine the problems which would be encountered in trying to effect this transition, thus reverting to the question posed at the end of the last chapter of why there were not more fundamental changes in economic policy after Nkrumah was deposed, when the economic case for more radical changes seemed obvious.

Problems of Transition

While Nkrumah was probably mistaken in perceiving his country as locked in a vicious circle of poverty, that diagnosis may be more valid now. Improved national saving and investment rates are indispensable conditions for improved long-term economic growth, but past stagnation has led to declining private living standards, small marginal and average propensities to save, and strong resistance to increased taxation. Worse, it has conditioned potential investors to perceive few promising new opportunities. Moreover, the political instability with which stagnation has – not coincidentally[67] – been associated has both generated cynicism about governmental promises of bread tomorrow and dulled economic responses to specific policy measures.[68] Improved economic performance is probably a necessary (but not sufficient) condition of greater political stability, just as greater stability is probably a necessary (but insufficient) condition for future growth. One should not push this pessimism too far, but it seems beyond doubt that the stagnation of the sixties has rather severely increased the difficulties of doing better in the future.

A similar argument could be stated from a different standpoint. Onto an already imperfect price system Nkrumah grafted a variety of distortions, among them an over-valued currency, an arbitrary set of import and industrial taxes, negative real rates of interest, a variety of inefficient direct controls, and non-economic investment criteria in the public sector. Two questions arise: Can large distortions best be treated by the use of marginalist policy instruments, when, almost by definition, marginal instruments are most efficient in inducing small changes? And can confidence be justified that measures to correct any one distortion will improve the allocation of resources so long as other distortions remain intact? The latter query is prompted by the 'problem of the second-best' which, it has been argued, demonstrates the futility of piecemeal welfare economics.[69]

These may seem rather fanciful points to raise here but their practical content can be illustrated by reference to the 1971 devaluation, in which this writer was involved as an adviser to the Ghana government. The economists involved in the preparation of this measure, which raised the cedi price of foreign exchange by 90 per cent, found themselves professionally unprepared for such a task. How could one prepare meaningful estimates of the effects of such a large change? Attempts to do so by the use of supply and demand elasticities raised the obvious objection that elasticities are only appropriate for relatively modest changes in the relevant variables, to say nothing of the fact that we could only guess at what value the elasticities might have. Attempts to employ an absorption approach raised similar difficulties with respect to marginal consumption, saving and investment propensities and, depending on the chosen assumptions, generated a range of estimates so wide as to be unusable. Moreover, and this brings in the 'second-best' problem, it was not at all certain that the government would combine the devaluation with a package of measures which would, more or less simultaneously, act upon the other major distortions holding back the economy and jeopardizing the success of the devaluation itself.[70] In essence, it was an act of faith with a large attendant risk of diminished human welfare.

The politics of transition are no easier than the economics – and here we come nearer to an explanation of why avowedly anti-Nkrumah governments continued with so many of the policies and institutions he originated. The first and probably most important reason for this continuity is that to a large extent Nkrumah's attitudes and policies were those of a nationalist. Those policies could only be undone at the risk of offending the nationalism which remained strong even though the Founding Father had been deposed. It would be a mistake to conclude from the popular rejoicing at his downfall that the Ghanaian people were out of sympathy with all Nkrumah's policies; far from it. He had asserted the supremacy of the national interest, had visibly accumulated new assets under Ghanaian ownership and control, had reduced Ghana's dependence on others. Of these feats, I believe, the Ghanaian public remained proud; it was the shorter-term hardships which they, in common with electorates everywhere, disliked.

On this view, Nkrumah's interventionism, especially his partial closing of the economy, might be seen as decolonization, with import and exchange controls, import substitution, and state participation in industry not merely symbols of a flexing of nationalist muscles but essential measures to translate political sovereignty into economic independence.[71] Attempts to open the economy, reduce the overvaluation of the cedi, sell off state enterprises, close down the most inefficient industries, and encourage foreign investment by allocating more foreign exchange for profit remittances could thus be seen as a reversion to a 'colonial' scheme of things, a betrayal of the country's recently won freedom. To the extent that Nkrumah's policies were nationalistic, attempts to undo them could only incur popular displeasure. In any case, Busia and some of his ministerial colleagues were themselves old-time nationalists.[72]

On the whole, the governments which succeeded Nkrumah trod cautiously and often sacrificed greater economic efficiency to nationalist sensitivities. Some of the ways in which they did depart from Nkrumah's orthodoxy, especially in the devaluations, were heartily despised by Ghana's intelligentsia. The NRC, which came to power after devaluation, quickly proved itself to be the most nationalist of all post-independence governments. It was a development predicted by the commentator who stressed most heavily the nationalistic nature of Nkrumah and his party:[73]

> Despite the fall and emphatic rejection of Nkrumah in Ghana, a complete abandon of his policies seems hardly conceivable. *Volens nolens,* the new regime will have to resume from what has been left by fifteen years of Nkrumaism . . . For the time being it would seem that Ghana is in a process of digesting these fifteen years – at the economic level, this takes the form of a most desirable streamlining and sorting out operation. But, it goes without saying that this economic consolidation cannot constitute a program of government nor can a negative and unattractive policy of simple anti-Nkrumaism. Sooner or later, the nationalist program of development will have to be resumed in Ghana on a large scale . . .

Besides the nationalist impulse, there was a further factor working against a wholesale dismantling of what Nkrumah had created, which is clarified by asking, who were the winners and who the losers from his policies? The general point is simple but has far-reaching implications: the economic costs of his policies tended to be diffused generally over the consuming public, but the benefits were enjoyed by highly specific groups of workers and businessmen. While pressure groups in Ghana have not yet attained great potency, they nevertheless have more influence on governments than the unorganized generality of consumers. This helps to explain why the experiences of the sixties failed to create social forces to make a more radically liberalizing approach to economic probems politically advantageous.

Perhaps the most obvious illustration of the point relates to the possibility of improving the efficiency of manufacturing. Chapter 8 showed that a large proportion of manufacturing industry was highly inefficient and would remain so even with improved capacity utilization and a more realistic exchange rate.[74] Chapter 11 showed that little was done about this after 1966 except for a politically costless policy of increasing the supply of imported materials and spares. To raise the efficiency of the manufacturing sector would have involved some major reorientations, including closure in the most hopeless cases, but to force that kind of change could only have been a politically thankless task, evoking strong resistance from trade unions and business interests. The general public paid the price of industrial inefficiency, being offered heavily protected, high-cost, low-quality substitutes.[75] But there was, and is, no effective consumer lobby in Ghana, nor a sophisticated public opinion on such matters. Thus a government contemplating a rationalization of industrial protection could expect strong resistance and few electoral compensations. The same could be said of government attempts to sell, close or rationalize public enterprises, the

348 DEVELOPMENT ECONOMICS IN ACTION

managements and labour forces of which had by 1966 become large enough to be of some political potency.[76] Moreover, Ghanaian private business interests were neither strong nor well regarded by the civil service, reducing pressure from those who might have benefited most from disengagement by the state.[77] That some of the most ill-considered public enterprises lingered on unmolested after 1966 is not, after all, so surprising; more noteworthy, perhaps, was the closure of state farms and the reduction of surplus labour in other public projects.

Much the same could be said of import controls, with the benefits concentrated among those fortunate enough to do well out of the allocation of licences and the costs much more widely diffused. (In this case, though, the controls were dismantled, despite resistance from particularist groups.[78]) And who except an unholy alliance of trading houses and a few academic economists could be in favour of removing price controls?

The Busia government's approach to the distribution of income unnecessarily aggravated the political difficulties of transition. Basing their policies on the mistaken view that urban-rural income inequalities were widening and ought to be narrowed, their stress on rural development and imposition of tax measures which hit the urban proletariat created resentment which was all the stronger for being based on genuine economic grievances.[79] To tell urban labourers trying to make do on a minimum wage which had never been generous and was worth only half what it had been a decade earlier that they were 'simply the less well-off members of a relatively wealthy urban minority . . .' contributed to a political climate in the towns which made the task of military usurpers all the easier.

Thus, economic and political factors conspired to produce a kind of *immobilisme* after 1966 and they will continue to have that tendency. Yet it is all too clear that *immobilisme* in Ghana is a precise synonym for more stagnation, so how can Ghana escape from this box?

Escape Routes
Possibly that question is based upon an invalid premise: that when all the costs and benefits are weighed, Ghanaians will wish to escape. To repeat, many of the apparent conflicts between economic objectives in the sixties – growth, employment, economic independence – arose essentially out of tensions between the interests of present and future generations. How can one decide on the time preferences of the Ghanaian people? In democratic theory that is the task of political processes, but that theory is largely irrelevant in present-day Ghana. The issue is rather one of national leadership. By whatever means, and with whatever claims to legitimacy, leadership emerges, it invariably names economic development among its primary objectives. The seriousness of such a claim is to be judged by the time preferences

which the leadership displays in the everyday decisions of state. A leader who succeeded where Nkrumah failed in marrying charisma with realism could successfully reconcile the competing claims of the present and future, but would require qualities which have not so far been conspicuous in Ghanaian politics and which political instability has done nothing to encourage.

If political leadership is seen as the critical variable, what kind of ideology might it embrace? First, a nationalist one, which will remain a *sine qua non* of political legitimacy for a long time, to consolidate a new nation whose solidarity through thick and thin cannot yet be taken for granted, and which would be brought under stress in the course of modernization.[80] But the term 'nationalism' does not take us much further, except to assert that policies should primarily be based upon the pursuit of Ghana's national interest (qualified, possibly, by the spirit of pan-Africanism). A wide variety of policies can be claimed as nationalistic and nationalism can have positive or negative effects on economic development.[81] Nkrumah's nation-building successes notwithstanding, the forms which nationalism took during the sixties had unnecessarily negative effects, partly due to the style of Nkrumah and his party. Although it had some of the characteristics of a mass party, the CPP had a highly centralized structure and was not organized to mobilize the economic potential of a participatory nationalism.[82] Nkrumah's government chose rather to stifle local participation by destroying democratic local government and voluntary co-operatives.[83] This was a personal rather than an organizational defect, originating in Nkrumah's own authoritarian style of leadership,[84] although governments which followed were also centralist,[85] just as colonial administrations had been earlier. One consequence of this history has been to create an attitude on the part of many Ghanaians which regards the central government as a universal provider, and state property as fair game for anyone who can make away with some.

To tap the economic potential of nationalism, the leadership of which we have spoken would do well to adopt a more participatory style.[86]

if nationalism is not made explicit, if it is not enriched and deepened by a very rapid transformation into a consciousness of social and political needs, in other words into humanism, it leads up a blind alley. The bourgeois leaders of underdeveloped countries imprison national consciousness in sterile formalism. It is only when men and women are included on a vast scale in enlightened and fruitful work that form and body are given to that consciousness. Then the flag and the palace where sits the government cease to be the symbols of the nation.

Then, perhaps, the enthusiasm and hope engendered by the successful struggle for political independence could be rekindled and harnessed constructively. To repeat, the trick is to adopt a strategy which harnesses the positive aspects of nationalism in the cause of development, rather than to perceive them as opposed objectives.

But this scarcely represents a development programme; there remain many unanswered questions about future policies, including the 'command versus market economy' controversy. No attempt will be made here to map out a comprehensive programme but one or two general principles may be suggested.

Nkrumah's strategy may be characterized as one which demanded large inputs of Ghana's scarcest resources: foreign exchange, capital, modern knowledge and skills, efficient potical decision-making capabilities, an effectual public administration, good information flows. An alternative principle speaks for itself: take what is there – abundant supplies of land and unskilled labour, and an economically responsive population – fashion a strategy based upon the maximum utilization of these attributes, and recognise the constraints which set the limits of effective action. Some of the implications are obvious: a strategy which builds upon and modernizes the traditional rather than imposing an alien technology; a strategy which gives more prominence to agriculture than Nkrumah did; a strategy which seeks always for the highest degree of labour intensity consistent with economic efficiency, and one which seeks always to ensure that activities are based upon local rather than imported resources; a strategy which, instead of defying the constraints, gives priority to removing or loosening them. These features scarcely need elaboration. Nor does the point that it is this type of strategy which offers the best chances of reconciling growth, equity, employment and economic independence; what we have just outlined is redistribution through growth.

But the same general principle also has clear implications for the role of the state. This study has argued that the state was an inefficient agent of modernization, with limited capacity to raise the standard of its own performance, that political processes resulted in a low quality of economic decision-making and may continue to do so, and that there is little realistic prospect of satisfying the enormous informational needs of an approach based upon centralized decision-making. If this is accepted, it follows that the state has tried to do too much and ought to attempt less. The point is not doctrinal, derived from an inbred distrust of the state; it is an obvious answer to the question, which kind of approach is the most realistic? It rejects the illusion that the power of the state is limitless, and is derived from an attitude similar to that urged by Mensah when he was trying to clarify what he meant by a 'pragmatic socialist':[87]

> Pragmatism would refer to two features of our programme. In the first place it would limit itself to the solution of a manageable

number of practical problems and in the second place it would observe the existing boundaries to practical action.

There is, of course, no question of a strategy of laissez-faire. Market imperfections, social injustices and the entrepreneurial gap eliminate that as neither practicable nor desirable. What is advocated is a reduced *degree* of intervention, a greater willingness to let the market do what it is being prevented from doing, a concentration of the resources of the state on a 'manageable number of practical problems'. This would specifically include much less dependence on direct controls and a reduction in the degree of state participation in the productive and service sectors. More positively, it would include policies designed to improve the operation of markets and to eliminate the grosser inefficiencies created during the sixties.

There is no point in pretending that this kind of pragmatism is ideologically neutral; it can satisfy no purist, right or left, and reducing the role of the state would be particularly alien to those who consider themselves of the left. But it is urged that pragmatism need not be incompatible with the ideology of a government which recognizes that its prospects of building the society which it desires will depend upon the efficiency with which it proceeds – the costs it imposes and the benefits it creates. What is surely clear is that there is no necessary connection between socialism and the policy instruments which Nkrumah chose to employ. This is not merely because there are many different definitions of socialism,[88] but also because the results achieved by these instruments had little to do with anyone's definition of socialism. Price controls which were supposed to protect the poor operated to the advantage of the rich; public enterprises were given no coherent social goals and were not effectively accountable to the people's representatives.

That the state must remain important is emphasized by a plea for the formulation of and steady adherence to, a package of policies which is viewed as a consistent, reinforcing programme. There are several advantages to a programme approach, as distinct from a set of separately considered *ad hoc* measures, even though each may be sound in itself. It can more easily provide for the interaction of separate policy instruments, such as the co-ordination of short-term economic management with longer-run development measures, or the consistency of measures relating to domestic and external probems. It can substantially ease the economic problems of transition discussed in the previous section, by providing for a succession of smaller measures rather than a few discontinuous jumps. And, by making each policy move a component of a larger scheme, it can diminish the force of 'second-best' arguments about the 'futility of piecemeal welfare economics.'

Again, steady adherence to a well-formulated programme would reduce the frequent occurrence of seemingly arbitrary changes of policy. Private businessmen may have been unsettled at least as much by the unpredictability of Nkrumah's government as by its espousal of public ownership.[89] Similar problems remained after Nkrumah, for although the previous chapter argued that there was much overall continuity of economic policy, there were also frequent changes in specific policy variables, such as tariff rates and import policies, a tendency facilitated by the British tradition of annual budgets. If instruments are used to influence decisions in the private sector they will only be effective – the elasticities will only be substantial – if the new signals are accepted as a reliable guide to the future. There is not likely to be much response if it is expected that the policy, even the government, will change again soon. Consider the experiences of a would-be exporter. In 1967 he was offered a new exchange rate seeming to offer a better deal, but discovered that it still discouraged exports and that it was rather quickly eroded by domestic inflation. Then the 1969 budget promised him an export bonus, which failed to materialize.[90] Eighteen months later a scheme was finally put into effect, but within the year it had been abolished because of the December 1971 devaluation. Our exporter was faced with a new set of signals. But not for long. Six weeks later the currency was revalued and not long after that a new export bonus scheme was introduced.[91] Could our exporter depend on its continued existence in making his investment decisions? He could not be blamed for being chary of this new inducement.

A Second Look at Mainstream Development Economics
The starting point of this book was the thesis that the development strategy adopted by Nkrumah had many affinities with the major policy recommendations of mainstream development economics. If Ghana's experiences represent a case study of applied development economics, what conclusions may we draw from those experiences for the economic theory of development?

Subject to the qualification that one should not generalize from a single observation, from the review of Nkrumah's strategy earlier in this chapter, elaborated in the main body of the study, it is not difficult to derive a critique of the ideas surveyed in chapter 2. Several of the points are becoming familiar in the recent literature on economic development, as a result of similar disappointments in other low-income countries. The excessive pessimism of a 'low-level equilibrium trap' analysis of the problems of low-income countries; the perils of a big investment push; the limitations of an import-substitution, closed-economy strategy – these are points which are now widely acknowledged. There is no point in treading this ground once more, but there are a few additional conclusions to be drawn which may, perhaps, be a little less familiar.

Firstly, it should be made more explicit than it has been in the past that the creation of disequilibria as stimuli to economic development implies a challenge-and-response model of interactions,[92] and that the *social systems, political processes and economic structures of low-income countries may often prevent adequate responses.* It has often been argued that large disequilibria are necessary because responses (elasticities) are insufficient to obtain acceptable results from small (marginal) inducements. On the contrary, it may be much easier to respond to new opportunities arising organically, as it were, from the existing economic system, rather than to artificially created imbalances imposed from without and owing little to local resources, knowledge or skills.

Secondly, I would stress the aridity of conceiving economic modernization as consisting essentially of the replication of past patterns of development. It is bad logic, poor history and unimaginative economics to extrapolate past experiences to form policy recommendations, not only because the developments of the past, having shaped present-day circumstances, are thereby affecting the opportunities and choices of today's low-income countries. Writers have rightly stressed the potential for developing countries of the discoveries of the last two centuries; but what has emerged here is the impotence of a technology transplanted into an environment which is quite different from the one in which the techniques were developed. The chief lesson to be drawn from historical and contemporary experiences is the crucial role of innovation in the development process – utilizing scientific advances, relating them to newly perceived economic opportunities, and *adapting them to local circumstances.* Organic development–growing from and improving upon what already exists; depending as much upon the expansion of existing productive units as upon the creation of new ones – has more to offer than an imitative concept of modernization which confuses technical with economic excellence.

Thirdly, the results of this study have served to emphasize the dangers of simplistic distinctions between the intrinsic merits of a given economic strategy and the efficiency with which it is executed. In the case of Ghana, the inefficiency of its implementation could not be distinguished from the strategy itself, which made such large administrative, informational and other demands that poor execution was inevitable, and consequently inseparable from the strategy. A further implication is that the absorptive capacity of an economy for productive investment is the product of a complex of elements, going beyond the conventional stress on the availability of co-operant factors of production, such as natural resources and an appropriately skilled labour force. Particularly in the public sector, it also concerns the political-institutional framework within which projects are identified, evaluated, constructed and managed; the motives, penalties and incentives which impinge upon those activities; the efficiency of the capital market; and the availability and allocation of foreign exchange. On a similar tack, the Ghanaian experience demonstrates the rather severe limitations of a view which sees human capital formation largely in terms of formal education. On-the-job experience gained in the context of systems of discipline, reward and promotion which reinforce productive motivations is also a key element. As with physical, so with human capital formation: it will not vitalize an economy in a social context antithetical to improving productivity.

Fourthly, there are no short-cuts. No better example could be given of the dangers of an attractive but ill-chosen analogy than the enormous influence exerted by the notion of a take-off into self-sustaining growth. The analogy, it seems to me, is wholly inappropriate, seeming to offer quick rewards and almost effortless progress on the strength of a herculean once-and-for-all effort to gain momentum. In truth, it is a notion no longer fashionable in the literature but its impact on the world of affairs remains lively. Ghanaians paid dearly for the influence of this view of development.

Fifthly, we should be suspicious of arguments to the effect that production and welfare losses arising from the misallocation of resources are generally small, by comparison with the effects of dynamic growth.[93] This study has emphasized that Nkrumah's highly imperfect allocations of capital and other resources not only imposed heavy costs in the short run but gravely reduced the *dynamic* potential of the resources he invested – resources which could have been used otherwise. Today's misallocation is tomorrow's slow growth.

Sixthly, I have tried to show how impossible it is to choose economic policies in a political vacuum, and how important non-economic factors are likely to be in the eventual outcome. This was important, for instance, in explaining the ineffectuality of planning and controls, and the course of events after Nkrumah had been deposed, with political and economic factors interacting to inhibit policy changes that seemed rather obviously desirable. Social factors were also seen to have a large bearing upon the elasticity of the economy and public administration in the face of manifest needs for improvements. This not only underscores the familiar point that an adequate theory of economic development must comprehend non-economic variables;[94] but also that the influence of planners and advisers who formulate 'optimal' economic policies without adequate reference to political realities will at best be small, and at worst mischievous.

Lastly, the common assumption that economic policy instruments are highly potent in the process of development deserves to be questioned. The strategy of mainstream development economics was a 'policy-intensive' one, diminishing the influence of the market and depending heavily upon state intervention, and even the more recent literature remains heavily oriented to policy questions. In Ghana, various policy instruments were tried, but were often ineffectual or dysfunctional, even though, among African countries, Ghana stood a better chance than most of making interventionism work. The frequently large gap in Ghana between the theoretical merits and practical achievements of a given policy is a universal tendency, deriving from a failure to recognize limitations on governmental power. It is perhaps an ironic conclusion to a study of policies to urge that there is far more to development than getting policies right.

NOTES

[1] *See* Foster and Zolberg, 1971; Woronoff, 1972; and Eshag and Richards, 1967.

[2] Rimmer, 1969, pp. 202–3 and *passim.*

[3] An unpublished draft by Chenery *et al.,* 1973, provides data showing six developing countries in which the growth rate of the GNP of the poorest 40 per cent of the population was slower than the overall growth of GNP, and another six in which the poorest 40 per cent did better than the average, and concludes that 'we do not really know what relationship exists between growth and income distribution'.

[4] I have borrowed the term from Chenery *et al.,* op cit. There is the further point argued by Crosland, 1956, Chapter XIII, that so long as some benefits of growth are enjoyed by the poor, felt, as distinct from objective, inequalities tend to diminish, and with it some of the political heat which surrounds the equity issue.

[5] One is reminded of the debate among economic historians about whether the British industrial revolution was associated with a decline in working-class living standards. The debate is entirely about short-run effects; in the longer term the beneficial effects are not in doubt.

[6] A number of writers have found productivity growth and employment to be positively correlated.

[7] Assume it was possible to raise the current level of employment by 5 per cent by measures which, by reducing saving and investment, reduced the future expansion of employment by 1 per cent annually. Ceteris paribus, the total volume of employment would be smaller by the end of the fifth year.

[8] *See* Manning Nash in Johnson (ed.), 1967, citing the Mexican example.

[9] *See* Kraus in Foster and Zolberg, 1971, p. 71; and Apter, 1973, chapter 15.

[10] *See* Grayson, 1972, who cites other examples of 'forced breeding' of indigenous entrepreneurs.

[11] For a forceful statement of this point of view *see* Berg in Foster and Zolberg, 1971.

[12] *See* Killick, 1966, Table 14.11.

[13] At the time of writing the government of Ghana is negotiating with foreign aluminium interests for the creation of a jointly-owned bauxite and alumina industry, and various companies are prospecting for oil.

[14] Wallich, 1958.

[15] Fiscal projections prepared in 1971 by the Ministry of Finance to the mid-seventies predicted current deficits in each year, getting larger over time, in the absence of major tax and expenditure policy changes.

[16] Balance of payments projections prepared in late 1971 indicate that the exchange rate established by the 1972 revaluation will lead to continuing long-term balance of payments difficulties, although a different result might be indicated if there was a favourable response to the export bonus scheme subsequently restored by the NRC, or if world cocoa prices were to remain at the extraordinary heights they reached in 1973–4.

[17] The type of argument outlined below is quite commonly heard in Ghana, and some elements of it are presented by Genoud, 1969, *passim,* and Hymer, 1971.

[18] Nkrumah stressed the unfavourable situation he inherited from the British: 'Those who would judge us by the heights we have achieved would do well to remember the depths from which we started.' (Nkrumah, 1968, p. 76). We might also record a more ideological type of argument, that Nkrumah failed because of a mistaken view that he could succeed on the basis of a mixed economy and 'without engaging in a life and death struggle' with the private sector (see Fitch and Oppenheimer, 1966, p. 113 and passim).

[19] See Foster, 1965, p. 296, for this type of argument.

[20] Professor Arthur Lewis, who served as his economic adviser for some years, says that Nkrumah practically rejected the word 'impossible' (Uphoff, 1970, p. 293).

[21] 'But the most striking flaw in the regime's responsiveness was Nkrumah's inability and unwillingness to demand accountability from those with responsibility or to exact some measure of discipline. The latter was the most elusive element in Nkrumah's rule and personal political behaviour' (Kraus, 1971, p. 62).

[22] The rationale I have in mind here is essentially one found in the writings of Hirschman (1958, and especially 1971, pp. 14–21), although he was no advocate of a big push view of development, seeking instead to develop a model of development operating through the creation of disequilibria at a more micro-economic level. His writings receive more attention in this chapter than those of others whose ideas were surveyed in chapter 2 because his more explicit and suggestive treatment of the interaction of political and economic forces is of particular interest for present purposes.

[23] The Valco management was inclined to boast that its plant was the most advanced and automated aluminium smelter ever built. On the economics of the smelter see Killick, 1966, pp. 401–10.

[24] Pozen, 1972, provides an interesting study of the inappropriate importation of legal 'technology' in Ghana and ways in which its actual working differed from the model upon which it was based. He makes the point that 'the process of remoulding corporate charters fostered an illusion of social change within Ghana, thereby diverting attention from the underlying problems . . .' (p. 844). There was, both during and after the Nkrumah period, a strong penchant for creating new bodies, re-naming others, and passing new laws irrespective of their enforceability, thereby erecting a facade of activity and progress while underneath little was changing.

[25] Myint, 1972, chapter 1, surveys the experiences of south-east Asian countries in the sixties and draws as his main conclusion 'the close connection between the economic development of the South-east Asian countries and the expansion of their exports and . . . how their domestic economic policies can help or hinder the process of export expansion' (p. 35). See Little et al., 1970, passim on the effects of inward-looking import substitution policies on the balance of payments and economic development.

[26] Hirschman, 1971, pp. 16–17; and 1967, chapter 2 and passim.

[27] Data obtained from annual budget estimates. The comparable figure for 1959 was twenty-nine senior staff. Between these years the average number of miles for which each senior officer was responsible rose from 155 to 289 miles.

[28] Nathan Sector Studies, General Report on Transportation, p. 49.

[29] Bezanson, 1973B, p. 65 and passim. He shows that the public sector absorbed about 88 per cent of the 1969 and 1970 outputs of the universities, a proportion which falls to 49 per cent if teachers are excluded (pp. 35–6).

[30] The soldiers drilled unpunctual officials outside their offices in the period immediately after the 1972 coup, sometimes rather severely, although the campaign was not sustained for long. The quotation is from West Africa, 1 September 1972.

[31] Price, 1971.

[32] Fifteen per cent of his civil servant respondents could find nothing at all good to say about the service, and only nine per cent stated that they would recommend a civil service career. Overwhelmingly the most frequent point given in favour of the

service was that it provided security. ibid., pp. 336, 351, and *passim.*

[33] Mensah, 1970, p. 1.

[34] Price, 1971, pp. 399–403, suggests changes in personnel policy which would improve matters but expresses doubt whether his suggestions would be accepted and enforced by the service. On the possibility of more effective discipline he states (p. 386), 'this is a contradiction in terms – the civil service is valued for the security it affords its members precisely because its internal incentive system is structured so as not to permit the manipulation of sanctions that would make the poor performer insecure.' Certainly, the service was successful in resisting Busia's attempts to tighten up discipline.

[35] One factor making for this result, as Goody points out, is that defeated (or deposed) politicians often have few employment alternatives, which increases the pressure upon them to do the popular thing, even though it may be unwise from a longer-run viewpoint (*see* Goody, 1968, p. 349).

[36] *Daily Graphic,* 18 March 1972.

[37] The studies of import and price controls which comprise chapter 10 originated, together with specific recommendations, as policy documents for the NRC in the first half of 1972, but were ignored. Later evidence suggests that many of the defects revealed in chapter 10 have duly reappeared.

[38] Green, 1971, p. 263.

[39] Lewis, 1965, pp. 23–4.

[40] During 1970 a substantial number of civil servants were dismissed under a special constitutional provision, and several of these promptly established themselves as businessmen. A similar development that has occurred in recent years is for relatively well-to-do urban dwellers to invest in substantial farms where a variety of improved practices are employed. Nkrumah's feat in depriving the traditional chiefs of much more than symbolic authority appears to have been a permanent reform and has much to do with the modernity of the new élite which emerged to replace the chiefs.

[41] *See* Knight, 1972, and Gill and Omaboe, 1963.

[42] Foster, 1965, p. 294.

[43] ibid., pp. 274 and 282–3; and Peil, 1972, p. 45.

[44] *See* Hill, 1963, especially chapter 1; and Szereszewski, 1965, especially chapter 5.

[45] *See* Killick, 1966, p. 377, for a brief survey of the findings of some of these.

[46] Nyanteng and van Apeldoorn, 1971, pp. 116–17, found that in response to an increase in the price of a particular crop, farmers were likely to increase their output of all crops, as a risk-spreading device. They also found farmers to be well informed about prices, except in the most inaccessible villages. Uphoff, 1970, p. 334, cites reports of positive farmer responses to suggested improvements in cultivation techniques so long as they promised to be profitable, and C. K. Brown, 1972, p. 41, found the beneficiaries of agricultural extension services to be much more likely to introduce innovations than farmers who had not sought or received this type of assistance. Further work by Hill, 1970, chapters 3–5, on the cattle trade and fishermen, similarly demonstrates responsiveness to financial incentives.

[47] Joseph J. Stern conducted a study of the elasticity of sales to the Diamond Marketing Corporation by small-scale diggers for January 1968 to August 1971 and obtained an elasticity of $2 \cdot 16$ ($R^2 = 0 \cdot 38$). The large value of this elasticity reflects switches between sales to the Corporation and illicit smuggling to other West African countries, rather than changes in production, but again suggests the Ghanaian to be a maximizer. I am grateful to Dr Stern for this information.

[48] *See* chapter 10, Part II, for evidence that the retail trading system is flexible and competitive. Mention might also be made of the enterprise with which lorry owners and taxi drivers have responded to the inadequacies of the urban public transport systems. Beckman, 1973A, pp. 9–11, shows how Ghanaians began to fill the vacuum left by the withdrawal of expatriate companies from cocoa buying, until frustrated by the grant of a monopoly in this trade to the Farmers' Council.

[49] Price, 1971, *passim;* and Garlick, 1971, p. 100.

[50] *See* Fortes, 1971, pp. 13–14, and Kilby and Hill, cited by Garlick, p. 100.

[51] Hirschman, 1971, p. 314.

[52] *See* a discussion of this by Dadson, 1970, pp. 62–3.

[53] Blanchard, 1971, p. 23.

[54] Owusu, 1970, p. 250.

[55] Garlick, p. 146.

[56] Peil, 1972, p. 118.

[57] Foster, 1965, Tables 32 and 33, found businessmen to rank eighth out of twenty-five occupations, below secondary school teachers and clergymen. He also found status rankings generally to be strongly correlated with perceived income (R=0·92 for boys and 0·87 for girls) but that, especially among boys, the status of businessmen was well below what would have been predicted from the incomes they were thought to receive.

[58] Garlick, pp. 111–12, 139 and 116 respectively. Along similar lines, the Chairman of the National Redemption Council complained that many Ghanaian limited liability companies existed only in name: 'Your operations are so personalised that it becomes almost impossible to survive in your absence. It is a sad fact that most Ghanaian enterprises have failed to survive the lives of their founder precisely for this reason.' (Reported in *West Africa,* 8 January 1973.)

[59] Killick, 1972–3, records the rather unsuccessful early attempts to provide loan finance to Ghanaian businessmen, which were persistently misused as a source of political patronage; a similar scheme ran into the same difficulties in the early seventies – *see* statement by S. O. Mensah in *Daily Graphic,* 8 January 1972, and an article in *The Spokesman* of 22 February 1972.

[60] Garlick, p. 151; also Schatz, 1968, and Kilby, 1969, chapter 10.

[61] Hakam, 1972. Harris, 1970, also takes a more positive view, discussing the Nigerian situation.

[62] *See* Lawson, 1967, p. 19, for a brief biography of one of these.

[63] For reasons given in chapter 4, it seems probable, however, that this gap narrowed and perhaps disappeared during the sixties (*see* pp. 82–3).

[64] Killick, 1966, pp. 279–80.

[65] The *Industrial Statistics, 1969* records a total of seventy manufacturing industries (at the four-digit level) in that year, containing an average of five establishments (note that more than one establishment may belong to a single company). A few of these industries, such as those making clothing, contain a relatively large number of establishments, so the average for the remainder must have been well below five.

[66] Marshall observed that the best of all monopoly profits may be a quiet life; a monopolist may be less responsive to new opportunities than the businessman in a highly competitive activity.

[67] Economic hardships were important factors in the timing of both the 1966 and 1972 coups, a fact which has put future governments on notice that somehow they must achieve better economic performance without squeezing the consumer further.

[68] The NRC was speaking nothing less than the truth when it stated that 'Several years of economic mismanagement and maladministration, corruption and nepotism, social injustice and exploitation, disappointment and frustration have shattered the dreams and expectations of Ghanaians.' (NRC *Charter,* 1973, p. 4). On returning to Ghana in 1973 it seemed to me that this judgment was beginning to apply to the NRC itself. *See also* Kilson, 1971, pp. 121–2.

[69] The general theorem of the second-best states that 'if there is introduced into a general equilibrium system a constraint which prevents the attainment of one of the Paretian conditions [of optimality], the other Paretian conditions, although still attainable, are, in general, no longer desirable.' (*See* Lipsey and Lancaster, 1956–57, pp. 11 and 17; also Fishlow and David, 1961.)

[70] I particularly have in mind here the effects of exchange and price controls and of the misallocation of resources through the government budget, which stood to receive

a large transfer of resources as a result of the devaluation. *See* Leith, 1973, chapter 5, for a discussion of the policy failings which undermined the 1967 devaluation.

[71] Recall that the introduction of import controls was justified to Parliament as 'a weapon of economic sovereignty'.

[72] It was from this stance that Busia in 1953 said of the planned Volta river project, 'it is against our interest as a nation to mortgage our entire economic future between the benevolence of the British and the restraint of the aluminium company,' (*Legislative Assembly Debates,* 23 February 1953, p. 498).

[73] Genoud, 1969, p. 228.

[74] Steel, 1972, Table VI, shows that even with a 50 per cent 'shadow' premium on foreign exchange and complete utilization of capacity about 43 per cent of total manufacturing output would still be 'inefficient' in terms of domestic resource costs.

[75] Ghanaians popularly describe locally fabricated import substitutes as 'made in here', an expression employed in a derogatory fashion. Local officials tend to describe the preference of the consumers for imported goods as irrational, but I suspect it is firmly based on comparative qualities of local and foreign goods.

[76] Pozen, 1972, p. 825, mentions that by 1968 the managing directors of public corporations had joined together to form their own lobby, although he also mentions an example in which they were unsuccessful in influencing government policy.

[77] *See* Esseks, 1971, *passim.*

[78] For example, there were pressures from within Busia's Progress Party resistant to the abolition of import licences for fish and other items.

[79] The chief of these tax measures was the National Development Levy, in effect an addition to the income tax, introduced in the 1971 budget. The Trade Union Congress was strongly opposed to this measure and its attempts to organize opposition led the Busia government to pass legislation abolishing the Congress.

[80] Paradoxically, continued stagnation would also be liable to introduce increasing political tensions, with the danger that tribal groupings would polarize as groups became more and more preoccupied with the sharing-out of national income.

[81] Rostow, 1960, pp. 26–7, draws attention to some of the positive effects. For useful essays on the economic effects of nationalism *see* Johnson (ed.), 1967.

[82] On the nature of the CPP, *see* Austin, 1964, chapter 1. Also Fitch and Oppenheimer: 'It was not a mass party in the sense of mobilizing large numbers of people and bringing them into the political arena as active and politically conscious participants. Many of the men and women who bought membership cards in the CPP did so for the same reasons that citizens in the United States buy tickets to a policeman's ball. In both cases, the sale involves a tax levied on the vulnerable by the powerful,' (p. 107).

[83] Beckman, 1973A, pp. 8–9.

[84] It is surely not without significance that on the opening page of his autobiography, published in 1957, Nkrumah quoted the following lines from Walt Whitman:
'Who is he that would become my follower?
Who would sign himself a candidate for my affections?
The way is suspicious, the result uncertain, perhaps destructive,
You would have to give up all else, I alone would expect
     to be your sole and exclusive standard,
Your novitiate would even be long and exhausting,
Your whole past theory of your life and all conformity to the lives
     around you would have to be abandon'd.'
Scarcely any leader could have been more explicit about his arrogance, not to say megalomania. Note also the presumption of the title he chose for his autobiography: *Ghana.*

[85] During the NLC period there was some attempt at a decentralization of decision-making, along lines recommended in the *Mills-Odoi Report,* but it quickly became apparent that the Busia government had little liking for the idea, and the NRC seems even more centralist in its thinking.

[86] Fanon, 1968, p. 204.
[87] Mensah, 1971. All too characteristically, it is clear from the context in which this passage occurs that Mensah did not intend it to be applied to the role of the state!
[88] President Nyerere of Tanzania is arguably just as serious about socialism as Nkrumah was, but his understanding of that ideology has led him to emphasize agriculture and labour-intensity, and to reject large-scale industrialization, central planning and control (*see* Helleiner, 1972B, particularly pp. 187-8).
[89] Garlick, 1971, p. 128.
[90] *Budget Statement, 1969/70,* pp. 17–19.
[91] The revaluation occurred on 7 February 1972 and the new export bonus came into force in September 1972 (*see* Export Bonus Decree, 1973; NRCD 148). It was to be paid at the rate of 20 per cent of gross export earnings as compared with 25 per cent under the 1971 scheme.
[92] Hirschman has been the most explicit on this point but, while he has stressed that there is nothing automatic or inevitable about the emergence of agents of change who will break the bottlenecks, the general thrust of his writings does appear to rest upon the premise that, in the general case, there will be an adequate response (*see* especially Hirschman, 1971, chapter 1).
[93] *See* Fishlow and David, 1961, for an example of this kind of conclusion, and Leibenstein, 1966, for an interesting criticism of the methodology of studies of this type.
[94] Among recent writings, Myrdal's *Asian Drama,* 1968, most fully mirrors a growing consciousness of the large importance of non-economic forces in the development process.

Bibliography of Works Cited

For reports of the various commissions/committees of enquiry *see* under *Report*, except for the *Amamoo Report* which is listed under *Government Policies towards the State Gold Mining Corporation*.

Government of Ghana Publications
Auditor-General, *Reports on the Accounts of Ghana*, Government Printer, Accra, periodic issues.
Bank of Ghana, *Annual Reports*, Accra, annually, commencing 1958.
Bank of Ghana, *Quarterly Economic Bulletin*, Accra, quarterly.
Census Office, *1960 Population Census of Ghana*, various volumes, Central Bureau of Statistics, Accra.
Census Office, *1970 Population Census of Ghana*, Vol. II, Central Bureau of Statistics, Accra, 1972.
Central Bureau of Statistics, *Annual Trade Reports*, Accra, periodical.
Central Bureau of Statistics, *Directory of Industrial Establishments*, Accra, September 1969.
Central Bureau of Statistics, *Economic Survey*, Government Printer, Accra, annual series.
Central Bureau of Statistics, *Industrial Statistics*, CBS, Accra, periodical series.
Central Bureau of Statistics, *External Trade Statistics*, Accra, monthly.
Central Bureau of Statistics, *Labour Statistics*, Accra, annual series.
Central Bureau of Statistics, *Motor Vehicle Statistics*, Government Printer, Accra, annual series.
Central Bureau of Statistics, *Statistical Handbook, 1969*, Accra, 1969.
Central Bureau of Statistics, *Statistical Newsletter*, mimeo, periodical, Accra.
Central Bureau of Statistics, *Statistical Year Books*, 1961, 1962, 1965–6, 1967–8, Accra.
Commissioner for Economic Affairs (E. N. Omaboe), *Developments in the Ghanaian Economy between 1960 and 1968*, Government Printer, Accra, June 1969.

Commissioner of Finance (J. H. Mensah), *Budget Statement for 1969–70*, Government Printer, Accra, 1969.

Development Planning Secretariat, *High Level and Skilled Manpower Survey in Ghana – 1968 and Assessment of Manpower Situation (1971)*, Accra, December 1971.

Gold Coast Agricultural Development Corporation, *First Report and Accounts, 1955–56*, Accra, 1957.

Government of Ghana, *Ghana Gazette*, Accra, periodical.

Government of Ghana, *One-year Development Plan: July 1970 to June 1971*, Government Printer, Accra, September 1970.

Government of Ghana, *Second Development Plan, 1959–64*, Government Printer, Accra, 1959.

Government of Ghana, *Sessional Address* (by Brig. A. A. Afrifa), Ghana Publishing Corporation, Accra, October 1969.

Government Policies Towards the State Gold Mining Corporation, a report by an inter-departmental committee under the chairmanship of the Hon. J. G. Amamoo, M.P., mimeo, Accra, May 1971 (the '*Amamoo Report*').

Labour Department, *Employment Market Situation Report*, mimeo, Accra, monthly.

Legislative Assembly Debates, see under Parliament.

Manpower Unit, *Survey of High-level Manpower in Ghana, 1960*, Government Printer, Accra, 1961.

Minister of Finance (F. K. D. Goka), *1963–4 Budget Statement*, Accra, October 1963.

Minister of Finance (K. Amoako-Atta), *1965 Supplementary Budget Statement*, Accra, 10 September 1965.

Minister of Finance (K. Amoaka-Atta), *1966 Budget Statement*, Accra, 1966.

Minister of Finance (J. H. Mensah), *Budget Statement of 1971–2*, Government Printer, Accra, July 1971.

Ministry of Agriculture, *Report on Ghana Sample Census of Agriculture, 1970*, Government Printer, Accra (two volumes), 1972, 1973.

Ministry of Finance, *The Budget, 1965*, Government Printer, Accra, 1965.

Ministry of Finance, *The Budget, 1966–7*, Accra, 1966.

Ministry of Finance, *Financial Statement*, issued annually with the budget, Accra.

Ministry of Finance, *Foreign Exchange Budget, 1966*, Accra, 1966.

National Investment Bank, *Evaluation Report: State Cannery Corporation*, mimeo, Accra, 1968 ('*NIB Cannery Report*').

National Investment Bank, *Evaluation Report: State Footwear Corporation*, mimeo, Accra, May 1968 ('*NIB Footwear Report*').

National Investment Bank, *Evaluation of the State Boatyards* (partial report), mimeo, Accra, 1968 ('*NIB Boatyard Report*')

National Liberation Council, *Ghana's Economy and Aid Require-*

ments in 1968, Government Printer, Accra, 1968.

National Liberation Council, *Ghana's Economy and Aid Requirements; January 1969–June 1970*, Government Printer, Accra, March 1969.

National Liberation Council, *Ghana's Industrial Policy Statement*, Government Printer, Accra, 1968.

National Liberation Council, *New Deal for Ghana's Economy* (containing statements by Brig. A. A. Afrifa and E. N. Omaboe), State Publishing Corporation, Accra, July 1967.

National Liberation Council, *Outline of Government Economic Policy*, Government Printer, Accra, August 1967.

National Liberation Council, *Population Planning for National Progress and Prosperity*, Government Printer, Accra, March 1969.

National Liberation Council, *Rebuilding the National Economy*, Government Printer, Accra, March 1966.

National Liberation Council, *Two-year Development Plan: From Stabilization to Development: A Plan for the Period mid-1968 to mid-1970*, Government Printer, Accra, July 1968.

National Redemption Council, *Charter of the National Redemption Council*, Government Printer, Accra, n.d. (ca. January 1973).

National Redemption Council, *Outline of Ghana's Investment Policy*, State Publishing Corporation, Accra, 1973.

Office of the Planning Commission, *Annual Plan for the Second Plan Year, 1965 Financial Year*, Government Printer, Accra, 1965.

Office of the Planning Commission, *Seven-year Development Plan, 1963–4 to 1969–70*, Accra, 1964.

Office of the Prime Minister, *Report of the Housing and Town Planning Committee*, mimeo, Accra, October 1971.

Parliament, *National Assembly Debates* (official record of the proceedings of Parliament), Accra. Also referred to as *Legislative Assembly Debates* and *Parliamentary Debates*.

Public Accounts Committee of the National Assembly, First and Second Report, State Publishing Corporation, Accra, 1965.

Report of a Commission of Enquiry into Alleged Irregularities and Malpractices in Connection with the Issue of Import Licenses, Government Printer, Accra, February 1964 (*'Akainyah Report'*).

Report of the Commission Appointed to Enquire into the Function, Operations and Administration of the Workers Brigade, Ministry of Information, Accra, 1967 (*'Kom Report'*).

Report of the Commission to Enquire into the Kwame Nkrumah Properties, Ministry of Information, Accra, 1966 (*'Apaloo Report'*).

Report of the Commission of Enquiry into Irregularities and Malpractices in the Grant of Import Licenses, Ministry of Information, Accra, 1967 (*'Ollenu Report'*). *See also White Paper No. 4/67*, Accra, 1967 issued by the government commenting on the *Ollenu Report*.

Report of Commission of Enquiry into Trade Malpractices in Ghana,

Government Printer, Accra, 1965 (*'Abrahams Report'*).

Report of the Commission on the Structure and Remuneration of the Public Services in Ghana, Ministry of Information, Accra, 1967 (*'Mills-Odoi Report'*).

Report of the Committee of Enquiry on the Purchase of Cocoa, United Ghana Farmers Co-operative Council (UGFCC) during the Nkrumah Regime, Government Printer, Accra, 1966 (*'de Graft-Johnson Report'*).

Report of the Committee of Enquiry into the State Furniture and Joinery Corporation, Ministry of Information, Accra, 1967 (*'Tsegah Report'*).

Report by Fishing Consultants, *The State Fishing Corporation*, mimeo, Accra, 1969.

Report of the Investigation Team which probed the Star Publishing Company and The Guinea Press Limited, Ministry of Information, Accra, 1969 (the *'Quist Report'*).

Report of the sub-committee on Education, Manpower and Employment, National Planning Commission, mimeo, Accra, n.d. (ca 1962).

State Enterprises under the work schedule of the State Enterprises Secretariat for the period 1964–65. A report, mimeo, Accra, December 1966.

Volta River Authority, *Annual Reports*, Accra, annually.

Other Sources

Abban, J. B. and Leith, J. Clark. *Protection of Ghanaian Manufacturing Due to Tariffs and Indirect Taxes*, mimeo, Accra, n.d. (ca. 1971). (Published in Leith, 1973.)

Acheampong, Col. I. K., Chairman of the National Redemption Council. *Speeches and Interviews*, Vol. 1, Ghana Information Services, Accra, 1973.

Addo, N. O. 'Demographic Aspects of Manpower and Employment in Ghana,' *Economic Bulletin of Ghana*, 1967, no. 3.

Addo, N. O. 'Employment and Labour Supply on Ghana's Cocoa Farms in the Pre- and Post-Aliens Compliance Order Era,' *Economic Bulletin of Ghana*, 1972, No. 4.

Agarwala, A. N. and Singh, S. P. (eds.), *The Economics of Underdevelopment*, Oxford U. P., Bombay, 1958.

Ahmad, Naseem. 'Some Aspects of Bugetary Policy in Ghana,' *Economic Bulletin of Ghana*, 1966, no. 1.

Ahmad, Naseem. *Deficit Financing, Inflation and Capital Formation:*

The Ghanaian Experience, 1960–5, Weltforum Verlag, München, 1970.

Apter, David E. *The Politics of Modernization*, Chicago U.P., 1965.

Apter, David E. *Choice and the Politics of Allocation*, Yale U.P., New Haven, 1971.

Apter, David E. *C₁ ana in Transition*, Princeton U.P., 2nd revised edition 1973 (First published 1955.)

Arndt, H. W. 'Development Economics Before 1945' in Bhagwati, J. N. and Eckhaus, R. S., *Development and Planning; Essays in Honour of Paul Rosenstein-Rodan*, Allen and Unwin, London, 1972.

Ashanti Pioneer (daily newspaper), Kumasi, Ghana.

Austin, Dennis. *Politics in Ghana, 1946–60*, Oxford University Press, London, 1964.

Bahl, Roy W. 'A Representative Tax System Approach to Measuring Tax Effort in Developing Countries', IMF *Staff Papers*, March 1972.

Baran, Paul A. 'On the Political Economy of Backwardness', *Manchester School*, January 1952 (reproduced in Agarwala and Singh whose page numbers are referred to in the text).

Baran, Paul A. *The Political Economy of Growth*, Monthly Review Press, New York, 1957.

Bartels, J. E. M. *Supply Position of Copra to Esiama Copra Oil Mill (1961–9)*, Food Research Institute, mimeo, Accra, 1970.

Bauer, P. T. *West African Trade*, Routledge and Kegan Paul, London, reissued 1963.

Bauer, P. T. *Dissent on Development*, Harvard University Press, Cambridge, Mass., 1972.

Bauer, P. T. and Yamey, B. S. *The Economics of Under-developed Countries*, Cambridge U.P., 1957.

Beckman, Björn. *The Distribution of Cocoa Income, 1961–5*, Department of Economics, University of Ghana, mimeo, Legon, June 1970.

Beckman, Björn. *The Political Economy of Cocoa*, mimeo, Stockholm, 1972.

Beckman, Björn. 'The Internal Marketing Monopoly of the Farmers' Council', Paper presented to Cocoa Economics Research Conference, mimeo, University of Ghana, April 1973.

Bell, Philip W. and Todaro, Michael P. *Economic Theory: An Integrated Text with Special Reference to Tropical Africa and Other Developing Areas*, Oxford U.P., Nairobi, 1969.

Berg, Elliot J. 'Socialism and Economic Development in Tropical Africa', *Quarterly Journal of Economics*, November 1964.

Berg, Elliot J. 'Structural Transformation versus Gradualism: Recent Economic Development in Ghana and the Ivory Coast' in Foster and Zolberg (eds.), 1971.

Bezanson, Keith A. *Secondary School Leaver Research Project: Report of the Pilot Project*, mimeo, Accra, March 1971.

Bezanson, Keith A. *Survey of Middle Continuation School Leavers*, mimeo, Ministry of Education, Accra, 1973 (Bezanson 1973A).

Bezanson, Keith A. *Survey of University of Ghana Graduates*, mimeo, Ministry of Education, Accra, 1973 (Bezanson 1973B).

Bhagwati, Jagdish. 'Immiserizing Growth: A Geometrical Note', *Review of Economic Studies*, June 1958.

Bhatia, Rattan J. 'Import Programming in Ghana, 1966–9', *Finance and Development*, March 1973.

Bing, Geoffrey. *Reap the Whirlwind*, MacGibbon and Kee, London, 1968.

Birmingham, Walter, Neustadt, I. and Omaboe, E. N. (eds.), *A Study of Contemporary Ghana*: Vol. I. – *The Economy of Ghana* (1966) Vol. II. – *Some Aspects of Social Structure* (1967) Allen and Unwin, London.

Bissue, I. I. *An Appraisal of Ghana's Seven-year Development Plan*, B. Litt. thesis, Oxford University, July 1965.

Bissue, I. I. 'Ghana's Seven-year Development Plan in Retrospect', *Economic Bulletin of Ghana*, 1967, No. 1.

Blanchard, David. 'Some Problems of Increasing Output with Peasant Production Units', mimeo, Department of Economics, University of Ghana, Legon, n.d. (ca. 1971).

Blomqvist, A. G. 'Price Inflation in Ghana: A "Monetarist View",' mimeo, n.d. (ca. 1971).

Brown, C. K. *Some Problems of Investment and Innovation Confronting the Ghanaian Food Crop Farmer*, Institute of Statistical, Social and Economic Research, University of Ghana, 1972.

Brown, T. Merritt. 'Macroeconomic Data of Ghana', *Economic Bulletin of Ghana*, 1972, Nos. 1 and 2.

Bruton, Henry J. 'Growth Models and Underdeveloped Countries', *Journal of Political Economy*, August 1955.

Bruton, Henry J. *Principles of Development Economics*, Prentice Hall, New Jersey, 1965.

Bruton, Henry J. 'The Import-substitution Strategy of Economic Development: A Survey', *Pakistan Development Review*, Summer 1970.

Buxton, T. K. 'The Cash Income of Cocoa Farmers in Ghana'. Paper presented to the Cocoa Economics Research Conference, mimeo, University of Ghana, April 1973.

Cairncross, A. K. *Factors in Economic Development*, Allen and Unwin, Lor.don, 1962.

Caldwell, J. C. in Birmingham *et al.* (eds.), 1967, Chapters I to IV.

Cantor, D. *Import-replacing Industrialisation and Economic Development in Ghana*, Ph.D. thesis, Harvard University, 1966.

Chambers, Robert (ed.) *The Volta Resettlement Experience*, New York, Praeger, 1970.

Chelliah, Raja J. 'Trends in Taxation in Developing Countries', IMF *Staff Papers*, July 1971.

Chen, N. R. and Galenson, W. *The Chinese Economy under Communism*, Aldine, Chicago, 1969.

Chenery, Hollis B. 'The Interdependence of Investment Decisions' in Abramovitz *et al.*, *The Allocation of Economic Resources*, Stanford U.P., 1959.

Chenery, Hollis B. 'Patterns of Industrial Growth', *American Economic Review*, September 1960.

Chenery, Hollis B. (ed.) *Studies in Development Planning*, Harvard U.P., Cambridge, Mass., 1971.

Chenery, Hollis B., John Duloy and Richard Jolly. *Redistribution with Growth: An Approach to Policy*, unpublished draft, Washington, D.C., August 1973.

Clower, R., Dalton, M. Harwitz and Walters, A. A. *Growth without Development: An Economic Survey of Liberia*, Northwestern U.P., Evanston, 1966.

Convention People's Party. *Programme for Work and Happiness*, Government Printer, Accra, 1962. (CPP, 1962).

Coombes, David. *State Enterprise: Business or Politics*, Allen and Unwin, London, 1971.

Coppock, J. D. *International Economic Instability*, McGraw Hill, New York, 1962.

Corden, W. M. *The Theory of Protection*, Oxford U.P., London, 1971.

Crosland, C. A. R. *The Future of Socialism*, Jonathan Cape, London, 1956.

Dadson, J. A. *Socialised Agriculture in Ghana, 1962–5*, Ph.D dissertation, Harvard University, October 1970.

Daily Graphic (newspaper), Accra.

Dennison, E. F. *Why Growth Rates Differ*, Washington, 1967.

Deutsch, K. 'Social Mobilisation and Political Development', *American Political Science Review*, September 1961.

Dobb, Maurice. *An Essay of Economic Growth and Planning*, Monthly Review Press, New York, 1960.

Dobb, Maurice. *Economic Growth and Underdeveloped Countries*, Lawrence and Wishart, London, 1963.

Domar, Evsey. *Essays in the Theory of Economic Growth*, Oxford U.P., 1957.

Due, Jean M. 'Agricultural Development in the Ivory Coast and Ghana', *Journal of Modern African Studies*, 1969, No. 4.

Dumont, René. *False Start in Africa*, André Deutsch, London, 1966 (first published in French, 1962).

du Sautoy, Peter. *Community Development in Ghana*, Oxford U.P.,

London, 1958.

Dutta-Roy, D. K. *The Eastern Region Household Budget Survey*, Institute of Statistical, Social and Economic Research, University of Ghana, Legon, 1969.

The Echo (newspaper), Accra.

Eicher, Carl K. and Leidholm, Carl. *Growth and Development of the Nigerian Economy*, Michigan State U.P., 1970.

Eisenstadt, S. N. *Modernisation: Growth and Diversity*, Department of Government, Indiana University, Bloomington, 1963.

Eshag, Eprime and Richards, P. J. ' Comparison of Economic Developments in Ghana and the Ivory Coast since 1960', *Bulletin of the Oxford University Institute of Statistics*, November 1967.

Esseks, John D. 'Government and Indigenous Private Enterprise in Ghana', *Journal of Modern African Studies*, May 1971.

Ewusi, Kodwo. *The Distribution of Monetary Incomes in Ghana*, Institute of Statistical, Social and Economic Research, University of Ghana, Legon, 1971 (Ewusi, 1971A).

Ewusi, Kodwo. 'Road Transport Facilities and their Effects on Local Food Prices in the Sixties', *Economic Bulletin of Ghana*, 1971, No. 3. (Ewusi, 1971B).

Faber, Mike and Seers, Dudley (eds.). *The Crisis in Planning*, Chatto and Windus, London, 1972 (two volumes).

Fanon, Frantz. *The Wretched of the Earth*, Grove Press, New York, 1968 (first published in French in 1961).

Fei, J. C. H. and Ranis, G. *Development of the Labour Surplus Economy: Theory and Policy*, Homewood, Illinois, 1964.

Fishlow, Albert and David, Paul. 'Optimal Resource Allocation in an Imperfect Market Setting', *Journal of Political Economy*, December 1961.

Fitch, Bob and Oppenheimer, Mary. *Ghana: End of an Illusion*, Monthly Review Press, New York, 1966.

Folson, B. D. G. 'The Development of Socialist Ideology in Ghana, 1949–58', *Ghana Social Science Journal*, Vol. 1, Nos. 1 and 2, 1971.

Fordwor, Kwame Donkoh. *An Evaluation of Ghanaian State-owned Industrial Projects: A Study in Cost-Benefit Analysis*, Ph.D. dissertation, University of Pensylvania, 1971.

Fortes, Meyer. 'Some Aspects of Migration and Mobility in Ghana', *Journal of Asian and African Studies*, January 1971.

Foster, C. D. *Politics, Finance and the Role of Economics: An Essay on the Control of Public Enterprise*, Allen and Unwin, London, 1971.

Foster, Philip. *Education and Social Change in Ghana*, Chicago U.P., 1965.

Foster, Philip and Zolberg, Aristide R. (eds.). *Ghana and the Ivory Coast: Perspectives on Modernisation*, Chicago U.P., Chicago, 1971.

Frank, Charles R., Jr. 'Public and Private Enterprise in Africa' in Ranis (ed.) 1971.

Frankel, S. Herbert. *The Economic Impact on Under-developed Societies*, Blackwells, Oxford, 1953.

Friedland, William H. and Rosberg, Jr., Carl G. (eds.). *African Socialism*, Stanford U.P., 1964.

Friedmann, W. G. and J. F. Garner. *Government Enterprise: A Comparative Study*, Columbia U.P., New York, 1970.

Frimpong, J. H. S. *The Ghana Parliament, 1957–66: A Critical Analysis*, Ph.D. dissertation, Exeter University, 1970.

Frimpong-Ansah, J. H. 'Stabilisation and Development: Ghana's Experience', *Economic Bulletin of Ghana*, 1971, No. 1.

Furtado, Celso. 'Capital Formation and Economic Development', *International Economic Papers*, No. 4, 1954 (reproduced in Agarwala and Singh, 1958, whose page numbers are referred to in the text).

Gaisie, S. K. 'Estimation of vital Rates for Ghana' (publication details unknown).

Gaisie, S. K. *Dynamics of Population Growth in Ghana*, Department of Sociology, University of Ghana, Legon, 1970.

Gantt II, Andrew H. and Dutto, Giuseppe. 'Financial Performance of Government-Owned Corporations in Less Developed Countries', IMF *Staff Papers*, March 1968.

Garlick, Peter C. *African Traders and Economic Development in Ghana*, Oxford U.P., London, 1971.

Genoud, Roger. *Nationalism and Economic Development in Ghana*, Praeger, New York, 1969.

Ghana Commercial Bank, published by the Bank on its 10th anniversary, Accra, 1963.

Ghanaian Times (daily newspaper), Accra.

Gill and Duffus Ltd., *Cocoa Market Reports*, London, periodical.

Gill, B. and E. N. Omaboe. 'Internal Migration Differentials from Conventional Census Questionnaire Items – Ghana', paper presented to the International Statistical Institute, 1963.

Godfrey, E. M. *Demand and Supply in the Food and Labour Markets of a Low-income Country: A Model for Ghana*, Ph.D. dissertation, Unversity of Manchester, 1971.

Golding, P. T. F. 'An Enquiry into Household Expenditure and Consumption and Sale of Household Produce in Ghana', *Economic Bulletin of Ghana*, 1962, No. 4.

Goodman, Stephen H. 'Eastern and Western Markets for the Primary Products of Ghana', *Economic Bulletin of Ghana*, 1966, No. 4.

Goody, Jack. 'Consensus and Dissent in Ghana', *Political Science Quarterly*, September 1968.

Grayson, Leslie E. 'The Promotion of Indigenous Private Enterprise

in Ghana.' Paper presented at annual meeting of African Studies
Association, November 1972.

Grayson, Leslie E. 'A Conglomerate in Africa: Public Sector
Manufacturing Enterprises in Ghana, 1962–71', *African Studies
Review*, 1973 (Grayson, 1973A).

Grayson, Leslie E. 'The Role of Suppliers' Credits in the Industrialisation of Ghana', *Economic Development and Cultural Change*, April
1973 (Grayson 1973B).

Green, Reginald H. 'Political Independence and the National
Economy' in Allen, C. and Johnson R. W. (eds.), *African Perspectives*, Cambridge U.P., 1970.

Green, Reginald H. 'Reflections on Economic Strategy, Structure,
Implementation, and Necessity: Ghana and the Ivory Coast,
1957–67' in Foster and Zolberg (eds.), 1971.

Grundy, Kenneth W. 'Nkrumah's Theory of Underdevelopment: An
Analysis of Recurrent Themes', *World Politics*, April 1963.

Hakam, A. N. 'Impediments to the Growth of Indigenous
Entrepreneurship in Ghana: 1946–1968', *Economic Bulletin of
Ghana*, 1972, No. 2.

Hancock, W. K. *Survey of British Commonwealth Affairs*, Vol. II, Part
2, Oxford U.P., London, 1942.

Hanson, A. H. *Public Enterprise and Economic Development*, Routledge and Kegan Paul, London, 2nd edition, 1965.

Haq, Mahbub ul. Article in *Development Digest*, October 1971.

Harlander, H. and Mezger, D. *Development Banking in Africa*, Weltforum Verlag, München, 1971.

Harris, John R. 'Nigerian Entrepreneurship in Industry', in Eicher and
Liedholm, 1970, Chapter 16.

Harrod, R. F. *Towards a Dynamic Economics*, Macmillan, London,
1948.

Hart, Keith. 'Informal Income Opportunities and Urban Employment
in Ghana', *Journal of Modern African Studies*, 1973, No. 1.

Healey, Derek T. 'Development Policy: New Thinking About an
Interpretation', *Journal of Economic Literature*, September 1972.

Helleiner, G. K. 'Beyond Growth Rates and Plan Volumes – Planning
for Africa in the 1970's', *Journal of Modern African Studies*,
October 1972 (Helleiner, 1972(A)).

Helleiner, G. K. 'Socialism and Economic Development in Tanzania',
Journal of Development Studies, January 1972 (Helleiner, 1972(B)).

Henderson, P. D. 'Investment Criteria for Public Enterprises' in
Turvey, R., (ed.), *Public Enterprise*, Penguin Books, London, 1968.

Higgins, Benjamin. *Economic Development*, Constable, London, 1959
(1st edition).

Hill, Polly. *The Migrant Cocoa Farmers of Southern Ghana*, Cambridge University Press, London, 1963.

Hill, Polly. *Studies in Rural Capitalism in West Africa*, Cambridge University Press, London, 1970.

Hirschman, Albert O. *The Strategy of Economic Development*, Yale U.P., New Haven, 1958.

Hirschman, Albert O. *Development Projects Observed*, Brookings Institute, Washington, 1967.

Hirschman, Albert O. 'The Political Economy of Import-Substituting Industrialization in Latin America', *Quarterly Journal of Economics*, February 1968. (Reproduced in Hirschman (1971), and page numbers refer to this volume).

Hirschman, Albert O. *A Bias for Hope*, Yale U.P., New Haven, 1971.

Hurd, G. E. 'Education' in Birmingham *et al.* (eds.), 1967 (Chapter VI).

Hymer, Stephen. 'The Political Economy of the Gold Coast and Ghana' in Ranis (ed.), 1971.

International Bank for Reconstruction and Development. *Appraisal of the Volta River Hydroelectric Project*, Washington, 1961.

International Bank for Reconstruction and Development. *Public Sector Development Problems and Programs in Ghana*, (8 volumes), mimeo, Washington, March 1966.

International Bank for Reconstruction and Development. *Annual Report, 1968*, Washington, 1969.

Issac, J. E. *Questions of Wage Policy in Ghana*. International Labour Office, mimeo, 1962.

Johnson, Harry G. *Economic Policies Towards Less Developed Countries*, Praeger, New York, 1967.

Johnson, Harry G. (ed.). *Economic Nationalism in Old and New States*, Chicago U.P., Chicago, 1967.

Jolly, Richard. *Planning Education for African Development*, East African Publishing House, Nairobi, 1969.

Kilby, Peter. *Industrialisation in an Open Economy: Nigeria 1945–66*, Cambridge U.P., London, 1969.

Killick, Tony. 'Ghana's Balance of Payments Since 1950', *Economic Bulletin of Ghana*, 1962, Nos. 2 and 3.

Killick, Tony, 'The Economy in 1962', *Economic Bulletin of Ghana*, 1964, No. 1.

Killick, Tony. 'The Performance of Ghana's Economy: 1963 and After', *Economic Bulletin of Ghana*, No. 1, 1965.

Killick, Tony. Chapters 6, 7 and 9 to 17 of Birmingham *et al.* (eds.), 1966.

Killick, Tony. 'Unemployment as an Indicator of Prosperity: A Statistical Curiosity', *Economic Bulletin of Ghana*, 1972, No. 3.

Killick, Tony. 'The State Promotion of Industry: The Case of the

Ghana Industrial Development Corporation', *Ghana Social Science Journal*, Vol. 2, No. 1 and Vol. 3, No. 1, 1972 and 1973.

Killick, Tony. 'The Benefits of Foreign Direct Investment and its Alternatives: An Empirical Exploration', *Journal of Development Studies*, January 1973 (Killick, 1973A).

Killick, Tony. 'Price Controls in Africa: The Ghanaian Experience', *Journal of Modern African Studies*, September 1973 (Killick, 1973B).

Killick, Tony and Szereszewski, Robert. 'The Economy of Ghana', in Robson, P. and Lury, D. (eds.), *The Economies of Africa*, Allen and Unwin, London, 1969.

Kilson, Martin. 'The Grassroots in Ghanaian Politics' in Foster and Zolberg (eds.), 1971, Chapter 5.

Kindleberger, Charles P. *Foreign Trade and the National Economy*, Yale U.P., New Haven, 1962.

Kindleberger, Charles P. *International Economics*, Richard D. Irwin, Homewood, Illinois, 3rd Edition, 1963.

King, John A., Jr. *Economic Development Projects and Their Appraisal.* Johns Hopkins, Baltimore, 1967.

Klein, Thomas M. 'Economic Aid through Debt Relief', *Finance and Development*, September 1973.

Knight, J. B. 'Rural-Urban Income Comparisons and Migration in Ghana', *Bulletin of the Oxford Institute of Economics and Statistics*, 1972, No. 2.

Knight, J. D. 'Mechanisms of Income Distribution in Ghana', mimeoed draft, 1972.

Kpedekpo, G. M. K. *Studies on Vital Registration Data from the Compulsory Registration Areas of Ghana, 1962–67*, University of Ghana, Institute of Statistical, Social and Economic Research, Legon, 1970 (2 volumes).

Kraus, Jon. 'Political Change, Conflict and Development in Ghana' in Foster and Zolberg (eds.), 1971.

Kraus, Jon. 'The Political Economy of Trade Union-Government Relations in Ghana: The Struggle over Minimum Wages under Four Regimes'. Draft paper prepared for conference on Workers, Unions and Development in Africa, University of Toronto, April, 1973.

Kurihara, K. K. *The Keynesian Theory of Economic Development*, Allen and Unwin, London, 1958.

Kuznets, Simon. *Postwar Economic Growth*, Harvard U.P., Cambridge, Mass., 1964.

Kuznets, Simon. *Economic Growth and Structure*, Heinemann, London, 1965.

Kuznets, Simon. *Modern Economic Growth: Rate, Structure and Spread*, Yale U.P., New Haven, 1966.

Landau, Luis. 'Saving Functions for Latin America', Chapter 13 of

Chenery (ed.), 1971.

Larbi-Odam, S. *Production of Coconut Oil at Esiama*, mimeo, Esiama, 1970.

Lawson, Rowena M. 'Inflation in the Consumer Market in Ghana', *Economic Bulletin of Ghana*, 1966, No. 1 (Lawson, 1966A).

Lawson, Rowena M. 'Transport Charges on Local Foodstuffs', *Economic Bulletin of Ghana*, 1966, No. 2 (Lawson, 1966B).

Lawson, Rowena M. 'The Growth of the Fishing Industry in Ghana', *Economic Bulletin of Ghana*, 1967, No. 4.

Legon Observer, journal published by the Legon Society of National Affairs, Accra.

Legum, Colin 'Socialism in Ghana: A Political Interpretation' in Friedland and Rosberg (eds.), 1964.

Leibenstein, Harvey. *Theory of Economic-Demographic Development*, Princeton U.P., 1954.

Leibenstein, Harvey. *Economic Backwardness and Economic Growth*, Wiley, New York, 1957.

Leibenstein, Harvey. 'Allocative Efficiency vs. "X-Efficiency,"', *American Economic Review*, June 1966.

Leith, J. Clark. 'Export Concentration and Stability: The Case of Ghana', *Economic Bulletin of Ghana*, 1971, No. 1 (Leith, 1971A).

Leith, J. Clark. 'The Competitive performance of Ghanaian Exports in the Nkrumah Period', *Ghana Social Science Journal*, May 1971 (Leith, 1971B).

Leith, J. Clark. *Foreign Trade Regimes and Economic Development: Ghana*, National Bureau of Economic Research, Columbia University Press, 1975.

Lewis, W. Arthur. *The Theory of Economic Growth*, Allen and Unwin, London, 1955.

Lewis, W. Arthur. 'Economic Development with Unlimited Supplies of Labour', *Manchester School*, 1954 (reproduced in Agarwala and Singh (eds.) 1958, and page numbers refer to this volume).

Lewis, W. Arthur. 'On Assessing a Development Plan', *Economic Bulletin of Ghana*, 1959, No. 6–7.

Lewis, W. Arthur. *Politics in West Africa*, Allen & Unwin, London, 1965.

Leys, Colin (ed.). *Politics and Change in Developing Countries*, Cambridge U.P., 1969.

Lipsey, R. G. and Lancaster, Kelvin. 'The General Theory of the Second Best', *Review of Economic Studies*, 1956–57, No. 63.

Little, Ian; Scitovsky, Tibor and Scott, Maurice. *Industry and Trade in Some Developing Countries*, Oxford U.P., London, 1970.

Lotz, Jørgen R. and Elliott R. Morss. 'Measuring "Tax Effort" in Developing Countries', IMF *Staff Papers*, November 1967.

Macbean, Alasdair I. *Export Instability and Economic Development*,

Allen and Unwin, London, 1966.

Mandlebaum, K. *The Industrialisation of Backward Areas*, Blackwell, Oxford, 1947.

Meade, J. E. *Trade and Welfare*, Oxford U.P., London, 1965.

Meier, Gerald M. and Baldwin, Robert E. *Economic Development*, Wiley, New York, 1957.

Mensah, J. H. 'A Perspective Plan for Ghana', *Economic Bulletin of Ghana*, 1962, No. 2.

Mensah, J. H. 'The Relevance of Marxian Economics to Development Planning in Ghana', *Economic Bulletin of Ghana*, 1965, No. 1.

Mensah J. H. (Minister of Finance and Economic Planning), *The State of the Economy and the External Debts Problem*, Ghana Publishing Corporation, Accra, April 1970.

Mensah, J. H. 'Incomes Distribution in Ghana', *Business Weekly*, Accra, 31 May and 7 June 1971.

Michaely, M. *Concentration in International Trade*, North-Holland, Amsterdam, 1962.

Miedema, Sieb. 'Cocoa Fluctuations and Fiscal Policy in Ghana', mimeo draft, Accra, May 1972.

Miracle, Marvin P. and Seidman, Ann. *State Farms in Ghana*, Land Tenure Center, University of Wisconsin, mimeo, March 1968 (Miracle and Seidman, 1968A).

Miracle, Marvin P. and Seidman, Ann. *Agricultural Co-operatives and Quasi-Co-operatives in Ghana, 1951–65*, Land Tenure Center, University of Wisconsin, mimeo, July 1968 (Miracle and Seidman, 1968B).

Mishan, E. J. 'The Postwar Literature on Externalities: An Interpretative Essay', *Journal of Economic Literature*, March 1971.

Mohan, J. 'Nkrumah and Nkrumaism' in *Social Register, 1967*, Merlin Press, London, 1967.

Myint, H. 'An Interpretation of Economic Backwardness', *Oxford Economic Papers*, June 1954.

Myint, H. *Economics of the Developing Countries*, Hutchinson, London, 3rd edition, 1967 (first published 1964).

Myint, H. *Southeast Asia's Economy*, Penguin Books, London, 1972.

Myrdal, Gunnar. *The Political Element in the Development of Economic Theory*, Routledge and Kegan Paul, London, 1953.

Myrdal, Gunnar. *An International Economy*, Harpers, New York, 1956.

Myrdal, Gunnar. *Economic Theory and Under-Developed Regions*, Methuen, London, 1964 (first published 1957).

Myrdal, Gunnar. *Asian Drama*, Twentieth Century Fund, New York, 1968 (3 vols.).

Nathan, Robert R., Associates. *Sector Studies on Transportation, Agriculture and Water Resources*, various volumes, Accra, 1970.

Newman, Peter. 'Capacity Utilisation and Growth', reproduced as Appendix A of *Economic Assumptions and Co-ordination* by the Nathan Consortium for Sector Studies, Accra, May 1970.

Nkrumah, Kwame. *Ghana, An Autobiography*, Nelson, London, 1957.

Nkrumah, Kwame. 'African Prospect', *Foreign Affairs*, October 1958.

Nkrumah, Kwame. *I Speak of Freedom*, Heinemann, London, 1961.

Nkrumah, Kwame. *Towards Colonial Freedom*, Heinemann, London, 1962 (first written 1947).

Nkrumah, Kwame. *Africa Must Unite*, International Publishers, New York, 1972 (first published 1963).

Nkrumah, Kwame. *Consciencism*, Monthly Review Press, New York, revised edition, 1970 (originally published 1964).

Nkrumah, Kwame. *Neo-Colonialism: The Last Stage of Imperialism*, International Publishers, New York, 1966 (first Published 1965).

Nkrumah, Kwame. *Dark Days in Ghana*, Panaf Publications, London, 1968.

Nkrumah, Kwame. *Class Struggle in Africa*, International Publishers, New York, 1970.

Nurkse, Ragnar. *Problems of Capital Formation in Underdeveloped Countries*, Blackwell, Oxford, 1953.

Nurkse, Ragnar. *Patterns of Trade and Development*, Wicksell Lectures, 1959 (reproduced in Nurkse 1961, and page numbers refer to this volume).

Nurkse, Ragnar. *Equilibrium and Growth in the World Economy*, Harvard U.P., Cambridge, Mass., 1961.

Nyanteng, V. K. and van Apeldoorn, G. J. *The Farmer and the Marketing of Foodstuffs*, Institute of Statistical, Social and Economic Research, University of Ghana, Legon, 1971.

Nypan, E. 'Demand for Imported Products in Ghana and Demand for Ghanaian Products in Other Countries', *Economic Bulletin of Ghana*, 1960, No. 1.

Odling-Smee, J. 'The Public and Private Sectors', mimeo, Accra, May 1972.

Ofori-Atta, Jones. 'Some Aspects of Economic Policy in Ghana, 1957–61', *Economic Bulletin of Ghana*, 1967, No. 3.

Okali, C. and Kotey, R. A. *Akokoaso: A Resurvey*, Institute of Statistical, Social and Economic Research, University of Ghana, Legon, 1971.

Omaboe, E. N. 'Some Observations on the Statistical Requirements of Development Planning in the Less-developed Countries', *Economic Bulletin of Ghana*, 1963, No. 2.

Omaboe, E. N. Chapters 1 and 18 of Birmingham *et al.* (eds.), 1966.

Ord, H. W. *et al. Ghana: Projected Level of Demand, Supply and Imports of Agricultural Products in 1965, 1970 and 1975.* Report prepared for U.S. Department of Agriculture, Edinburgh, 1964.

Owusu, Maxwell. *Uses and Abuses of Political Power; A Case Study of Continuity and Change in the Politics of Ghana*, Chicago U.P., 1970.

Page Engineering Consultants. *Telecommunications Sector Study*, Accra, 1969.

Pantanali, Romano. *Review of Economic Development in Ghana*, mimeoed draft, Accra, 1970.

Papanek, Gustav F. *Pakistan's Development: Social Goals and Private Incentives*, Harvard U.P., Cambridge, Mass., 1967.

Pearson, Lester B., *et al. Partners in Development: Report of the Commission on International Development*, Pall Mall Press, London, 1969.

Pearson, Scott R. and Page, John M. *Development Effects of Ghana's Forest Products Industry*. Report prepared for U.S.A.I.D., mimeo, Accra, December 1972.

Peil, Margaret. *The Ghanaian Factory Worker: Industrial Man in Africa*, Cambridge U.P., London, 1972.

Pickett, James, Forsyth D. J. C. and McBain, N. S. 'The Choice of Technology, Economic Efficiency and Employment in Developing Countries', in E. O. Edwards (ed.), *Employment in Developing Nations,* Columbia U. P. New York, 1974.

Please, Stanley. 'Saving through Taxation – Mirage or Reality', *Fund and Bank Review: Finance and Development*, March 1967.

Pozen, Robert C. 'Case Study: Ghana Distilleries', mimeographed draft, 1973.

Pozen, Robert C. 'Judicial Relations with Public Corporations', mimeographed draft, 1973.

(N.B. The materials in the above two references have since been incorporated in Pozen's *Legal Choices for State Enterprises in the Third World*, New York University Press, 1976.)

Pozen, Robert C. 'Public Corporations in Ghana: A Case Study in Legal Importation', *Wisconsin Law Review,* Fall 1972.

Prebisch, Raul, *see* United Nations, 1950, 1964A.

Price, Robert M. *The Social Basis of Administrative Behaviour in a Transitional Polity: The Case of Ghana*, Ph.D. dissertation, University of California, December 1971.

The Progress Party Manifesto, New Times Press, Accra, August 1969.

Quansah, S. T. 'The Gonja Settlement and Development Scheme – Ghana', *Economic Bulletin of Ghana*, 1972, No. 1.

Ranis, Gustav (ed.). *Government and Economic Development,* Yale U.P., New Haven, 1971.

Reusse, Eberhard, *Ghana's Food industries, 1968*, Food and Agriculture Organization, mimeo, April 1968.

Richardson, S. D. 'Aspects of Forestry in Ghana', mimeo, Accra, July 1969.

Rimmer,D. 'Schumpeter and the Underdeveloped Countries', *Quarterly Journal of Economics*, August 1961.

Rimmer, D. 'The Crisis in the Ghana Economy', *Modern African Studies*, May 1966.

Rimmer, D. 'The Abstraction from Politics', *Journal of Development Studies*, April 1969. *See also* the same author's *Macromancy*, Institute of Economic Affairs, 1973.

Rimmer, D. *Wage Politics in West Africa*, Faculty of Commerce and Social Science, Occasional Paper No. 12, University of Birmingham, 1970.

Robinson, E. A. G. (ed.). *Economic Consequences of the Size of Nations*, Macmillan, London, 1963.

Robinson, Joan. *Economic Philosophy*, Watts, London, 1962.

Roemer, Michael. 'Relative Factor Prices in Ghanaian Manufacturing 1960–70', *Economic Bulletin of Ghana*, 1971, No. 4.

Roemer, Michael. *The Neoclassical Employment Model Applied to Ghanaian Manufacturing*, Harvard University Economic Development Report No. 225, mimeo, November 1972.

Rosenstein-Rodan, P. N. 'Problems of Industrialisation of Eastern and South-eastern Europe', *Economic Journal*, June–September 1943.

Rosenstein-Rodan, P. N. 'The International Development of Economically Backward Areas', *International Affairs*, 1944.

Rostow, W. W. *The Stages of Economic Growth*, Cambridge U.P., 1960.

Rostow, W. W. (ed.). *The Economics of Take-off into Sustained Growth*, Macmillan, London, 1963.

Rourke, B. E. 'The Value of Agricultural Production by Region in Ghana, 1970–1: Some Provisional Estimates', ISSER, mimeo, University of Ghana, 1973 (Rourke, 1973A).

Rourke, B. E. 'Relative Profitability of Cocoa and Alternative Crops: Some Provisional Estimates for the Eastern Region, Ghana'. Paper presented to Cocoa Economics Research Conference, mimeo, University of Ghana, April 1973, (Rourke, 1973B).

Rourke, B. E. and Obeng, F. A. 'Seasonality in the employment of Casual Agricultural Labour in Ghana', *Economic Bulletin of Ghana*, No. 3, 1973.

Rourke, B. E. and Sakyi-Gyinae, S. K. 'Agricultural and Urban Wage Rates in Ghana', *Economic Bulletin of Ghana*, 1972, No. 1.

Schatz, Sayre P. 'The High Cost of Aiding Business in Developing Economies: Nigeria's Loan Programmes', *Oxford Economic Papers*, November 1968.

Schlesinger, Arthur. *A Thousand Days*, Houghton Mifflin, Cambridge, Mass., 1965.

Schultz, Theodore W. *Transforming Traditional Agriculture*, Yale U.P., New Haven, 1964.

Schumpeter, Joseph A. *The Theory of Economic Development*, Oxford U.P., New York, 1961 (first published in English in 1934).

Schumpeter, Joseph A. *Capitalism, Socialism and Democracy*, Harper and Row, New York, 3rd edition, 1960.

Scitovsky, Tibor. 'Two Concepts of External Economies', *Journal of Political Economy*, April 1954 (reproduced in Agarwala and Singh (eds.), 1958, and page numbers refer to their volume).

Scott, Douglas A. *Growth and Crisis: Economic Policy in Ghana, 1946–65*, Ph.D. dissertation, Harvard University, 1967.

Seers, Dudley. 'The Limitations of the Special Case', *Bulletin of the Oxford University Institute of Statistics*, November 1963.

Seers, Dudley. 'What are We Trying to Measure?', *Journal of Development Studies*, April 1972.

Seers, Dudley and Ross, C. R. *Report on Financial and Physical Problems of Development in the Gold Coast*, Government Printer, Accra, 1952.

Sharpston, M. J. 'The Regional Pattern of Health Expenditure', mimeo, n.d. (ca. 1969).

Singal, M. S. and Nartey, J. D. N. *Sources and Methods of Estimation of National Income at Current Prices in Ghana*, Central Bureau of Statistics, Accra, 1971.

Singer, Hans W., 'The Distribution of Gains between Investing and Borrowing Countries', *American Economic Review Papers and Proceedings*, May 1950 (reproduced in Singer, 1964, and page numbers refer to this volume).

Singer, Hans W. *International Development: Growth and Change*, McGraw Hill, New York, 1964.

The Spark: *Some Essential Features of Nkrumaism*, Lawrence and Wishart, London, 1964.

The Spokesman (newspaper), Accra.

Steel, William F. *Import Substitution Policy in Ghana in the 1960's*, Ph.D. dissertation, Massachusetts Institute of Technology, September 1970.

Steel William F. 'Import Substitution and Excess Capacity in Ghana', *Oxford Economic Papers*, July 1972.

Stern, Joseph J. *Towards a More Rational Tariff Policy*, mimeo, Accra, May 1971.

Stern, Joseph J. 'Ghana's Exports and Terms of Trade: 1955–70', *Economic Bulletin of Ghana*, 1972, No. 4.

Stevens, Chris. 'In Search of the Economic Kingdom: The Development of Economic Relations Between Ghana and the USSR', *Journal of Developing Areas*, October 1974.

Stewart, Frances. 'Appropriate, Intermediate or Inferior Economics', *Journal of Development Studies*, April 1971.

Stoces, Ferdinand. 'Agricultural Production in Ghana, 1955–65', *Economic Bulletin of Ghana*, 1966, No. 3.

Streeten, Paul. *The Frontiers of Development Studies*, Macmillan, London, 1972.

Sutcliffe, R. B. *Industry and Underdevelopment*, Addison-Wesley, London, 1971.

Szerezewski, R. *Structural Changes in the Economy of Ghana, 1891–1911*, Weidenfeld and Nicolson, London, 1965.

Szereszewski, R. Chapters 2–5 and 8 of Birmingham *et al.* (eds.), 1966.

Tinbergen, Jan. *On the Theory of Economic Policy*, North-Holland, Amsterdam, 1955 (2nd. edition).

Tinbergen, Jan. *Design of Development*, Johns Hopkins Press, Baltimore, 1958.

Tyner, R. *Survey of Aboso Glassworks*, Report for GIHOC, mimeo, Accra, 1969.

United Nations. *Relative Prices of Exports and Imports of Underdeveloped Countries*, New York, 1949.

United Nations. *The Economic Development of Latin America and its Principal Problems*, New York, 1950 (attributed in the text to Raul Prebisch).

United Nations. *Community Trade and Economic Development*, New York, 1953.

United Nations. *Towards a New Trade Policy for Development*, New York, 1964 (attributed in the text to Raul Prebisch) (UN, 1964A).

United Nations. *World Economic Survey*, 1963, Vol. I, New York, 1964 (UN, 1964B).

United Nations. *World Economic Survey, Parts I and II*, New York, 1966.

United Nations, Department of Economic Affairs. *Measures for the Development of Under-developed Countries*, New York, 1951.

U.N. Economic Commission for Africa, *Economic Survey of Africa*, Addis Ababa, 1966, ref. 66.II.K3.

Uphoff, Norman T. *Ghana's Experience in Using External Aid for Development, 1957–66*, University of California, Berkeley, 1970 (mimeo). A revised version of this work is to be published under the title, *Foreign Aid and the Political Economy of Development in Nkrumah's Ghana*.

Viner, Jacob. *Studies in the Theory of International Trade*, Harper and Brothers, New York, 1937.

Viner, Jacob. *International Trade and Economic Development*, Free Press, Glencoe, Illinois, 1952.

Wall, D. *Chicago Essays in Economic Development,* Chicago U.P., 1972.

Wallich, Henry C. 'Some Notes Towards a Theory of Derived Development', reproduced in Agarwala and Singh (eds.) 1958.

Walters, D. *Report on the National Accounts of Ghana, 1955–61,* typescript, C.B.S., Accra. 1962.

Waterston, Albert. *Development Planning: Lessons of Experience,* Oxford U.P. London, 1966 (Waterston, 1966A).

Waterston, Albert. *Practical Program of Planning for Ghana,* State Publishing Corporation, Accra, 1966 (Waterston, 1966B).

Weisskoff, Richard. 'Demand Elasticities for a Developing Economy: An International Comparison of Consumption Patterns' in Chenery (ed.), 1971.

Weisskopf, Thomas E. 'An Econometric Test of Alternative Constraints on the Growth of Underdeveloped Countries', *Review of Economics and Statistics,* February, 1972.

van der Wel, P. P. *The Development of the Ghana Sugar Industry, 1960–70,* n.d. (ca. 1972).

West Africa (weekly journal), Overseas Newspapers, London.

Wiles, P. J. D. *The Political Economy of Communism,* Blackwell, Oxford, 1962.

Williams, T. D. and Ntim, S. M. 'Public Employment Centres as a Source of Data on Unemployment in Ghana', *Economic Bulletin of Ghana,* 1973, No. 1.

Wills, J. Brian (ed.). *Agriculture and Land Use in Ghana,* Oxford U.P., London, 1962.

Woronoff, Jon. *West African Wager,* Scarecrow Press, Metuchen, N.J., 1972.

Yotopoulos, Pan A. and Nugent, Jeffrey B. 'A Balanced Growth Version of the Linkage Hypothesis', *Quarterly Journal of Economics,* May 1973.

Young, Allyn. 'Increasing Returns and Economic Progress', *Economic Journal,* December 1928.

INDEX

390 · · · DEVELOPMENT ECONOMICS IN ACTION

b